From Liberation to Conquest

From Liberation to Conquest

THE VISUAL AND POPULAR CULTURES
OF THE
SPANISH-AMERICAN WAR OF 1898

Bonnie M. Miller

UNIVERSITY OF MASSACHUSETTS PRESS
Amherst and Boston

LC 2011032774
ISBN 978-1-55849-924-9 (paper); 905-8 (library cloth)

Designed by Sally Nichols
Set in Sabon
Printed and bound by Thomson-Shore, Inc.

Library of Congress Cataloging-in-Publication Data

Miller, Bonnie M., 1977–
From liberation to conquest : the visual and popular cultures of the Spanish-American
War of 1898 / Bonnie M. Miller.
p. cm.
Includes bibliographical references and index.
ISBN 978-1-55849-924-9 (pbk. : alk. paper) — ISBN 978-1-55849-905-8 (library cloth
: alk. paper) 1. Spanish-American War, 1898—Public opinion. 2. Spanish-American
War, 1898—Press coverage—United States. 3. Spanish-American War, 1898—Causes.
4. Press and politics—United States—History—19th century. 5. Popular culture—
United States—History—19th century. 6. United States—Territorial expansion—Public
opinion. I. Title.
E721.M58 2011
973.8′9–dc23
2011032774

British Library Cataloguing in Publication data are available.

*This book has been published with the assistance of a grant from
the University of Massachusetts Boston through the
Office of the Vice Provost for Research and Strategic Initiatives.*

For Jonathan

ILLUSTRATIONS

Acknowledgments

It is with great pleasure that I express my gratitude to those who have helped make this undertaking possible. My interest in the Spanish-American War dates back to my undergraduate studies at the University of Delaware, where I was privileged to work with Jesus Cruz. I ventured into his office as a freshman History major eager to learn about historical research, and at his suggestion began reading all I could about the war of 1898. He guided me through the earliest stages of this project and inspired me to broaden the pursuit at the graduate level. I owe a great debt to Jesus and to my other undergraduate professors Carol Hoffecker, James Curtis, Kathleen Therrien, Jean Pfaelzer, and Bernie Kaplan, who opened my eyes to the study of history, literature, and visual culture and gave me something to aspire to in my teaching and research.

In my graduate education in the History Department at Johns Hopkins University, I was blessed with extraordinary teachers and mentors who created a rich and stimulating intellectual environment. Ronald Walters, my dissertation director, contributed to every aspect of this process from dissertation to book. His generous spirit, enthusiasm, and warmth made a sometimes tedious and daunting process enjoyable. I also thank Paul Kramer for his keen editorial insights and invaluable advice throughout the publication process. Finally, I am grateful for the rigorous intellectual training I received from Toby Ditz, Judith Walkowitz, and Michael Johnson, who taught me what it means to think as a cultural historian.

It has been a great joy working with the University of Massachusetts Press, and I am thankful for the thoughtful assistance I have received from editor Brian Halley, director Bruce Wilcox, copyeditors Amanda Heller and Mary Bellino, and managing editor Carol

Betsch, who have guided this book through to publication. I also want to acknowledge the publication subvention support provided by the Office of the Vice Provost for Research and Strategic Initiatives at University of Massachusetts Boston, which has helped to defray the expense of publishing the large quantity of images in this book.

I have received the generous aid of many friends and colleagues who have given me the gift of their time and wisdom by reading drafts of the chapters written here and providing invaluable suggestions. Much thanks to David Brody, Judith Smith, Lois Rudnick, Aaron Lecklider, Betsy Klimasmith, Kristin Hoganson, Joshua Brown, Tara Kelly, Catherine Jones, Caleb McDaniel, and Marguerite Hoyt. I also thank Matthew Bokovoy of the University of Nebraska Press, along with readers Robert Rydell and John Nieto-Phillips, for constructive feedback that unquestionably strengthened this book.

When I reflect on this experience, I think of the hundreds of reels of microfilm of newspaper print I had to sort through in order to compile my data. My ever-thickening glasses are testament to it. I thank the Inter-Library Loan departments of the libraries at the University of Delaware, Johns Hopkins University, and University of Massachusetts at Boston for processing a staggering number of requests on my behalf. One Inter-Library Loan librarian once told me that I kept their office in business, and I take pride in that.

I give special thanks to Jeffrey Spencer, Dave Wells, and Burnice Fiedler, who welcomed me to Omaha, Nebraska, and into their homes. They graciously shared their expertise as well as their personal collections of Spanish-American War and Omaha world's fair materials in the early stages of my research.

I appreciate the financial assistance I received along the way from the University of Massachusetts at Boston, the Jacob K. Javits Fellowship Program of the U.S. Department of Education, the Western Association of Women Historians, the University of Delaware Undergraduate Research Program, and the Johns Hopkins University History Department, with special thanks to the generosity of William and Lois Diamond and Arthur O. Lovejoy.

My deepest thanks go to my family. My parents, Janet and Eddie Goldenberg, have shared their love of history and teaching with me from a young age. Along the way, they have kept me company in the archives and helped me collect materials. But most important, they have sustained my efforts with their encouragement and unshakable confidence in me. I am most fortunate to have them in my life.

I dedicate this book to my husband, Jonathan, whose unfailing love and support gave me the strength to see this project to its conclusion. I could never repay him for the remarkable patience he has shown me and sacrifices he has made through every stage of this process, but it will be my greatest pleasure spending the rest of my life trying. I have also found inspiration in the love of my two little ones, Alexander and Sarina. I would have to concede that this book came into being not because of them but in spite of them. But I love them all the more for it, because they keep me balanced and smiling.

From Liberation to Conquest

Introduction

In a cartoon titled "One Type of Patriot" published in October 1898, the *Chicago Inter Ocean* commented on the effects of media during the Spanish-American War in mobilizing Americans into political action (figure I.1). The first frame depicts a prototypical white male patriot caught up in the exhilaration over the battle of San Juan Hill. Such fervor befit a reader of the *Chicago Inter Ocean,* a newspaper that prided itself on the motto "Republican in everything, independent in nothing."[1] As he reads his popular magazine, the American patriot imagines himself sporting the Stars and Stripes, brandishing his sword, and charging up the hill with shellfire bursting around him. But in the second frame his fantasy of patriotic participation fails to energize him to vote in the November elections. Despite a picture on his wall commemorating victory at the battle of Manila, he sits idly smoking a pipe and enjoying the paper. The caption states: "When he reads of San Juan he imagines himself glorying in the storm of shot and shell. But on election day he guesses it looks rather stormy and he doesn't bother about going to the polls."

The cartoonist recognizes that the sensory and psychological enticements of patriotic media need not require engagement with the politics surrounding U.S. actions. He derides the ballyhoo of media production in the Spanish-American War, which, he claims, seems to provide a virtual reality that obviates the necessity for citizens to act or think. This is a remarkable reflection on the failure of media influence to galvanize popular political sentiment given the era of sensationalistic journalism from which it came and the swell of popular interest in the war. It challenges the assumption that readers consumed war- and imperial-related media out of support for those policies and inspires the central questions of this book:

ONE TYPE OF PATRIOT.

When he reads of San Juan he imagines himself glory-ing in the storm of shot and shell.

But on election day he guesses it looks rather stormy and he doesn't bother about going to the polls.

I.1. "One Type of Patriot." *Chicago Inter Ocean*, October 27, 1898, 3.

How did cultural producers promote attention to the projects of war and empire? Were their political messages effectively delivered?

This book aims to show the strengths and limitations of media spectacle as a mechanism for manufacturing popular consent to war and imperialism in 1898–99. Upon its decision to intervene in Cuba's struggle for independence from Spanish colonial rule in 1898, the United States demonstrated a willingness to use military force to exert its influence in the Western hemisphere. This significant turning point in American foreign policy culminated in a major step in the nation's rise to power: the acquisition of an overseas empire. Editors, journalists, cartoonists, playwrights, filmmakers, advertisers, photographers, and showmen set the frames of reference for the way readers and viewers came to understand the implications of these actions. These "media makers" differed in their political inclinations, motivations, and methods of communication, but nonetheless, repetitive patterns of imagining the war and its participants emerged across all spheres of media production. Tracking this media content before, during, and immediately after the war illuminates how media makers shifted their strategies of representation in relation to unfolding political developments and emerging debates over colonial possession.

This book moves beyond the presumed impact of "yellow" journalism to explore the interaction of a much wider array of cultural forms in the promotion of war and empire as spectacle.[2] My analysis of the press includes news content, political cartoons, editorials, and advertisements from over forty newspapers and periodicals in both rural and urban settings across the country.[3] I also examine a range of popular amusements, including stage plays, world's fair attractions, Wild West shows, battle reenactments, parades, public celebrations, early cinema, souvenirs, and photography. As a commercial medium seeking readers and advertisers, the press often conveyed the news as entertainment for a mass audience. Functioning interdependently with the press, creators of popular amusements reproduced prominent news stories and presented them in an emotionally captivating way. But analyzing visual media in mainstream, high-circulation newspapers and mass entertainments inevitably yields only a partial picture. Although a wider international context shaped U.S. actions in 1898, I focus primarily here on media that white Americans produced for broad consumption.[4]

The media's ideological power lies in the ability to "define" a situation and assign meanings to it. In their selection, emphasis, omission, and framing of media content, cultural producers decide what is (and is not) newsworthy and designate the most salient factors for consideration.[5] Media producers played a significant role in constructing the story of the Spanish-American War, identifying the key issues and protagonists of a complicated international crisis, even though these media perceptions were not always in accordance with one another or with governmental policies. While analyzing media content brings to light the strategies of its makers for capturing and holding audience interest, we cannot say definitively what recipients of this content actually took away from its consumption.[6] Given the scarcity of historical evidence of popular response, the closest we can get to seeing how individuals across the nation found meaning in the war is to analyze what they read, viewed, and experienced in order to comprehend the frameworks offered to direct their understanding.

For media makers, the key to maximizing the appeal of war-related cultural productions was to harness the dynamics of spectacle —its elevated sensory impact, theatrical scaffolding, blend of the "real" and the imaginative, and shock value.[7] Sensationalized depictions of the events and participants of the war overlapped in printed accounts, live shows, retail spaces, parades, and fair attractions, creating multiple social contexts for audiences to consume them. The pervasiveness of these spectacular productions of the war made alternative possibilities harder to see, even for selective or skeptical media consumers.

The political and commercial motivations of creators vary, but what unifies their storytelling is their reliance on and perpetuation of prevailing cultural norms and shared conceptions of what audiences want. In 1898, regardless of their stance on war or empire, image makers framed their views of the conflict through shared visual typographies of race, gender, and sexuality as well as conventions of melodrama, romance, and spectacle. Cultural producers made their subjects compelling through the storylines, symbols, and categories they borrowed and reshaped, and occasionally invented. They mobilized these visual cues to encode messages of power within a shifting political terrain: to mark the good guys from the bad and to designate the boundaries of racial and cultural inclusion. These patterns of ideological production helped to unify, and sometimes divide, the nation on questions of enormous political, military, economic, and cultural importance, not only for the United States but also for the peoples of Cuba, Puerto Rico, Guam, and the Philippines.

The Spanish-American War left a lasting influence on American visual, print, and popular culture by inspiring cultural innovation and boosting consumption. Millions of Americans attended public celebrations of the war and watched reenactments of its most prominent battles. Urban crowds gathered outside news headquarters to read the latest press bulletins. The slogan "Remember the *Maine*" appeared on chewing gum wrappers, loaves of bread, matchboxes, spoons, and buttons. In the summer of 1898 over 2 million Americans watched reproductions of the battleship *Maine* burst into flames daily in the serene lagoon of the Omaha world's fair. Vaudeville houses across the nation passed off motion picture depictions of staged battle scenes as actual war footage, and minstrel shows incorporated military themes and colonial characters, such as singing Filipinos or dancing Hawaiians, into their performances.

Although Americans came into contact with war-related imagery in countless ways, these acts of consumption did not necessarily engender support for the Republican political agenda, as the *Chicago Inter Ocean* cartoonist had hoped. The American patriot imagined in the *Inter Ocean* cartoon is a media consumer. His magazine shapes his mental picture of what fighting on San Juan Hill looks and feels like so that he can envision himself taking part, but he relinquishes his stake in foreign affairs as quickly as he acquired it. The cartoonist criticizes the "patriot" for getting sucked into "the medium" without getting "the message," that is, without translating his participation into political engagement.[8] Media makers transformed the Spanish-American War into popular spectacle, complete with its share of drama, emotion, heroics, and scandal. This story of the entanglement of political power, popular culture, and the production of public knowledge takes place at a critical moment in American history, when the nation was asserting itself globally and the country's popular culture industries were emerging and consolidating. But the fusion of politics and entertainment had potentially unstable and contradictory effects; commercializing political messages obscured political meanings at the same time that it helped to fortify ideologies of racial supremacy and enhance aspirations for a greater U.S. presence at the table of world powers. The consequences of this convergence would reverberate in the media politics of future U.S. wars of the twentieth and twenty-first centuries.

Historical Perspectives of the Spanish-American/Cuban Conflict

The crisis of 1898 has roots in the history of Western colonization and land appropriation. In the sixteenth century, Spain took colonial possession of vast portions of North, Central, and South America. After a wave of revolutions in the early nineteenth century procured independence for all of Spain's colonies in the West Indies and in Central and South America, only Cuba, Puerto Rico, Guam, and the Philippines remained under Spanish dominion. Centuries of Spanish control and the popular accommodation and resistance it engendered shaped the histories of these territories long before U.S. intervention in Cuba in 1898.

Just over ninety miles from Key West, the island of Cuba was in a state of crisis in the 1890s, torn apart by decades of colonial resistance. Frustrated by high taxes and little possibility of home rule,

Cuban lawyer and intellectual Carlos Manuel de Céspedes had orga-
nized a movement for reform that ripened into violent revolt in 1868.
In the Ten Years' War, from 1868 to 1878, the Cuban Liberation
Army unsuccessfully fought its first war for independence. The Peace
of Zanjón in 1878 left Spanish rule intact and produced little change.
Cuba also faced a high tax burden in subsequent years to compensate
Spain for the costs of the Ten Years' War. Economic conditions in
Cuba deteriorated further in the early 1890s, when a global depres-
sion led to a tightening of U.S. tariff policies. These conditions helped
to reignite the Cuban independence movement. In 1895 a small group
of Cuban revolutionaries reinstated the fight, and their strategic use
of guerrilla warfare and economic destruction provoked a brutal
Spanish response. Spanish premier Antonio Cánovas replaced the
more moderate Cuban governor-general Arsenio Martínez Campos
in early 1896 with General Valeriano Weyler y Nicolau. Weyler issued
a decree of reconcentration to destroy rebel supply lines and isolate
the insurgency, transporting civilians, mostly women and children,
into concentration camps. The war had a devastating impact; caught
between a Liberation Army that laid waste to the Cuban economy
and forced many Cubans to become refugees from their homes and
a Spanish campaign of repression that concentrated civilians without
meeting basic needs, Cuban civilians died in multitudes, with numbers estimated at 100,000 or more.[9]

The American preoccupation with Cuba began much earlier than
this immediate crisis. Cuba's strategic location, proximity to U.S.
borders, and status as the world's largest sugar producer made it a
highly attractive prospect for U.S. annexation. There were multiple
failed attempts to purchase it from Spain by Presidents John Quincy
Adams in 1825, James K. Polk in 1847, Franklin Pierce in 1854, and
James Buchanan in 1858. The 1854 Ostend Manifesto, drawn up by
minister to Great Britain and future president James Buchanan, testi-
fies to the American aspiration to incorporate Cuba, stating that "the
Union can never enjoy repose, nor possess reliable security, as long
as Cuba is not embraced within its boundaries." The Senate affirmed
this sentiment five years later, reporting that the American people
supported annexation "with a unanimity unsurpassed on any question of national policy which has hitherto engaged the public mind."[10]
Although Buchanan was unable to acquire Cuba, late-nineteenth-

century policy, such as the Sugar Act of 1871, wove Cuban and Puerto Rican markets deeper into the U.S. economy. The topic of Cuba resurfaced in 1895 when exiled Cuban poet José Martí, along with Cuban generals Máximo Gómez and Antonio Maceo, resumed the war for independence from Spanish colonial rule. But between 1895 and 1898 there was surprisingly little talk of Cuban annexation in American popular media on account of the intensity of feeling for "Cuba Libre"(Free Cuba).

Propelling perceptions of Spanish misconduct were the efforts of the Cuban Junta, an organization based in New York and Washington that raised money, supplies, and awareness for Cuban independence. The Junta fed U.S. press editors stories of Spanish atrocities, sculpting the portrait of Spanish villainy that emerged in the "yellow" press on the eastern seaboard. These efforts spawned more than seventy illegal filibustering expeditions that sailed from U.S. shores to supply arms to the Cuban revolutionaries. U.S. authorities did little to stop them, nor did the Spanish, who feared reprisals if hostile measures were taken. News reports on the Cuban revolution, alleged Spanish atrocities, and numerous filibustering missions kept the Cuba story in the headlines throughout 1896 and 1897.

In August 1897 an Italian anarchist assassinated the Spanish premier, and Spanish political leadership turned to Liberal Party leader Práxedes Mateo Sagasta. Sagasta sought to alleviate tensions by recalling Weyler and promising Cuban autonomy. Although President McKinley urged Cuba to give Spain a chance for these reforms to take effect, it became evident that the Cuban nationalists would accept nothing short of independence. After rioting broke out in Havana in January 1898, McKinley ordered the U.S.S. *Maine* to Havana harbor on a peaceful call to protect American citizens and property in Cuba. On February 15 the battleship mysteriously exploded in port, killing 266 American sailors on board. After completing its investigations, a naval board of inquiry concluded that the explosion had an external cause, most likely a mine in the harbor, but could not definitively prove that Spain was responsible. Amid continuing reports of the humanitarian crisis in Cuba, the *Maine* report was enough to compel the majority of newspaper editors and policymakers, along with President McKinley, to support military intervention.

With little popular or political opposition, on April 25, 1898, the

United States declared war against Spain. After suffering defeats in land and naval campaigns in Cuba and the Philippines, Spain surrendered in less than three months. A cease-fire was signed on August 12, and official peace negotiations were held in Paris that November. The Senate ratified the peace treaty in February 1899, stipulating the transfer of the remaining Spanish empire to U.S. possession. The U.S. Army occupied Cuba until May 1902 and granted independence only under provision of the Platt Amendment, which limited Cuban authority to dictate foreign policy, secured a U.S. military base in Guantánamo, and gave the United States the right to intervene at will. In exchange for $20 million, Spain ceded the entire Philippine archipelago, which remained in U.S. hands until World War II, achieving independence in 1946. Into the bargain the United States also acquired (and still retains) the Spanish holdings of Puerto Rico and Guam.

When McKinley seized upon a war with Spain to further U.S. global interests, he was accelerating a deeply rooted expansionist agenda. The primary emphasis of America's first century of national existence had been on continental expansionism, involving the dispossession of Native American lands as well as the acquisition of French territories in the Louisiana Purchase, Spanish Florida, and the land cession of the Mexican War. Tensions over slavery and its expansion into newly created western states kept the nation fixated internally, even as southern planters looked to the Caribbean and West Indies, and especially Cuba, to expand their slave-based plantation economy. During and after the Civil War, many Americans migrated westward, propelled by the incentives of the Homestead Act of 1862 and the construction of the transcontinental railroad system.

During this period of rapid settlement of the trans-Mississippi West, the world's greatest powers—Great Britain, France, Germany, Spain, Belgium, and Japan—were extending their empires into Africa and Asia and rapidly building their arsenals. In the last decades of the nineteenth century, American financiers and politicians also sought to expand foreign markets in the Caribbean, Pacific, and Latin America. The State Department established protective tariffs and trading rights with Hawaii, Cuba, and Puerto Rico. In the early 1890s Alfred T. Mahan's influential works on the importance of sea power, and Frederick Jackson Turner's speech declaring the U.S. frontier closed, helped create a framework for U.S. policymakers to rationalize strengthening U.S. naval power and seeking new frontiers outside continental borders.[11] The United States secured the Western Hemisphere as its sphere of influence by risking war with the British in the Venezuela border dispute of 1895 to enforce the Monroe Doctrine, upholding the nation's right to intervene in Latin America to protect its interests. The Spanish-American War was the next step in the expansion of American geopolitical and commercial interests overseas, soon to be followed by Secretary of State John Hay's "open door notes" in 1899 to ensure trade access to China.

The war with Spain began as a quest to liberate Cuba from Spanish colonial rule, but its scope immediately broadened after the war first began in the Philippines. Fought in Cuba, the Philippines, Guam, and Puerto Rico, the Spanish-American War became a launching pad for American overseas imperialism in the Western Hemisphere and the Far East. From a twenty-first-century perspective, it seems an all too familiar story of the striking disconnect between the rhetoric of wartime objectives and the realities of its outcomes. It was the advancement of U.S. strategic interests, not the media-constructed moral pretext, that ultimately determined the fate of those involved. Historians have debated what led the United States into a war with Spain in 1898: some emphasize the war as a pathway to an increased U.S. presence in the Caribbean and the Pacific, while others look at social, cultural, and psychological factors to explain the outcry of support for Cuba Libre. The question, at its simplest, hinges on whether one examines the Spanish-American War from the front or the back: Do we judge the war on the humanitarian concerns seemingly motivating its origins or for the imperial grab that followed it?

The best way to make sense of this incongruity is to separate the media's representations of U.S. actions from the designs of the McKinley administration. Notwithstanding the ambiguities and inconsistencies of mass cultural production, the makers of American visual, print, and popular culture largely framed the conflict in plain idealistic terms—to "free Cuba" from a colonial predator. U.S. press coverage of the Cuban crisis almost invariably took the side of the Cuban revolutionaries. While there were political, diplomatic, and economic incentives for the United States to intervene in Cuba, these reasons were rarely articulated, and perhaps not even realized, in prewar media campaigns. Media makers consolidated popular support for war around the symbolic ideal of

Cuban liberation without explicit consideration of the politics of its postwar settlement. In order to justify war for purely selfless reasons, the press purposely excised discussions of the political or material gains from intervention.

For President McKinley, however, the Cuban situation was closely linked to the strategic problem of enhancing U.S. commercial power in the Pacific. After the Chinese defeat in the Sino-Japanese War of 1894–95 prompted the leading world powers to seize spheres of influence in China, the president was eager to stake a claim for the United States. For McKinley and his advisers, the war opened possibilities of expanding trade lines and attaining key coaling, cable, and naval stations. In this context it makes sense that after asking Congress for the power to end Spanish rule in Cuba, McKinley ordered the first strike against Spain to occur in Philippine waters and then directed the navy to take Guam and Wake Island before the U.S. Army even landed in Cuba.[12] Following Admiral George Dewey's naval victory in Manila in early May, McKinley fortified U.S. power in the Philippines by creating the Department of the Pacific under the command of Major General Wesley Merritt. This set in motion the U.S. occupation of the Philippines months before McKinley demanded that Spain cede the entire archipelago. With Germany, Japan, and Great Britain vying for power in the Far East, McKinley recognized the primacy of the Pacific in the war with Spain, but few Americans saw the war through this lens. McKinley's war message to Congress resolved only to end Spanish rule in Cuba without any definitive exposition of his broader aspirations.

One of the persistent myths in historical accounts of the Spanish-American War is that the primary impetus came not from President McKinley but from the pressure of a war-hungry public manipulated by a sensationalistic press and jingoist political culture.[13] This theory places too much weight on the sensationalism of the "yellow" press, particularly William Randolph Hearst and Joseph Pulitzer, without consideration of the larger media environment. At the same time, its proponents too easily assume an equivalency between press and public opinion and fail to provide any evidence to substantiate that press accounts directly affected congressional or executive decision making.[14] The theory of a "yellow" press–made war absolves McKinley of his own designs and paves the way for his administration, and a century of historians after him, to dismiss imperialism as an unexpected by-product of the war.[15]

This book will not provide yet another reprise of Hearst's famous entreaty to artist Frederic Remington: "You furnish the pictures, I'll furnish the war." This exchange, if it even happened, has littered too many Spanish-American War histories and has been used as grounds to overstate Pulitzer's and Hearst's influence in shaping political actions. While Pulitzer and Hearst may have been the most extreme in their use, they did not hold a monopoly on the sensationalistic conventions defining the "yellow" brand, such as large multicolumn headlines, extensive use of pictures, experimental layouts, question-able journalistic practices, and lengthy colorful Sunday supplements.[16] There were numerous high-circulation papers in the United States at the time that were various shades of "yellow," including the *New York Journal,* the *New York World,* the *New York Sun,* the *San Francisco Examiner,* the *New York Herald,* the *Chicago Tribune,* and the *Chicago Record.*[17] These were not the only papers to use sensational-istic tactics. But they had large enough budgets to send correspondents on fieldwork and disseminate their reports to nationwide newspapers through subscription wire services, which gave them an advantage in shaping media depictions of the Cuban crisis.

Yet the editorial power of the yellow press did not drown out the range of other news outlets and other cultural forms shaping local interpretations of the events. In 1898 there were about 2,200 daily newspapers, 13,000 weeklies, and 600 semiweeklies across the coun-try.[18] With a combined circulation at the height of war of about 2.25 million, the *New York Journal* and *New York World* had a readership that consisted of at most 3 percent of the national population in 1898.[19] What is more, many newspapers repeatedly primed readers to be wary of yellow press accounts, which may have further limited their impact. The *Baltimore Sun* claimed their reports to be "entirely imaginary and out of touch with the facts."[20] The *New York Evening Post* affirmed, "Every one who knows anything about 'yellow journals' knows that everything they do and say is intended to promote sales."[21] The yel-low press therefore did not have the reach or the authority to dictate public opinion; rather, the key to its significance lay in its establishing important visual and discursive precedents for how a broader network of print, visual, and popular culture mass-marketed war and empire.

The complement to this conventional historical portrait of a rabble-rousing yellow press is that of a haggard and sleep-deprived president forced into war by the clamor coming from Congress, the press, and public opinion. McKinley had claimed in his inaugural address that "peace is preferable to war in almost every contingency."[22] His exposure to the brutal realities of battle during his service in the Civil War became the cornerstone of his pacifistic image, which he used to justify his reluctance to use force to end the Cuban crisis. As a result, Theodore Roosevelt ridiculed McKinley's lack of manly resolve; he asserted, "McKinley has no more backbone than a chocolate éclair!" This infamous comment drowned out alternative descriptions of McKinley in the historical record, such as that of Secretary of State John Hay, who noted that McKinley had "a very strong will" and "likes to have things his own way."[23]

Scholars of McKinley's presidency disagree over his imperialist ambitions. Some claim he was genuinely disinclined, while others see him as a brilliant mastermind who took advantage of the public outcry for "Cuba Libre" to advance his imperial agenda.[24] Historians arguing for McKinley's reluctance often cite Chicago newspaper publisher Herman Kohlsaat's descriptions of private conversations he had with McKinley in 1898. Kohlsaat claimed that when McKinley confided in him about his hesitations in going to war, he "broke down and cried like a baby of thirteen." Following Dewey's victory in Manila Bay, McKinley reportedly told him: "When we received the cable from Admiral Dewey telling of the taking of the Philippines I looked up their location on the globe. I could not have told where those darned islands were within 2,000 miles!"[25] This vision of McKinley scanning the globe to find the Philippines substantiated the perception that he did not wage war with an informed view of its commercial importance. McKinley clinched his self-representation as a reluctant imperialist when he conveyed to the nation how he came to the decision to retain the Philippines: "I went down on my knees and prayed Almighty God for light and guidance. . . . And one night late it came to me this way—I don't know how it was, but it came." It was at this moment, McKinley claimed to a group of Methodist bishops, when he realized he had no choice but to take all of the Philippines.[26]

These well-rehearsed accounts of the motivating factors guiding the decisions of 1898 grant too much power to a select group of editors and not enough to McKinley, and altogether fail to recognize the wider set of cultural, political, and economic forces that compelled U.S. actions. The private industries of the press and commercial amusements did not have to be in the pocket of the government for them to do McKinley's bidding. Whether media makers latched onto the Cuban crisis for its attention-grabbing quality or were truly committed to Cuba Libre, or both, the sum total of their cultural productions was a compelling script for U.S. intervention. What they created, in effect, was war propaganda, but it had no centralized design or government oversight, which would come later in World War I and World War II. With the makers of print, visual, and popular culture generating enthusiasm for war, the president could avoid making his agenda explicit and deflect responsibility. Once entrenched in the war, however, McKinley claimed that adhering to popular demands to intervene in Cuba (an intervention he chose to initiate in Manila Bay) left him no other "responsible" choice but to retain the Philippines and other Spanish colonies. He argued that the Filipinos were incapable of self-government, and in light of the barbarities of Spanish rule, it would be "cowardly and dishonorable" to return them to Spain.[27]

Historians have labeled this public demand for intervention a case of "war fever" or "hysteria," a product of the "psychic crisis" of the 1890s, as Richard Hofstadter called it.[28] Cold war bureaucrat George Kennan and the realist school of the 1950s argued that the United States "resorted to war for subjective and emotional reasons" while interpreting popular support as irrational and impulsive because it was driven by a moral compass, not in terms of U.S. strategic interests.[29] This diagnosis of "war fever" implies a psychological and physical inability to think and reason clearly, but the painstaking efforts of many media makers to provide proof of their allegations suggest the opposite, that readers were not easily swayed. The Spanish-American War took place in a cultural period that thrived on claims of authenticity, as Miles Orvell has shown, compelling media creators to corroborate the "reality" of their cultural productions to establish credibility with readers and viewers.[30] Media marketing repeatedly invoked the "expert" testimony of government officials and military personnel, pseudoscientific theories of race and social development, accounts by eyewitnesses and actual participants, and photographic "evidence."

The concern that "war fever" drove the nation to war was raised during the war period itself. Charles H. Ames, in turn, wrote a letter to the *Boston Transcript* in 1898 affirming the integrity of popular sentiment. Having studied the "motives and feelings of people in different parts of the country," he found that the popular clamor for war was based not on "selfishness or greed or desire for military glory" but rather "a genuine sentiment of pity for the oppressed and righteous indignation at the long history of cruelty and infamy perpetrated at our very doors."[31] Ames's assessment of public opinion reiterates a recurring theme in media accounts of the conflict: the Cuban crisis at the nation's doorstep (see figure 1.2). This image was vital to differentiate Cuba's plight from other humanitarian concerns in the world, such as the concurrent famine in India, as America's problem. Physical proximity became the imagined connection to warrant U.S. involvement, creating, as Ames noted, a sincere popular determination for war.

Media Production in the Spanish-American War

The Spanish-American War has often been touted, especially in its own time, as having healed the rift of the Civil War by uniting the North and the South against a common enemy. But there is another narrative of nationalism created here, one in which media makers across the country created a collective, though conflicted, national vision of the events and participants of the U.S.-Cuban-Spanish war.[32] The shared "community" of public participation in this national wartime culture had perhaps as much unifying force as the powerful image of the Blue and Gray fighting side by side for the first time since the Civil War.

Late-nineteenth-century print culture as a whole saw an expansion of visual content. Over the course of the nineteenth century, the press became more commercially driven. Whereas political parties typically funded early American newspapers, beginning in the 1830s and 1840s the press increasingly sought advertising revenue, encouraging editors to see readers as "consumers" as well as potential "voters."[33] Alice Fahs argues that the Civil War was a turning point in press consumption as more Americans read newspapers on a daily basis in order to follow events.[34] Still, cost and technology limited wartime visual production to a handful of illustrated periodicals and independent sources.

AN UNDESIRABLE NEIGHBOR.

UNCLE SAM: "No use talking—there'll never be peace in this neighborhood so long as that Spaniard is here."

I.2. Boz, "An Undesirable Neighbor." *Boston Globe,* March 19, 1898, 4.

This changed in the last decades of the nineteenth century as the relationship between the press and its audiences grew more dependent on visual content.[35] Alan Trachtenberg noted that by the 1890s, "steam-powered printing presses, [and] improved methods of lithography and photoengraving . . . led to an unprecedented quantity of visual data," creating what Neil Harris has called "an iconographical revolution of the first order."[36] Newspaper and magazine distribution reached higher circulations owing to improvements in printing and transportation as well as cheaper postal rates. In response to market demands, magazine editors incorporated more material on public affairs and made greater use of illustration. Magazines like *Century* and *Harper's* began publishing halftone photographs in the 1880s, and a few mass-circulation newspapers also acquired this capacity by 1898.[37]

Political cartoons became a key feature in newspapers and illustrated magazines, thanks to the influential work of a cohort of graphic artists in the 1870s and 1880s, including Thomas Nast, Joseph Keppler, and Frederick Opper. Many mass-circulation newspapers featured a daily cartoon, often on the front page, which was likely the first thing to meet the eye of a reader coming in contact with the newspaper. As one writer of the period noted, cartoons "were more than ever in demand" during the Spanish-American War. By the turn of the century, graphic artists often commanded larger salaries than reporters, averaging about $25 a week, while a top cartoonist for the large New York papers could earn over $200 a week.[38] Reporter Earl Mayo observed in 1898: "A dozen years ago the cartoonist had no place in daily journalism. . . . Today the cartoonists of the big dailies occupy offices adjoining those of the editors-in-chief, and their daily pictures are the subjects of careful editorial consultation."[39]

The reiteration of war-related themes on the popular stage and screen broadened their circulation beyond the world of print, expanding the quantity, range, and reach of information to a diverse public. The Cuban crisis and war with Spain spurred the creation of world's fair attractions, stage melodramas, vaudeville skits, Wild West show acts, and battle reenactments that transformed the characters and events of press reports into highly pleasurable entertainments. The Spanish-American War also inspired the rise of early film, and many spectators experienced the novelty of watching motion picture footage of what was presented as actual war events. Press editors, journalists, and cartoonists in turn integrated the modes of storytelling and spectacular effects of these war-related amusements into the way they expressed the political stakes of war and empire to their readers. Watching a stage play depicting a Cuban heroine endangered by a brutal Spaniard, a live reenactment of the battle of Manila Bay in all its naval glory, or a film of the Rough Riders allegedly charging up San Juan Hill gave an unprecedented visual immediacy to events occurring overseas while bonding Americans on the home front in shared patriotic consumption.

Creators of war-related cultural productions made strategic efforts to meet the needs of a nation coping with the economic and social turbulence of the 1890s. Their efforts addressed the cultural longing to heal the residual wounds of the Civil War, reaffirmed notions of masculine vigor, and built patriotic unity and national pride. They hit on the right ingredients to mobilize and maintain support for U.S. actions abroad: drama, sex, and spectacle fused into a moral framework that turned action into a show of noble and manly purpose. Largely on the basis of his observations during World War I, Walter Lippman argued in his pathbreaking study *Public Opinion* (1922) that readers and viewers needed to be "exercised" to feel invested in public affairs.[40] Media makers in 1898, whether they were conscious of it or not, endeavored to achieve this effect, although the representations they created were not necessarily motivated toward consistent or coherent political positions. This master narrative urging U.S. intervention contained three essential elements: (1) a sympathetic victim, in the form of endangered and suffering women and children; (2) a brutal villain convicted by the court of public opinion for greed, corruption, rape, and murder; and (3) an altruistic, manly savior. To magnify the drama, cultural producers drew on the romantic belief that pure evil could be overcome only through violent means.[41] The complete and utter vilification of Spain accentuated American moral decency while in actuality masking the actual gains of victory. The Cuban nationalists were the ambiguous component in these prewar campaigns; the melodramatic scheme in some cases recognized their efforts to liberate themselves and at other times dismissed them entirely. Once the war began, however, discussion of Cuba's humanitarian crisis and struggle for independence took a back seat to American military glory.

Amidst a rising tide of public sentiment against colonial acquisition as the war drew to a close, the imperialist ambivalence latent in the media content of prewar campaigns became more pronounced. Imperialist fantasies and postwar military scandals diverted media attention from Cuban independence, the primary cause of intervention in the first place alongside the desire to avenge the *Maine*. The

melodramatic paradigm underwriting the iconography of intervention was no longer sustainable, and the narrative of rescuing oppressed
women and children was replaced by the moral logic of the "white
man's burden." Pro-imperialist image makers abandoned the symbols of Cuban nationalism and borrowed conventions of ethnic and
racial caricature to re-create images of former Spanish subjects into
candidates for American guardianship. Critics of imperial acquisition had the more difficult position to defend, going against the currents of nationalistic and militaristic sentiment. They had to visualize
the threat that the colonies posed to American politics, race, and
culture. Ultimately it was the racialized spectacle of colonialism that
predominated media visions of empire on both sides of the imperialist debate, not the political, diplomatic, and economic considerations
at stake. Pro- *and* anticolonialist propaganda seemed more invested
in satisfying the popular appetite for exotic, sensationalized depictions than in conveying the density of the issues to audiences.

The chapters that follow trace the patterns of representation that
gained prominence (and the ones that did not) across a variety of
cultural forms and probe the relatively unscripted and contingent
nature of their political meanings, which undermined their capacity
to be simple tools of top-down persuasion. The narrative proceeds
chronologically from the period building up to U.S. intervention
in Cuba (chapters 1 and 2), through the duration of the Spanish-
American War (chapters 3–5), and ending with the imperial debates
and resumption of war in the Philippines (chapters 6 and 7). It maps
the paradoxical shift in the purpose of U.S. intervention from liberation to conquest: How did a war that media makers initially promoted as a mission to stop imperialist exploitation end with the
taking of America's first overseas possessions? The overlaps and
incongruities between media and political agendas depicted in these
pages have broad implications, past and present, for thinking about
the motivations and impact of media producers seeking to frame
the purpose, performance, and effects of U.S. foreign policy actions,
which were not always in accordance with, or determined by, dic-
tates from Washington. In their promotion of war as spectacle, media
producers fomented patriotism along with a sense of moral imperative, and eventually an ambivalence toward imperial expansion.

1

The Spectacle of Endangered Bodies

THE VISUAL ICONOGRAPHY OF WAR

> Here at the Nation's Capital, as well as in the country
> at large, popular sympathy is overwhelmingly in favor
> of the independence of Cuba. . . . The existence of this
> sentiment was strongly disclosed yesterday when
> the people of Washington expressed their feelings on
> the subject in mass-meeting, following the example
> of other cities. . . . This monster Cuban demonstration
> and mass-meeting by the citizens of Washington was
> held in the Columbia Theater. . . . The stage and boxes
> were decorated with United States and Cuban flags,
> and in front of the speaker's stand on the stage was
> a crayon picture of Gen. Antonio Maceo.
>
> *Washington Post,* May 17, 1897

Prior to the U.S. declaration of war against Spain, American editors, journalists, cartoonists, writers, and playwrights framed the Cuban crisis almost entirely from a Cuban nationalist perspective. This is not surprising given Spanish governor-general Weyler's combative relationship with U.S. press correspondents in Cuba and the influence of the Cuban Junta in propagating stories of Spanish atrocities. But this outlook had deeper roots; America's long-standing preoccupation with Cuba and desire to incorporate it into the United States meant that Spain's exit was already deemed inevitable and in Cuba's best interests. Between 1896 and April 1898, however, sympathies for Cuban independence largely overshadowed the clamor for annexation. This was a direct result of the formal conventions organizing the media production of this political crisis, which found substantial narrative power in the cause of Cuba Libre. American media makers provided a rationale for intervention, which the McKinley administration seized, through visions of Cuban women brutalized and bound by Spain. Framing U.S. actions as a riveting tale of dashing heroes, dark villains, and alluring damsels in distress transformed intervention into a dramatic rescue.

This narrative design had more to do with manufacturing popular interest than with consideration of the long-term political implications of U.S. involvement. Media coverage made U.S. political objectives in Cuba explicit only insofar as they conformed to the script of "playing savior." Ambiguity about the consequences of U.S. actions and the imperialistic prospects of intervention was symptomatic of the press campaigns from the start. It was the commercial popularity of spectacular melodrama more than any political agenda that turned the Cuban rebellion into the object of cartoonists' pens, the plot device of romantic novelists, and the latest theme of entertainment.

The Cuban insurrection was an ideal fit for stage melodrama's escalation of sensation in the 1890s, offering themes of battle, martyrdom, and suffering.[1] In order to save an endangered heroine, plot constructions revolved around thrilling and suspenseful "situations" that featured extravagant rescues and escapes. Spectacle was intrinsic to melodrama, with its emphasis on peril and action, particularly in "sensational" as opposed to family-oriented melodrama.[2] Popular romance novels of the period employed similar narrative conventions, telling stories of Americans triumphing over evil in foreign lands. A study of book loans from American public libraries in 1893 demonstrated that romance novels were the favored choice among readers, and not surprisingly, Cuba became a popular fictional setting in the late 1890s.[3] Stage melodrama and popular romantic fiction offered the narrative ingredients for framing the Cuban crisis through the formula of romantic rescue. Beginning in the last decades of the nineteenth century, as cultural critics began distinguishing between "high" and "low" forms of cultural expression, these genres were increasingly categorized as "lowbrow" for their hackneyed, maudlin content.[4] In fact, the tendency to write off the importance of the conflict, which has come to be remembered as but a "splendid little war," as Secretary of State John Hay termed it, may be due in part to the derision surrounding the very forms underwriting it.

Weyler's policy of reconcentration provided the basis for cultural producers to vilify Spain for abusing its power and endangering

Cuban lives, when in actuality the crisis conditions stemmed from strategic decisions made on both sides of the Spanish-Cuban conflict. The renewal of popular uprising in 1895 began with only limited support in eastern Cuba. Frustrated by Spain's failure to institute the reforms agreed to after the Ten Years' War, the commander in chief of the Cuban army, General Máximo Gómez, called for total war until Spain relinquished Cuba. Gómez advanced into western Cuba, advocating guerrilla strikes and the wholesale destruction of Cuba's economic resources, including the burning of plantations, the symbols of capitalized agriculture. He forced civilians to strike under penalty of death, leaving thousands without any means to support themselves. Women and children fled into neighboring towns and cities, while many able-bodied men joined the growing ranks of the Liberation Army. John Lawrence Tone has argued that this was the "informal beginning of reconcentration."[5] This unrest also provoked a severe Spanish response, beginning with Weyler's appointment in 1896. He divided the island into war zones to suppress insurgency in the western and central regions of the island and required civilians, already displaced by the dislocation of the rebellion, to move into fortified camps. His intent was to cripple the insurgency by removing the rebels' source of food and shelter provided by civilians in the countryside. Already strained by the military budget for pacification, Weyler could not equip these camps with adequate food, water, and shelter, forcing civilians to fend for themselves and placing them at great risk of starvation, exposure, and disease.

The effects of war and reconcentration on the Cuban people were real and horrific, with mass casualties of men, women, and children. The American press did not have to fabricate or exaggerate this human suffering in order to stir empathy in its readers, but how they spun the story was critical in assigning accountability. They simplified and distorted the complex realities of the conflict in how they framed it. They held the Spanish solely responsible for the heartrending state of Cuban affairs and proclaimed the right of the Cuban nationalists to seek liberation. Their initial outcry for U.S. intervention was anti-imperialist at core, and the motto—"Cuba Libre"—spread widely throughout American print, visual, and popular culture. Weyler and Spanish autocracy were vilified, and General Gómez was celebrated as a brave and self-sacrificing liberator (figure 1.1). The *New York*

LIBERATORS OF SPANISH AMERICA.

1.1. "Liberators of Spanish America." *Chicago Times-Herald,* June 5, 1898, 17.

World called Gómez "the Washington of Cuba, the patriot who can and will lead Cubans to . . . freedom."[6]

Cuba, the Tormented Victim

Newsmakers presented Spain's pacification of Cuba as a brutal campaign waged against Cuban families, particularly unarmed women and children, in which combatants and noncombatants were indistinguishable. Headlines across the nation read "Women and Children Condemned to Filth and Disease" (*Boston Globe*), "Thousand Agonies of Starvation's Slow Deaths Inflicted by the Spaniards upon the Women and Little Children of Cuba" (*New York Journal*), and "The Spanish Butcher Wages Brutal Warfare on Helpless Women and Children" (*Cleveland Plain Dealer*), to cite a few. "It is not war; it is murder by starvation; the extermination of a people; 'the destruction of a breed,'" charged the *New York World*.[7]

Even though only a handful of major metropolitan newspapers, such as the *New York World, Herald, Sun,* and *Journal,* as well as the *Chicago Tribune and Record,* had the resources to afford foreign war correspondents, their wire services enabled newspapers around the country to reproduce their reports. Many editors also subscribed to the Associated Press (AP) instead of or in addition to the leading New York and Chicago journals.[8] During the war Hearst spent $50,000 weekly (equivalent to more than $1 million per week in present terms) to cover the mounting costs of cable fees, dispatch boats, and travel expenses.[9] Most newspapers could not compete and opted instead to furnish their readers with up-to-date reports obtained from the leading news sources.

These press services enabled Americans from all parts of the country to learn about the ongoing crisis from the perspective of a cohort of dynamic young war correspondents, including Sylvester Scovel, Richard Harding Davis, James Creelman, George Bronson Rea, and Stephen Crane. William Paley of Edison's Biograph in late March–early April 1898 shot motion picture footage of a pack of press correspondents racing through the streets of Key West, competing to be first at the cable office to transmit their reports.[10] In this popular film that season, Paley tapped into and helped perpetuate the glamour and excitement of international travel and press correspondence surrounding the Cuban conflict. These journalists, in turn, narrated the crisis as if it were the plot of a dime novel, telling of their personal adventures alongside the Cuban revolutionaries. Alternating roles of reporter, soldier, celebrity, and spy, they fashioned themselves as the heroic protagonists in America's rescue mission, documenting Cuba's devastation and Spain's destructiveness at extreme personal risk.[11]

Graphic artists, who in most cases did not go to Cuba, did the work of translating the correspondents' reports into visual representations.[12] Many took the form of pictorial editorials or political cartoons, intent on delivering a specific point of view in a concise visual statement. As a popular art, cartooning makes use of symbols and allusions circulating broadly and relies on a reader's familiarity with the pressing concerns of the day.[13] Although renowned cartoonists may have wielded some influence in shaping graphic content, managing editors retained decision-making power in editorial matters. When President McKinley called long-standing *New York World* cartoonist Walt McDougall a Democrat, McDougall corrected him. "Working for a Democratic paper doesn't make me a Democrat!" he retorted, adding, "Cartoonists have no politics." A cartoonist, said McDougall, must have an "ability to see two sides" and "a curious elasticity of mind that permits him to make cartoons for either party without doing violence to his own private opinions."[14] Editorial columns in the 1890s rarely included bylines, making it difficult to determine authorship, but cartoonists fixed their signature on their art, taking credit for their work regardless of whether or not their cartoons were in line with their own political or personal inclinations.

A small community of cartoonists, working for daily newspapers and illustrated weeklies, created a shared pictorial narrative of the effects of Spanish brutality on Cuban civilians. In one of C. G. Bush's cartoons reproduced in the *New York Herald*, Uncle Sam stands dolefully, holding his hat behind his back, before the makeshift hut of a distraught Cuban family, with several dead and dying, including a child, on the ground (figure 1.2). He comments, "And This Is War!" The *Houston Post* published a similar image, demonstrating a gleeful General Weyler standing before a burning house, having just written the proclamation "Another Cuban Family Pacified."[15] These cartoonists strove to elicit sympathy for Cuba by illustrating the impact of Spanish repression on Cuban families. At the same time, they functioned to erase the "real" war that Cuban insurgents were waging against Spain for their independence. Designating the Cubans as objects of pity rendered them powerless.

Halftone photographs and graphic illustrations in the popular press replicated images of Cuban poverty and displacement. *Chicago Record* correspondent Crittenden Marriott made Cuban homes the object of his camera in Havana in 1897, and graphic artists converted his photographs into illustrations for the *Record*. The day before the *New York Herald* published Bush's cartoon, the *Herald* printed a sketch drawn from one of Marriott's photographs of Cuban families standing before makeshift dwellings. It depicted "a village of concentrados" in the same type of hut that appeared in Bush's cartoons, though these Cubans were alive and standing upright.[16]

For Marriott, these images of Cuban destitution were all the more heartbreaking given the "whiteness" of their occupants. He wrote: "An American traveler is surprised and a little shocked to see the peo-

—New York Herald.

1.2. Charles G. Bush, "And This Is War." *New York Herald,* May 17, 1897, 1.

ple who live in these huts, which remind him of negro cabins at home, for he rather expects to see negroes living in them here; but the people in these huts are as white—and a good deal whiter—than nine out of ten Americans. One can easily see the blue veins through their very fine and white complexions."[17] He was appalled at the squalor that these "white" families had to endure. Despite Cuba's racial diversity, media campaigns prior to U.S. intervention consistently coded Cuban victims as "white" in order to define them as worthy of rescue according to the melodramatic script. Their "whiteness" heightened the tragedy of their circumstances and warranted action on their behalf.

Graphic artists and playwrights also expressed Cuba's vulnerability through the visual codes of gender, producing a common symbol of Cuban suffering: the feminized victim. She was often depicted prostrate, chained, on her knees, emaciated, and/or wounded. Cuba was not always represented as female. But since gender functioned to signal its status as an endangered body, image makers chose the female form when emphasizing Cuba's need to be rescued. When artists wanted to project an image of Cuba actively struggling against

Spain, they used the male form.[18] They did so infrequently, however, since a male Cuba potentially rendered the American hero unnecessary. This important iconographic exclusion foreshadowed the later political marginalization of the Cubans in the processes of war, peace, and postwar reconstruction.

One important exception to the general suppression of the male Cuban icon was in Buffalo Bill's Wild West Show. William F. Cody, better known as Buffalo Bill, added an international dimension to his productions in the 1890s. Although the western cowboy theme gave his shows a distinctly American flavor, his cast became more multinational in this period, including Mexicans, American Indians, Russian cossacks, Arabs, and others, hailed as a Congress of Rough Riders from around the world. As part of this exhibition, Cody showcased fifteen Cuban insurgents on leave because of combat injuries. Their wounds enhanced the spectacle, becoming badges of courage and signs of authenticity, of their having actually fought in Cuba. "Every man of them bears the mark of bravery; scars . . . and gashes give testimony to devotion to Cuba, to heroism in the struggle for its liberty," declared the *New York World.* In introducing each of them, Buffalo Bill focused on the man's wounds as a means of telling his story, each more fantastic than the next. The "public favorite," as the *World* claimed, was Sergeant Eleadoro Hernandez, shot twice in the foot in battle and taken prisoner. Spanish officers tortured him for information, cutting his body with a machete and needlessly amputating his leg, but he refused to speak. With open wounds, he was left in prison for months until General Ramón Blanco issued a general amnesty to promote compliance with home rule. Hernandez's triumphant ride on horseback around the ring with the other Cubans elicited loud cheers.[19] His tortured body, paraded before the crowd, bore the marks of his suffering and sacrifice, but he posed no threat to the rescue narrative. He could no longer fight, making room for the manly American hero to step in and finish the job.

A female Cuba more suitably fit the "chivalric paradigm," to borrow Kristin Hoganson's phrase, of Cuban liberation.[20] Images of Cuba as a virtuous, meek, and chaste woman affirmed the normative power of the feminine, signaling her patriarchal dependence and reconstituting the white manhood of her saviors. By submitting to her rescuer, Cuba demonstrated her need for U.S. protection. Yet, some

SPAIN'S "SENSE OF JUSTICE."

1.3. Charles G. Bush, "Spain's 'Sense of Justice.'" *New York World,* March 29, 1898, 1.

graphic artists and playwrights recognized the narrative appeal of empowering a female Cuba, thus complicating the political assumptions of imperial dominance embedded in the image.

At one extreme, graphic artists rendered Cuba as a passive victim at the mercy of the misogynistic Latin male, as in C. G. Bush's "Spain's 'Sense of Justice'" in the *New York World* (figure 1.3). In the tradition of its most notorious leaders, Spain callously tramples a mute and prostrate female Cuba, who projects the utmost in subjection and vulnerability. Bearing his phallic torch and sword dripping with blood, he symbolizes the brutal rape and conquest of Cuba.

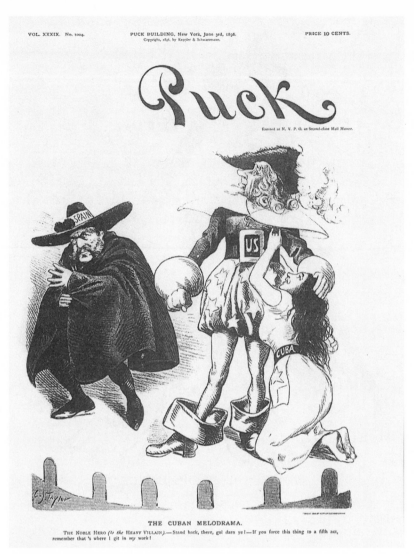

VOL. XXXIX. No. 1004. PUCK BUILDING, New York, June 3rd, 1896. PRICE 10 CENTS.
Copyright, 1896, by Keppler & Schwarzmann.

Entered at N. Y. P. O. as Second-class Mail Matter.

THE CUBAN MELODRAMA.

THE NOBLE HERO (to the HEAVY VILLAIN).— Stand back, there, gol darn ye!— If you force this thing to a fifth act, remember that's where I git in my work!

1.4. C. J. Taylor, "The Cuban Melodrama." *Puck* 34 (June 3, 1896): 1.

Graphic artists, in other instances, acknowledged Cuba's sexual power as a source of resistance.[21] Although it was up to the American male hero to free her from Spain's sadistic grasp, at times Cuba enlisted her sexuality to lure him in. The cover of *Puck* magazine in June 1896 may have been the earliest incarnation of this romantic plot: the American hero protecting the white Cuban female from the dark and evil Spaniard (figure 1.4). The artist, C. J. Taylor, exposes the ballyhoo of the Cuban narrative in his satirical use of melo-dramatic conventions; the caption reads "The Cuban Melodrama: The Noble Hero (to the Heavy Villain)—Stand back, there, gol darn ye!—If you force this thing to a fifth act, remember that's where I git in *my* work!" The voluptuous Cuban woman, however, does not fit the melodramatic ideal of sexual modesty. Dressed in rags, she kneels barefoot at his side in a sexually suggestive pose and gazes at him with pleading eyes. Her long wavy hair and unkempt body evoke a racialized and exotic sensuality, leaving one only to imagine what kind of "work" the hero refers to when the play reaches its climax in the fifth act.[22] Taylor mocks the Anglo-Saxon hero, effeminized in Elizabethan costume, in his role as her defender. Although American men may have envisioned themselves as protectors of the Cuban damsels in distress, Taylor's satirical tone highlights the iconic tension: Is the seducer the American hero or the Cuban enchantress? Who is wielding the power?

When Taylor's cartoon was published in 1896, the feminized image of Cuba was still relatively rare. By early 1898 she appeared in cartoons nationwide.[23] On February 20, 1898, the cover of the *Los Angeles Sunday Times* magazine featured the image (figure 1.5). A barefoot Cuba beseeches the Statue of Liberty for her freedom. "Have We Degenerated?" asks the title. The specters of American generals of the Revolutionary War and the Civil War chide, "Her appeal would not have been in vain in our day." The artist portrays a female Cuba as a kneeling, chained supplicant, though coded white, drawing on the familiar likeness of the abolitionist emblem "Am I Not a Woman and a Sister?" (figure 1.6).[24] This typifies how image makers refigured the visual language of African enslavement in depicting a female Cuba. Exposing the figure's bound wrists, bare breasts, and scars of whippings on her face and back underscores her sexual bondage. Still, she is not depicted as passive. She is a brave, muscular warrior—a kind of Cuban Amazon—who perseveres through her pain.[25] There are limits to her agency, nonetheless; the most she can do is beseech aid.

Stage performances also imprinted suffering on the body of a female Cuba. At the Academy of Music in Richmond, Virginia, in April 1897, a team of local organizations produced a series of vignettes on the crisis. In one, the Confederate Memorial Association

Veterans of 1776 and 1865: "Her appeal would not have been in vain in our day."

1.5. "Have We Degenerated?" *Los Angeles Times Illustrated Magazine*,
February 20, 1898, 1.

depicted the Cuban nationalists in a spectacular charge against the
Sons of Confederate Veterans, who played the Spanish cavalry. In the
final scene, "Cuba is seen appealing with hands outstretched in mute
appeal to America, asking for aid."[26] As a subaltern, she does not
speak for herself; her endangered body constitutes the spectacle of
suffering and visually signifies her cry for help.[27]

1.6. Abolitionist Emblem, "Am I Not a Woman and a Sister?" From George Bourne, *Slavery Illustrated in Its Effects upon Woman and Domestic Society* (Boston: Isaac Knapp, 1837). Manuscripts, Archives and Rare Books Division, Schomburg Center for Research in Black Culture, The New York Public Library, Astor, Lenox and Tilden Foundations.

Other dramatists enabled female Cuba to facilitate her own liberation. By the mid-1890s, graphic artist Charles Dana Gibson's construction of the "Gibson Girl," an athletic, smart, daring, and attractive young woman, emerged as the era's epitome of feminine beauty and character, the "New Woman." Romance novels as well as "serial-queen" stage melodramas increasingly incorporated this image of the heroine as an intelligent, assertive defender.[28] Many theatrical productions fit the Cuban heroine to this paradigm as a woman who, far from being fragile or helpless, bravely and skillfully defeats the Spanish villain. One could argue that her capacity to rescue herself undermined the imperialist fantasy of "playing savior," which warranted colonial occupation.

Take, for example, the play *Cuba's Vow,* appearing in New York, Philadelphia, and Boston in 1897. It begins as Miss Cuba, the young heroine, sees her parents killed at the order of the "Tigress," the Spanish villainess. One reviewer described the Tigress in gothic language as a "devil of the tombs," leading audiences to "hiss" each time she appeared onstage. Reviewers described Miss Cuba, by contrast, as attractive and vibrant, with loosely flowing hair, wearing short skirts that left her "ambitious young legs . . . free and untrammeled."[29] Her sexual assertiveness contrasts with the dominant mode of stage melodrama, which relied on female chastity and virtue. Passionate and strong, she vows to avenge the murder of her parents. She falls in love with an American sympathizer with the Cuban rebellion, who is also the object of the Tigress's desire. In a moment of comic relief, the American (played by Harrington Reynolds) rescues an extra-large Cuban flag during a Spanish attack and gets lost inside its folds. Literally trapped within a symbol of Cuba Libre, the American hero is rendered helpless. Miss Cuba's situation worsens when the Tigress imprisons her out of jealousy. At this point in the play she wore a long skirt and her hair tied up to symbolize her fettered spirit, highlighting her sexuality as her source of strength. After a jailer unlocks her cell, Miss Cuba fulfills her vow and pushes the Tigress off a balcony to her death, delivering herself from bondage. While the show consistently ended with Cuba's self-liberation, theatrical manager Harley Merry adapted the plot to fit the demographics of local audiences, varying the severity of Spanish oppression according to the numbers of Cuban or Spanish people in area communities.[30]

The conflicting expressions of a female Cuba's agency in prewar visual culture demonstrate that these images of gender and rescue had no single, consistent meaning. Cuba's sexual allure can be understood as an imperial metaphor for her political and economic desirability, increasing the manly vigor of her rescuer. But it also signified empowerment, making her an active participant in her own liberation. The motivation for mass-producing Cuban liberation through the icon of the endangered Cuban woman had little to do with U.S. imperialist ambitions; rather, media makers recognized the commercial appeal of storylines involving sexual danger and valiant rescue. The emotional power of endangered femininity has inspired Americans to take aggressive measures throughout U.S. history, from the rallying calls of lynch mobs to the battle cries of the twentieth and twenty-first centuries, impelled by narratives ranging from colonial captivity tales, to charges of German brutalities against Belgian women during World War I and reports of the Taliban's mistreatment of Afghan women in the war on terror.[31] Deploying the moral mission of rescue, with its compelling claims of rape, starvation, and vulnerability, particularly with women and children as victims, has long persisted because it turns action into manly, noble purpose and inaction into irresponsibility and abandonment. The imperial subtext and long-term political ramifications of this rescue narrative were at best an afterthought.

Spain, the Barbaric Villain

To arouse audiences from apathy to anger, media makers constructed an image of the Spanish villain as pathologically and inhumanely cruel.[32] They borrowed from a well-established visual and textual repertoire of imagery, the Black Legend, dating back to the period of New World colonialism and Catholic-Protestant antagonism in the sixteenth century. Spain's northern European rivals constructed this series of stereotypes to associate Spain with the evils of Catholicism, the brutal conquest of Spanish America, and the barbarities of the Dutch war and the Spanish Inquisition.[33] The Black Legend offered vivid imagery to designate Spain as exceptionally evil, fanatical, and degenerate.

Branded "the butcher," Captain-General Valeriano Weyler y Nicolau became the chief icon of Spanish brutality. In early 1897 the *Denver Post* depicted the "Butcher General Weyler" bearing a large knife and an angry scowl (figure 1.7). Thrusting his large belt buckle forward and holding his knife like a torch, he stalks as if on the hunt for blood, confident of his power to inflict retribution. This image was similarly mobilized by comic opera comedian Montjoy Walker, who won acclaim for his burlesque of Weyler's swaggering pride and cruelty on the vaudeville stage.[34]

Image makers most typically pictured Spain as a pirate or demon, surrounded by symbols of gothic horror such as skeletons, bloody knives, and skulls. By 1898 this portrait became increasingly grue-some in the yellow press. A classic example of this image appeared on the front page of the *New York World* (figure 1.8), where C. G. Bush depicts Spain as a skeleton with a black cape and a machete dripping with blood. He embodies the Four Horsemen of the Apocalypse all in

He still continues to slaughter the innocents, setting at naught the provisions of treaties, trampling under foot the rights of American citizens and flying in the face of humanity.

1.7. "Butcher General Weyler." *Denver Post,* February 19, 1897, 1.

one as he spells out the terms of his rule: "Slaughter, Pestilence, Rapine, Starvation." He carries a fiery torch to burn the homes and farms of the *reconcentrados* and speaks the words of Rudyard Kipling: "Lord, God of Hosts, Be With Us Yet, Lest We Forget—Lest We Forget!" The religious overtones play on the accusations of superstition and deviltry implied in the Black Legend, which constructed Spain as a grisly and diabolical enemy.[35] Even the less sensationalistic *New York Times* shared this language in depicting Spain, declaring: "Cortez and Pizarro in Peru were the prototypes of successive brutal, bloodthirsty, and extortionate colonial and viceregal tyrants even down to the time of Weyler. The history of Spanish occupation in America is a record

"LORD, GOD OF HOSTS, BE WITH US YET,
LEST WE FORGET—LEST WE FORGET!"

1.8. Charles G. Bush, "Lord, God of Hosts." *New York World,* March 23, 1898, 1.

of perverse and bigoted misrule."[36] Media accounts imagined Spain in the image of the Black Legend to heighten the sense of impending threat against the imperiled female victim Cuba, the latest prey of this "perverse and bigoted" monster.

Extending the caricature, news outlets and image makers documented in horrific detail the physical effects of Spanish oppression on the bodies of Cuban *reconcentrados.* The *Tennessee Commercial Appeal,* in what it termed a "sickening spectacle," spoke of "infants vainly tugging at famine-withered breasts," calling this physical and spiritual disintegration of body and soul "a crime against Almighty God."[37] The appalling effects of starvation on the bodies of the victims became proof of Spanish inhumanity. As described by Julian Hawthorne in the *New York Journal,* they were a horrifying sight to witness: "There is little difference in the expressions of skulls, but a skull seen through drawn and wrinkled skin, and with the ghastly eyes still in their sockets, is a more terrible spectacle than naked bones." Fannie B. Ward, a female correspondent for the *Chicago Inter Ocean,* published a drawing of an open pit full of human bones, a mass grave she discovered at Havana Cemetery. She describes her trip to the cemetery in gruesome detail: "Hundreds of broken coffins were piled in one corner, and thousands of skulls—some white and shining with long exposure to the sun, others with grave mold green upon them—grinned from every side."[38]

The image of thousands of grinning skulls in this mass grave is horrific enough, but it may only have heightened readers' feelings of outrage that it was an American woman who ventured upon such a ghastly sight. Like the assertive Cuban heroine or evil Spanish villainess, war reporter Fannie Ward undercut any neat division of gender in the cultural production of the crisis in which "female" was code for frailty and "male" signified action. Still, female journalists were in the minority, making up only 7.3 percent of the profession in 1900 and primarily slated to write on topics designated for female readers. Only three other female journalists went to Cuba: Kathleen Blake Watkins of the *Toronto Mail and Empire,* Anna Benjamin of *Leslie's Illustrated Weekly,* and Katherine White of the *Chicago Record.*[39] Their limited role is not surprising, given that the very act of being a foreign correspondent in Cuba was gendered. Reporters styled themselves rescuers in the melodramatic scheme (a role *Journal* correspondent Karl Decker adhered to literally), risking incarceration or worse to bring to light the "truth" about Spain's trail of destruction.

The Tango of Representation and Reality

Press coverage of the Cuban crisis countrywide was sporadic between 1895 and 1897. In September 1897 the Cuban-sympathizing *Cleveland Plain Dealer* worried that "the cause of poor Cuba is likely to be lost sight of" because of its subordination to other news topics. Looking back, the *Atlantic Monthly* claimed that even six months before the war began, the public was "not greatly aroused" and "gave little thought to Cuba," and that a prediction of war "would have seemed wild and foolish."[40] It took the destruction of the battleship *Maine* in February 1898 to catapult Cuba into the national spotlight. Prior to that time, the vilification of Spain and clamor for Cuban independence had appeared primarily in the yellow press. These journals attempted to draw attention to the Cuban crisis through human interest stories about actual afflicted women and families to authenticate narratives of Spanish cruelty and sexual danger. The significance of Pulitzer's and Hearst's influence (as well as that of other editors of large urban dailies) lies in their setting the agenda to determine how Cuba's story should be told, an agenda that took root more broadly in American print, visual, and popular culture after the *Maine* incident.

In February 1897 Richard Harding Davis cabled a dispatch from Cuba reporting that Spanish officials had strip-searched two women aboard the U.S.S. *Olivette* on suspicion of plotting rebellion. Well-known artist Frederic Remington illustrated Davis's story for the *New York Journal* with a five-column drawing that re-created the episode into a near-pornographic scene (figure 1.9). Under the headline "Spaniards Search Women on American Steamers," Remington depicts a fair-skinned woman standing, completely naked, with her buttocks exposed to the viewer, surrounded by three fully clothed men. The dark shading of the men's suits and the background of the ship contrasts starkly with her white skin. The men stand dangerously close, scrutinizing her body. A *New York Times* editorialist described the image as "a thrilling tableau of a young and unclad female, surrounded by tall and mustached hidalgos of peculiarly villainous Spanish types." It was "a great opportunity," claimed the *Times,* "for in this case was not the nude 'legitimate news'?—and greatly the artist rose to it."[41] The woman's sexual violation is seemingly doubly imposed, for she is allegedly forced to undress not only before these men but also before a wide reading public.

After the piece was published, the House of Representatives promptly passed a resolution calling for an investigation into the matter, which is not surprising, considering that the press served

SPANIARDS SEARCH WOMEN ON AMERICAN STEAMERS.
—DRAWN BY FREDERIC REMINGTON.

1.9. Frederic Remington, "Spaniards Search Women on American Steamers." *New York Journal,* February 12, 1897, 2.

as one of the government's predominant sources of intelligence on Cuban affairs. But the *New York World* soon charged the *Journal* with falsifying the story, claiming that the woman had been searched by a female officer in private. After this was confirmed, Davis quit the *Journal.* The *World* quoted Davis's angry response to the illustration: "Mr. Frederick [*sic*] Remington, who was not present and who drew an imaginary picture of the scene, is responsible for the idea that the search was conducted by men. Had I seen the picture before it appeared I should never have allowed it to accompany my article."[42] Despite the controversy, few editors nationwide commented on the incident. While the national impact of the sketch may have been insignificant, it reveals the *Journal*'s project to sensationalize Cuban affairs through the iconography of sexually violated women. It suggests that Hearst kept his ears pricked for a bona fide distressed female to personify Cuba.

Less than a week after Remington's sketch appeared, a naturalized American citizen and practicing dentist, Dr. Ricardo Ruiz, died in his prison cell in Guanabacoa, Cuba. Ruiz was one of the many Americans the press claimed were being held indefinitely in Spanish prisons on the charge of rebellion. His death became a point of national interest in part because the U.S. consul-general in Cuba, Fitzhugh Lee, a former Confederate general and nephew to Robert E. Lee, had threatened to resign if the U.S. government did not provide him with the resources to prevent such tragedies. Spanish officials called Ruiz's death a suicide, but an autopsy revealed that he had received a blow to his head causing "congestion of the brain," leading Lee to suspect murder. To the *New York Herald,* Spain was guilty either way; "the only question is whether it is a case of murder in cold blood by an inhuman jailer or of suicide by a sufferer driven to despair and madness by barbaric treatment."[43]

Press reports called Ruiz's cell a "dungeon," a term reminiscent of Spain's legendary inquisitorial past, and described it as "filled with filth, vermin, and flies."[44] The *Chicago Tribune* alleged that after Ruiz denied having ties to the insurgents, the guards had subjected him to the "componte," meaning that a guard had struck him with a piece of iron until he fainted or bled, then let him revive, and struck him again. "The design is to kill him by degrees, and when the climax of cruelty is reached then a powerful and decisive blow on the head puts an end to the poor victim's sufferings."[45] There was no proof that Ruiz underwent such torture, but it is not surprising that the *Tribune* imagined such an experience for Ruiz; it fit the profile of mythic Spanish medievalism.

The *Journal,* the *Herald,* and the *World* constructed the story as a domestic tragedy. They published numerous sketches (drawn from photographs) of Rita Lesca V. de Ruiz, the doctor's widow, veiled in mourning, and her five children arriving in the United States, attending church services, and meeting with President McKinley.[46] Press reports draped her tale of woe in sentimentalist rhetoric, painting her as a defenseless, grief-stricken widow; the *Herald* reported, "While caressing her children, the poor widow gathered about her, too, the inanimate objects which recalled her husband and protector who was gone." Described as "slight and fragile looking," Rita Ruiz and her children personified a major theme in the iconography of the Cuban crisis, that of shattered family.[47]

The yellow press further claimed that Rita Ruiz possessed proof of her husband's murder. According to reports, Dr. Ruiz's jail cell was completely bare, without even a bed, and Rita Ruiz persuaded the guards to let him have an old chair she brought from home. Officials returned the chair to her after his death, and on the bottom she reportedly discovered this message from her late husband, etched by his fingernails: "To Mercedes, Evangeline, Ricardito, Rene and Gloria: Farewell, children of my life. Be obedient to your mother. I bless you all. I shall be killed. To Rita, my wife, my soul, adios. If I am removed, tell all. Ricardo."[48] The yellow press printed illustrations of the chair as proof of murder, but its existence was improbable. Consul-General Lee's report to the State Department on the murder investigation failed to mention it. A skeptical editorialist for the *San Francisco Chronicle* called the evidence "absurd."[49] But the chair was essential in crafting the narrative of a family torn asunder. The *New York Journal* described the chair as "the means of his [Ruiz's] sending a last loving message to his wife and children" before facing death.[50] Playwright Dazie Noel dramatized the Ruiz story in a stage play titled *A Spaniard's Revenge or The Death of Ricardo Ruiz.*[51] Noel manufactured a desire on the part of the Spanish jailer, Lt. Col. Eulate Fondesveila for Rita Ruiz, prompting Ricardo's incarceration. Fondesveila murders Ricardo, and Rita murders Fondesveila in retribution. Although the love triangle and the revenge plot were not part of the historical script, the play used the element of the chair and Ruiz's dying message, which audiences likely recalled from press accounts, to confirm Fondesveila as the killer. In the aftermath of the scandal, even without official proof, the U.S. State Department requested that the Spanish government make reparations to Rita Ruiz to compensate her for her suffering.

Despite the sensationalized narrative of Dr. Ruiz's death, the episode did not create a press consensus for war. Other than the major dailies of New York and Chicago, few newspapers covered the ongoing Ruiz story with front-page articles and illustrations. Even the *Journal*'s companion paper, the *San Francisco Examiner,* devoted more attention to the concurrent Bob Fitzsimmons–James Corbett boxing match. The impact, if any, of the Ruiz affair on arousing public opinion was at best localized to the readership of a limited set of newspapers. And even that was short-lived, for the Spanish government acted quickly to pacify popular indignation by releasing General Julio Sanguilly, another naturalized American citizen imprisoned in Cuba for insurrection. Congress had demanded Sanguilly's immediate release, but before a resolution could be passed, the Queen Regent of Spain signed his pardon. When Sanguilly left Cuba and arrived in Philadelphia, press illustrations celebrated his reception and joyous reunion with his wife and children.[52] The parallel narrative of Sanguilly's release in effect defused the need to avenge Ruiz's death. In the same moment when Spain ripped Ruiz's family apart, another family was put back together. In an ironic footnote to the story, it took less than a month before Sanguilly was caught breaking the terms of his pardon by sneaking back into Cuba to incite rebellion.

In the months following Ruiz's murder, the press lost interest in Cuba. Feature articles shifted to the Greco-Turkish War and the search for gold in the Klondike. From April to early August 1897, even the yellow press published few pieces on Cuba. It was during this interval, in mid-May, that the U.S. government passed its only piece of legislation to aid Cuba that year. After receiving consular reports documenting famine among U.S. citizens living in Cuba, President McKinley asked Congress to appropriate $50,000 in relief, but stipulated that only Americans residing in Cuba would be eligible for aid. The Senate in turn passed the Morgan Resolution, recognizing that a state of war existed in Cuba. But McKinley chose not to act on it. The timing of this relief bill is particularly revealing, for it was passed not in the midst of a well-publicized crisis in Cuba but during a moment of relative silence in the news industry's Cuban war coverage. This suggests that government leaders were not taking their cues from the press or, by extension, public hype.

Prior to the summer of 1897, McKinley's administration had yet to focus on the Cuban problem. McKinley kept a scrapbook of newspaper clippings from all across the nation, and only two articles in total on Cuban affairs appeared prior to June of that year. During that summer, McKinley formulated his Cuban policy of pressuring Spain into reform by threatening intervention with the hope of preventing war.

His Cuban policy thus crystallized at a time when Cuba was not occupying the headlines, not even in the yellow press. McKinley devoted significantly more energies than his predecessors had into galvanizing public support for his agenda, but at no point did he allow press or popular opinion to dictate his decisions regarding Cuba.[53]

On August 9, 1897, the lull in the press was broken; headlines nationwide announced that an Italian anarchist had assassinated the Spanish premier, Antonio Cánovas, leaving the government in crisis. That October the Queen Regent turned the leadership over to Liberal Party leader Práxedes Mateo Sagasta. But even before this transition of power took place, an event occurred with great sensationalistic appeal. On August 16, correspondent James Creelman of the *Journal* claimed, a copyboy entered Hearst's office with a cable from Havana stating the details of the arrest of Evangelina Cisneros, a beautiful seventeen-year-old Cuban girl. Hearst reportedly slapped his knee and yelled to his managing editor, "We've got Spain, now!"[54]

According to the story told by the *New York Journal,* Evangelina was the niece of the self-proclaimed president of the Cuban Republic, and she had joined her father, a revolutionary of the Ten Years' War, on the Isle of Pines, where he had been exiled. The Spanish governor, Colonel Berriz, viewed her with a lustful eye, and when she refused his advances and screamed for help, her brothers and friends rushed to her aid. When the police arrived, they arrested Evangelina on the charge of conspiring to assassinate Berriz. She was incarcerated in the Casa de Recojidas, a prison for "degraded" women (often described as "negresses" in American press accounts), where she remained for months. The *Journal* reported that Spain had sentenced her to twenty years' imprisonment in the African penal settlement of Ceuta, where no woman had ever been sent (this was a fabrication, as she had not yet been officially sentenced). There, the *Journal* elaborated, the prisoners "are tortured, with all the ingenuity and ferocity of the Inquisition."[55] The *Journal* thus molded Evangelina into an "authentic" example of the feminized victim of Spanish depravity.[56]

The Spanish ambassador to the United States, Enrique Dupuy de Lôme, however, reported an alternate version of the Cisneros story. "The facts show," de Lôme stipulated, "that Miss Evangelina Cossio Cisneros lured to her house the military commander of the Island of Pines, and had men concealed in it, who tried to assassinate him in connection with an uprising of the prisoners in the island."[57] De Lôme's account of the story did not turn U.S. press opinion against Evangelina, but it may have lent credibility to the observations of the well-respected U.S. consul-general, Lee, who disputed the *Journal*'s report that Evangelina had been sentenced to Ceuta. After visiting her in prison, Lee told the press that she was not being subjected to indignities. His reports led some papers, such as the *San Francisco Chronicle*, to condemn the *Journal* for "press hysterics," alleging that Evangelina was a victim not of Spanish brutality but of sensationalistic journalism:

> It seems that their appeal went to the wrong quarter, as the people really to blame for the continued incarceration of Weyler's beautiful captive do not live in Havana and Madrid, but in New York and San Francisco. According to Consul-General Lee, the real culprits are the yellow journalists. "Were it not for the hubbub which has been raised about her in this country," says General Lee, "the girl would probably have been released long ago. In fact I was given to understand that her name was on the pardon list."[58]

But even if editors were conscious of the effects of American media coverage in prolonging Cisneros's ordeal, they did not abandon the story; they recognized that Spain's incarceration of this "beautiful captive" would marshal the attention of their readers.

Nearly every press account lingered over her physical beauty. Her most striking feature, claimed reporters, was her eyes, which the *Richmond Times* described as "large and liquid, at one time melting into a translucent glow, with only a spark in the center like a dim light at the end of a chasm of ebony blackness, and again flashing fire, like the sparks from an electric machine." The *Chicago Times-Herald* quoted a fellow inmate's impression of her: "Her large eyes, shaded by brows that could not be more artistic if a master hand had painted them, are soulful and expressive to a degree that baffles description." The *Washington Post* concurred: "Her eyes are of a liquid black, with just a touch of dash and fire in their penetrating glance. The lines of her nose are finely drawn and rather acute—aquiline. An abundance of curling, waving black hair, that at times glints with a tinge of chestnut bronze, and a complexion, although dark, quite clear, and a transparent skin—the picture of this heroine is complete."[59] Writers and artists accentuated her physical attractiveness and aristocratic birth to amplify interest in her misfortune.

At first, Spanish villainy threatened her sexuality, but now her vibrancy of body and spirit was at risk. The *New York Journal* published before-and-after sketches claiming to reveal "The Effect on Senorita Cisneros of One Year's Incarceration in a Spanish Prison," the first (supposedly drawn from a photograph) depicting her in the prime of health and the second (allegedly drawn from a physician's description) portraying her as weary and defeated (figure 1.10). *Journal* artists embellished the personal impact of her incarceration by drawing her with drooping eyebrows, giving her smaller eyes and disheveled hair, and shading her cheeks, nose, neck, and forehead. Another image depicted her on her hands and knees scrubbing the prison floor. "This is the work which beautiful Evangelina Cisneros, gently born, daintily reared, is forced by vile negress overseers to do each day," charged the *Journal*.[60] "The consumptive's flush is already showing itself upon her typical delicate complexion" lamented the *Examiner*.[61] Consul-General Lee refuted these characterizations and told reporters that she was housed in two clean rooms, with more than adequate food and clothing. Editors nationwide also resisted Hearst's elaborations. Because the *Journal* and the *Examiner* had a combined circulation of only about 423,000, these sensationalistic depictions did not reach a nationwide audience.

The *Journal* nevertheless urged women across sectional and national boundaries to come to her aid and publicized the responses of many prominent women who recognized her cause, such as President McKinley's mother, Jefferson Davis's widow, Julia Ward Howe, and Clara Barton. The *Journal* couched appeals for its petition campaigns in the maternalist language prevalent in the female moral reform movement.[62] After amassing the signatures of 20,000 American and 200,000 British women petitioning for Evangelina Cisneros's immediate release, the *Journal* claimed the movement to be "an uprising of womanhood such as, perhaps, has never been seen before."[63] The romantic construction of women as active maternal agents caring for a vulnerable Cuba paralleled the logic of the dominant narrative—that of the American male hero coming to the rescue of a sexualized female Cuba.[64]

Despite these women's efforts, it was hearty male bravado that

THE EFFECT ON SENORITA CISNEROS OF ONE YEAR'S INCARCERATION IN A SPANISH PRISON.
(The first picture is from a photograph, the second from a description given a Journal correspondent at Havana by a physician.)

1.10. "The Effect on Senorita Cisneros of One Year's Incarceration in a Spanish Prison." *New York Journal,* August 23, 1897, 1.

transformed the Cisneros story into a "spectacle of international acclaim," as the *St. Louis Republic* put it.[65] After pleas to Spain failed, Hearst sent press correspondent Karl Decker to fulfill the *Journal*'s motto—"the journalism of action"—and break Evangelina out of jail. Decker's team claimed to have found their way into an adjoining cell and supplied her with drugs to incapacitate the guards. Then they scaled the wall with a ladder and wrenched apart the iron bars covering a window. The mission was a success. On October 6, 1897, she successfully escaped from prison and, posing as a man, tricked Spanish customs officials into letting her board the *Seneca,* bound for New York. The *Journal*'s headline read in big bold letters "An American Newspaper Accomplishes at a Single Stroke What the Red Tape of Diplomacy Failed Utterly to Bring About in Many Months." Overflowing with self-congratulation, Hearst promoted the rescue as exemplary of his journalistic paradigm, asserting an active role for the press in forging necessary change, even when the government was unable or unwilling to do so.[66]

The construction of Karl Decker's rescue as a valiant act of medieval-style chivalry illuminates the power of melodrama in structuring how the press and its readers interpreted events. The *Washington Times* praised Decker for his "gallant deed of knight-errantry" and for rescuing "a forlorn damsel from the foul castle of the dragon-hyena Weyler." Julian Hawthorne in the *Journal* called him a "hero of the most romantic and daring episode of modern times," elaborating, "From time to time, as the hours went by, I had to remind myself, 'This is true; it is all real.'"[67] David Rich, a real estate agent and reader of the *Examiner,* wrote in, "It is a most interesting, I might say thrilling, story from beginning to end, and reads more like fiction of the Middle Ages than sober fact." The wife of Supreme Court Justice Stephen J. Field concurred: "The affair in all its details read like some medieval romance."[68]

The Cisneros affair not only illustrates how journalists used the power of melodrama and spectacle to shape the way their readers interpreted historical events but also shows how the wider popular culture recapitulated these sensationalized narratives for a broader audience. Within weeks of the rescue, it was "restaged" for theater audiences. Proctor's Theater in New York presented a one-act play titled *For Liberty,* written by and starring Mrs. Hoffman-Neil as Evangelina. Proctor offered Cisneros $500 a week to occupy a box during performances.[69] The *Atlanta Constitution* had this cynical take on the Cisneros spectacle:

> Already she has commenced to be besieged with offers to go on the stage by enterprising managers. Not content with sending her boxes to their shows in order to draw crowds to the performance, they now want the poor little Cuban to make a spectacle of herself just to satisfy that abnormally developed desire to see some one who has done something out of the ordinary, no matter whether it be a beast who has slugged some one into insensibility, an idiot who has jumped from some unearthly height or a poor little girl who has been rescued from prison. The chances are that Cisneros can no more act than a cow, but that will not matter, if a good Cuban play is written, painting the Spaniards as black as can be and making her the heroine; that will be enough for American audiences and the chances are that she could retire after one season with a comfortable bank account to her credit.[70]

Disparaging the mass-produced dramatic formula of the popular stage, this editorialist echoes the dismissive tone of some contemporary critics toward the forms of cultural expression capitalizing on the Cuban rescue narrative. As long as the theatrical script conformed to the portraits of good and evil, laments the editorialist, the audiences and box office would be satisfied.

For the "savior" narrative to play out fully, however, Cisneros had to learn the ways of American society. Cella Wallace, a wealthy childless widow, offered to serve as her benefactor. In a statement brimming with imperialist maternalism, she asserted, "All I have in this world is plenty of money and I long for some loving child to educate and teach to enjoy it when I pass away."[71] For unknown reasons, Cisneros declined Wallace's offer in favor of one from Mrs. John A. Logan, who successfully petitioned the Orphans' Court for legal guardianship. To effect her acculturation, the court mandated that Cisneros apply for citizenship and attend school, which the *Journal* later documented with images of her naturalization ceremony and of Cisneros learning to speak English.

In a classic finale, in June 1898 Cisneros married Carlos Carbonell, who had assisted in her rescue. Carbonell, a Cuban American banker who was part of a clandestine network supporting the revolution, had hidden Cisneros in his house until she could be safely conveyed to the *Seneca*. The melodrama thus ended in formulaic fashion, with the marriage of hero and heroine. But in real life, Cisneros chose to marry not Decker, her American rescuer, but one of the Cuban heroes whose invisible efforts had ensured her release. Soon after Spain's defeat, she and her new husband left the United States and settled in Cuba.

The Spectacle of Mass Death

Just as Decker was making his rescue of Cisneros in October 1897, the transfer of power in the Spanish government took effect. Sagasta announced his plan for Cuban autonomy and replaced Captain-General Weyler with Ramón Blanco, who had a reputation for a softer, more diplomatic style. Despite the relaxation of censorship under Blanco's regime, press coverage of the Cuban crisis declined.

In his message to Congress in December of that year, President McKinley urged Americans to give the policy a fair trial. In the meantime, Blanco established relief committees throughout Cuba to alleviate suffering and won praise from the more conservative American press. Unlike his predecessor, Blanco "does not war on women," declared the *Chicago Times-Herald.*[72] Blanco also accepted U.S. support, leading government agencies and private organizations to organize mass aid drives for Cuba.

After Cuban insurgents murdered a Spanish envoy for bringing word of home rule, it became clear that the rebels would accept nothing less than independence. Accordingly, the yellow press resumed its campaigns to stir sympathy for Cuba. At the same moment, two books by former *New York Herald* correspondents, *The Real Condition of Cuba* by Stephen Bonsal and George Bronson Rea's *Facts and Fakes about Cuba,* entered public circulation and exposed the fabrication of Spanish atrocities in yellow press accounts. The popularity of these books may have raised the level of skepticism toward yellow journalism, perhaps in part prompting the yellow press to rely more fully on visual evidence to authenticate its allegations.

The spotlight returned to the ongoing physical anguish of the *reconcentrados* in spite of official repeal of the policy. The *Journal* launched its "Human Documents" campaign, which Julian Hawthorne described as a "spectacle of death," writing: "You do not have to read in order to appreciate the ghastly meaning of the pictures of Cuban 'reconcentrados' published in the Journal to-day. . . . The pictures of human misery which the Journal publishes are drawn from photographs. Their publication is a duty, not a pleasure. They are selected from a hundred or more in the possession of this paper, and are far from being the most ghastly, the most horrifying of all, for some are too frightful to print."[73] Reference to the "duty" of providing visual proof is highly significant here, for it speaks to the public's need for corroboration that Cuba's suffering was in fact "real." By noting that the sketches were "drawn from photographs," the *Journal* affirmed the accuracy of its graphic imagery by association with photography, which readers often perceived as transmitting the truth. The paper offered the images as evidence, suggesting that one must "see" these pictures, or better yet "see" the suffering firsthand, to grasp the extent of the misery. The *Journal* went so far as to claim

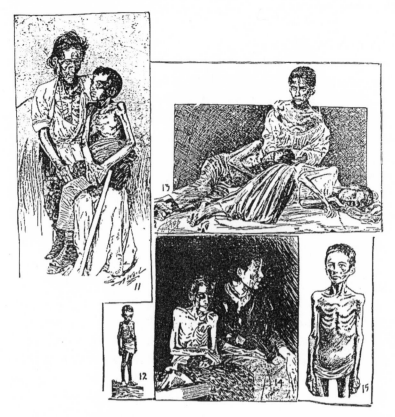

1.11. *New York Journal,* March 14, 1898, 5.

to be censoring its own images and not showing those "too frightful to print" for fear of distressing readers. Those who witnessed the horrors firsthand reiterated the primacy of the visual in this matter. "Language is inadequate to describe the suffering and misery seen here," claimed Congressman William A. Smith of Michigan; Congressman W. H. King of Utah concurred: "I found that no one has ever half depicted the awful horrors of the reconcentrados. . . . To realize just what this means, one must see for himself."[74]

The "Human Documents" campaign consisted of shocking depictions of the emaciated bodies of dead and dying Cubans. "It is not exaggeration to say that every house has become a hospital and every garden a graveyard," reported the *Denver Post.* In March 1898 the *Journal* published a full-page spread illustrating dying women and children with clearly defined ribs and distended stomachs. In an excerpt from this montage (figure 1.11), we see women and children in the last stages of starvation. Meticulous shading accentuates their fragile form, shrunken limbs, and gaunt faces. After viewing images like these, Congressman Peter Otey of Virginia told the *Journal,* "These photographs represent such an unspeakable horror that they would be incredible, but for the fact that their truth cannot be challenged."[75]

Heightening the horror of this humanitarian crisis was that it was occurring close to American borders (see figure 1.2). By characterizing Cuba as America's neighbor, U.S. news and image producers used geographic proximity to justify America's historical interest in Cuba and its moral responsibility to intervene. The *Houston Post* argued that when the people of Armenia and India suffered from famine, the United States "in the name of Christianity and humanity" generously donated "to relieve the suffering in those far off lands." "Now we are to be asked to assist the destitute and miserable thousands right at our door, the starving and persecuted non-combatants in Cuba."[76] Alongside images of Cuban poverty and starvation were nearly identical illustrations of famine-stricken people in India. What separated the former from the latter in the mobilization of U.S. military efforts was the repeated theme in the prewar campaigns that the Cuban conflict was taking place at America's doorstep—and therefore could not be ignored.

Testimonials from government officials, consuls, aid workers, journalists, visitors, and congressmen confirmed the images of Cuban suffering circulating in the press. The one that did the most to corroborate press accounts was a speech given by Senator Redfield Proctor, a Republican from Vermont, on the floor of a packed Senate chamber on March 17. Proctor described the "desolation and distress, misery and starvation" that he had witnessed in Cuba:

> I went to Cuba with the strong conviction that the picture had been overdrawn, that a few cases of starvation and suffering had inspired and stimulated the press correspondents, and they had given free play to a strong, natural, and highly cultivated imagination. Before starting I received through the mail a leaflet, published by the *Christian Herald,* with cuts of some of the sick and starving reconcentrados, and took it with me, thinking these were rare specimens got up to make the worst possible showing. I saw plenty as bad and worse; many that should not be photographed and shown.[77]

Proctor's claim that press accounts were not embellished, despite his expectations to the contrary, had a profound impact on public opinion, and in particular on the American business community. The conservative *Wall Street Journal* credited Proctor's speech with having "converted a great many people on Wall Street who have heretofore taken the ground that the United States had no business to interfere in a revolution on Spanish soil."[78] In his short statement he validated the melodramatic conception of the Cuban crisis on a national scale. Proctor's influence was based on his reputation as a sincere observer "of unimpeachable integrity." Accounts praised his ability to speak "without prejudice or even sentiment," such that "every element of sensationalism had been studiously eliminated." According to the *Boston Herald*, "he shows that he has endeavored to control, and succeeded in controlling, his emotions, and has made, and is making, an effort to deal fairly and dispassionately with the subject; hence his statements have touched those who have not been greatly moved by what they thought were the exaggerated reports of professional correspondents."[79]

In the week following Proctor's speech, the Senate heard the corroborating accounts of the other senators who had observed conditions in Cuba. John Thurston, a Republican senator from Nebraska, spoke tearfully about his visit to Cuba with his wife, who died during the course of the trip. He ascribed her death to the shock of witnessing such devastating scenes. Mobilizing the pain of his personal tragedy, Thurston urged the nation to take action: "We cannot refuse to accept this responsibility which the God of the universe has placed upon us as the one great power in the New World. We must act!" The *New York Journal* memorialized his wife's alleged dying words in an illustration showing a plaque draped with the iconic image of the woeful and helpless Cuban woman: "Oh! Mothers of the Northland, who tenderly clasp your little ones close to your loving hearts! Think of the black despair that filled each mother's heart as she felt her lifeblood ebb away, and knew that she left her little ones to perish from the pains of starvation and disease."[80]

In these influential and highly publicized speeches, congressional leaders intertwined political arguments for intervention in Cuba with popular imagery of Spanish brutality. These speeches authenticated the caricatured visual symbols from press accounts, novels, and stage plays and helped solidify public sentiment for ending Spanish rule in Cuba, whatever the cost. Reference to these images in congressional debates reinforced their power of persuasion and led to their mass proliferation. In downtown Washington, D.C., for example, shop owners began posting pictures of Cuban victims from newspapers in their store windows. An older man looking upon the images reportedly exclaimed: "The inquisition! The inquisition! Just another form of it, sir. The same bloody work of a bloody country. Can't sleep at night without a grave-yard yawning under their beds."[81]

Retrospective accounts of the period leading up to the declaration of war recalled the profusion of Cuba Libre sentiment throughout American political and popular culture. Editor William Allen White of the Emporia, Kansas, *Gazette* wrote of a local politician in 1898: "Charley Curtis made some speeches, as did most of our Congressmen in Kansas, about the oppression of the Cubans. . . . 'Our Charley' knew nothing about the deeper currents of imperialism. . . . He was out after votes to hold his job, and 'free Cuba' was a vote-getter. I wrote editorials about 'free Cuba,' just as casually as Charley Curtis wrote speeches."[82] On the eve of World War I, Ellen Maury Slayden, a native Virginian and wife of a Texas congressman, recalled the nation's mood in 1898, remarking, "What a difference there is in the public mind today" from "when we went to war with Spain." Back then, she observed, "we were on edge with excitement and enthusiasm . . . we saluted one another with 'Viva Cuba Libre,' and called our red hats and dresses by Cuban names."[83] While these reflections call attention to the power of Cuba Libre as a commercial and political draw, neither White nor Slayden noted any substantial engagement with the long-term implications of Cuban independence. This helps explain why the commitment to Cuba Libre dissipated so quickly once U.S. imperial ambitions became manifest.

    In shaping a war around Cuba Libre, media makers tapped into an emerging staple of American national identity—the perception of being an active advocate for moral righteousness in the world. Justifying intervention in this framework, however, reduces the complexities of U.S. motivations and obscures the actual political, military, and economic results of such actions. Any argument for war as an avenue for commercial or strategic gain was purposely muted in order to maintain the purity of American motives, and there is little reason to doubt the altruistic intentions that many Americans expressed. But an important side effect of playing savior in 1898 was that it eclipsed the two decades of fighting in Cuba that preceded American involvement. Cuba's persistent struggle to attain independence mattered only in so far as it created a pretext for U.S. entrance into the war. To rouse support for intervention, media makers substantiated the depths of human misery in Cuba with visual evidence and reputable testimonies, like that of Senator Proctor. Having demonstrated the actual distress of the Cuban people, the press attributed sole responsibility to Spain. There was no place in the master narrative for complicated assessments of accountability, recognition of Cuban participation, or postwar planning. As in any conventional melodrama, the story climaxed with the blissful wedding of hero and heroine upon her rescue. Nobody cares what happens after that.

Still, the preconditions for an imperial mentality were already built in to the graphic language of intervention. Embedded in the humanitarian impulse to "save" Cuba was a conception of America as the conveyor of humanity and civilization. There was an inherent arrogance and presumption of superiority in America's belief that it could step into this role so effortlessly after Cuban revolutionaries had been fighting Spain for years. While the war in 1898 was thankfully short, the same faulty assumptions would be used to rationalize the actions of the United States toward many of the peoples and places it has since sought to "save," with much less definitive results. Despite the clamor for Cuba Libre, exponents of the U.S.-centered rescue narrative at times reduced Cubans to objects, not agents, of their own liberation. But the logical extension of this worldview was not necessarily imperialistic. Although imperialists would later run with this colonial perception and frame America's imperial career in terms of "duty" and "destiny," anticolonialists would later denounce acquisition using the same set of ethnocentric and racist beliefs. In effect, the political implications of the distinction between empowering and disempowering Cuban nationalists in prewar media campaigns were inconsequential without explicit recognition of the war as a pathway to imperial gain.

Still, by the end of 1897, war with Spain was far from inevitable. Historical accounts that treat the yellow press as a causal factor for the Spanish-American War generally approach the conflict as a culmination of incidents dating back to the resumption of hostilities in 1895 which brought the United States to the verge of war. They allege that incidents like the Ruiz and Cisneros affairs were the cumulative building blocks of mounting public agitation for war that by April 1898 could no longer be contained. But an alternative way of looking at these episodes is that while they helped the yellow press sell papers, they constituted a string of failed attempts to provoke a military response. If the yellow press had had the power to incite public hysteria and force the hand of a reluctant president, then the United States would have gone to war earlier than it did. Evidence suggests rather that McKinley paid little heed to Pulitzer and Hearst in assessing popular support for war. His scrapbooks of newspaper clippings contained few from the *Journal* and the *World*.[84] The primary legacy of the yellow press, then, is best understood in terms of its crafting a narrative of the Cuban crisis with theatrical appeal and harnessing the power of images and firsthand accounts to authenticate it.

Prior to February 1898, most dailies outside New York and Chicago were not clamoring for war. It was difficult to justify, because Spain had colonized Cuba for nearly four centuries and posed minimal threat to U.S. security, despite the current disorder. Some argued that the insurgency placed American lives and property in Cuba at risk, but McKinley addressed this concern by sending the *Maine* to protect them. It was only after the explosion of the *Maine* that the cultural production of the Cuban crisis began to engulf a broader spectrum of print, visual, and popular media. The destruction of the battleship provided the impetus for media makers to add another level of emotional magnitude to the spectacle of the international crisis. The sense of urgency for war was no longer just about rescuing Cuba from a dire situation. The United States had to make Spain pay for attacking the nation's honor brutally and without provocation through its alleged act of treachery.

2

The Spectacle of Disaster

THE EXPLOSION OF THE U.S.S. *MAINE*

Awake! United States!
How proudly sailed the warship *Maine,*
A nation's pride, without a stain!
A wreck she lies, her sailors slain
By treach'rous butchers, paid by Spain!
Eagle, soar on high
And sound the battle cry!
Wave the starry flag!
In mire it shall not drag!
Marie Elizabeth Lamb
(April 1898)

Press campaigns to raise awareness of Cuba's humanitarian crisis had been growing steadily since 1895, but the single incident that irrevocably focused media attention on Cuba occurred at precisely 9:40 p.m. on the evening of February 15, 1898, when the U.S. battleship *Maine* exploded in Havana harbor, killing 266 of the 354 American sailors on board. Pulitzer and Hearst immediately named Spain as the culprit, but many editors around the country urged their readers to withhold judgment before a thorough investigation could be made. It was not the jingoist calls of a few high-circulation "yellow" papers that unified the nation on a belligerent course. The *Maine* explosion set in motion a consolidation of support for the Cuban cause across American print, visual, and popular media that transformed audience engagement with events in Cuba. Following the incident, cultural producers incorporated the *Maine* and Cuba's plight into nearly every venue of American popular culture, including stage plays, early motion pictures, advertisements, material displays, and world's fair attractions.

The *Maine* affair poses a revealing case study in how late-nine-teenth-century visual and popular forms interacted within the culture of spectacle to consolidate patriotic sentiment by means of a powerful narrative of national disaster.[1] Historians who argue that the yellow press prepared the public psychologically and emotionally for war point to the *Maine* affair as the prime example of sensationalistic journalism. This chapter will show, however, that Americans were exposed to the *Maine* catastrophe through a much broader cultural framework than merely reacting to a handful of warmongering newspapers and politicians. If the cultural production focused on the *Maine* had ceased with the declaration of war, one could make the case that the media hype surrounding the explosion was a propagandistic tool to rouse support for war. But the enduring popularity of the *Maine* in film, theater, and world's fair attractions during and after the war demonstrates that it was more than a political instrument. American culture reoriented itself in the 1890s around values of pleasure, consumerism, and spectacle, and this entertainment-based culture collided with the politics of the *Maine* disaster.[2]

On January 24, 1898, President McKinley ordered the U.S.S. *Maine* to Havana harbor to protect American life and property in Cuba after rioting broke out on the streets of the city in mid-January. Many Americans first heard of the battleship the next day, when press headlines and illustrations broke the announcement. As the *Maine* settled into its stay in Havana, Captain Charles D. Sigsbee reported no indication of tensions. The ship seemed to attract more attention, rather, as a tourist destination for Cubans; "there must have been three or four hundred of them on board from time to time," wrote Sigsbee.[3] Back in the United States, however, hostilities escalated when, on February 9, the *New York Journal* published an intercepted personal letter written by the Spanish ambassador to the United States, Dupuy de Lôme, characterizing President McKinley as "weak and catering to the rabble, and, besides, a low politician" and admitting to duplicitous diplomatic dealings with Washington.[4] De Lôme immediately resigned, but the incident heightened suspicions of Spain just days before the *Maine* explosion.

On the morning of February 16, an eight-year-old boy from an upper-class family in Milton, Massachusetts, came down for breakfast and glanced at the newspaper headline in the *Boston Herald*:

"*Maine* Destroyed!" He looked up at his father, who told him, "That means war." Years later he wrote, "Whenever the battleship *Maine* is mentioned, my memory leaps to that dining room scene and to the excitement aroused by the word 'war.'" He recalled overhearing his parents discussing that night whether they should rethink their summer vacation plans on Cape Cod in favor of a safer destination, such as Alaska, in the event of Spanish military strikes against the North Atlantic coast.[5] For many Americans, the destruction of the *Maine* represented an attack on the United States and made war seem inevitable. "The average American dates the beginning of hostilities from 9:40 o'clock p.m. Feb. 15, when the explosion occurred," claimed the *Chicago Record*.[6]

Press Coverage of the *Maine* Disaster

In the days and weeks after the *Maine* explosion, press reports and illustrations provided a framework for Americans to visualize what took place and frame judgments accordingly about how the nation should respond. Because of the limitations of technology and transportation in the 1890s, the process of transmitting an image in the press from its point of creation to its final printing involved multiple layers of translation and social mediation. Immediately after the *Maine* explosion, graphic artists produced visual images from secondhand descriptions arriving by telegraph; later, once enough time had elapsed for photographs to be sent back to the United States, artists produced hand-drawn images from photos taken on location. Seeing these images of the wreckage and the recovery efforts may have deepened the connection that Americans felt to the events taking place in Cuba, which, in turn, may have helped to generate support for military action.

On the evening of February 15, only two correspondents, F. J. Hilgert of the Associated Press and Sylvester Scovel of the *New York World*, were able to send dispatches with word of the explosion.[7] Because the news came over the wire late, most editors did not have time to order the production of new images, so they drew from their archives the most recent sketches of the *Maine*, published on January 25, announcing the ship's departure for Havana. For this reason, most of the first pictures published of the *Maine* after the explosion showed the mighty warship intact. The *Louisville Courier-Journal* is a case in point. At 1:20 A.M. on the morning of February 16, news of the explosion came over the wire from the AP. The morning edition, however, was ready to go to print, so the managing and telegraph editors in great haste revamped the first and second pages to make room for the breaking news. To supplement the headline, they reprinted a four-column picture of the *Maine* that had been previously published on January 25. In ten minutes the editors set up the story, placed it in form, and sent the paper to the stereotypers. The *Courier-Journal* thus became one of the few papers in the region to cover the story in its first edition the next morning.[8]

In the following days, graphic artists manufactured images of the explosion based on verbal wire descriptions—what the *Houston Post* called "thrilling word pictures."[9] Pulitzer and Hearst immediately framed the explosion as an attack on the United States. The *Journal* printed a giant headline on February 17: "Destruction of the War Ship *Maine* Was the Work of an Enemy." The same day the *World* headlined "*Maine* Explosion Caused by Bomb or Torpedo" and presented an action-packed image of the stern of the vessel exploding in a huge cloud of smoke and fire with men falling from the flames into the surrounding water and pieces of steel and iron flying into the air (figure 2.1). The caption attributed the image to an eyewitness description of the explosion received via cable from *World* correspondent Sylvester Scovel of the "volcano of fire and showers of boats, bodies, iron and guns." One year earlier, however, the *World* had published a large drawing of the battleship *Maine* in a gale, hit by giant waves that carried three men overboard to their death.[10] The angle, scale, and detail of the vessel along with the placement of the fallen men are nearly identical to those in the *World*'s drawing of the *Maine* explosion, suggesting that the graphic department used this earlier incident as a visual template for depicting the current disaster.

The telegraphed "word pictures" of other large urban dailies resulted in dramatically different visual conceptions of the ship, the explosion, and the human loss involved. They were all inaccurate, based solely on secondhand tidbits of verbal description. Foreign correspondents, who paid by the word to cable reports, often sent only succinct bits of information, but these few words enabled illustrators

2.1. "*Maine* Explosion Caused by Bomb or Torpedo." *New York World,* February 17, 1898, 1.

to proclaim legitimacy through "telegraphic description" from an eyewitness source. The same day the *World*'s drawing was published, the *Dallas News* offered its viewers a simpler view of the explosion, showing the ship's stern exploding in a cloud of smoke with a few pieces of debris in the air but no dead bodies (figure 2.2). The late edition of the *Boston Globe* on February 16 presented an unembellished image of "The Sunken Warship" drawn from cabled description in seeming contrast to its own lurid headline, "Heaping Up Horror" (figure 2.3). The *Globe* artist depicts a petite ship half above the surface, as if still sinking, with little structural damage and no flames, smoke, or flying debris; instead, small rescue boats surrounding the ship seem to mitigate the fallout. The inconsistency of these early illustrations reveals the wide-ranging visual reports of the incident. At this moment the medium was not yet fully "modern," meaning that images were not instantaneous and widely shared; rather, they varied according to editorial agendas, locality, and access to technology.[11]

In conjunction with illustrations of the wreckage, there was a proliferation of political cartoons in newspapers across the country debating the implications of the *Maine* disaster. Six days after the explosion, cartoonist Clifford Berryman of the *Washington Post*

THE EXPLOSION ON THE MAINE—DRAWN FROM TELEGRAPHED DESCRIPTION.

2.2. "The Explosion on the *Maine.*" *Dallas News,* February 17, 1898, 1.

portrayed Uncle Sam using binoculars to examine the *Maine* wreck from U.S. shores, while a refined and demure Columbia stands at his side with eyes cast downward, mourning those lost in the explosion (figure 2.4). Cartoonists typically chose Uncle Sam to emphasize political or military authority while utilizing his female counterpart, Columbia, to represent abstract principles of humanity, morality, and freedom.[12] By gendering the viewing field, Berryman's "double vision" correlates masculinity with national vigilance and femininity with sentiment, while at the same time calling attention to the difficulties of having to calibrate a U.S. response to events taking place overseas, out of visual range. In giving Uncle Sam the binoculars, Berryman places the responsibility to do right by the *Maine* into the hands of masculine American power. But he provided no caption, as it was too early yet for him to declare what that course of action should be.

THE GLOBE EXTRA!

LATEST

HEAPING UP HORROR.

Sigsbee Telegraphs That 238 Lives Were Lost by Disaster to the Maine.

THE SUNKEN WARSHIP.
(Drawn from Cabled Descriptions of the Scene in Havana Harbor Today.)

2.3. "The Sunken Warship." *Boston Evening Globe,* February 16, 1898, 1.

At this point, President McKinley assembled a naval court of inquiry to investigate the cause of the explosion. It did not make its final report until March 28. To sustain readers' attention until then, the press preserved the illusion of continuous "breaking news." This was and is one of the great challenges for news media, to maintain interest in the midst of slowly developing events. With the exception of McKinley's successful request to Congress for a $50 million war appropriation (passed on March 8 and 9 in the House and Senate respectively), the weeks leading up to the release of the report were relatively uneventful. For the first time in presidential history,

2.4. Clifford Berryman, *Washington Post*, February 21, 1898, 1.

however, McKinley ordered his staff to provide routine statements to the press, ensuring reporters a constant stream of material on the ongoing *Maine* investigation and Cuban crisis.[13]

Contrary to the belief that "war fever" took hold of America, many editors displayed remarkable reserve as the investigation got under way.[14] A survey of 160 newspapers nationwide for the last two weeks of February revealed that little more than half blamed the explosion on Spain, while the rest encouraged their readers to await the outcome of the investigation.[15] Ellen Maury Slayden, wife of a Texas congressman, noted in her private journal on February 20 that "the country on the whole" was "behaving well" and that "people of importance" were "withholding opinions."[16]

Cries for war and calls for restraint occurred simultaneously, at times within the same news source, confusing media messages and dividing public opinion.[17] Even though many newspapers subscribed to the press services of Pulitzer and Hearst, they did not necessarily replicate their warmongering positions. Instead of simply reprinting images from the leading yellow papers, editors often directed their own artists to produce new drawings using the press service images as models, thus granting local artists flexibility to modify visual content to meet the needs of their readership. It was also common practice for newspapers to assail the reliability of the yellow press in their editorial columns in an effort to bolster their own credibility.[18] The *Chicago Times-Herald*, for example, reproduced sensationalistic news content from the *Journal* and the *World* but at the same time printed a series of cartoons from the *Philadelphia Times* criticizing yellow journalism for colluding with stock speculators to mastermind a push to war.[19] Denunciations of the yellow press did not prevent appropriation of their newspaper content. Frustrated by the extensive borrowing of its news stories without acknowledgment, Hearst's news service set a trap early in the war, reporting the supposed death in Cuba of an Austrian artillery expert named Colonel Refilpe W. Thenuz. After the *World* fell for it and printed the story, the *Journal* revealed that Thenuz did not exist and was in fact an anagram for "We Pilfer the News."[20]

Historians describe this journalistic moment as one in which newspaper editors, particularly of the yellow press, tried to outdo their rivals through excessive fabrication and sensationalism, when in fact claims to authenticity became one of the most important assets in this competition. Press illustrations became an important means for editors to assert their credibility, particularly once enough time had elapsed for photographs from Havana to arrive in the United States. Consequently, newspapers no longer cited "telegraphic description" and now claimed that images were based on actual photographic evidence. Press coverage of the *Maine* affair fell in the midst of the transition from hand-drawn illustration to photojournalism. One year earlier, the *New York Tribune* had published the first "halftone" photo in the main news pages. The *New York Times* and *New York Tribune* began publishing halftone supplements, but it was still cost-prohibitive for most papers to print photographs in regular news sections. Although the technology was available to publish photographs, editors chose to print graphic replications while taking advantage of popular conceptions of photography as a mechanical and therefore "objective" representation of reality to substantiate the authenticity of drawn images. Most illustrations contained a byline either crediting a photographic source or misrepresenting the drawing as an actual photograph. Many editors were reluctant to displace hand-drawn art because it put the power in the hands of the artist to invent detail without the formal constraints of accuracy. Drawings based on verbal descriptions from the newswire could also be produced quickly, unlike photographs, which had to be transported to newspaper headquarters before appearing in print. Still, the rise of photography changed the pictorial style of illustrated journalism, placing greater demands on graphic artists to deliver more visual precision through use of detail, perspective, and tonal shading to mimic the "realism" of photography.[21]

The yellow press took the lead in garnering images of the wreck and advancing two major theories to convince its readers that there had been a deliberate attack. The first asserted that a torpedo had pierced the *Maine* on the starboard side, causing the ship's powder magazines to explode. *New York Journal* correspondent George Eugene Bryson reported that three days after the explosion (before U.S. divers began their work), Spanish naval divers found a torpedo hole in the wreck. Arthur Brisbane, managing editor of the *Journal,* printed Bryson's story under an exceedingly large headline that required staff artists to draw the letters, for the paper did not own brass type big enough to meet Brisbane's demands.[22]

To support the torpedo theory, editors across the country made extensive use of technical language and scientific drawings as a further claim to visual authority.[23] The *Chicago Tribune* printed a sectional diagram of the *Maine* to demonstrate how a projectile could generate such damage, which was reproduced in papers around the country (figure 2.5). The diagram dissects the infrastructure of the ship, indicating placement of crew quarters, boilers, magazines, turrets, guns, and masts. The detail of the sketch, taken from the official naval scheme of the ship, gives the illusion of accuracy, indicating the exact spot where the torpedo entered the ship. The *Tribune,* however, published the diagram three days after the explosion, well before investigators had time to gather sufficient evidence. In response to a

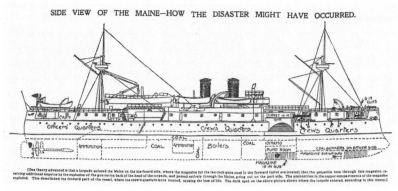

SIDE VIEW OF THE MAINE—HOW THE DISASTER MIGHT HAVE OCCURRED.

2.5. "Side View of the *Maine.*" *Chicago Tribune,* February 18, 1898, 2.

set of mechanical drawings of the *Maine* that appeared in *Scientific American,* one reader, an engineer from Cornell, wrote to the editor: "I was very much impressed and stirred by your illustrations of the '*Maine*' report. . . . I have just been writing to the leading English engineering papers, calling the attention of their readers to your issue of this date and to the fact that you give in those illustrations proof, absolute and unchallengeable, of the major fact that that unfortunate crew was murdered."[24]

Increasing use of photographs enabled the press to offer considerably more detailed and accurate images of the wreckage to support their allegations. Between February 20 and 25, many metropolitan newspapers published large front-page graphic illustrations of the "first actual photographs" of the wreck. The *New York World* headlined on its front page on February 20 "The *World's* Latest Discoveries Indicate *Maine* Was Blown Up by Submarine Mine. Here Are the First Actual Photographs of the Wreck" (figure 2.6). To substantiate the authenticity of its photo, the *World* included a precise travel itinerary: "The photograph left Havana by steamship *Olivette* at 2 P.M. Wednesday, arrived at Key West at 10.30 P.M.; at Port Tampa, Fla., 4 P.M. Thursday; left Tampa by New York express at 7 P.M. Thursday, and arrived at New York at 2:15 yesterday afternoon. It is here reproduced exactly." The photograph included in the official report of the board of inquiry (figure 2.7) shows that the *World's* drawing was accurate, down to the slight rightward tilt of the remaining topmast and the arc and orientation of specific pieces of bent steel and iron. The drawing clearly matches the cropped

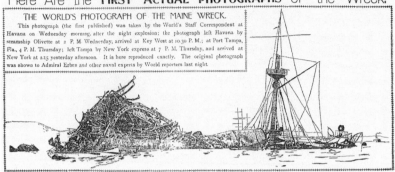

THE WORLD'S LATEST DISCOVERIES INDICATE MAINE WAS BLOWN UP BY SUBMARINE MINE.

Here Are the FIRST ACTUAL PHOTOGRAPHS of the Wreck.

THE WORLD'S PHOTOGRAPH OF THE MAINE WRECK.

This photograph (the first published) was taken by the World's Staff Correspondent at Havana on Wednesday morning, after the night explosion; the photograph left Havana by steamship Olivette at 2 P. M. Wednesday, arrived at Key West at 10.30 P. M.; at Port Tampa, Fla., 4 P. M. Thursday; left Tampa by New York express at 7 P. M. Thursday, and arrived at New York at 2.15 yesterday afternoon. It is here reproduced exactly. The original photograph was shown to Admiral Erben and other naval experts by World reporters last night.

2.6. "First Actual Photographs of the Wreck." *New York World*, February 20, 1898, 1.

2.7. Photograph of the *Maine* from the Official Naval Court of Inquiry, 1898. From *Message from the President of the United States, Transmitting the Report of the Naval Court of Inquiry upon the Destruction of the United States Battle Ship "Maine" in Havana Harbor, February 15, 1898, Together with the Testimony Taken before the Court* (Washington, D.C.: Government Printing Office, 1898).

frame and vantage point of the photograph. The *World* supplied the expert reading of Rear Admiral Henry Erben to shape viewers' interpretation of the image. "My God! . . . Is that the *Maine?*" he exclaimed. "You see the heavy armor plates are bent. It is frightful. I don't see how a torpedo could have done so much damage."[25] On the basis of this testimony, the *World* abandoned the torpedo theory, as did the naval board soon after, once the theory was deemed untenable owing to the nature of the damage.

As the work of the naval investigation unfolded, the yellow press shifted its visual frame to support the mine theory. On February 23 one of the official military divers discovered that the exterior bottom plates on the port side of the ship were bent upward, which he reported to Ensign Wilfrid Van Nest Powelson. Powelson testified to the board about his theory that a mine had triggered the explosion, citing the evidence of an uplifted inward bending of the keel and bottom plates. Commissioned by Secretary of the Navy John D. Long, photographer John C. Hemment assisted in the investigation. Despite his official role in the proceedings, Hemment was also on the payroll of multiple newspapers. Having known many *Maine* crew members, Hemment felt personally invested in proving what he had already determined was an act of "Spanish treachery." He had lunched a week before the tragedy with one ill-fated sailor, a Lieutenant Jenkins, and was present when the divers recovered his body. "The features were all but unrecognizable," he wrote, adding, "[I] was so much affected that I had not the heart to photograph it." His photos of the recovered bottom plates became the central evidence to support the board's finding of an external cause and were included in the report sent to Congress. "I did not know at the time I made them how important these pictures were," he claimed.[26]

Hemment also furnished Hearst and other editors with his photographs, which were then circulated through subscription services, allowing graphic artists across the country to copy them and present them to viewers as conclusive proof of Spanish culpability. The *Chicago Tribune* published a graphic series based on these photographs titled "Parts of *Maine* Wreck Which Indicate External Explosion (from photographs taken by the *New York World* correspondent in Havana)." One image shows the bottom plates as an indistinguishable mass of iron and steel with text to frame its viewing: "This remnant of the battleship did more to convince the board of inquiry that the explosion was external than any other evidence discovered. It is considered almost absolute proof of that position." It is juxtaposed with another illustration of bent iron and steel in the water. The final image presents a ten-inch powder magazine retrieved from the wreckage; intact, it stands as evidence against internal detonation.[27]

In addition to offering theories and evidence of the cause of the explosion, the press also reported in vivid visual detail the divers' efforts to recover the bodies after the explosion. In a *New York World* illustration purported to have been "drawn for the *World* from a scientifically correct picture in *Cassier's Engineering Magazine*," two men in full diving gear descend the ship's ladder, ax in hand, to scour the wreckage for a dead sailor trapped beneath debris. The sailor lies prostrate, seemingly peering upward though lifeless; only his head and arm are visible.[28] In an illustration appearing in the *San Francisco Examiner, New York Journal,* and *Dallas News,* the caption explains that *Maine* chaplain John P. Chidwick is "bending over to peer more closely into the blurred features of a dead sailor."[29] It pictures his struggle to recognize the sailors, having to lean over in close inspection of the disfigured bodies before preparation for burial, which Sigsbee temporarily arranged in Havana and Key West cemeteries.

Printed descriptions by the official *Maine* divers of their gruesome work amplified the visual impact of the lurid images of dismembered bodies in the press. The *Richmond Times* published this account from diver John Wall:

Cutting into the wreck I threw my light ahead and examined each point. It was an awful sight. I saw detached arms and legs and skulls ripped bare of hair. I saw bodies that were drowned by the water and bodies that were not drowned at all, but held down by great pieces of piling wood. . . . As I approached the wreck this time I saw something moving inside. . . . As I came nearer, for the object was in the inner room, I was startled to see it was the most greedy of ocean monsters—a shark! He had in his teeth a body and was swimming rapidly toward the door. I took up an axe, resolved to recover that sailor or die in the attempt. . . . When he was within ten feet of me I aimed a blow which struck him in the side, and a great yellowish streak of shark blood followed the axe handle. He gave a queer gulp, which I could hear and, dropping his victim, fled with swift strokes of the tail. I carried this man above. He was in a worse shape than the other poor fellow, but I got him up to a soldier's burial.[30]

His ghastly descriptions of severed body parts and skulls provided a new face of horror to the disaster. His sensory language engaged readers in the terror of men meeting death in a most brutal form, their bodies ripped apart and now subjected to the predators of the seas. Captain Sigsbee's response to requests for the bodies to be brought back to the United States added confirmation to these descriptions, as he explained that "friends of the dead should understand we are in the tropics."[31]

The visual production of the divers' work kept the focus on the spectacle of death and destruction, sustaining the anticipation of a U.S. response and the link between the *Maine* explosion and Cuba's struggle for independence. On the front page of the *Minneapolis Journal* on February 22 (figure 2.8), cartoonist Charles Bartholomew depicts Uncle Sam as a diver descending a ladder into the *Maine* wreckage, equipped with his diving gear, signature hat, coattails, and striped pants. "While Uncle Sam Has His Diving Clothes on He Might Do a Thorough Job of This Investigation in Cuban Waters," reads the caption. Mimicking scientific drawings of the divers in their investigations, the cartoon shows Uncle Sam in rounded helmet and boots receiving oxygen through long supply tubes. Like the diver John Wall, Uncle Sam comes upon a "suspicious looking fish" labeled Spain, but this long-snouted fish has snared not a sailor but rather the feminized Cuba Libre, piercing her midsection in a phallic thrust. Cuba takes the form of a shapely mermaid with flowing hair. Uncle Sam faces the same challenge as Wall, to save his victim from a marine aggressor, an allegorical message in favor of U.S. intervention to free Cuba from Spain. In an article adjoining the cartoon, the horrific realities of the divers' work are again reiterated, as the text reports that many of the bodies recovered in the forward part of the ship "are said to have been mutilated in the struggle for life."[32]

With detailed drawings of the funeral cavalcade on the streets of Havana, illustrators further framed the *Maine* tragedy as an extension of the Cuban humanitarian crisis. Artists magnified the pres-

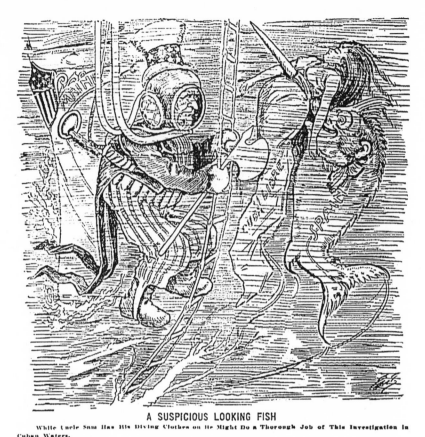

A SUSPICIOUS LOOKING FISH

While Uncle Sam Has His Diving Clothes on He Might Do a Thorough Job of This Investigation in Cuban Waters.

2.8. Charles Bartholomew, "A Suspicious Looking Fish." *Minneapolis Journal,* February 22, 1898, 1.

ence of the Cuban *reconcentrados* in the funeral processions. "Their reverent attitudes and sympathetic bearing told how they appreciate the support their cause has received from the people of the United States," reads the caption to one such drawing published in the *San Francisco Examiner.*[33]

The extensive press coverage of the *Maine* affair was not only politically motivated, to legitimate U.S. intervention in Cuba, but also commercially driven; in fact, the destruction of the *Maine* proved a great boon to newspaper sales. The daily circulation of the *Philadelphia Inquirer* climbed in 1898 from an average of 139,000 in January to 211,000 in May. The *Boston Herald* also prospered, selling 166,000 copies in January and 285,000 in March. The *New York*

Journal's circulation, averaging 420,000 issues in January, swelled to 1,025,600 immediately after the *Maine* disaster, and the *New York World*'s sales of 711,622 in December 1897 increased to over 1 million in April and May 1898. Large urban dailies further boosted these rising circulation numbers by issuing multiple extras per day with up-to-date war-related news. The *Journal* at its height issued as many as forty-three editions in a single day.[34]

Once images supporting Powelson's mine theory flooded newspapers nationwide in March 1898, editors across the country proclaimed with certainty that Spain had blown up the *Maine*. In the majority of editorial commentaries, substantiations of an "outside explosion" translated into conviction of the Spanish government.[35] Contemporary military analyst Frederick Jane was less certain and voiced a much less popular view. He recognized that the perpetrator or perpetrators could have been Spanish officials, a renegade Spanish fanatic, or a Cuban insurrectionist; or the explosion could have been accidental.[36] The final report of the naval court of inquiry merely confirmed the expected: that the *Maine* exploded from an external cause. Investigators did not, however, find evidence to fix responsibility on Spain. The board concluded that there had been two explosions, the first of which was caused by a mine, lifting the ship and fracturing the keel at frame number eighteen on the port side of the ship, forcing the keel to invert in a V shape. A second explosion, of even greater magnitude, came from two or more of the forward magazines.[37] The Spanish board of inquiry performed an independent investigation and reached a different conclusion. It declared the cause of the explosion to be internal, citing the lack of dead fish in the harbor, the absence of any visible geyser after the blast, and the fact that surrounding ships did not report a shock wave.[38] U.S. press accounts gave these considerations little weight. The Spanish leaders' repeated pleas of innocence, their active assistance in the rescue and recovery operations, and their request for peaceful arbitration (which President McKinley denied) did not muffle the chorus of voices for U.S. military retribution.

Despite the allegations of visual proof, the cause of the explosion has never been definitively ascertained. In 1911, after the ship was recovered from the bottom of Havana harbor, a second board of inquiry's investigation supported the initial finding that an external cause (most likely a mine) had produced the explosion. Unsatisfied with these prior investigations, Admiral Hyman G. Rickover reopened the matter in 1974. He hired two navy experts on ship design who found no evidence of an external explosion and postulated that the cause was likely an accidental fire in the coal bunker. In 1998 David W. Wooddell, a senior researcher for *National Geographic,* reexamined the mine and coal bunker theories using computer-generated modeling and argued in favor of the original finding—an external cause. With such conflicting reports, it is unlikely that we will ever know with certainty the true cause of the explosion or the specific parties responsible.[39]

The *Maine* in Motion Pictures

Widespread interest in the destruction of the *Maine* inspired the rise of a relatively new medium of visual communication: motion pictures. Lauren Rabinovitz argues that the "glut on the [motion picture] market might have led to movies' dismissal as only a passing fancy or fad had it not been for the outbreak of the Spanish-American War in 1898."[40] The war came at a very early stage in film history. It was only two years earlier that the first motion picture was projected onscreen for commercial use. Before then, the only available medium for public film viewing was through various kinds of peep-show apparatus at sideshows and amusement parks.[41]

In contrast to later Hollywood motion pictures, early cinema operated under a different conception of spectatorship that thrived on capturing intense "instants," not developing complex plots.[42] Press reports provided filmmakers with shooting scripts, and audiences relied on a live orator or knowledge from newspapers to fill in the narrative gaps.[43] President McKinley's inauguration in March 1897, for example, was the first to be captured on film.[44] Many exhibitors took advantage of a brand new technology first appearing in November 1897—a "motion picture slide projector"—that enabled them to intersperse still and motion pictures in their presentations. They often obtained the photographs directly from newspapers, but as Jonathan Auerbach has argued, motion picture presentations "gave news the power and immediacy of a photographic realism that could not be matched by print."[45]

The Spanish-American War significantly boosted the nascent film industry. In film's earliest years, motion pictures were primarily shown in the nation's largest cities at amusement parks, opera halls, vaudeville houses, carnivals, and fairs, but there was also a growing market for film in small-town America. The business of traveling exhibitors, like Lyman H. Howe, John R. Dibble, Charles H. Oxenham, and others, swelled with the popularity of war pictures. Whereas Howe primarily targeted a more conservative, religious audience prior to the Spanish-American War, public interest in war scenes enabled him to expand into venues such as theaters and opera houses in smaller cities and towns. The pool of available motion pictures was limited, but itinerant exhibitors varied their selections, using scenes of regional regiments to give shows a local flavor. Still, larger cities offered greater immediacy, and smaller-town audiences often experienced delays in seeing war-related events pictured on screen.[46]

Filmmakers provided another medium for the *Maine* disaster narrative to find visual expression. Although these films were invariably marketed as "realistic," many of them manufactured images for public consumption. Wallace McCutcheon's American Mutoscope Company, or Biograph, which by 1897 had a national exhibition circuit, took its footage of the U.S. battleships *Iowa* and *Massachusetts* and renamed the *Massachusetts* the *Maine*. Shown just weeks after the explosion took place, McCutcheon's film instantly gratified audiences. The *New York World* reported that in Chicago "there was fifteen minutes of terrific shouting . . . when the battleships *Maine* and *Iowa* were shown in the biograph."[47] Its success led McCutcheon to send cameramen G. W. Bitzer and Arthur Marvin to Cuba to film the ongoing investigation and recovery efforts, resulting in the films "Divers at Work on the Wreck of the *Maine*" and "The Wreck of the *Maine*," displayed in Keith's Theatre in Boston and other venues in March 1898. Chicago's Hopkins' Theatre also had a successful run of the Biograph film "After the Burial of *Maine* Victims, Key West—Leaving the Graves." New York's Proctor's Pleasure Palace advertised the claim of "Taking New Yorkers Practically to Cuba by Photography" through daily showings of Bitzer and Marvin's footage of the wreck and the divers at work.[48] By the start of the war, motion picture footage of the *Maine* and its crewmen's funeral processions reached at least seventeen U.S. cities.[49]

Filmed images of the wreckage, recovery operations, and funeral cavalcades helped sustain the emotional intensity of the conflict as the nation awaited the findings of the official investigation. In competition with Biograph, F. Z. Maguire of the Edison Manufacturing Company sent cinematographer William Paley, then with Hearst's organization, to Cuba. In a short film titled "Wreck of the Battleship 'Maine'" (filmed in late March), Paley presented audiences with a panoramic view of Havana harbor and the remains of the *Maine* in less than a minute of running time. His camera pans the wreck from the vantage point of another ship in the harbor, which makes the devastating scene appear all the more intimate and authentic. In a second film, titled "Burial of the 'Maine' Victims" (filmed March 27, 1898), Paley depicted the funeral procession of hearses carrying the flag-draped coffins of the *Maine* dead in Key West with American sailors walking beside them with solemn expressions.[50] Audiences watched the hearses coming toward them in succession, flanked by the surviving sailors.

The *Maine* affair provided a great impetus for Albert E. Smith and Jim Blackton's Vitagraph Company, which rivaled Biograph and the Edison Manufacturing Company. Smith wrote, "The *Maine* disaster opened a new cycle, the newsreel movie, and proved that a wave of patriotism can be as valuable to a picturemaker as a wave of passion." Smith and Blackton produced a three-minute film of the *Maine* funeral parade. To intensify the movie-going experience, they reopened a vacant opera house in New York in March and, for the first time, hired an orchestra to accompany the film with heartrending music. After the show, claimed Smith, "spectators filed wordlessly from the theater, faces grave, here and there eyes blinking furiously to press back the tears."[51] Its success gave Vitagraph the boost it needed to produce more war pictures. Vitagraph incorporated photographs of the *Maine* from the *New York Herald* into its picture presentations.[52] Film and press imagery complemented each other in substance and content, but the novelty of the new cinematic medium, its presence in interactive public spaces, and its artificial "reality effect" amplified the emotional magnitude of the *Maine* disaster as the nation came closer to war.

The *Maine* as Commodity

The slogan "Remember the *Maine*" appeared everywhere, even on chewing gum wrappers, matches, paperweights, and dinnerware. The commodification of the *Maine* tragedy prior to and during the war is evident in the creative ways that retailers appropriated it for commercial gain. There was no hesitancy in situating national calamity in the sphere of commerce, which added a different dimension to the ways in which Americans imagined and coped with the incident.

Just as editors ratcheted up the intensity of the disaster to sell papers, advertisers capitalized on public interest in the *Maine* affair to sell products. In an era of rapid economic and industrial growth, the culture industries of the late nineteenth century became ever more adept at reaching mass audiences to boost sales. Advertisers increasingly privileged visual modes of expression over informative text to attract the attention of buyers.[53] The R. S. Crutcher Furniture Company of Atlanta printed a large drawing of the battleship *Maine* in an ad appearing just days after the explosion, embedded in text that read, "The terrible explosion of the U.S. Man of War *Maine* ... is causing a great deal of excitement among the American people, but for the next 30 days we are going to have an 'explosion of prices' on Furniture, Carpets and Baby Carriages that will startle the entire population of Georgia." The Whittlesey Hardware Company of Houston ran an ad in April with a large bold print header "The '*Maine*' Question," and then in smaller type "To be considered is, Who will give you the best value for your money?"[54] Even though the political situation had no bearing on the companies or the products sold, advertisers relied heavily on the visual power of *Maine*-related images and slogans (printed in conspicuous type) to draw in readers. Thus war-related news and pictorial content were not confined to the layout of the main news and editorial pages.

Of even greater attraction value in the period leading up to the war were actual pieces of *Maine* wreckage put on display. The M. R. Emmons & Company department store in Atlanta displayed a fragment of the ship in its store window, and claimed it was "examined with interest by all who saw it." Painted white, the splintered wood showed signs of smoke and fire. In March the *New York World* placed a piece of the *Maine* wreckage outside its headquarters.

Encased in glass, the six-by-eight-inch chunk of concrete, the *World* alleged, "created a sensation."[55]

With the onset of war, ad campaigns sought to lure customers by offering souvenirs with a purchase, enabling buyers to broadcast their patriotism. In May, Raphaels Incorporated, a clothing store in San Francisco, furnished customers with a "Remember the *Maine*" badge, which appeared in the store's advertisement along with a colored representation of the vessel on the high seas. "The MAINE REMEMBERED FREE . . ." appears in large boldface type. The Queen Shoe Store of Los Angeles offered buyers a commemorative spoon: "'Remember the Maine.' THIS WEEK ONLY, The Queen Shoe Store . . . will give to each purchaser of One Dollar's worth or more of Shoes A BEAUTIFUL SOUVENIR SPOON, REPRESENTING THE BATTLESHIP MAINE. See them in our show windows. . . . 'Remember the Queen.'"[56]

Because the *Maine* symbolized American loss, resilience, and military purpose, advertisements continued to exploit its attention-grabbing qualities for the duration of the war. In a July 1898 ad the M. J. Cull grocery store of New Orleans trumpeted in oversized bold print, "Remember the Main," continuing in small print, "point about our groceries is that they are all guaranteed—guaranteed to be clean, fresh, and wholesome."[57] Images of the *Maine* circulated on badges, glassware, buttons, spoons, flags, and ribbons. Louise Imogen Guiney, a writer in Massachusetts, wrote to a friend in June 1898: "I stopped at a street-corner the other day, and bought some penny badges for the boys. . . . I didn't dare get two alike! but I think you'd better give the only immoral one, 'Remember the *Maine!*' to Baby, and so confine it to the domestic circle."[58] Although Guiney purchased the badge, her remark about its "immorality" suggests her disapproval of the war and reminds us that consumption of war-related goods did not necessarily signify political support for government policies.

If advertisers and retailers capitalized on the symbolic power of the *Maine,* it was not necessarily with the political intent to incite or maintain support for war but rather to seize the attention of potential buyers so that other commercial messages could be communicated. Advertently or not, they helped sustain the staying power of the *Maine* affair for American consumers in the spring and summer of 1898.

The Spectacle of the *Maine* in Popular Culture

It may not be surprising that the public relived the *Maine* disaster through various media platforms, but what is remarkable is the extent to which misfortune and amusement were intertwined in the realm of popular culture. The mythification of the *Maine* occurred almost immediately; its tragic elements, though always present, gradually receded as the incident blended into the martial spirit of patriotism consuming the nation.

The *Maine* affair permeated American religious culture, particularly as many church leaders used the explosion to call their congregations to action in the period leading up to the war. Pastors of various denominations reinforced the political narrative of Spanish oppression in their sermons. The Reverend E. E. Franke of the Church of the Seventh-Day Adventists in Brooklyn declared, "We sent the *Maine* down there and the world at large is now re-echoing what Cuba said long ago, 'Treachery!'" As he spoke these words to his congregation just a week after the *Maine* exploded, he displayed on a stereopticon screen Charles G. Bush's cartoon "And a Nation Mourned" (figure 2.9), published on February 17 in the *New York World*.[59] The image enhanced the emotional impact of his message, showing a dead American sailor, outfitted with a U.S.S. *Maine* cap, washed up on shore. Franke, perhaps, saw in the image a religious context that he could put to use for the martyred sailor lies with his arms stretched out like those of Jesus Christ on a crucifix. The soldier's hand falls limp, a possible analogue to Christ's hand in Michelangelo's *Pietà*. The sunken *Maine* appears in the background with the American flag at half-mast. Franke was among many religious leaders to connect the national mission of avenging the *Maine* and liberating Cuba to Christian values of compassion, duty, and self-sacrifice. The Reverend A. M. Sherman from Morristown, New Jersey, claimed that he and his fellow pastors did what they could "from pulpit and platform" to rouse their congregations to support military intervention in Cuba. The Reverend W. E. Dugan in San Francisco shared his enthusiasm in a sermon: "Circumstantial evidence in the *Maine* disaster left no doubt in my mind that Spain deliberately blew up that ship. . . . We should teach Spain that she cannot insult us and trifle with our honor as a nation."[60]

AND A NATION MOURNED.

2.9. Charles G. Bush, "And a Nation Mourned." *New York World,* February 17, 1898, 7.

As America anticipated the start of war, the story of the *Maine* became a crowd-pleasing subject in mass entertainments. Theater managers scrambled to include *Maine* segments in their comedy, vaudeville, and dramatic skits. Popular music ballads and marches integrated it into their lyrics, eulogizing the dead, unifying Americans on behalf of Cuba Libre, and glorifying U.S. militarism.[61] Increasing demands for wartime spectacle pushed the boundaries of theater production. This was evident in the enlargement of theaters and the use of grander sets, larger casts, and elaborate scenery and special effects. In New Orleans, for example, war plays were presented in the new Crescent Theater, built to hold 1,800 spectators and fitted with an extended stage capacity, acoustics, and electric lighting.

The *Maine* affair also unleashed a surge of performances in its honor in February and March 1898. The *New York Journal* and *San Francisco Examiner* spearheaded a campaign to raise money to erect a monument in memory of the *Maine* and organized a committee of theater managers to promote benefit performances in twenty-five cities. The Denver Tabor Theater put on a show, attended by Colorado's governor and the city's elite, featuring Henry Clay Barnabee singing with the First Regiment Band. The *Denver Post* celebrated the "glow of patriotism" of the "thrilling scene" with a large front-page drawing of the exuberant crowd in a packed theater, having raised $467.90 for the *Journal*'s *Maine* fund.[62] San Francisco held a succession of fund-raising performances, the first of which took place at the Baldwin Theater and featured a minstrel show, complete with a new war song, "Uncle Sam, Why Are You Waiting?" The chorus repeated, "Down with their ships in shell and fire / And avenge our gallant *Maine!*"[63] This *Maine*-inspired string of national performances turned cultural producers into leading public advocates for Cuban liberation and enabled audiences to support the cause financially and psychologically while enjoying the pleasures of light entertainment.

Well after war had been declared, the translation of the *Maine* incident into popular spectacle kept its memory alive and nurtured patriotic sentiment. It also eclipsed more sober forms of remembering, at times descending to garish depths, such as in popular minstrel shows. West's Big Minstrel Jubilee closed its performances with a spectacular bit titled "Remember the *Maine*" in which the head of the company, William West, playing Captain Sigsbee, led his troupe of sailors in a comical drill to the sounds of a naval band. It is remarkable and even peculiar that audiences found entertaining a parody of a military drill by sailors who would presumably have died in the explosion. At the McVicker's Theater in Chicago, Haverly's European-American Minstrels revamped the first part of their production to suit the patriotic mood. Minstrels dressed as naval officers rejoiced over U.S. victories in Manila while shouting "Remember the *Maine*" to the accompaniment of a marine band.[64]

Dramatic productions based on the *Maine* tragedy also toured the country. One of the more successful was Lincoln J. Carter's "spectacular nautical melodrama" titled *Remember the "Maine,"* which reviewers claimed delighted audiences in Boston, Chicago, Houston, Dallas, Cleveland, Galveston, and Louisville. In New York, the Star Theater presented in the fall of 1898 the melodrama *The "Maine" Avenged*. For a ticket price of seventy-five cents, spectators watched the *Maine* explode onstage at the hands of a spiteful Spaniard. One reviewer described the show as "four acts teeming with instances of Yankee prowess, Cuban patriotism, and Spanish cowardice."[65] The spectacle of the *Maine* continued to attract consumers of American popular culture during and after the war. Postwar cultural productions of the *Maine* affair may have retrospectively confirmed the righteousness of U.S. actions, but its political meanings were filtered by, or perhaps lost altogether to, the principal goal of amusement.

The *Maine* at the Omaha World's Fairs, 1898–99

The events of the Spanish-American War converged with the makings of the Trans-Mississippi and International Exposition of 1898 in Omaha, Nebraska, and the Greater America Exposition, held on the same grounds the following summer. The Trans-Mississippi Exposition opened on the first of June, shortly after the Spanish-American War began. Under the presidential leadership of Gurdon W. Wattles, vice president of the Union National Bank and board member of the Omaha Commercial Club, fair management acquired a congressional appropriation of $200,000 and secured the assistance of the Departments of State, War, and the Navy in the collection and organization of exhibits.

Inspiring the makings of an Omaha exposition was a series of nineteenth-century European and American world's fairs preceding it. The first, the Greater Exhibition of 1851, took place in the Crystal Palace in London and was soon followed by fairs in Paris and Vienna. In the United States, the two most prominent late-nineteenth-century fairs were the Philadelphia Centennial Exposition in 1876 and the World's Columbian Exposition in Chicago in 1893. Packaged in architectural grandeur and showcasing America's progress in technology, agriculture, and the arts, these expositions communicated to fairgoers the value of civilization on a spectacular scale. They fed the rise of mass tourism and consumerism, providing a large souvenir market and enticing fairgoers with exotic amusements. In celebrating America's material advancements while couching depictions of native cultures in primitive and grotesque displays, the world's fair was an important medium in negotiating conceptions of race and empire for a mass audience.

Fair planners initially feared that the outbreak of war would eclipse interest in the Omaha world's fair, but to the contrary, the fairgrounds almost immediately became a center of Spanish-American War–inspired popular culture, taking shape in government exhibits, midway attractions, military parades, special day events, and souvenirs. John L. Webster, a prominent lawyer and one of the fair's organizers, announced on opening day, "A month ago it was a serious question whether the war with Spain would not injure this exposition; but within a month it has become an accentuation of the expansive power of the American nation."[66] The fair closed on the first of November with a total attendance of 2,613,508 people.[67] Although attendance drew disproportionately from the local region, fair publicity reached a broader national audience.[68]

The Omaha fairs helped sustain popular attention on the *Maine* disaster not only throughout the summer of 1898 but also the following year when the fair reopened. One of the most-frequented displays was a glass-encased model of the *Maine* (as it looked prior to the explosion) in the Government Building, regally draped with the Stars and Stripes. One observer noted, "Perhaps nothing in the immense building attracts the attention that does this beautiful model of the noble craft." To stir up interest, the *Omaha World-Herald* described to its readers the reactions of spectators: "Sometimes men swear audibly to give vent to their feelings while women relieve their pent-up emotions in tears. Nowhere else on the grounds is such intensity of feeling manifested."[69]

The Omaha fairs also reenacted the *Maine* explosion daily on the "lagoon," offering the promise of great entertainment through "realistic" display. A slideshow told the story of the *Maine,* presenting stereopticon pictures of the wreckage, recovery operations, and funeral processions.[70] Then spectators shared in the dramatic experience of watching the ship blown to bits before their very eyes. One photograph (figure 2.10), taken by an unknown photographer, captured the sensational instant when wood and armament flew into the sky in a burst of fire and smoke. Fair organizers touted the attraction in their advertising as a reality show; "Roltaire's Explosion of the *Maine* is one of the most realistic reproductions ever presented to the public. It is not a picture nor an illusion, but simply a miniature reality," read one piece in the *Omaha World-Herald*.[71] Despite the marketing of the show as "realistic," the ship's miniature scale, the lack of casualties, the minimal fallout, and the palatial backdrop of the White City grossly distorted perceptions of the actual disaster. One reviewer noted the excitement and anger that the show aroused, appealing to audiences' patriotic and martial sensibilities: "The Destruction of the *Maine* show was accorded a hearty reception, the bitter vengeance meted out to the ship's destroyers, as announced in the morning papers, being the incentive to cheers alike for the show and the boys at Santiago."[72] Alice French, a writer from Iowa, however, described the show as "one of the very prettiest things on the grounds," elaborating: "The scene, the ships riding at anchor in Havana Harbor ('on real water, ladies and gentlemen,') the tropical storm, the illumination of the city and the sunrise are remarkably pretty. As for the explosion, it wouldn't disturb a rabbit."[73]

Cultural producers, from newspaper editors to filmmakers to theatrical entertainers, recognized in the international incident a powerful combination of drama, action, loss, and heroism and kept it in the forefront of American popular culture as long as it still held the public's interest, even after the war had come and gone.

"Remember the *Maine*" in its countless manifestations throughout American visual, print, and popular culture became shorthand for the larger themes propelling U.S. intervention in Cuba: the infamy of Spain for allegedly attacking the United States, Cuban vulnerability, and American fortitude and manly honor. Media production surrounding the *Maine* affair certainly had an impact on consolidating national sentiment for war. "Now, there can no longer be doubt that after the blowing up of the *Maine* public opinion moved forward instinctively to a strong pitch of indignation," declared the *Atlantic Monthly*.[74] Statements by ordinary citizens supported that observation. George L. Jewett, an insurance agent from Macon, Georgia, said, "I am in favor of demanding instant satisfaction for the *Maine* and the freedom of Cuba." A coal operator from Kansas identified

2.10. Reenacted *Maine* Explosion at the Omaha World's Fair. Courtesy Jeffrey Spencer.

as Captain Beck argued, "We should demand satisfaction, because no one at Havana could obtain 500 pounds of dynamite to blow up the *Maine* if they did not get it from the Spanish government." M. L. Bevus, a judge from Des Moines, Iowa, asserted: "The nation has been insulted and our sailors murdered. If the President is afraid to act let Congress assume the responsibility."[75]

Despite the pervasiveness of the *Maine* disaster narrative, some Americans did not believe that the destruction of the *Maine* constituted grounds for war. The Unitarian Ministerial Union and the Women's Educational and Industrial Union in Boston jointly denounced the mass-marketing of the motto "Remember the *Maine*," claiming that its spirit of revenge undermined the true cause of the war, the "deliverance of a neighboring people."[76] Marian Lawrence Peabody, a young woman from Massachusetts, expressed doubts in her diary in 1898 that Spain was at fault: "I think nothing is bad enough for whoever blew up the *Maine* but no one knows who did it.... It seems absurd to go to war 'for humanity's sake,' which is the accepted cause, and then start off by killing three hundred brave sailors and wounding six hundred more."[77] Helen Keller, in a private letter to a friend, also denounced a policy of blood revenge, proposing instead the construction of a college in Havana to memorialize the *Maine* without resorting to the "old-time belief that might makes right."[78] Many Americans supported nonmilitary intervention in Cuba; for example, a reading of Southern Methodist newspapers suggests that they largely opposed military action and urged readers to help the Cubans through charitable fundraising and the construction of soup kitchens.[79]

Nonetheless, in March 1898 three important events converged to push the United States toward war: the naval board's report of its findings of an external attack, Senator Proctor's speech in Congress confirming the state of crisis in Cuba, and President McKinley's public release of consular reports documenting the plight of the Cuban *reconcentrados*. Proctor's speech was perfectly timed, coming just days before the naval board released its report. Across the nation, cartoons made it appear that war was inevitable, documenting a national sentiment of nervous anticipation, the dogs of war itching to be unleashed, the tension building with each passing day.[80] Many Americans, in fact, expressed frustration with McKinley for not acting soon enough; crowds burned his image in effigy in many cities, and audiences hissed his picture in New York theaters.[81] What media makers and their audiences did not expect, however, was that upon heeding the call to "avenge the *Maine*" and end Cuban suffering, McKinley would order the first strike against Spain not in Cuba but in the Philippines.

On April 11, McKinley asked Congress to grant him the authority to go to war to end Spanish rule in Cuba but did not clarify his long-term policy. As a lawyer, he knew the importance of ambiguous language when setting out his intention: "In the name of humanity, in the name of civilization, in behalf of endangered American interests which give us the right and the duty to speak and to act, the war in Cuba must stop."[82] Ellen Maury Slayden commented in her private journal that the president's war message was "long and vague and weak," adding, "If he has a definite policy, he managed to conceal it under a stream of weak English."[83] Congressional leaders welcomed the president's request to intervene in order to renew their commitment to Cuban liberation. Congress had voted multiple times in the preceding years to grant belligerent rights to the Cuban nationalists (which McKinley and his predecessor, Grover Cleveland, rejected). While there was strong congressional support for formal recognition of the Cuban Republic, McKinley instead sought a free hand in determining Cuba's status: "To commit this country now to the recognition of any particular government in Cuba might subject us to embarrassing conditions of international obligation toward the organization so recognized."[84] In the declaration of war passed April 25 a compromise was reached; Henry Teller, a Republican senator from Colorado, proposed an amendment disclaiming "any disposition or intention to exercise sovereignty, jurisdiction, or control" over Cuba and promising to "leave the government and control of the island to its people."[85] From the perspective of most media accounts, this amendment confirmed the noble purpose of intervention: to secure Cuban independence and avenge the *Maine*.

For leaders such as Assistant Secretary of the Navy Theodore Roosevelt and Senator Henry Cabot Lodge, the *Maine* was an ideal pretext for war. As early as February 25, Roosevelt sent orders on his own accord to the commander of the U.S. Asiatic Squadron, Commodore George Dewey, to station his fleet at Hong Kong and prepare for an attack on the Spanish navy at Manila. But despite his neglect of protocol, Roosevelt did not unilaterally facilitate the possibility of fighting Spain in the Philippines. As early as June 1896, Lieutenant William W. Kimball of the Office of Naval Intelligence urged this military strategy should war commence, a course of action the Navy Department considered during the summer of 1897. These plans likely account for why Naval Secretary Long did not rescind the order after learning of Roosevelt's actions while he was away from Washington.[86] In April 1898 General John M. Schofield further advised the president to attack Spain in Puerto Rico and the Philippines, not in Cuba, where Spanish military forces were strongest. This military approach was not widely publicized, and it came as a great surprise to the nation when the war began on the other side of the world. Slayden wrote in her journal on May 2, after hearing about the U.S. naval presence in Manila Bay: "Maps are searched to find the Philippines—few people ever heard of them before. I am sure I never did."[87]

Biographers and presidential scholars may never know McKinley's true intentions for entering the conflict, especially since he left little record of it. What matters, however, is that the Spanish-American War became "McKinley's War" as soon as Congress granted him the authority to fight it, and he launched a different kind of war from the one the press had envisioned. From the moment that the war began, the *Maine* was heralded as the nation's rallying call. One regiment leaving Dallas for the front epitomized this martial spirit; on the side of their train car they wrote: "Remember the *Maine*. To hell with Spain!"[88]

3

Socializing the Politics of Militarism

THE SPANISH-AMERICAN WAR IN POPULAR CULTURE

> This is an awfully funny war. . . . What a great big
> burlesque it all is! What a caricature poor old rickety
> Spain has made of herself. She is the champion
> cartoonist of the nineteenth century, with herself as
> the subject. It is funny, awfully funny, at every step, and
> from whatever point you look at it. Spain started out
> with several hundred thousand men to whip a handful
> of half armed subjects and made a glorious fiasco of
> that. . . . Funny? Well I should say it was! I have been
> laughing ever since the darned thing started.
> *Cleveland Plain Dealer,* July 18, 1898

After the declaration of war, President McKinley called for 125,000 volunteers to supplement regular army units. The response was staggering. The *Maine* disaster and the humanitarian crisis in Cuba inspired thousands of young men across the nation to enlist. "This is one of the most popular wars we have ever had," claimed a small midwestern paper. "Everybody wants to go to Cuba."[1] This spirit led newspapers across the country to embed illustrations of flags, eagles, and the phrase "Remember the *Maine*" in their front-page banners.[2] Many young men conveyed their enthusiasm for the war by inscribing patriotic tattoos on their bodies. One Philadelphia man got a panorama of the battle of Santiago inked across his chest. Many others had portraits of Admiral George Dewey, "Fighting Bob" Evans, and Consul-General Fitzhugh Lee tattooed on their arms along with icons of patriotism such as flags and eagles.[3] This popular fad reveals the creative ways in which military imagery of the Spanish-American War found expression in American visual culture.

With special emphasis on the war's three central battles (Manila

Bay, San Juan Hill, and Santiago), this chapter examines the construction and dissemination of the spectacle of war in a range of popular forms and maps its lingering effects through public consumption.[4] Cultural producers promoted a heightened national feeling of triumphant militarism by shaping war as a spectacular diversion in an array of cultural forms for audiences of all ages.[5] In the proliferation of battle reenactments, motion picture views, and other war-themed amusements during and after the conflict, cultural entrepreneurs framed battle representations within a theatrical rubric of flamboyant spectacle, manly heroics, and thrilling action. They fashioned an aesthetic of "spectacular reality" that utilized sensational effects and staging to produce the *illusion* that the images and actions were taking place in reality, involving actual participants, places, and events.[6] Popular newspapers substantiated these reality claims in their advertisements for these mass entertainments while they reproduced the same sensationalistic narratives in their own accounts of U.S. military achievements. Despite their insistence on the accuracy of their battle scenes, media makers ultimately furnished audiences with strikingly "unreal" visions of war.

President McKinley took steps to invite the press into the White House in order to manage media relations, but he did not create a government agency to direct the production of war propaganda as President Woodrow Wilson would later do in World War I with the creation of the Committee on Public Information. McKinley's administration installed censors in U.S. colonies to prevent war correspondents from printing vital military information but left the production of war-related imagery and commercial amusements on the home front virtually unfettered.[7] This left cultural producers free to design war-related media to suit their own political or financial agendas. They exploited the political circumstances in order to establish their particular craft as a reliable apparatus for informing the public of political events. Having already fixed audience attention on the impending conflict through the narratives of Cuba Libre and "Remember the *Maine*," the makers of American print, visual, and popular culture exploited the patriotic and military spirit of wartime to boost their consumer appeal. Intentional or not, this had the effect of accentuating the nation's military successes and masking its failures.

SOCIETY MEN AND WOMEN TURN OUT TO WITNESS THE COMPANY DRILLS OF THE LEGION.
The popular and patriotic interest in the work of Louisville's crack military company to steadily on the increase. Nearly every night the past week thousands of men and women have flocked to the Legion Armory to witness the maneuvers of the soldier boys.

3.1. "Society Men and Women Turn Out to Witness the Company Drills of the Legion." *Louisville Courier-Journal,* May 1, 1898, 1.

The Battle of Manila Bay

As the army mobilized for war, local military organizations stirred public anticipation by turning the drilling of new recruits into a spectator sport. Press imagery enhanced the appeal of these military entertainments by sensationalizing the excitement of the crowds at these events. These scenes illustrate the military exercises, but more important, they foreground the spectator experience.[8] In one such illustration published on May 1, the *Louisville Courier-Journal* depicted an amphitheater full of "society men and women" watching the militiamen perform their drills (figure 3.1). The caption states, "Nearly every night of the past week thousands of men and women have flocked to the Legion Armory to witness the maneuvers of the soldier boys." The artist frames the scene from the vantage point of a fellow spectator, encouraging viewers to imagine themselves in the crowd.[9]

Commercial entrepreneurs capitalized on the most publicized military events of the Spanish-American War to create exciting, pleasurable entertainments, and in turn, the press promoted these amusements as a reliable and compelling source for war news and information. While there were many skirmishes and bombardments during the land and naval campaigns of the war, these small-scale events were not ideal for producing spectacular attractions. Media makers instead conveyed the military operations of the war as the story of a few decisive battles, beginning with Admiral Dewey's naval victory in Manila Bay. In a revealing moment of interaction between cultural forms, news and image producers transformed this battle into a spectacular naval extravaganza.

The singular emphasis on Cuban liberation in prewar press campaigns did not prepare the nation for the war to commence in the Philippines. Prominent South Carolina businessman and reformer Frederik Holmes Christensen wrote in his diary after the victory at Manila Bay: "When this war was declared no one had any idea it would involve us in the Eastern trouble but the very first battle which came with in a few weeks after the commencement of hostilities made us the masters of the richest islands in the East. . . . [T]he question which is likely to confront us at the termination of hostilities will be what shall we do with the Philippines. The matter has taken every one so much by surprise that they don't seem to know what to say."[10] The press shared Christensen's surprise. With over a hundred press correspondents stationed in Cuba waiting for the action to start, only three were positioned in the Philippines: Joseph L. Stickney of the *New York Herald*, Edwin W. Harden of the *New York World*, and John T. McCutcheon of the *Chicago Record*.[11] This significant disparity in coverage is in itself strong evidence that the press did not foresee the objectives or operations of the war expanding beyond Cuba. It was only in the days immediately preceding the commencement of battle that some newspapers even suggested the possibility that the United States might attack Spain in the Far East.

The battle of Manila Bay took place on May 1, but it was not until May 4 that Dewey ordered one of his ships to Hong Kong to send home word of victory. Dewey ordered the cutting of Manila's telegraph cable on the day of the battle in order to isolate Spain, forcing the three eager U.S. press correspondents to wait three days before they could transmit their dispatches. From Hong Kong, Harden cleverly sent a brief message at an urgent press rate ($9.90 per word), scooping his rivals and even beating Dewey's official dispatch. Harden's message arrived in New York at five thirty Saturday morning, too late for the morning edition, so the *World*'s news service passed it on to the *Chicago Tribune*. Jim Keeley, editor of the *Tribune*, called the White House and was the first to relate the news of victory to Washington. McCutcheon sent his cable at the regular commercial rate ($1.80 per word), but there was nobody at the *Record* office at that late hour to prepare it for the Saturday edition, and since the paper had no Sunday edition, his story had to wait for Monday. After requesting permission from the *Record*, the *New York Journal*'s Sunday edition published McCutcheon's dispatch (rewritten in "garbled" form, to McCutcheon's dismay). Although the *Record* was last to publish his dispatch, it was first to publish his complete story.[12] Despite the expectation that the telegraph could transmit news immediately, the path of communications in this case reveals its limitations in reaching government and news sources instantaneously but nonetheless illuminates a remarkable degree of collaboration between rival newspapers through news services that shared highly valued dispatches from the front.

Even before Dewey reported the outcome of the battle, news outlets on the home front had already set the expectation for a historic victory. Before Dewey ordered Manila's cable cut early on in the battle, a Spanish official had cabled a dispatch to Madrid hinting at great losses for the Spanish fleet and prompting rumors of a U.S. victory. Without any substantiation of what had actually taken place, graphic artists immediately began preparing illustrations to sensationalize the victory. On May 3 the *Houston Post* published "The Fight between the Two Fleets in Manila Harbor," a vivid drawing of Dewey's ship, the *Olympia*, in battle against the Spanish fleet in the rough waters of Manila Bay, amidst a sea of burning ships and floating wreckage. The *Post* claimed that the source of the drawing was "from a telegraphic description," which of course was impossible at that early date,

THE OLYMPIA AS SHE APPEARED AS THE REINA CHRISTINA STEAMED OUT OF THE SPANISH FLEET TO MEET HER.
[Copyright, 1898, by The Chicago Record.]

3.2. John T. McCutcheon, "The *Olympia*." *Philadelphia Inquirer,* June 19, 1898, 34.

typifying the strategy of fabricating "realism" to enhance the truth claims of imagery.[13] It would not be until over a month later that the *Philadelphia Inquirer* published four full-page spreads of Stickney's and McCutcheon's sketches of the battle, dubbed "a complete panorama of 'Dewey at Manila.'" McCutcheon's sketches foreground the pyrotechnics of battle with strong black and white contrasts to highlight smoke and fire. Framed as the only "authentic" pictures of the engagement from eyewitnesses, the series portrays the *Olympia* under siege from bursting shells (figure 3.2), the wreckage of the Spanish squadron, and views of Manila Bay and Cavite. "The four pages of pictures will place you in *immediate* touch with our new possessions in the far East, and will give you a more practical idea of the awful engines of modern warfare than any pictures ever printed," declared the *Inquirer.*[14] This emphasis on the creation of immediacy suggests the ability of pictures in this cultural moment to break down the distance of space and time for viewers. And yet, despite such claims, these thrilling graphic reproductions of the battle offered strikingly limited information about the fight.[15]

Just weeks after the battle of Manila took place, even before the *Inquirer* published its eyewitness accounts, commercial entrepreneurs began marketing spectacular reenactments of the naval battle. Pyrotechnics expert Henry J. Pain produced "The Battle of Manila," a widely popular attraction that toured the country in 1898, first appearing in Manhattan Beach in late May. Pain constructed a stage over three hundred feet wide to accommodate Manila Bay, the forts at Cavite, and reproductions of over twenty U.S. and Spanish battleships. Called a "thrilling mimic war panorama," Pain's production went to great lengths to create the semblance of real warfare. Claimed Pain:

> I can confidently assert that the battle of Manila . . . will be the most elaborate exhibition of fireworks ever seen in this or any other country. I regard it as a masterpiece in the pyrotechnical line. In my latest work I have sought not only to amuse, but to instruct. Every incident connected with Admiral Dewey's achievements in Manila have [sic] been faithfully and accurately reproduced. . . . With startling ingenuity the battle is reproduced, and the effects of the screeching shells, the firing of cannon and the burning of ships will be sensationally startling, and will explain in a more convincing manner than could be had through any other means the terrors of naval warfare as it really exists.[16]

Pain's reenactment reproduced the themes of U.S. naval supremacy and manly heroism put forth in press accounts of the naval confrontation. To edge out the competition, Pain advertised the ability of his spectacular production to convey the total experience of the battle. But in fact, not only did the rapid turnaround between the actual battle and the show's opening hamper his access to military information about the battle, but also he suppressed any signs of human casualties during combat to meet the needs of his family-centered audiences.

The "spectacular reality" of his productions drew power from the synergy between newspaper accounts and live reenactments. The overlap between news and entertainment was evident in newspaper illustrations of Pain's spectacles, such as those in the *New York Journal,* which were nearly identical to press depictions of the actual battle (figure 3.3). In lending legitimacy to the authenticity of Pain's reenactment, editors bolstered the credibility of their own graphic representations of the battle. While producing a show that was "sensational in the extreme," the *San Francisco Examiner* told its readers, Pain aspired to "historical fidelity," publicizing his careful library

3.3. "Scene from Pain's Fall of Manila." *New York Journal,* August 6, 1898, 5.

research in order to model ships and maneuvers "faithfully" after actual events. "Nothing has been left undone to make the drama absolutely realistic in every detail," according to the *Journal.*[17]

Pain's production toured the country after its tremendous commercial success in New York.[18] To heighten the dramatic tension, Pain introduced a land attack on the forts in Manila, which did not actually take place. Despite their promises of "realism," commercial entrepreneurs were not bound to remain true to the historical script.[19] In Atlanta, as in other cities, Pain's battle reenactment was intertwined with other popular entertainments, preceded by a sequence of novelty acts, including a trapeze artist, acrobats, and a man walking the high wire. The show was a "record breaker" in Dallas with battle scenes replete with roaring cannons, flashing gunfire, exploding bombshells, and flying wreckage. "Only those enlisted to support a country's cause ever have an opportunity to witness a real battle, but this production . . . is so realistic that one witnessing it is for the time being transported to the scene of the original and during the duration of the battle is kept in a frenzy of excitement and anticipation," said a *Dallas News* reviewer.[20]

The battle of Manila remained a popular theme of attractions even after the war ended. During the fall of 1898 a commercial vendor in Chicago produced at a cost of $75,000 an "electro-cyclorama" of the battle, which depicted the events on a great circular canvas. Viewers looked out on Manila Bay from an observation platform on the *Olympia*, which undulated as if tossed by real waves, thanks to a sophisticated wiring system. Red lights flashing from behind the canvas simulated the effect of exploding shells and mines. The scenes, changed by electrical apparatus, conveyed the spectator through each successive phase of battle.[21] The stirring visual panorama of the "electro-cyclorama" attempted to give audiences the feeling of being inside the battle as a participant, not merely a spectator.

The combined effect of press reports, illustrations, and popular entertainments turned the battle of Manila Bay into a visual spectacle that blended the "real" and the "imaginative" in a pleasing sensory experience and helped viewers not just imagine but feel the thrill of taking part in a triumphant naval victory fought on the other side of the globe.

The Battle of San Juan Hill

Nothing stands out more in the public memory of the Spanish-American War than Theodore Roosevelt's troop of Rough Riders on San Juan Hill. The name conjures up the image of a band of manly cowboys, led by Roosevelt, charging up a steep grassy hill to great American victory. And yet war correspondent and witness to the battle Richard Harding Davis described the assault on San Juan Hill in a much more somber tone, as a "chute of death" that came at great cost to American lives. He wrote:

> I have seen many illustrations and pictures of this charge on the San Juan hills, but none of them seem to show it just as I remember it. In the picture-papers, the men are running up the hill swiftly and gallantly, in regular formation, rank after rank, with flags flying, their eyes aflame and their hair streaming, their bayonets fixed, in long, brilliant lines, an invincible, overpowering weight of numbers. Instead of which I think the thing which impressed one the most, when our men started from cover, was that they were so few. It seemed as if someone had made an awful and terrible mistake.

One's instinct was to call to them to come back. You felt that some-
one had blundered and that these few men were blindly following
out some madman's mad order. It was not heroic then, it seemed
merely terribly pathetic.[22]

Davis's description of the attack as "terribly pathetic" was in drastic
contrast to popular representations of the battle. In fact, Davis had
written a dispatch to the *New York Herald* describing the maneuver as a chaotic series of blunders, but the *Herald* refused to print
it.[23] Image makers instead rendered the battle as a brilliant victory,
with Rough Riders charging valiantly, holding their weapons upright
and waving the American flag through the air. The other regiments
that participated, especially the African American divisions, were
generally forgotten.[24] The crafting of this battle into a decisive U.S.
military victory illuminates the sense of invincibility typifying these
representations and the conscious exclusion of images that did not
fit the aura of spectacular victory emanating from war-related mass
media.

Graphic artists depicted the chaotic and deadly maneuver on the
foothills of Santiago as a highly theatrical moment of American
manly heroics. Patriotic visual renditions of American valor in battle
were not new; this tradition in American art went back to the famous
historical paintings of the Revolutionary War by artists such as
Benjamin West, Emanuel Leutze, and John Trumbull. Between May
and July 1898, glorified depictions of Americans at war, on land and
sea, inundated pictorial papers and magazines. Frederic Remington,
Henry Reuterdahl, B. West Clinedinst, W. A. Rogers, and other artists invariably depicted U.S. soldiers unleashing their weapons with
resolution in scenes of impending victory and intense action. In his
studio in New York, W. G. Read painted a classic example of Teddy
Roosevelt brandishing his sword and leading a stampede of cavalrymen into battle on San Juan Hill amidst exploding shells and bugles
blowing.[25] The conception of the Rough Riders as cowboys led many
artists, like Read, to fabricate an image of the men on horseback.
Press accounts and illustrations constructed them as a brigade of
polo-playing millionaires and western types straight out of a Wild
West show, dubbed "Cow-Punchers" and "Fifth Ave. Dudes."[26] In
July 1898 a sketch artist for the *Charleston News and Courier* pic-

COLONEL ROOSEVELT LEADING HIS "TERRORS" IN THE FAMOUS CHARGE AT SAN JUAN

3.4. "Colonel Roosevelt Leading His 'Terrors' in the Famous Charge at San Juan." *Charleston News and Courier,* July 24, 1898, 13.

tured Roosevelt standing before his men confidently coordinating the attack on San Juan Hill (figure 3.4). Titled "Colonel Roosevelt Leading His 'Terrors' in the Famous Charge at San Juan," it presents a boisterous pack of Rough Riders wearing cowboy hats, ascending the hill. Some carry the flag; others hold weapons poised to shoot. Despite the bullets whizzing past them, no men appear to be hit. Nearly all of these images frame the charge from below, accentuating the spectacle of their upward climb to glory.

Photographers on location hoped to capture actual battle scenes but had little success. William Randolph Hearst hired photographer John C. Hemment, after his successful work during the *Maine* naval investigation, to return to Cuba. Chartering a boat, the *Sylvia,* as a makeshift floating darkroom, Hearst accompanied Hemment in Cuba to procure firsthand war pictures. Hemment armed himself with his weapons of choice: a six-by-ten, an eleven-by-fourteen, and a twelve-by-twenty camera, each with a long-focus lens, along with hundreds of glass photographic plates. He placed himself at the closest possible range, sometimes at great personal risk, but the moisture from rainy weather and poor lighting conditions were not ideal for producing glass plate negatives. Getting pictures at the bombardment of Morro Castle was "impossible," he wrote, because of the "long range" and the "large volumes of smoke." He witnessed the charge at El Caney, but inclement weather forced him to concede that "the pen had the advantage of the camera's eye." He wrote with disappointment, "What an inspiring picture to have impressed upon a negative—the soldiers making this noble charge!"[27] Hemment and other photographers instead sought out more suitable subjects: soldiers in transit or in camp, naval vessels at sea, and hospital scenes.

While photography was relegated to other purposes, motion picture footage reinforced the romantic power play of San Juan Hill. It became the subject of the first news footage of a battle ever made and was shown in cities nationwide. For the first time in American history, spectators could watch seemingly "real" military operations of the nation at war unfold onscreen in their own hometowns. After successfully covering the *Maine* disaster, Jim Blackton and Albert E. Smith of Vitagraph received requests from Tony Pastor's theaters and other venues for war films. Having accompanied the Seventy-first Regiment to Cuba, Blackton and Smith, toting their camera, tripod, and film, had the opportunity to film the charge at San Juan Hill firsthand. In their attempt to film the actual battle, Smith quickly retreated after "the shattered camera door brought with it the realization that bullets, not bugs, were whining past our heads."[28] When capturing the action on film failed, Blackton and Smith arranged for Roosevelt and the Rough Riders shortly after the battle to stage a charge up the hill. Shown within weeks after the battle took place, this seemingly authentic film footage of a disciplined charge by Roosevelt leading his men with their bayonets raised on San Juan Hill validated the mythic construction of the event proliferating throughout American visual culture.[29] The *Boston Herald* claimed that the "pictures of the bloody battle of San Juan hill" were "so realistic that audiences watch[ed] them with breathless attention."[30]

Theater owners enhanced the battle pictures onscreen with war-themed decoration to further intensify the film-viewing experience. As Amy Kaplan has demonstrated, "the spectacle of war . . . suffused every aspect of attending the theater." The Eden Musee, a major cinematic center in New York City, enhanced the movie-going experience by transforming its interior into a model battleship, supplemented with "realistic" wax models of leading war figures, including Dewey and Admiral William T. Sampson. Some theaters, in fact, used mock gunfire and smoke to heighten the sensory impact of war scenes.[31] Not only did the novelty of the medium itself corroborate claims of realism for what we now know to have been manufactured depictions, but also the entire experience of attending the theater became another means for audiences to immerse themselves in the spectacle of war.

Throughout 1898 and 1899 spectacular reenactments of the battle of San Juan Hill entertained viewers in cities across America. One of the largest productions, which took place in Chicago in 1899, utilized actual military personnel. In an arena accommodating forty thousand people, the set was eight hundred feet long, complete with a sixty-foot-high hill. Painters provided fifty thousand feet of canvas depicting scenes of the trenches, blockhouses, and Santiago Bay. The U.S. Army's First Regiment played the roles of both American and Spanish soldiers, although the men playing the Spaniards did so only "by force," alleged the *Chicago Times-Herald*. The final scene depicted the Americans charging up the hill "resistlessly"; reaching the top, they proudly raised the flag as the band played "Rally 'round the Flag, Boys." It was followed by an elaborate fireworks display of whistling rockets and fiery portraits of Dewey and Roosevelt. After seeing the show, Major Larry Ennis of the Seventh Regiment told reporters that "if San Juan Hill had been so near him that he could almost pick the stones off it with his hand he would have believed he saw a real battle."[32]

What is more, over 10 million Americans in almost three hundred cities saw Buffalo Bill and his Congress of Rough Riders' spectacular production of the battle of San Juan Hill in the Wild West Show tours of 1899 and 1900.[33] William F. Cody (Buffalo Bill) advertised the event as a "vivid, truthful, thrilling, heart-stirring dioramic reproduction . . . presented by some of the genuine participants in the famous battle." Cody publicized the participation of sixteen genuine Rough Riders (and two warhorses, Knickerbocker and Lancer).[34] Cody's choice of featuring San Juan Hill stemmed from his genuine interest in the Cuban campaigns. Just as he styled himself an "Indian fighter" for having killed Yellow Hair at Little Big Horn, which he habitually reenacted in his shows, he saw the war in Cuba as a great opportunity.[35] He volunteered to lead a regiment of thirty thousand Native Americans into battle, claiming they would fight to avenge themselves against Spain for initiating the white man's conquest of their lands and peoples. In all likelihood he hoped to reproduce his part in the war as a feature in shows down the line. Wrote Cody:

> There are in the United States to-day fully 30,000 full-blooded Indian warriors and at least 30,000 more youths and aged Indian men who can fight. With the 30,000 young redmen, mounted on their wiry ponies, acting in conjunction with the insurgents with an adequate amount of artillery, and using the same military tactics that they and their fathers used in fighting the whites in the wild West, I do not think that the Spaniards would last more than sixty days in a land war in Cuba. . . . If these 30,000 shouting Indian braves on horseback, resplendent in brilliant war paint, the eagle feathers on their war bonnets fluttering in the wind . . . sweep down on Havana in a grand charge what a *picture* it would make![36]

Cody already had a vision in mind for creating a battle "picture" with great theatrical appeal that would be ideal for future reenactment, but McKinley rejected his offer.

Cody's talent for self-promotion may not have landed him on the battlefield, but he played an even more important role in shaping the war in the likeness of a Wild West show. This is best exemplified in Theodore Roosevelt's appropriation of the name of Cody's famed "Rough Riders," which rendered the heroes of the war in the image of the western frontier. At the same time, as Christine Bold argues, contemporary newspaper reports, historical accounts, and Roosevelt's own writings constructed the Rough Riders in battle as "the Wild West version of war as a game" and warfare as "a vigorous, rule-bound, character-building sport" for America's male youth.[37] Cody certainly capitalized on the war, but his framework also helped transform popular understanding of the war as an extension of the Wild West.

The spectacular display of manly heroics in popular representations of the battle of San Juan Hill superseded acknowledgement of the high numbers of casualties (about 10 percent of all U.S. forces engaged on July 1), military mismanagement, and imperial under-pinnings of the campaigns.[38] Image makers transformed the battle into a symbol of America's emergence on the world stage.

Popular Celebrities of the Spanish-American War

Media producers sustained audience attention by turning war heroes into popular celebrities. This process of personalization countered the abstraction of overseas events by centering the spotlight on a few leading protagonists. Theodore Roosevelt was the most adept at playing the part of "war celebrity," shaping his persona as a rough-riding cowboy to his own political advantage. Several Rough Riders traveled with him on his campaign circuit for the New York gubernatorial race in 1898 to draw in crowds and speak of his war exploits.[39] Admiral Dewey and Lieutenant Richmond P. Hobson also became highly visible celebrities during the war, possibly even sur-passing Roosevelt in popularity, but they were much less adroit at fulfilling this role. Newspaper columns recounted in detail their war stories, childhood experiences, family life, and romantic encounters. Illustrated press coverage of Dewey and Hobson facilitated an "illu-sion of intimacy" with these public figures for home audiences, which Richard Schickel argues is central to the construction of celebrity in modern America. Their heroic stories also became an instrument for selling newspapers, as public fascination with them grew.[40]

In the instant that the press declared triumph for the Pacific fleet at Manila, Dewey, much to his surprise, became a national attrac-tion. Thousands of babies were named George Dewey (or Georgiana Dewey for girls); New Orleans changed Spain Street to Dewey Street; the Postal Department received applications from all over the coun-try to rename towns after Dewey, such as the newly established town of Deweyville, a suburb of Topeka, Kansas; music stores nationwide sold hundreds of Dewey songs, waltzes, and marches; a wide range of goods took the Dewey brand name; street vendors sold souve-nirs displaying his portrait in the form of buttons, badges, stickpins, and paperweights; many New York hotels added Dewey ices in the shape of battleships to their menus; and Dewey cocktails outstripped

WHEN DEWEY COMES MARCHING HOME AGAIN.

A Hint for His Reception.

3.5. "When Dewey Comes Marching Home Again." *Chicago Inter Ocean*, August 18, 1898, 3.

the martini and the highball as the most popular drinks in many saloons.[41]

A few cartoonists took aim at the mass-marketing of Dewey. A satirical cartoon in the *Chicago Inter Ocean* in the summer of 1898 titled "When Dewey Comes Marching Home Again" depicted a grand parade of consumer goods bearing Dewey's name, including soap, baking powder, umbrellas, clothing, pork and beans, stoves, and bicycles (figure 3.5). The nation had rewarded him, according to the cartoon, by making him a trademark and calling a generation of babies after him, here known as the "Young America Named after Dewey Society," positioned in military formation, ready to serve in his next mission.[42] One might think that as a fervent advocate of McKinley's Republican agenda, the *Inter Ocean* would have been first in line to idolize a military leader who had advanced its party's objectives. The cartoonist instead seems skeptical of the effects of the Dewey craze, hinting at the dilution of political meaning that might accompany the commodification of his image.

Dewey did not encourage the attention and was far from eager to embrace his overnight celebrity. In his autobiography he wrote: "My career as a hard-working naval officer scarcely equipped me for a role as the central figure of public applause. On the 30th of April,

1898, I had been practically unknown to the general public. In a day my name was on every one's lips."[43] After Spain surrendered, newspapers reported that Dewey "dreaded" returning home and had asked to remain in the Philippines. The *Chicago Times-Herald* reported, "He shudders at the very thought of being converted into an exhibit or a kissing post."[44]

The final naval confrontation of the war, the battle of Santiago Bay, presented another opportunity for a war hero to emerge. On May 19 the U.S. Navy received intelligence that the Spanish fleet was in port at Santiago Bay, Cuba, under the authority of Admiral Pascual Cervera y Topete. Rear Admiral William T. Sampson ordered Richmond P. Hobson to sink the American collier the *Merrimac* in the narrow outlet of the harbor to prevent Admiral Cervera's fleet from exiting. It was expected to be a suicide mission, but Spanish artillery damaged the *Merrimac*'s steering gear during the operation, making it impossible for Hobson to reach his target and block the channel. Although Hobson and his crew sustained no injuries, Spanish authorities took them prisoner, releasing them soon after the battle ended.

Media producers sensationalized Hobson's actions, despite his inability to carry out his assignment. A *New York Herald* artist created what became the iconic representation of his noble feat, and imitations of this sketch appeared in print across the country, penned by different artists (figure 3.6). Titling the sketch were the words of the Commander of the U.S. "Flying Squadron" during the battle at Santiago, Commodore Winfield Scott Schley: "History does not record an act of finer heroism." In the foreground, Hobson and his crew appear on a raft on the raging sea watching the *Merrimac* blow up in a stunning explosion. Despite having risked their lives, the men are calm and observe the explosion like spectators before a fireworks display. The image appeared in many forms, including its adaptation as a float in Denver's state parade to celebrate the culmination of peace.[45]

The national advertising campaign for Dr. R. V. Pierce's "Golden Medical Discovery" made use of the spectacle of Hobson's bravery. For the duration of the war, each of Dr. Pierce's ads borrowed from the repertoire of war iconography, with illustrations of scenes such as an American soldier protecting an imperiled female Cuba from a Spanish pirate, Clara Barton caring for sick Cubans, men charg-

3.6. H. Dart, "Richmond Pearson Hobson." *New York Herald,* Section 5, June 12, 1898, 1.

ing up San Juan Hill, and Spain surrendering at Santiago. The title, graphics, and opening text feigned the appearance of a war news column; not before the third or fourth paragraph was the product introduced. The advertisement, appearing in many urban dailies less than a week after Hobson's noble feat, asserted, "Give Full Honor Where Due: 'Remember the *Merrimac*!'" (figure 3.7) The ad read:

Lieutenant Hobson has proved himself the greatest hero of modern times. . . . Almost every man in the entire fleet begged to be allowed a place on the *Merrimac*—a forlorn hope for their country's glory—for none who went expected to get out alive through the hell that would surely pour from the cannon mouths of Morro and Zocapa. It was a scene of heroism and heroes which will do more to convince the world that Americans are not "a nation of shopkeepers," but that they are built of the material from which heroes are made. It takes a man with good blood, strong nerves and a healthy condition of heart, brains, and stomach to be a hero.

Dr. Pierce's medication, according to the logic of the advertisement, would give a person the stamina and physical resolve to become a hero. It claims to create "pure, rich blood" and cleanse the body of germs and disease. For this reason the artist alters the paradigmatic *Herald* illustration to iconify Hobson's heroism and masculine fortitude. The visual emphasis on his physique exemplifies the deployment of "manliness" as symbolic of American military potential. Centering on Hobson distills the complexity of the maneuver to the action of a single heroic superstar.

In contrast to Dewey, Richmond P. Hobson embraced his celebrity wholeheartedly, and his scandalous behavior added fuel to press sensationalism. Instead of acting as "the popular idol of soldierly nerve and Christian manhood," as the *Philadelphia Inquirer* hailed him, Hobson refashioned himself as a sex symbol.[46] Upon his return from Cuba, he reportedly stopped at each train station to kiss his waiting female admirers. In St. Louis, the *Chicago Times-Herald* reported, "the whole city is ringing with the story of the kiss imprinted on the cherry lips of Miss Emma Arnold."[47] Arnold, the first woman Hobson kissed, became a local celebrity in her own right: "The kiss of the hero of Santiago has made of her the arbiter of fashions, the director of the latest fads. In a word, the pressure of his bearded lips has made her the 'rage,'" proclaimed the *New York Journal*.[48] The press meticulously tracked the kissing circuit of Hobson's national lecture tour, which produced long lines of eager women. The *New York World* declared that his "triumphal tour" had "no parallel in the history of this country," estimating that he had kissed more than 1,400 women from Chicago to San Francisco.[49] In his efforts to please his fans, Hobson brought the "illusion of intimacy" in his celebrity to a new level.

While the press turned Hobson's escapades into front-page news, nicknaming him the "hero of the merry smack," the unanticipated

3.7. "Dr. Pierce's Golden Medical Discovery." *Houston Post,* July 8, 1898, 2.

turn of Hobson's kissing spectacle brought denunciation from military officials and editorialists alike.[50] "We don't want an ass for an Admiral," claimed one officer to the *San Francisco Chronicle.*[51] "One kiss did not make the Hobson scandal. It was the promiscuous public kissing of all classes and conditions of silly women that shattered the idol of modest heroism his countrymen had made of Hobson," argued the *Chicago Times-Herald.* "Even the laurel leaves that honored an act of heroism have withered in this atmosphere of sicken-ing *sentimentality*," claimed the *New York World*. In his defense, Hobson proclaimed the patriotic motivations for his actions; he told reporters: "I have kissed a large number of women, mostly young schoolgirls, who have thus expressed their patriotism. It was simply a matter of enthusiasm that found vent that way. It was not a tribute to Hobson, the man, but to Hobson, the navy's representative."[52] How lucky for American women that Hobson, "the navy's represen-tative," stood up to the task!

Whether it involved buying Hobson cigars, wearing Dewey suits, or dancing the Hobson or Dewey waltz, the cultural production of Dewey's and Hobson's celebrity enabled audiences to idolize them, read about their private lives, purchase goods bearing their name, and attend dramatic productions that told and retold their stories. Their tenure as national celebrities kept the media frame around American militarism and manhood and helped to mask the contribu-tions of other military participants, including the Cuban and Filipino forces fighting alongside the Americans to ensure Spain's defeat.

The Battle of Santiago Bay

The definitive naval victory over the Spanish squadron at Santiago became the climax in the media's promotion of the war as spectacle. This achievement marked a turning point in the war; Spain no longer commanded Cuban waters. Fortuitously, news of the triumph came on the Fourth of July, enabling media makers to mobilize the nation-alist sentiments of the holiday to transform the victory into a broadly shared celebration of American militarism. Put best by a headline in the *Cleveland Plain Dealer*, the defeat of Spain at Santiago was "Sampson's Fourth of July Present to the Nation."[53]

News of victory enabled organizers of the Trans-Mississippi and International Exposition in Omaha to turn the Fourth of July festivi-ties at the fairgrounds into an elaborate demonstration of patriotism. After Illinois governor John M. Tanner's address, the manager of the Associated Press took the speaker's stand and announced the news. The official historian of the exposition described the scene: "The crowd went wild with enthusiasm in an instant. . . . Men and women mounted the seats and waved their arms in the air as though carried away, and the music was almost drowned beneath the flood of glad acclaims."[54] The news sparked a spontaneous eruption of the crowd of over 44,000 people at the fair that day. The president of the Omaha fair, Gurdon Wattles, remembered the scene vividly over twenty years later: "When, on July 4, the news of the destruction of Cervera's fleet and the capture of Santiago came over the wires, enthusiasm knew no bounds."[55]

The heightened emotional state in which the public received news of the victory stimulated the demand for spectacular battle imagery. Jim Blackton and Albert E. Smith of the Vitagraph motion picture company rose to the task. Having left Cuba before the battle of Santiago took place, they chose to manufacture footage of the event in secret. The miniature reproduction of the battle that Blackton and Smith cleverly devised was in fact a forerunner to the special effects techniques of modern filmmaking. They purchased large photographs of U.S. and Spanish ships from a street vendor, cut out the ships, and placed them in a frame filled with water one inch deep, before a painted background of clouds and sky. Behind each ship they placed three pinches of gunpowder and attached a fine thread to pull the ships past the camera. To add smoke effects to the scene, Blackton asked his wife to smoke a few cigarettes. With the camera rolling, Blackton sparked the gunpowder with a wire taper. Blackton's wife, concealing her fits of coughing, blew smoke into the scene as each ship passed before the camera. In total, the film ran for two minutes. Smith wrote: "It would be less than the truth to say we were not wildly excited at what we saw on the screen. The smoky overcast and the flames of fire from the 'guns' gave the scene an atmosphere of remarkable realism."[56]

Still photographs, appearing in photographic portfolios and pictorial papers, enhanced the visual celebration of American naval power in the weeks after the battle took place. Although photographers were unable to take functional photographs of the actual siege, they compensated by taking portraits of nearly every U.S. cruiser and battleship that saw action, bedecked with flags and in their glory on the high seas, in juxtaposition with photographs of their destroyed Spanish counterparts (see figures 3.8 and 3.9). In picturing the fallen Spanish fleet, photographer John Hemment commented, "What had

3.8. The U.S.S. *San Francisco*. From *Through the War by Camera: A Weekly Artfolio of Current Events, on Land and Sea, in the Spanish-American War of 1898* (New York: Pearson Publishing, 1898).

Reina Christina, Flagship of Spanish Admiral Montojo. Completely destroyed by Dewey, May 1, 1898.

3.9. F. Tennyson Neely, photograph of the wreckage of the *Reina Christina*. From Neely, *Fighting in the Philippines: Authentic Original Photographs* (London: F. Tennyson Neely, 1899).

once been the bright and buoyant hope of the Spanish navy were now helpless hulks strewn along Cuba's southern shore."[57]

Biograph's motion picture, "Wreck of the 'Vizcaya,'" visually proclaimed that the United States had avenged the destruction of the *Maine* in Santiago Bay. Press reports commonly touted the cruiser *Vizcaya* as the Spanish equivalent to the *Maine*. The *Vizcaya* actuality film, filmed July 3 or 4, 1898, exactly mirrored the visual construction of its predecessor a few months earlier, the highly acclaimed "Wreck of the Battleship '*Maine*.'"[58] The distance from the wrecks, the timing of the camera pan, and the angle of vision and panoramic view of the two films were nearly identical, both seemingly shot from the perspective of another ship at sea. A *Chicago Record* correspondent expressed a common perception as he proudly stated when reporting the naval victory: "The *Maine* is remembered. Spain's fleet in these waters has been annihilated."[59]

It took less than a month after the battle before cultural entrepreneurs had created mass entertainments reenacting the naval confrontation at Santiago Bay. One of the largest was Imre Kiralfy's reproduction of the battles of Manila Bay and Santiago at Madison Square Garden in New York. Kiralfy learned of the victory at Santiago Bay while attending a banquet at the American Society in London, and he remembered thinking at that moment: "The finale to my play was found! History had given it to me!" Kiralfy mimicked his rival Henry Pain in his pronouncements of research and attention to "actual facts" to bolster the authenticity of his shows.[60] As in Pain's production, fulfilling his promises of "realism" were less important to Kiralfy than creating an entertainment with broad appeal, leading to the absence of any references to death or injury in the reconstruction of the battle. "There is nothing in the whole entertainment to cause sadness or gloom," the *New York Journal* assured its readers.[61]

Kiralfy indentified the *New York Herald* and other papers as his source of "accurate" information, again demonstrating the collaboration of the press in circulating and legitimating the production of military spectacle. His goal, to create a "life-like representation" of events, required elaborate staging, with a tank four feet deep, 120 feet wide, and 370 feet long that held over 175,000 cubic feet of water. Models of U.S. and Spanish battleships, each twenty-five feet long, "plow the waters of the lake, go ahead, stop, back, turn and maneuver in every way exactly as though they were real war vessels, impelled by steam and operated by real crews," reported the *Cleveland Plain Dealer*. The *New York Journal* bolstered the image of its own firsthand reporting by likening the spectator's perspective at the show to the privileged visual access of their war correspondents in Cuba: "The floor of the big amphitheatre has been ripped up and an ocean flooded in. On this ocean every manoeuvre of our fleets . . . will be represented in such a realistic manner and with such historic accuracy that New Yorkers can see the blockades and battles as effectively almost as though they had been on board a *Journal* dispatch boat."[62] The show was so successful that Kiralfy later reconstructed it as a private concession on the midway of the Omaha world's fair at the end of that summer.[63]

Media production of the Spanish-American War centered on U.S. victories at Manila Bay, San Juan Hill, and Santiago Bay. Although the impact of this cultural production on audiences is difficult to measure, the material effects are clearly evident in the countless ways in which war-related themes became a part of American home life and consumer choices.

Popular Consumption of the War

The spectacular rendering of war-related media bred a culture of patriotic diversion that rapidly engulfed the nation for the duration of the war. Political wife Ellen Maury Slayden noted in her private journal the flurry of wartime patriotic enthusiasm, which she described as "deafening," adding, "Most people talk as if the war was to be a gigantic picnic."[64] Taking part in this militaristic culture enabled Americans to articulate patriotic sentiment without necessarily internalizing the deeper political implications.

Theaters served as an important site for disseminating war information, further blurring boundaries between the informative function of news and the desire to entertain. During the war, a succession of war plays opened in theaters across the country. Cuban war dramas became a hot commodity because they managed "to tickle the public where it hungers for tickling just now," claimed the *Courier-Journal* of Louisville, Kentucky.[65] Many shows incorporated patriotic music, such as "The Star-Spangled Banner," "Yankee Doodle," and other national hymns into their productions. Even when the dramatic content was not war-related, some theaters interrupted performances with news bulletins from particular papers. Koster & Bial's theater in New York, for example, installed a wire service to the *New York Journal* to convey news from the front directly to audiences in between vaudeville skits. The Harlem Music Hall discontinued the reading of *Journal* bulletins after noting a negative response: "From all parts of the house came cries of 'Lie!' 'Fake!' 'Rats!' accompanied by catcalls. Then came a bombardment of hisses, and the stage manager, evidently disgusted with the result of his dip into sensational journalism, apologized for the sensational report."[66]

Military and patriotic themes became an integral, and perhaps inescapable, part of daily life across America, affecting people of all ages, including children. The day after Congress declared war, New York State passed a law mandating public schools to arrange for children to salute the flag every morning.[67] The superintendent of Williamson Trade School in Pennsylvania, however, discontinued the school's regular flag-raising ceremony. The flagstaff was bare for the first two months of the war, with the exception of Memorial Day, because he feared that the intense patriotism of the boys would lead them to enlist at the sight of the flag. While he encouraged volunteering, he feared that he might lose his entire student body.[68]

The proliferation of naval imagery in the press furnished children with a treasure trove of visual information on military and wartime matters. Children constituted an important segment of the newspaper reading audience, and a twentieth-century study of newspaper reading patterns found that young readers, from ages six to sixteen, were mostly drawn to pictorial content.[69] A seventh grade teacher, Miss Isabel Richman, told the *Chicago Inter Ocean* that most of her students read the war news regularly. "Nine of every ten boys and half of the girls have given vent to their feelings by making pictures of battle-ships," she noted, and these drawings "demonstrate a wonderful familiarity with vessels that is almost incredible."[70] Eight-year-old Gregory Mason from Milton, Massachusetts, put aside his marbles and baseball bats that spring and constructed wooden ships, which he named *Vizcaya* and *Colon*.[71] In Cincinnati a group of enterprising schoolboys raised money to build a battleship to replace the

Maine, which they named *The American Boy.* They secured President McKinley's approval for the project, and their efforts throughout the fall of 1898 generated over $35,000.[72]

Children increasingly consumed an accretion of war-related games and pastimes. The *Chicago Times-Herald* advertised a parlor archery game that came with a detailed map of Cuba along with a set of projectiles to bombard the fortifications. The large map depicted twenty-three U.S. battleships, which the *Times-Herald* argued would provide valuable visual context "to follow the war news." The *Youth's Companion,* a family-oriented magazine, advertised an activity called "Shooting the Spaniard," in which players threw darts at a likeness of the archetypical Spanish villain. "The Sunday *World*'s Havana Blockade Game" purported to be "a war game for every American boy and girl," in which players rolled the dice and followed their fleet on its patrol course, dodging torpedoes and searchlights in hopes of running the blockade. A puzzle, "How Would You Have Taken Santiago?" in the *New York Journal,* challenged readers to devise how U.S. troops should storm the city, offering a $10 prize for the best proposal.[73]

The flurry of war-related activities, merchandising, and imaginative war play demonstrates that children were encouraged to become active participants in the military culture unfolding around them. A five-year-old named Joey Lorentz invented the game "Manila" and organized his friends into Spanish and American militia units. "I'm Dewey," he proclaimed, "and youse kids is the Spanish guys. Now I turn my guns on you like this and blow you all to pieces. Boom! boom! I only wisht I had some firecrackers!" This war play at times turned violent, as in the case of a ten-year old boy named Henry Mendelssohn, who was pretending to direct the Spanish army in a sham battle against U.S. forces, led by his friend Leonard Davidow. Leonard commanded Henry to surrender, and when he did not, Leonard pointed a pistol at him and shot him in the leg. He was arraigned in court the next morning.[74]

Young boys may also have participated in this wartime culture by wearing one of the latest fashions, "Dewey suits," made of blue material with white trim.[75] This "Admiral" style for boys was just one of many new war-related fads that season. Trends in fashion increasingly favored a military or nautical style, with red, white, and blue colors in women's attire. Suits in the style of naval cadet uniforms became popular—a short blue jacket buttoned up to the collar with white frill at the neck. Many women adorned their clothing with imitation military buttons, insignia from local regiments, parasols decorated with hand-embroidered eagles, quasi-military capes, "army leggins," and military hats that mimicked the headgear of army privates. Complementary trends in men's fashion took hold, such as "Rough Rider" overcoats "made of black, blue and brown kersey and covert cloth," as one ad proclaimed.[76] Wearing patriotic fashions became an outward indicator of participation in this shared culture of patriotic diversion.

Retailers capitalized on war-related themes to draw attention to their products and stores. An advertisement for the Foreman Shoe Company of Chicago featured Uncle Sam using his new shoes to kick Spain across the Atlantic; it read "While Uncle Sam kicks the Dons from Cuba We'll Kick the Prices Off of Our High-Art Footwear." A Dallas department store converted six large show windows into a "Grand Camping Ground" with sets of military-style tents, each filled with sale items from different departments. A store in Savannah placed large colorful pictures of the *Maine* and the battle of Manila in its shop window. In Cleveland a number of corner grocery stores displayed in their windows sculptures of flags, boats, and other war-related images constructed out of their goods to spark attention.[77]

Related to this surge of marketing was another up-and-coming pastime, the widespread collecting of military souvenirs such as soldiers' gear, camp items, and flags. Retailers offered free war trinkets with a purchase for consumers to put on display in their parlors. One indicator of the pervasiveness of the wartime souvenir market was that by the time the war had ended, there was a prevailing feeling in the press, even among newspapers in favor of the war, that the "souvenir craze" had spun out of control. A cartoon in the *New York Journal,* for example, depicts General William Shafter leading soldiers overloaded with war accouterments to take back home, noting, "If all souvenirs are genuine, our returning army must have looked like this." Exaggerated views of "the 'souvenir' collecting mania" in the *Journal,* the *New York Herald,* and other papers struck a critical tone toward the nation's newfound obsession with military culture.[78]

During the war, many newspapers advertised photographic port-folios for purchase with photographs of the *Maine* and other U.S. battleships, portraits of major generals, pictures of troop movements and army camp life, and scenes from the colonies. To receive them, readers had to mail in inquiries and pay an additional charge. The *Los Angeles Times* supplement "The War by Camera," depicting all "the pomp and circumstance of glorious war," claimed to offer "the finest set of war views ever collected." New installments came out weekly, each containing sixteen pages of eleven-by-fourteen-inch photographs on fine paper. One reader of the *Times,* T. E. Gibbon, wrote in to say, "I have been very much entertained by the collec-tion, and value it so highly that I propose, when completed to have it bound." After receiving her *Chicago Times-Herald* folio, one woman wrote in: "You may send me the entire series. . . . I would rather go without my summer bonnet than be deprived of your offer. Why, my children are perfectly charmed and my neighbors' children flock in to see the portraits and read the footnotes."[79] Advertisers emphasized the utility of these folios as a way for Americans on the home front to gain familiarity with events and peoples overseas and to share in their patriotic consumption with friends and family.

The replication of Spanish-American War iconography and par-aphernalia throughout the streets, stores, and homes of America altered the colors, styles, and activities of everyday life. Anne Smith, writing for the *Philadelphia Inquirer,* satirically sketches its effect on the American home: "She [a typical American homemaker] makes of her house a national anthem, from the flags at the front and the wooden eagle over the hall-door to the military corner in her den, where she lounges under a flag canopy, surrounded by pictures of sea fights and photographs of military celebrities. . . . Her piano is draped with the tri-color, with a picture of the same ill-fated vessel [the *Maine*]. She rearranges her menu and gives patriotic luncheons with ices in the shape of the American eagle or Uncle Sam."[80] Popular consumption of the war does not get more literal, or perhaps more farcical, than eating its primary icons in the form of frozen desserts! While drawing a hyperbolic picture, Smith calls attention to interior decoration as a means by which homemakers could participate in the wartime culture.[81] Purchasing war-related home decor, wearing patriotic colors, perusing a war-themed store window, or placing a photographic album celebrating U.S. military accomplishments in one's parlor were among the many ways in which American consumers cultivated a nationalistic and martial spirit within their homes and communities.

The Success of Spectacle: The Unanticipated Effects

Turning war into entertainment under the pretext of historical accuracy had unexpected and unsettling consequences. The line between reality and fantasy was a fine one. Motion picture footage during the war confirmed the original purpose of U.S. intervention, solidifying visions of Spanish oppression. In one Edison film, "Cuban Refugees Waiting for Rations" (filmed in early May 1898 in Tampa, Florida), William Paley displayed the victims of Spanish reconcentration, showing a line of listless Cubans, tin cups in hand, waiting for relief from the United States. In another film, titled "Shooting Captured Insurgents," cameraman William Heise filmed the alleged death of Cuban rebels before a Spanish firing squad. The Spanish soldiers line up the insurgents in front of a large building, raise their weapons, and shoot. The film ends as the Cuban men fall dead amid the gun smoke. In fact this film, probably recorded in New Jersey in July 1898, reenacted the spectacle of Spanish brutality for home audiences to see.[82]

On the popular stage, most war plays adhered closely to the chronology of the conflict reported in the headlines and featured impersonations of actual military leaders. The emotional intensity of war dramas may in some cases have ventured too close to "reality." Such was the case of the Neil Stock Company's play *The Ensign,* dubbed a "thrilling realistic naval drama," which appeared at the Alhambra Theater in Chicago in May 1898. What was striking about this play was that its publicity warned, "The actors who represent Spaniards wish to state that they are not of that nationality, and that their sentiments are fully in accord with those uttered by Americans against Spain." The concern that audiences would not be able to distinguish actors from actual Spaniards was later validated, for the *Chicago Inter Ocean* reported that police officers had to prevent audience members in the upper tiers from hurling "missiles" of some kind at the actors, and "a riot was narrowly averted."[83] At Havlin's Theater in Chicago, police did not arrive in time to prevent an attack against an actor who played the part of an evil Spaniard in the play *Cuba*. An unknown assailant stabbed actor Edward Grady in the chest at the theater, leaving him in critical condition. Grady complained that even before the incident, boys on the streets had cursed him for playing a Spanish role. Ironically, Grady's loyalties were far from suspect, since he also served as a regular in the Seventh Regiment of the U.S. Army.[84] These violent manifestations reveal the instabilities at work in this merger of war and performative culture.

A similar setback plagued the opening of William L. Roberts's naval drama *The Commodore* at the Lincoln Theater in Chicago. The play toured U.S. cities after Spain had surrendered, and yet still a group of actors went on strike shortly before the first performance, not for higher pay but from "patriotic motives." The actors "could not bring themselves to pull on the cursed crimson trousers of the Spaniard," reported the *Courier-Journal*. Consequently, on opening night the Spanish forces were few and ill-trained, drawn at the last minute from available stage crew. Fortunately the show went on and achieved critical success. Reviewers praised its elaborate reproduction of naval warfare as well as the comic relief provided by a few of the characters—old drunken sailors repeatedly interjecting that they, too, had not forgotten the *Maine*.[85]

Actors playing Spanish roles were not the only targets of popular antagonism. On the streets of New York after war had commenced, an artist for the *Tribune* drew in chalk a likeness of General Weyler to supplement a headline on the paper's news bulletin board. A crowd bombarded the drawing with mud, eggs, stones, bananas, and anything else readily available, prompting a riot. The *Tribune* removed the drawing and resisted further visual illustration of Spanish leaders on the bulletin boards.[86] The heightened emotionality connected to Weyler's likeness led to a moment of public disorder that the *Tribune* did not expect or condone. Serving as a visual proxy for the "real" Spanish villain, these images became an outlet for the crowd to project aggression against Spain, no different, perhaps, from parlor games that positioned the Spanish villain at the bull's eye.

Although it is difficult to ascertain exactly how Americans responded to war-related media, these moments of violent civil unrest register the extremes of popular expression. The repetitive claims of realism in war-related performances may have hindered spectators from being able to sort out the real from the imaginary, or at the very least, it perhaps made any distinction inconsequential.

A contemporary critic of empire, John A. Hobson, put his finger on the pulse of a wider culture of spectatorship in 1902 when he wrote, "Jingoism is merely the lust of the spectator."[87] Audience participation in spectacles of war did not conclusively point to martial or imperial commitments. On the one hand, the celebration of U.S. militarism in visual and popular media was so widespread that escaping its influence was nearly impossible. Producers magnified and emotionalized war-related content for a broad popular base of viewers, including those without voting rights, such as women and children. Because readers and viewers often defined their patriotism through acts of consumption, downplaying or criticizing U.S. actions may have been socially constraining. The reproduction of patriotic and military themes in multiple forms of media helped to create the illusion that potentially controversial political choices were established and inevitable facts of national life. On the other hand, while promoting militaristic and patriotic values, war-related media were not generally programmed to have a specific political effect. The cultural production of the war served as an escape from the struggles of modern industrial life. Its amusement value complicates any simple reading of popular participation as a signal of support for government policies. Transforming war into an instrument of spectacle obscured political meaning or made it irrelevant altogether.

One effect of this consolidation of popular sentiment was a kindling of national unity. "In these warlike spectacles everywhere manifested it has already united us as nothing else could—as emancipating both sections of the union from the mistaken impression that we ever were, or ever could be, anything else than one people," wrote Henry Watterson.[88] As a prominent southern editor (of the *Louisville Courier-Journal*), Watterson urged war, and later imperialism, as a means of advancing the South's interests, and his editorials consistently praised the war for uniting the sections against a common enemy.[89] Fritz W. Guerin, a Union army veteran and St. Louis photographer, staged a photographic tableau that celebrated this pervasive sentiment (figure 3.10). With the U.S. and Cuban flags draped as backdrop, the image unites the Blue and Gray in a handshake

3.10. Fritz W. Guerin, "Cuba Libre." 1898. Courtesy Library of Congress.

that breaks the chains of a young, white female Cuba.[90] Widespread engagement with these narratives of war nationalized audiences at two levels: it strengthened individual ties to the nation and bonded Americans across sectional divisions.[91]

This familiar account of sectional reconciliation inspired by the war, however, may not be the only salient narrative of nationalism at work here. The collective result of this array of war-related images in American print, visual, and popular culture was the ascension of a glorified portrait of U.S. militarism. Readers and viewers from all parts of the country and from all political perspectives were encouraged to share in its consumption. Thus the merger of popular and political cultures had a paradoxical effect; while consuming war-related media may have fostered a shared patriotic culture among diverse publics, the ideological meanings attached could also be elusive, particularly when the spectacular display itself, and not the underlying political cause, defined its popular appeal.

The instability of political meaning had important consequences in shaping the public climate for the reception of empire. In rendering war a diversion, the spectacular construction of the war concealed its underlying imperial implications. Even if the spectacular production of the war did not necessarily align Americans with the politics of imperialism, it framed issues in a way that heightened interest in U.S. foreign policy and militarism, consolidated white masculinity, raised the patriotic consciousness of the public, and kept the focus on the American nationalist perspective (as opposed to Cuban, Hawaiian, Puerto Rican, Filipino, or other non-U.S. points of view). From the moment the war began, it became one fought for and about the United States. The ambivalence toward Cuban liberation in prewar media campaigns manifested itself as the promotion of American military glory supplanted Cuban independence on the media agenda. Cuban and Filipino participation was peripheral to the spectacular production of American manly heroics. The fact that the war earned the name the "Spanish-American War," leaving out Cuba entirely, reveals the power of the spectacle to drown out its imperial context.[92]

This by no means minimizes the deep-seated imperialist assumptions of mainstream American media, for the patterns of representation that came to dominate war-related productions fostered a culture of patriotic and martial sentiment to support empire, even if they were not consciously programmed for that effect. It suggests, however, the complexity and inconsistency of meaning underlying the fact. As we shall see, it would not be until the final moments, when the spectacle of war began to unravel, that the divisive issue of imperialism made a significant impact on media conceptions of the war.

4

The Visual Script Changes

THE ANNEXATION OF HAWAII
AND THE LURE OF EMPIRE

In the meantime, the Spanish War was raging. . . .
The country was excited. Emporia was thrilled to the
core. We celebrated the fall of Santiago with a big
public meeting outdoors at the corner of Fifth and
Commercial, and Ike Lambert, our leading lawyer and
most accomplished orator, spoke to the multitude.
He rang the changes of noble patriotism, the band
played "The Star Spangled Banner," and we sang
"Hail Columbia" and threw out a full-throated hymn
to imperialism with the verses of "America" and
were most pleased with ourselves. . . . We were
the chosen people; imperialists always were—from
Moses to McKinley. The *Emporia Gazette* was just as
crazy as any of the newspapers, no better.

The Autobiography of William Allen White (1946)

Upon the opening of hostilities, Blackton and Smith of Vitagraph
produced America's first war motion picture—"Tearing Down the
Spanish Flag" (1898). When Blackton's hand was seen tearing down
the Spanish flag and hoisting the American flag in its place, he and
his partner had hit upon a powerful visual image to electrify patriotic sentiment.[1] Dewey's naval achievement at Manila Bay on May
1 inspired the *New York Journal* to transform this image into a new
national vision: *not* to haul down the American flag. The *New York
Journal* called on its readers to support the full realization of U.S.
military potential. To do this, the nation needed to assert itself in the
arena of foreign policy, beginning with annexing Hawaii, building a
canal in Nicaragua, strengthening the U.S. Navy, and expanding U.S.
influence in the Western Hemisphere.[2]

Media sensationalism of U.S. victories at Manila Bay, San Juan Hill, and Santiago Bay played a decisive role in transforming perceptions of U.S. goals in the Spanish-American War from liberation to conquest. Liberation, which media accounts had defined prior to the war as culminating in a free Cuba, shifted to include the remainder of the Spanish empire and the exertion of long-term U.S. political, military, and commercial influence in the Caribbean and the Pacific. The battle of Manila Bay was presented as proof that the United States had become a formidable global power. The president of Stanford University, David Starr Jordan, in addressing the graduating class in May 1898, expressed his worry that victory would have an addictive effect: "What will be the reflex effect of great victories, suddenly realized strength, the patronizing applause, the ill-concealed envy of great nations, the conquest of strange territories, the raising of our flags beyond the seas? All this is new to us. . . . [I]t is delicious; it is intoxicating."[3] Dewey's "delicious" victory generated a swell of national pride that stirred media makers to invest the war with an entirely new mission. Cuban independence took secondary importance to the new priority of setting a place for the United States at the table of world powers.

In the early weeks of the war the press had toyed with the notion of imperial gain, but without serious reflection. Out of hundreds of war-related political cartoons published nationwide in May and June 1898, very few had raised considerations about imperial acquisition.[4] The national debate over this question did not begin in earnest until two months into the war, after America's naval victory in Santiago Bay in early July. While the nation celebrated Spain's defeat and impending surrender, Congress ratified a joint resolution annexing Hawaii and General Nelson Miles seized Puerto Rico. These events pushed U.S. foreign policy in a direction the media had not foreseen, or at least made explicit, prior to the war. The absence of such forethought in the prewar campaigns became evident in the increasing polarization of media opinion after the potential for imperial conquest was fully actualized. This chapter examines the reverberations of the surging military spirit on the master pictorial narrative of war that followed on the heels of U.S. victories at Manila Bay, San Juan Hill, and Santiago. The quickness to abandon, reverse, or adapt the narrative elements of the storyline underwriting U.S. intervention in this imperial reconfiguration confirms that media conceptions of the political goals of U.S. actions were ambiguous and multifaceted from the start.

Although we now often define "imperialism" and "empire" more broadly to encompass both direct and indirect mechanisms of control, the imperial debate in 1898–99 centered on whether or not the United States was entitled or obliged to exercise formal political and military sovereignty over part or all of the Spanish colonies. There is a gap between this more narrow view of "imperialism" as synonymous with political control, which is how historical actors of that time primarily understood it, and the more recent New Left conception that widens the understanding of empire to include informal modes of dominance. Many anti-imperialists in the postwar debates who argued against formal colonialism nevertheless supported policies extending cultural, economic, and diplomatic influence, making them imperialists of another sort. For this reason I call them "anticolonialists" to underscore the broader imperial vocabulary underlying the iconographies on both sides of the debate. In other accounts the same people I refer to as "anticolonialists" are labeled "anti-imperialists," and indeed some of them—but not all—were.

The Bridge to Empire: The Annexation of Hawaii

In early July, Congress passed a joint resolution annexing Hawaii at McKinley's request, citing reasons of military necessity. The ratification of Hawaiian annexation came before Congress and the nation at an ideal moment, when the spectacular production of U.S. victories at Manila Bay, San Juan Hill, and Santiago was at its height in multiple media platforms. The magnification of patriotic and militaristic sentiment engendered by this convergence of war-related news and entertainment eased the nation into shifting focus away from Cuban independence and toward establishing a greater U.S. presence in the Pacific, East Asia, and the Caribbean.

Prior to the Spanish-American War, all attempts to annex Hawaii had failed. President Franklin Pierce and Secretary of State William H. Seward (serving under President Andrew Johnson) had made unsuccessful attempts to solidify support for annexation in 1854 and 1867. Further attempts in 1893 and 1897 had similarly stalled. Despite America's growing missionary, political, and commercial influences in Hawaii during the second half of the nineteenth century, incorporation required a cultural and political climate favoring expansion, and this was not present until the Spanish-American War began. Protestant missionaries from New England had arrived in Hawaii in the 1820s, and by 1848, Western investment and the establishment of a plantation economy began to transform the islands. The integration of capitalist systems of private landownership, taxation, and wage labor displaced traditional agricultural practices and jeopardized Hawaiian sovereignty, particularly once sugar became the mainstay of Hawaii's economy. Talk of annexation began as early as the 1850s, during the rule of King Kamehameha III, as Hawaii's whaling and sugar industries increased ties to U.S. trade. Fearing internal revolution and the impact of filibustering activities from the coast of California, Kamehameha supported annexation, but his successor, Liholiho, abandoned the effort.[5]

In 1875 Hawaii and the United States signed a renewable reciprocity agreement granting Hawaii duty-free access for certain exports, such as sugar, to the United States in exchange for exclusivity (which meant that Hawaii could make this agreement only with the United States). While this gave the Hawaiian sugar industry an advantage, it also cemented Hawaii's economic dependency on the United States. By 1890, 99 percent of Hawaii's exports were shipped to the United States, and 76 percent of Hawaii's imports came from the United States.[6] The passage of the McKinley Tariff in 1890, however, annulled the terms of reciprocity by enabling other foreign entities, such as Cuba, to export sugar to the United States without any duties. Hawaii no longer retained an edge over other sugar-producing states, which led to an immediate drop in the price of sugar and gave Hawaiian sugar interests added incentive to press for annexation. In the midst of this crisis, Queen Liliuokalani ascended the throne in 1891, determined to break Hawaiian dependency on the United States.

After Liliuokalani called for a new constitution to restore native rights, a group of white property-holding businessmen in Hawaii, most of whom were Americans, overthrew her regime in January 1893. The U.S. minister to Hawaii, John L. Stevens, supported this action by installing an American warship, the U.S.S. *Boston*, just offshore. The presence of the U.S. Marines compelled the queen to abdicate her throne, and the new leadership made immediate appeals to President Benjamin Harrison for annexation. In February 1893, toward the latter part of his term, Harrison submitted a treaty of annexation to the Senate, but it did not come to a vote. Harrison's successor, Grover Cleveland, opposed annexation and withdrew the treaty upon coming into office. In the interim, a provisional government ruled in Hawaii until an administration friendly to annexation came to power in Washington.[7]

From 1893 to 1898 the debates over annexation previewed many of the same political, economic, and racial arguments that would shape the larger imperialist debate of 1898–99. Supporters of annexation argued that Hawaii could serve as a gateway to the Far East and provide rich commercial advantages. Critics questioned the involvement of Stevens in the coup, viewing it as merely a ploy on the part of the sugar industrialists. They claimed that the United States could reap commercial rewards without the burdens of annexation and raised concerns about the impact of annexation on American republican ideals, particularly if "inferior" Hawaiian natives were granted citizenship. Hopes for annexation resurfaced in McKinley's presidential campaign of 1896. His official platform urged that Hawaii be "controlled" by the United States, which implied his intention to annex it.[8] McKinley also argued for a revision of tariff policy. While the Hawaiian sugar industries urged the resumption of reciprocity, the American "sugar trust," the Western Sugar Refining Company of San Francisco, was strongly opposed for fear that this would endanger its sugar monopoly in the U.S. market.[9] Despite opposition by American sugar interests, President McKinley submitted another annexation treaty to the Senate on January 16, 1897. The Senate failed to achieve a two-thirds majority, leading annexationists to try to get the treaty passed through a joint resolution (which required only a simple majority in each house). But even the joint resolution did not have enough support to pass, marking yet another annexation failure.

The Spanish-American War proved decisive in furnishing the political conditions necessary for annexation. The joint resolution that had remained pending since 1897 was resubmitted immediately after reports of the victory in Manila Bay. McKinley justified annexing Hawaii as a necessary war measure in order for it to serve as a coaling station and naval base en route to the Far East. On June 15, 1898, the House passed the resolution by a vote of 209 to 91, with practically unanimous Republican support. It then went to the Senate on July 6 and passed by a vote of 42 to 21. The inflation of national pride coupled with the immediacy of the war tipped the balance in favor of annexation when all prior attempts had failed. McKinley established the tone of U.S. imperial authority by failing to solicit consent from or provide compensation to the native rulers and people in the territorial incorporation of Hawaii. McKinley's policy in Hawaii was one of the first steps toward outwardly shaping the imperialist agenda of the Spanish-American War.

While the war with Spain supplied the pretext for immediate annexation, the vote still inspired fierce debate in the Senate and in the press. Dissenting arguments anticipated the concerns that arose later with regard to acquiring Cuba and the Philippines. As Eric Love has argued, race was one of the most important "barriers" that annexationists "had to anticipate, account for, and remove if their imperialist plans would succeed."[10] Critics of annexation emphasized the incompatibility of incorporating native and Asian peoples into American racial stock and political culture. Throughout the nineteenth century, the native Hawaiian population had declined owing to the pathological effects of disease. From a population of over 130,000 in 1832, the native population dropped to fewer than 35,000 in 1890. Labor shortages resulting from this decline led to the importation of workers from China and later Japan, called "coolie laborers." By 1897 the Japanese were the second-largest ethnic group in Hawaii after the native population, and the Chinese were third. In an age of exclusionary policies toward Chinese and Japanese immigrants, the annexation treaties coming before the Senate explicitly prohibited future immigration from East Asia into Hawaii to alleviate domestic concerns about a rising Asian presence.[11]

Because of the prevalence of race as a factor in U.S. expansionist debates (which can be traced to the Mexican War conquest as well as justifications for Native American wars), political cartoonists drew on conventions of racial caricature to represent the stakes of Hawaii's candidacy for annexation. Images of African peoples as wild savages have a long history, one that Jan Nederveen Pieterse dates back to ancient Greece, but the modern image came into popular use in the eighteenth and nineteenth centuries in connection with the discourse of colonialism. Early images produced during the European exploration of Africa portrayed African peoples as heathens and ferocious warriors, but as European colonial policy matured in the nineteenth century, the savage warrior was transformed into the tractable but dependent child-savage as a way to rationalize long-term occupation.[12] Studies of physiognomy and anatomy in the eighteenth and nineteenth centuries as well as the theories of Charles Darwin, Herbert Spencer, and the "science" of race empowered Western societies to demarcate the world's peoples according to the physical attributes of race.

In the United States, the politics of slavery further institutionalized the image of African Americans as infantile and inferior. Representations of the lazy, carefree, contented slave (the Sambo) in need of paternalistic care proliferated in political cartoons, sheet music, and minstrel shows. During and after Reconstruction, resistance to African American political participation and economic advancement helped propel the image of the ignorant, superstitious, happy-go-lucky, immoral, and irresponsible African American as the dominant representation of that racial group. Many cartoons, such as Nathaniel Currier and James Ives's "Darktown" series in the 1880s, characterized the African American as "nigger," "niggah," "darkey," "coon," "pickaninny," "auntie," "uncle," or "buck."[13] Image makers in the 1890s drew on these images rooted in slavery, Reconstruction, and European imperialism to imagine the peoples of Hawaii, Cuba, Puerto Rico, and the Philippines.

Blackening the Hawaiian image had the effect of naturalizing the legitimacy of the white American planter elite in their competition for power with native monarchs. The racialized representation of Queen Liliuokalani became an argument in itself for America to keep its distance from Hawaii. On February 3, 1893, soon after Liliuokalani's abdication, *New York World* cartoonist Walt McDougall depicted her as a heavy Africanized woman with nappy hair and large white lips, giving visual expression to the editorialist's opposition to "the incorporation of alien territory and populations" (figure 4.1).[14] McDougall positions the queen in between two rival powers, Uncle

THE SITUATION IN HAWAII.

QUEEN LILLY—If you'se gwine take it at all, you best take it foh it's wilted.

4.1. Walt MacDougall, "The Situation in Hawaii." *New York World*, February 3, 1893, 1.

Sam and John Bull, holding a bouquet of flowers labeled "Hawaii"; the caption reads: "Queen Lilly—If you'se gwine take it at all, you best take it foh it's wilted." McDougall's racial characterization of the queen calls into question her capacity to rule, thereby validating the claim to power of the white planters, but he makes clear that it was not the place of England or America to intervene.

As long as cartoonists rendered Hawaii in the image of a black savage, the presumption was that annexation would be detrimental to U.S. interests. Like many of his contemporaries, political cartoonist Charles Bartholomew—better known simply as Bart—of the *Minneapolis Journal* chose to utilize the stereotypical iconography of African and African American peoples to represent Hawaii. He stressed the importance of available visual repertoires in designing new images: "When an idea is needed along any special line, sketches, studies and clippings form the tangible working material upon which to build. They are spread about the artist's desk."[15] In 1895 Bart produced a cartoon of Uncle Sam with an Africanized child, labeled Hawaii, tugging at his leg (figure 4.2). Bart's racialized depiction of Hawaii encapsulates his stance against annexation, but he is willing

ANNEXATION.

Uncle Sam—Want me to take you up, do you? Want me to be uncle to you, too, do you? Well, I'll think about it.

4.2. Charles Bartholomew, "Annexation." *Minneapolis Journal,* April 4, 1895, 1.

to consider embracing Cuba, depicted as a white child. "Want me to take you up, do you?" says Uncle Sam. "Well, I'll think about it." The racial distinction between Hawaii and Cuba is crucial for annexation even to be a possibility.[16] Even if infantalized, Cuba was coded white to make the point that it was potentially annexable or considered capable of independence. Graphic depictions of Cuba as white prior to the declaration reflected the initial conceptualization of U.S. intervention as a fight to liberate Cuba. These portrayals soon switched. Black images of Hawaii whitened in the press campaigns for annexation while the white image of Cuba darkened with the solidification of U.S. imperial ambitions. The effectiveness of visual language in these debates stemmed from its adaptability and flexibility to changing needs and arguments.

In a political context transformed by nationalistic fervor, one graphic strategy to justify annexation was whitening the Hawaiian image. Contrary to the conventional imperialist narrative of the "white man's burden" which justified dominion for the sake of uplifting perceived inferior races, a popular argument in favor of annexation was to protect the growing white minority.[17] As the pro-annexation *New York Journal* declared, "by the time the native population has died out, the Chinese and Japanese have gone back to Asia and a hundred thousand Americans have settled the islands it will be time enough to talk about statehood."[18] Annexationists made the case for statehood by picturing Hawaii's ascent into white society. For example, Robert Clyde Swayze, the *Philadelphia Inquirer*'s leading cartoonist, depicted Hawaii shortly after annexation as a miniature Uncle Sam with a "certificate of adoption" at his feet (figure 4.3), as the real Uncle Sam prepares to teach his young white apprentice about U.S. national development, law, and government. Uncle Sam promises, "Now, behave son, and as soon as I've walloped the Spanish, I'll begin your education."

While some artists whitened representations of Hawaii, others used sexual fantasy to draw their audience's attention. "Many a young man . . . will forget the maiden with whom he went to school," wrote a pro-annexationist *Boston Globe* editorialist, "as he temporarily dreams and whispers sweet things in delicate ears, that can't understand English, under murmuring palm trees."[19] Pro-annexationist cartoons often depicted Hawaii in the shape of a scantily clad native woman, selling empire as a medium for commercial tourism. World's fair attractions featuring "native" women from the Pacific Islands established an important context for the reception of this image. Jennie Wilson, whose mother was a native Hawaiian, performed hula dances at both the World's Columbian Exposition in Chicago in 1893 and the Trans-Mississippi and International Exposition in Omaha in 1898, occurring simultaneously with the debates over annexation. Performing on the Midway Plaisance in an exhibit called "South Sea Islanders," Wilson danced alongside other non-European

UNCLE SAM :—"Now, behave son, and as soon as I've walloped the Spanish, I'll begin your education."

4.3. Robert Clyde Swayze, "Now, behave son, and as soon as I've walloped the Spanish, I'll begin your education." *Philadelphia Inquirer,* July 10, 1898, 1.

female performers, including the well-known "hootchy-cootchy" dancers, offering audiences sexually suggestive and exotic shows.[20] Such performances enticed viewers to think about imperial subjects as objects of sexual pleasure and playful amusement.

Graphic artists also drew from popular images of Hawaii circulating in late-nineteenth-century postcards, commercial photographs, and travel guides which objectified Hawaiian women as tourist commodities. Embedding attractive women in a lush landscape to connote overseas expansion combined the attractions of sexual desire

4.4. "Hawaiian Women Picnicking." From *Through the War by Camera: A Weekly Artfolio of Current Events, on Land and Sea, in the Spanish-American War of 1898* (New York: Pearson Publishing, 1898).

and escape in a powerful visual package. The "native" hula girl image emerged as the most popular visual sign to stand in for the islands as a whole, typically shown on sandy beaches or surrounded by tropical foliage (figure 4.4).[21] This Hawaiian type embodied what Bernard Smith calls "soft primitivism," meaning she was presented as animalistic in a carefree, sexually uninhibited, natural sense, not in a more threatening, brutish form. Smith connects this image to the European American construction of the "noble savage" type inspired by the ideals of the Enlightenment. The "native" hula girl typified the erotic charge of imperial rhetoric, rendering the islands as desirable bodies to be possessed through the Western colonialist gaze. The illustrated magazine *Leslie's Weekly* depicted a U.S. soldier gawking at a "native" Hawaiian girl in a tropical locale (figure 4.5). The image is boldly sexual, as this bare-breasted woman, wearing only jewelry and a grass skirt, stares beckoningly at the soldier, poised with his gun, the instrument of his manhood. Read politically, her sexual advances symbolized a consensual desire for

HIS FIRST CHRISTMAS IN HAWAII.

4.5. C. Budd, "His First Christmas in Hawaii." *Leslie's Weekly* 87 (December 15, 1898): 477. Courtesy New York State Library, Manuscripts and Special Collections.

long-term incorporation in and deference to U.S. colonial domination. But for *Leslie's Weekly,* a journal that did not have an explicit editorial agenda on Hawaiian annexation, the reference to Hawaii could have been merely a pretext for publishing a near-pornographic illustration. Sexual spectacle may have been a compelling metaphor for political desirability, but it also sold papers.

Visual constructions of Hawaii reflect the malleability of race and gender as implements of empire. The *Leslie's Weekly* cartoonist presented the Hawaiian girl not as white or black but in an intermediary category of "brown." Phrenologist Samuel R. Wells in the early 1880s was one of many to substantiate this categorization using the science of race, claiming that the Hawaiian skull showed signs of more civilized development in its physical similarities to that of the Caucasian race as opposed to the Malay. Available and nonthreatening, the image of the "brown" Hawaiian girl was not visual code for exclusion (as the "Africanized" black image had been), and in fact seemed only to heighten her sexual magnetism. Depictions of the hula dancer as the "little brown gal" type helped galvanize support for annexation in 1898 and persisted throughout the twentieth century as the dominant image of the Hawaiian tourist industry.[22] The proliferation of this symbol of accommodation differed markedly from the blackened, grotesque images of native women rulers like Queen Liliuokalani, who challenged foreign encroachment on the identities and rights of the Hawaiian people. Image makers disparaged native claims to sovereignty by designating the queen as "black," not "brown," and depriving her of the womanly qualities of beauty, grace, and sex appeal, while at the same time naturalizing the embrace of the "brown" masses.[23]

Photographic folios and stereopticon views of the new colonies promoting the commercial possibilities of acquisition with images of verdant landscapes, waterways, and agricultural bounty were readily available during and after the Spanish-American War. An editorialist in the *Denver Post* noted this new "fad": "The American people are now to be dazzled with thoughts of conquest and with visions of warm isles in the southern seas, where life takes on a dreamy languor and the problem of existence solves itself."[24] Photographs of hula dances, village streets, and productive plantations were invested with imperial purpose, justifying U.S. occupation with the potential for economic abundance (see figure 4.6). Taking photographs was itself an act of

4.6. "A Pineapple Plantation." From *Through the War by Camera.*

colonization, a means of taking visual possession of new lands and peoples. Almost invariably, these photographs focused exclusively on "native" Hawaiians in their daily labors and homes and rendered invisible the substantial populations of people of North American, Portuguese, Chinese, Filipino, or Japanese descent. Published photographs of Hawaii and the other new colonies gave visual expression to the fantasies of acquisition while at the same time they advanced the moral urgency of acquisition as a means to modernize infrastructure and bring civilization (figure 4.7). Photographer William Dinwiddie, who spent two months in Puerto Rico after the Spanish evacuation in 1898, published photographs of the island's mills, cigar factories, and sugar, coffee, and tobacco plantations. While representing the "artistic loveliness and fertile possibilities" of Puerto Rico, his depictions of the sugar industry were intended to show its "precarious condition," necessitating American oversight (figure 4.8). "The promise of a successful future," he claimed, "lies in a more profound centralization of the industry."[25]

Opponents of taking Hawaii, however, resisted the efforts of annex-

4.7. "Filthy Condition of Marine Street, Santiago, Showing the Pressing Need of a Sewerage System." From *Leslie's Official History of the Spanish-American War: A Pictorial and Descriptive Record of the Cuban Rebellion, the Causes that Involved the United States, and a Complete Narrative of our Conflict with Spain on Land and Sea* (Washington, D.C.: War Records Office, 1899), 409.

4.8. William Dinwiddie, "Typical Sugar-Mill Near Ponce—Antiquated and Modern Machinery Combined." From Dinwiddie, *Puerto Rico: Its Conditions and Possibilities* (New York, Harper & Brothers, 1899), 110.

ationists to sidestep the racial implications of incorporation, instead framing their critique in explicitly racial terms. Joseph Pulitzer, an outspoken critic of imperialism, denounced Hawaiian annexation as the incorporation of "leprosy and loot." His *New York World* argued: "In a population of 105,000 there are less than 10,000 English-speaking whites—Germans, French, English, and Americans. . . . There are now 40,000 Chinese and Japanese coolies, 15,000 ignorant and shiftless human beings from the slums of Portuguese cities, [and] 40,000 leprosy-cursed native Hawaiians and half breeds."[26] Because of contemporary fears about maintaining the purity of racial bloodlines, critics cast annexation as a dual threat to American society—as the bearer of miscegenation and disease—in line with campaigns to place strict limits on immigration in the United States. *World* cartoonist C. G. Bush depicted Uncle Sam's revulsion for his two black subjects, the "Philippene" and "Hawaii" (figure 4.9). Dressed in a bowtie, top hat, and vest, the Hawaiian appears as a minstrel "darky" next to the primitive, machete-toting Filipino. Uncle Sam asks, "Who said annexation?" Anti-annexationists resisted the softening of the Hawaiian image and positioned the Hawaiian instead among his fellow racial "degenerates"—the Cuban and the Filipino.

Hawaiian annexation created the momentum for more extensive acquisitions and established the visual terms of debate surrounding them. The *Baltimore Sun* described Hawaii as "the entering wedge" to imperialism: "Standing alone, the mere question of annexing Hawaii, except for the principles involved, might not be considered as a vital matter. But it does not stand alone. Back of it is the question of the Philippines, of the Ladrone and Caroline islands, of Cuba and Porto Rico." The *Boston Transcript* affirmed that in urging annexation, the president "would open a door which he could not shut."[27]

Imperial Divisions: Delayed Engagement with the Colonial Question

In the weeks after the U.S. victory at Santiago Bay in early July, General Miles landed U.S. troops in Puerto Rico, President McKinley finessed congressional approval of Hawaiian annexation, and Spain surrendered. On August 12, Spain and the United States signed an

UNCLE SAM· "Who said annexation?"

4.9. Charles G. Bush, "Who Said Annexation?" *New York World,* May 20, 1898, 3.

armistice officially ending hostilities. News of the cease-fire had yet to reach Admiral Dewey in the Philippines, who was in the process of negotiating with Spanish governor-general Don Fermín Jáudenes y Alvarez for the surrender of Manila. In order to preserve the honor of his garrison, Jáudenes agreed to capitulate if the Americans staged a sham battle. As a result, the day after the armistice was signed, Dewey directed a naval bombardment of Manila, and General Wesley Merritt led a land "attack" against a Spanish pretense of resistance. Dewey gave orders not to inform Filipino leaders of the plan and to keep their forces outside the city walls, but the Filipinos interceded, and six Americans and dozens of Spaniards were killed. Still, the final battle brought the Spanish-American War full circle, for Dewey's victories at Manila had opened and now closed the war. Considering the spectacular production of the war on the home front, it seems especially appropriate that it ended with a battle put on for show. In a little over a hundred days and with relatively few combat losses, the United States emerged the victor. In effect, McKinley's decision to occupy Manila and not recognize the independence of the Philippine Republic, which Filipino nationalist leader Emilio Aguinaldo declared on June 12, laid the groundwork for his plans for long-term U.S. occupation. But he did not announce these intentions until the later that fall.

The end of military operations marked the beginning of more serious deliberation about the results of victory. Just a few months earlier, only a small minority of newspapers had opposed war with Spain, but the imperial debate generated a much greater divide. In December 1898 the *New York Herald* surveyed 470 papers nationwide and found that 288 supported formal colonial rule and 182 opposed it. The *Herald*'s study of national editorial opinion observed regional patterns, finding greater support for "expansion" in the middle western and western states than in New England, while the majority of southern states opposed it.[28] The *Literary Digest* compiled a similar survey of 192 newspapers and concluded, according to the *Philadelphia Inquirer,* that "84 express a preference for the American retention of the entire groups of the Philippines, 63 favor merely the retention of a naval station, and the rest are mostly divided in opinion as to the superior merits of an American protectorate and a joint protectorate. A few advocate the sale of the islands to some other nation, Japan or England, but it is significant that not one is in favor of returning the islands to Spain, an indication of public opinion that is going to make very difficult the adoption of any policy other than the retention of the islands."[29] The *Literary Digest* found that political party affiliation was the primary determinant of opinion on the imperial question. Democratic papers typically opposed expansion.[30] Nevertheless, the range of alternatives makes it problematic to discern two consistent positions. It was also not immediately clear if Philippine resisters would assent to American guardianship, and in some cases, editorial positions on empire changed as complications arose.

The debate over acquiring overseas colonies created dissension as to the meanings of "imperialism" and "expansionism" in the U.S. context.[31] Some advocates of formal colonialism claimed that taking control of the Spanish colonies was best expressed as "expansionism," not "imperialism," because it represented the next step in American territorial growth. The *New York Journal* drew this distinction: "An imperialist is 'one who favors the establishment or maintenance of an empire.' The expansionist does not favor the establishment or maintenance of an empire; he favors the expansion of republicanism."[32] Just as McKinley in December 1898 termed his policy in the Philippines "benevolent assimilation," the *Journal* and other pro-imperialist organs labeled overseas empire "expansionism" to accentuate its progressive intentions and escape the stigma of formal "imperial" rule of the European variety.

Others in the debate took issue with this semantic maneuver. The pro-imperialist *Boston Herald* argued that "imperialism necessarily implies expansion; but expansion by no means includes imperialism," meaning that expansion is not imperialistic if and only if the intention is to incorporate the territory into the union as a self-governing state, equal to all the others. "We can never make of the Philippine islands what we have made of Louisiana and California, states having an equal right and voice," declared the *Herald,* meaning that possession of the Philippines must be seen as an imperial action even if "enlightened" by good intentions.[33] Part of the confusion stemmed from the fact that even among those supporting acquisition of the Philippines, controversies arose regarding whether or not to retain all of the Philippines or just the main island of Luzon, and whether the Philippines would be held indefinitely as a colony, relegating the status of the Filipinos to that of subjects, not citizens, or annexed as a state and accorded full rights of citizenship, which was a much less popular option.

The media's iconographic frame for the war evolved in light of the imperial possibilities of victory. In the press buildup for war, opinion makers had declared the destruction of the *Maine* and the humanitarian crisis in Cuba to be the two leading reasons for U.S. intervention. Capturing this sentiment in May 1898, artist Victor Gillam in *Judge* depicted Uncle Sam standing before an oversized photograph album of war pictures (figure 4.10). To his right, photographs show

REMEMBER THE MAINE!
AND DON'T FORGET THE STARVING CUBANS!

4.10. Victor Gillam, "Remember the *Maine*! And Don't Forget the Starving Cubans." *Judge* 34 (May 7, 1898): 312.

the *Maine* before and after the explosion. To his left are two images of emaciated Cuban victims. The caption reads: "Remember the *Maine*! And Don't Forget the Starving Cubans!"

Just two weeks after the war began, Gillam already foresaw the evaporation of concern for Cuba's plight in U.S. media accounts. With each passing victory, headlines and political cartoons repeatedly affirmed the need to remember the *Maine,* while the topic of the humanitarian crisis all but faded. In a cartoon appearing in the *San Francisco Examiner* in July, less than a week after the battle of Santiago, Uncle Sam points a gun at a battered Spain and says, "Don, Do YOU Remember the *Maine*?" Uncle Sam reminds Spain of the lesson to be learned—that certain destruction follows an attack on the United States—but makes no mention of Spain's colonial transgressions.[34] By the end of the war, the imperial reconfiguration of the conflict prompted pro-imperialists to redefine the destruction of the *Maine* as the sole cause for intervention.[35]

Anticolonialist artists, by contrast, bemoaned the forgotten promises to Cuba. Joseph Pulitzer's *New York World* had initially called

"YOU'VE EARNED YOUR–INDEPENDENCE."

4.11. Charles G. Bush, "You've Earned Your Independence." *New York World,* March 12, 1898, 7.

for war to free Cuba from the fetters of Spanish colonial rule, as illustrated in a prewar cartoon published in March 1898 (figure 4.11). Uncle Sam stands on American shores with the instruments of war at his disposal: a naval fleet and a $50 million congressional appropriation. He calls out to Cuba on the opposite shore, saying, "You've earned your independence." The *World* editorialists alleged that the brave efforts of the Cuban nationalists warranted self-rule and urged the U.S. government to help Cuba acquire it. As the imperial possibilities of the war were realized, however, the same editorialists expressed their feelings of betrayal at the repudiation of the humanitarian objectives that had motivated them to advocate for U.S. inter-

UNCLE SAM: "Thought I was to free Cuba."

4.12. Charles G. Bush, "Thought I Was to Free Cuba." *New York World,* June 17, 1898, 7.

vention. Cartoonist Charles G. Bush reflected this disillusionment in a depiction of a gun-toting Uncle Sam carrying the American flag to a colossal "Conquest," with his cloak pinned by a stake satirically labeled "Kind-Hearted policy" (figure 4.12). "Thought I was to free Cuba," he remarks, as the image of a female Cuba remains bound to her master. Anticolonialist artists like Bush mobilized the same gendered script as their adversaries, but used it to chastise Uncle Sam for breaking his pledge to emancipate Cuba. In the process, Uncle Sam acquired undesirable racialized colonial subjects who came attached to the "conquest."

Another critical iconographic shift that took place after the battle of Santiago revised the media's initial campaign for U.S. intervention. Prior to the declaration of war, image makers had celebrated Cuban nationalism with repeated symbolic reference to Cuba Libre.[36] Published several weeks prior to the start of the war, a *Chicago Record* cartoon depicts a Cuban soldier, proudly holding the flag of Cuba Libre. The caption affirms, "The Victorious Insurgent Henceforth Shall Rule Cuba."[37] This prewar cartoon articulates that Cuba, not the United States, would determine Cuba's future. This is the same group of "insurgents" whom pro-imperialist news organs, like the *Record,* were declaring unfit for self-rule by the end of the war. Many newspapers that had pressed for Cuba Libre prior to the war later supported McKinley's decision to delay Cuban independence and finally offer it only in the form of U.S. supervision. The *Houston Post* wrote after the Spanish defeat at Santiago: "Of the Cubans, it is very apparent that it would have been impossible for the insurgents ever to win their freedom without our help. We were all deceived by reports from Cuba that reached us before the war began, and are forced to revise our conclusions as to the chances that then existed for Cuban success."[38] While it is evident that an important ideological shift had occurred, it was not without precedent. Imperialist media makers tapped into the underlying ambiguity over Cuba's part in securing its own liberation that materialized in prewar visions of the conflict.

After the battle of Santiago, Cuba's implied dependence became much more pronounced, and consequently the Cuba Libre motif disappeared almost entirely from graphic art nationwide.[39] In one revealing exception, a political cartoon in the *Syracuse Herald* called attention to this iconographic shift (figure 4.13). Set in Santiago after the surrender, the cartoon depicts Uncle Sam and Spain walking arm in arm as "comrades." The new image of Spain is stripped of the symbolism of the Black Legend, as he wears Uncle Sam's hat and enjoys some "hardtack," the familiar U.S. military ration, while Uncle Sam wears a Spaniard's hat and drinks a bottle of Spanish wine. As U.S. and Spanish soldiers festively embrace, a scrawny, dark-skinned Cuban broods in the background. He resentfully comments: "Say, ain't it time this ere shindig was stopped? Where in Cuba Libre do I come in?" American imperial ambitions now provided the foundation for "camaraderie" between Spain and the United States. Spain was no longer the villain; Cuba was now the outcast. The cartoonist's

COMRADES.

SANTIAGO AFTER THE SURRENDER.

THE CUBAN—" Say, ain't it time this ere shindig was stopped? Where in Cuba **Libre** do I come in?"—Syracuse Herald.

4.13. R. D. McKay, "Comrades." *Syracuse Herald,* 1898. From Marshall Everett, ed., *Exciting Experiences in Our Wars with Spain and the Filipinos* (Chicago: Book Publishers Union, 1899).

satirical comment on the quick turnaround in the image of the enemy reveals his cognizance of and distaste for the political indifference that enabled such a dramatic shift to take place with ease.

In view of the rising tide of militaristic spirit across the nation, press accounts accentuated Cuban incompetence in order to place exclusive credit for victory on U.S. actions. The press quoted extensively from participants in and observers of the Cuban campaigns who criticized Cuban military involvement. Trumbull White, a well-known historian and war correspondent of the period, described the Cuban troops as "of little military value to the American army." He cited a U.S. soldier who claimed, "The Cuban is our inferior, he is ragged, he is dirty, he is half-starved and steals our food whenever he can get it; he will not work and he will not fight when we tell him to."[40] Former Confederate general and commander of U.S. ground troops in Cuba, General Joseph Wheeler, also confirmed to reporters: "The average Cuban is uneducated. The animal instinct predominates. He looks for insults and harsh treatment because he has had little experience of the other sort. A combination of the lower qualities of human nature and nature educated to resentment is what we are dealing with."[41]

Blackening the portrait of the Cuban went hand in hand with the retreat from the mission to free Cuba that initially impelled Americans to support the war.[42] To justify denying Cuba full-fledged independence, cartoonists reinvented the Cuban nationalists as nonwhite barbarians, no longer representing them as self-sacrificial freedom fighters striving for the equivalent of their own American Revolution. To warrant independence, Cuban leaders in turn felt pressure to prove their "civility," which in late-nineteenth-century terms meant that they had to conform to imagined codes of whiteness. Cuban general Máximo Gómez told an associate: "We are before a Tribunal, and the Tribunal is formed by the Americans. . . . Our conduct should be worthy so that we are respected."[43] They endeavored to counter the racial shift in representation that justified the stance taken by many editorialists, such as the *Louisville Courier-Journal,* that self-government would "invite disaster and lead to the inevitable failure of our great humanitarian experiment."[44]

This new image of the Cuban as "irresponsible," "worthless," and having "the lower qualities of human nature" invoked the language of white supremacist ideologies justifying Jim Crow segregation, and were essential to the imperialist contention that intervention was necessary to secure Cuba's future. In a cartoon published in the *Chicago Tribune* and the *New York Times* (reproduced from the magazine *Punch*), Uncle Sam approaches an unkempt Cuban soldier saying: "See here! If I'd known what a durn'd, worthless, ill-conditioned

4.14. J. C. Hemment, "Cuban Scouts." From *Through the War by Camera.*

skunk you are, I wouldn't ha' lifted a hand for you! But—now I'm here—Guess I'm going to stay, and lick you into shape!"[45] J. C. Hemment's photographs of Cubans also reflected this racializing vision (figure 4.14). Calling the Cubans "scouts," not soldiers, Hemment reinforced their subordinate status to the U.S. Army in the military campaigns against Spain. He presented Cuban fighters poised to shoot in tattered camouflage attire and described them in animalistic terms as "ragged, down-trodden creatures" who "conceal themselves in tree-tops" and "crouch" behind palm trees. In the same way that Filipino guerrilla warfare was later disparaged, the visual association between the Cuban army and guerrilla tactics, as the military strategies of subhuman "savages," was intended to signify a lack of civilization. There was no recognition that these tactics had weakened the Spanish over years of rebellion, making a swift U.S. victory possible.

Pro-imperialist illustrations also dismissed the efforts of the Cuban leadership. In another rare exception to the disappearing emblem of Cuba Libre late in the war, *Puck* magazine published a cartoon in September 1898 depicting Uncle Sam sheltering a dark-skinned

4.15. L. Dalrymple, "Save Me from My Friends." *Puck* 44 (September 7, 1898): 8–9. Collection of The New-York Historical Society, neg. no. 83514d.

female Cuba Libre under the Stars and Stripes, alleging that Cuba's destiny was safest in the hands of American benefactors (figure 4.15). Rather than protecting Cuba Libre from brutal Spanish oppressors, Uncle Sam now had to stand against the Cubans themselves, even General Máximo Gómez, the leader of the Cuban rebellion, who formerly had been likened to Simón Bolívar and Miguel Hidalgo, the famous liberators of Spanish America (see figure 1.1). In postwar media, Gómez became a tyrannical and untrustworthy foe; as the *Washington Post* claimed: "What is Gomez but an adventurer—a soldier of fortune, a professional agitator—who thrives upon disorder and who would starve under a dispensation of peace and civilization? . . . Who knows what the patient, stupid, helpless rank and file of the so-called 'Cuban armies' want? Who has ever asked about or heard from them? . . . They are the dumb assets upon which the 'leaders' trade."[46]

Graphic artists defined American militarism not only in juxtaposition with colonial subjects now viewed as infantile racial inferiors, but also by discounting the participation of racial minorities at home. Despite the military participation of African Americans in the war effort, very few published images recognized their contributions. If shown in army camp imagery, they were most likely to be depicted serving, washing clothes, or cooking. The domestic service pictured in these images created a safe space to acknowledge African American participation in the war without exciting controversy.[47] The more general trend in print and visual accounts of the battles was to ignore or diminish African Americans' military service. Theodore Roosevelt assumed the inferiority of black soldiers when he proclaimed that he had had to interrupt the charge on San Juan Hill to prevent the African American cavalry from running away. With regard to the "colored infantrymen," he wrote, "no troops could have behaved better," yet qualified his praise by adding, "but they are, of course, peculiarly dependent upon their white officers."[48]

Many African American newspapers challenged the marginalization of African American military participation and urged able-bodied black men to enlist to prove their manhood and loyalty to the nation. African American editors found special meaning in the cause of Cuban independence, interpreting the struggle as a "black man's war" because many of its leaders, participants, and victims were men and women of color.[49] The high moral purpose of liberating an oppressed people convinced the *Indianapolis Freeman* that the needs of Cuba should, at least temporarily, supersede addressing the plight of black Americans: "The Negroes . . . will for the period deny [their] own crosses and help assume the heavier burdens of a maltreated neighbor." Many editors hoped that the loyal participation of African Americans in the war would improve the condition of their race at home. The *Colored American* asserted: "The races are drawn more closely together, and the Negro's manhood is placed directly in evidence. The black man has one more opportunity to prove his worth as a soldier, and to emphasize his title to all the privileges of citizenship." Despite these hopes, African American newspapers reported their disillusionment with the treatment of black soldiers in white press accounts. "We are to all intents and purposes ignored," complained the *Colored American*.[50]

Because most newspapers catering to black Americans in the 1890s were not equipped to publish illustrations, they could not provide an alternative vision of African American military service in newsprint. A notable exception was the *Indianapolis Freeman*,

the first "national illustrated colored newspaper," edited by George
L. Knox. Despite proclaiming that the paper had its "own force of
colored artists," financial constraints led Knox to reprint a number of wartime illustrations produced by and published in the white
press. Still, Knox was cognizant of the absence of representation of
black military achievements in American visual culture, and between
February and April 1899, he launched a series of front-page articles
titled "Special War Notes," featuring portraits of distinguished black
servicemen alongside engravings of black regiments in heroic combat
in Cuba. This was a rare moment when an African American newspaper, claiming to serve over eighty thousand subscribers, was able
to create a visual space in which African American military participation in the war could be recognized and truly celebrated, in opposition to the Jim Crow practices and white supremacist assumptions
of social inferiority impeding the inclusion of African Americans in
the projects of war and empire.[51]

But as U.S. war aims turned imperialistic in the final phase of the
conflict, many black newspapers retracted their support. It was one
thing to side with the cause of freeing Cuba from colonial exploitation; it was another to assent to U.S. imperialist domination, particularly in light of black Americans' own past and lived experience
with the policies and practices of subjugation. As the imperial debate
intensified, Edward Cooper, editor of *The Colored American*, recognized that "the anti-expansion sentiment, as evidenced in all of
our public gatherings, is growing among the Negroes."[52] African
American anticolonialists had a different perspective from that of
their white counterparts. They denounced imperialism, among other
reasons, because of the racist views justifying imperial conquest, and
to prevent the spread of white supremacist beliefs to the acquired territories. "It is the plain duty of this government to remedy our own
scandalous abuses rather than to extend the system under which they
have arisen to other people," declared the anticolonialist *Coffeyville
American*. The *Indianapolis Recorder* agreed: "If it was the duty of
our government to rescue Cuba from Spanish cruelty, it should be
its duty now to save her from the curse of color prejudice, the evil
effects of which [are] so keenly felt in our own country." A segment
of the black press, however, supported U.S. pacification and occupation of the Philippines. The *Indianapolis Freeman* argued, "The

Negroes must be taught that the enemy of the country is a common enemy and that the color of the face has nothing to do with it." As these opposing viewpoints illustrate, the imperial debate pressed African Americans to evaluate the racial politics of nation building and imperial conquest. Might they seek identification with the nation in the extension of U.S. power abroad or find common cause against the disempowerment of the newly acquired subjects? Most African American newspapers urged the latter, including the *AME Church Review* in Philadelphia, which called for a "world movement" among the "dark-skinned races" to "change the present relation of oppressor and oppressed."[53]

The U.S.-centered narrative of military achievement repudiated the efforts of those who did not fit the mass-produced vision of white Anglo-Saxon America, whether they came from inside or outside its borders. Calling U.S. imperialism "the dominating mastery of the Anglo-Saxon asserting itself," the African American *Indianapolis Recorder* recognized that colonial occupation would "be a gain to civilization" but also would be "the natives' loss."[54] Taking sole credit for victory, the McKinley administration proclaimed the right to determine the future of the Spanish empire, which it did without consulting the nationalist leaders of the colonies whose armies fought alongside the Americans to bring Spain to defeat.

From the vantage point of American print, visual, and popular media, the Spanish American War did not begin as an imperial war. Although William Randolph Hearst's *New York Journal* and Joseph Pulitzer's *New York World* were initially united as two of the leading advocates of intervention, the imperialist outcome of the war bitterly divided them. Even with his best efforts, Pulitzer was unable to divert the nation from an imperial course, revealing the limitations of his brand of journalism at the very moment when, historians claim, the yellow press had great power in influencing public opinion. Despite having championed the war months earlier, hundreds of papers joined Pulitzer in withdrawing support for McKinley once his imperialist aspirations were fully realized.

Calling attention to this shift by no means exonerates media makers for having entertained or promoted imperial policies, but it does suggest the power of spectacle and the patriotic consensus, particularly early in the war, to mask the controversies of empire. The emphasis on sensationalizing the military campaigns prevented news leaders and image makers from asking the hard questions about U.S. responsibilities to Cuba (or the rest of the Spanish colonies) after victory— what we might now call an "exit strategy." In the meantime, McKinley used military necessity to justify annexing Hawaii, which acted as a bridge to facilitate the taking of additional overseas possessions. The image battles surrounding Hawaiian annexation helped pave the way for new visions of the events and participants of the war to find prominence in mass media, beginning with the abandonment of Cuba Libre. The preconditions for this shift were already in place. Underlying the media campaigns from the beginning were conflicting images of Cuban capacity, veiled aspirations for Cuban annexation, and the hunger to prove U.S. manhood to the world. To frame the transition from liberation to conquest, media makers leveraged this earlier ambivalence, making explicit what before was implicit about the moral and racial imperative of U.S. guardianship. Even though a growing opposition resisted this shift, it failed to stem the tide. Whether or not President McKinley had explicit imperial designs from the outset, he refrained from publicizing those intentions. Instead he sat back while the cultural production of empire seduced the nation into imperialism.

5

The War's Final Phase

THE SHADOW OF MILITARY SCANDAL
ON GLORIFIED VICTORY

It is the general feeling that gross incompetency and mismanagement have marked the conduct of the war, and numerous investigations will undoubtedly be demanded. As the reports arrive the frightful conditions which exist in camp and on transports bring to light new stories of misery, starvation, and suffering which it is impossible to believe one human being would inflict upon another. . . . Every case which comes before the public is more startling than the last and great indignation is felt here over the inhuman treatment to which the defenders of the country's honor have been subjected. All of the glory which was earned by the brilliant victories of the American arms is being overshadowed by the frightful experience of the troops.

Chicago Tribune, August 27, 1898

Probably the most illustrious reporter to cover the Cuban rebellion was *New York World* correspondent Sylvester Scovel. Richard Harding Davis wrote of him, "A more manly, daring and able young man I have seldom met."[1] Scovel traveled with the Cuban army in 1897 and reported back to the *World* updates of his adventures in the field, one of which landed him in a Cuban prison in February 1897. Press petitions circulated across the country to secure his release, which Spain conceded after the State Department intervened. Scovel went to Cuba seeking fame and fortune and was eager to seize the spotlight. This he surely did in the ceremony that launched the U.S. occupation of Cuba, held at the governor's palace to officiate Spain's surrender of arms in July 1898. Striving to be photographed alongside the raised American flag, Scovel surreptitiously climbed to the roof of the palace during the proceedings. After he was ordered down, the commander of U.S. forces in Santiago, General William Shafter, slapped him for his insubordination. Scovel in turn punched back, grazing the general's chin. He was arrested, deported, and fired by the *World*, and was later reinstated only after making a humiliating and self-deprecating apology.[2] The great American hero in Cuba had "fallen" and the boundaries of manly bravado had been put in check—a fitting way to initiate the final phase of the war.

The sensationalistic production of U.S. military victories in the battles of Manila Bay, San Juan Hill, and Santiago Bay collectively reproduced in reenactments, plays, cinema, press accounts, and advertising initially overshadowed considerations of the implications of victory. The patriotic rhetoric celebrating U.S. military accomplishments inhibited debate about the policies those troops were fighting for. Exemplifying the consensual spirit prior to the Spanish defeat at Santiago, the *Indianapolis Sentinel* "refrained" from "questioning the motives or wisdom of the administration" and claimed that "in the face of the common enemy a united front should be presented."[3] U.S. entry into the Spanish-Cuban conflict would likely have engendered a more conflicted response had the imperial possibilities of victory been publicly recognized from the start. Instead, public and press opinion remained relatively united in support of the decision to intervene in Cuba until "without warning, without deliberation, and apparently without clear intention," the "burning question" of imperial acquisition arose, in the words of pastor and English professor Henry Van Dyke in his Thanksgiving Day sermon in 1898. He noted, "Nine months ago . . . not one American in five hundred could have told you what or where the Philippines were."[4] Daniel T. Pierce, editor of the periodical *Public Opinion,* similarly observed that several weeks after the battle of Manila Bay, "not ten 'great' city journals had at that time for a moment considered the annexation of the Philippines or any of the questions now grouped under the head of 'imperialism.'"[5]

This chapter tracks the emerging media dissension that broke the "united front" between the battle of Santiago (July 3, 1898) and the U.S.-Spanish armistice ending hostilities (August 12, 1898) in what I call the final phase of the war, when opposition arose to the management of the U.S. Army as well as to the potential for imperial acquisition accompanying U.S. victory in the war. Beginning in July–August 1898, press coverage of the return on hospital ships of U.S. servicemen sick and dying from disease and privation generated a media exposé of Department of War abuses and ineptitude. The main theme of graphic art production, particularly in Democratic-affiliated news sources, shifted from glorifying U.S. militarism to articulating the horrific negligence that U.S. soldiers allegedly faced in army camps, a charge that in effect fractured the bipartisan patriotic unity of the early war period.

The ramifications of this growing polarization are evident with regard to one of the most pervasive images in the media campaigns—the manly American savior—who went to war, according to the romantic narrative, to rescue female Cuba from the clutches of Spanish oppressors. U.S. victories at Manila Bay and in the Cuban land campaigns initially fortified the link between American manhood and the new martial spirit enveloping the nation, fueling nationalistic aspirations for world power. When cultural producers united images of U.S. militarism with those of white masculine power—creating the picture of the manly martial ideal—they implicitly expressed imperialist values by defining the U.S. soldier as an authoritative military presence.[6] Yet the deployment of this ideal flourished in the first two months of the fighting, *preceding* the recognition of the war's potential for imperialist gain. The widespread circulation of this portrayal in cartoons, photographs, and popular amusements may in fact have helped foster the necessary conditions for shifting popular desires away from Cuban independence and toward empire building. But because the military scandals undermining confidence in U.S. military preparations occurred simultaneously with public revelation of the imperial prospects of victory, the advancement of the male body as the icon of American military prowess became more conflicted in the very moment when the explicit imperialist context of these representations was fully realized.[7]

As political conditions changed after the battle at Santiago Bay, only then did media makers begin to grapple with the long-term effects of American actions in the war. In the midst of army scandals and imperial discord, the patriotic narrative unifying popular support began to unravel, even as the grand celebrations of peace took place around the nation.

Press Coverage of Army Maltreatment: The Shift to Exposé

During the final phase of the war, claims of War Department incompetence and negligence undermined the semblance of American military invincibility manifested by the succession of U.S. victories. Although there were early indications of inadequate conditions in the army camps, these allegations did not receive substantial press coverage until the final weeks of the war, after the battle of Santiago, as the troops returned home. The effect of these reports on press opinion was polarizing, and a considerable number of newspapers, many of which supported the Democratic Party, shifted their war coverage from the unifying mode of patriotic spectacle to the investigative style of the exposé. They became increasingly critical of the Republican administration's management of the war effort and attempted to publicize the dreadful state of the army camps, which they claimed unnecessarily subjected U.S. servicemen to the perils of disease and privation. This pre–Progressive Era muckraking style enabled these journalists to present themselves as guardians of the "public interest" by calling attention to the ills of society and insisting on reform.[8]

When the war first began, depictions of a strapping Uncle Sam, flexing and flaunting his muscles, became a popular visual metaphor to demonstrate America's newfound military might.[9] Even though cartoonists initially mobilized this image to emphasize America's ability to defeat Spain for humanitarian purposes (for Cuba Libre), not for explicit U.S. imperial gain, Uncle Sam's robust image indicated from the war's inception a nationalistic embrace of a more action-oriented role in global affairs. Cartoonist Fred Morgan of the *Philadelphia Inquirer* pictured a "Scene at the Champion's Training Quarters," featuring Uncle Sam exercising and accentuating his solid muscular form (figure 5.1). In front of the leading world powers, Uncle Sam prepares to strike a punching bag labeled "Increased Navy," with barbells labeled "Army" and "Navy" lying nearby. "After His Late Victory Uncle Sam Intends to Keep Always in

SCENE AT THE CHAMPION'S TRAINING QUARTERS.
After His Late Victory Uncle Sam Intends to Keep Always in Training

5.1. Fred Morgan, "Scene at the Champion's Training Quarters." *Philadelphia Inquirer,* August 20, 1898, 1.

Training," reads the caption. Uncle Sam's burliness also reflected the period's growing regard for sport, exercise, and dietary asceticism. By the 1890s, athletics had become a regular component of army training and was deemed essential to military effectiveness.[10] As with Theodore Roosevelt's ideology of "the strenuous life," cultural producers emphasized Anglo-Saxon vigor to counter class-based fears that American youth were falling victim to overcivilization and racial degeneration.[11]

Early war images conveyed visions of the nation's "boys" in tiptop shape, preparing for combat. Hundreds of newspaper illustrations in papers across the country chronicled daily life in various military camps in the South.[12] They depicted soldiers in training or engaged in ordinary activities such as eating, shaving, and attending prayer services. A drawing published in the *San Francisco Chronicle* in early May presents a regiment of men dining outdoors at a long table in a camp in Tampa (figure 5.2). Eating, drinking, and socializing, the men appear as a community. With food and bread abundant, one soldier reaches for a second helping. Motion picture footage of camp life was similarly reassuring, such as in Edison's short film "9th Infantry Boys' Morning Wash," recorded in May 1898 in Tampa. William Paley's camera work depicts a jovial scene of a group of soldiers in camp vigorously washing with towels and soap; a soldier in the foreground laughs playfully.[13] Both still and moving images gave home viewers a portrait of camp life as orderly and sanitary, conditions, it was believed, that would strengthen their resolve and avert the threat of yellow fever. Health officer Alvah H. Doty told *Leslie's Weekly* that because the "disease is almost always largely due to carelessness, and is consequently in a great measure avoidable," then "those who expect to see service in Cuba may well dismiss the subject of yellow fever from their minds."[14]

The rose-colored view of camp life in the early war period masked the actual problems that began at the outset of army mobilization. The military lacked experience in assembling and supporting an army of some 28,000 regulars and 182,000 volunteers, and could not sustain the agreeable image of camp life that news and image makers circulated.[15] In trying to mobilize quickly, Secretary of War Russell A. Alger and the other bureau chiefs of the War Department did not equip the army units evenly, leaving the reserve regiments in camps with inadequate accommodations and supplies. The Medical Department, under the direction of Surgeon General George M. Sternberg, underestimated its staffing needs as well as the medicine and hospital supplies that would be required. Furthermore, the camps were overcrowded and filthy, and fresh water was in short supply. The soldiers dug latrines and garbage pits adjacent to their

TROOPS MARCHING TO THEIR
CAMP GROUND AT TAMPA.

5.2. "Troops Marching to Their Camp Ground at Tampa." *San Francisco Chronicle*, May 2, 1898, 4.

living quarters, and sewage ran freely through the camps whenever it rained. Near the camp at Chickamauga, Georgia, a board of inspectors reported, "it was quite impossible to walk through the woods . . . without soiling one's feet with fecal matter."[16]

The lack of sanitation, insufficient supplies, and rapidity of mobilization established the conditions for disease to thrive. The primary killer was typhoid fever, a preventable disease under proper sanitary conditions. Over twenty thousand American soldiers contracted it, and it accounted for 87 percent of all deaths due to disease in the camps.[17] According to Sergeant Walter W. Ward of the Second Regiment of Massachusetts, the water in the army camp at Tampa "did not look much like water and tasted still less like it," and the men were fed "fat bacon and canned beans," which was "not the kind of food the sensible man going to spend a time in the tropics would select for his menu."[18] Many soldiers wrote home about the poor conditions, disease, and malnutrition, and some of these letters appeared in newsprint. One worried mother wrote to the *New York Journal*, "I am astonished to see . . . that this nation—supposed to be so impressed with the cruel want imposed on the Cubans that it asks its gallant boys to help to liberate the starving Cubans—is actually starving our boys at Chickamauga."[19]

The issue first achieved national attention in early June 1898, only one month into the war, when war correspondent Poultney Bigelow wrote an incendiary letter to the *New York Herald* and *Harper's Weekly* condemning the state of army camps in Tampa. "For downright neglect, I have seen nothing to beat the way the American is treated by Uncle Sam," he declared, arguing that the soldiers did not have suitable uniforms for tropical conditions, that they were forced to sleep on the ground, and that poor food rations kept the camp doctors overwhelmed with cases of dysentery. Bigelow urged immediate action, writing, "Just now it would do us all . . . good to discover why, thirty days after war is declared, our troops are losing their vitality in Florida, with not a single regiment fit to take the field."[20] Richard Harding Davis in the *New York Herald* censured Bigelow for his lack of patriotism and claimed that the chief surgeon of the Fifth Army Corps had reported that the army was "the healthiest in history" and "the rations served at Tampa are as good as those served to any continental army and in much greater quantity."[21] Army conditions, in fact, grew even worse in July with the onset of the rainy season. Bigelow's report and many soldiers' letters noted these problems early on, but it was not until the final weeks of the war that some reporters began to take these allegations seriously. Prior to that point, the heightened war spirit following the victories at Manila Bay and San Juan Hill made even the Democratic press hesitant to adopt a critical tone toward the administration.

The issue stayed buried until early August 1898, when Theodore Roosevelt wrote to Major General William R. Shafter, commander of U.S. troops in Cuba, demanding that he order the troops home immediately. Claiming that there were over 1,500 cases of malarial fever in his ranks, Roosevelt reported that "the whole command is so weakened and shattered as to be ripe for dying like rotten sheep . . . if we stay here." He argued against quarantining the troops in Cuba to prevent yellow fever from spreading to the mainland: "If we are kept here it will in all human possibility mean an appalling disaster, for the surgeons here estimate that over half the army, if kept here during the sickly season, will die."[22] To exert pressure on the

War Department, Roosevelt leaked the letter to the Associated Press, and it was reprinted in nationwide papers on August 4. Similarly, a number of officers in a "round robin" memo pleaded with the War Department to send the troops home. This came after the first case of yellow fever was discovered in U.S. ranks on July 6, and increasing numbers of soldiers were succumbing to malaria and dysentery. After the press publicly disclosed the "round robin" and Roosevelt's letter, the War Department had no choice but to comply. Secretary Alger arranged for the construction of Camp Wikoff at Montauk Point, New York, as the point of destination for the ailing troops. By the end of September, President McKinley appointed a commission, headed by Grenville M. Dodge, to investigate the allegations of neglect and mismanagement. Testifying before the Dodge Commission, General Nelson A. Miles further accused the War Department of distributing to the soldiers chemically treated beef—what he called "embalmed beef"—that was unfit for consumption. His statements led to a separate inquiry to investigate the quality of the beef that was being supplied to the army.

From Manly Ideal to War Victim: The Effects of the Army Scandal on Visual Depictions

The publicity surrounding Roosevelt's letter and the "round robin" occurred about a week before Spain and the United States signed the official cease-fire. As the War Department carried out the order to bring home the troops, press reports and illustrations replaced the hypermasculine icon of the American soldier with images of frailty, sickness, and incapacitation. In Massachusetts, the independent *Springfield Republican* gave this somber description of the returning troops:

> It was a solemn and pathetic day in Springfield yesterday, the farthest possible remove from those occasions when the 2d regiment used to gather for its sham fighting exercises. Those were festive, jubilant, picturesque days, when we all reveled in the holiday spirit. This was different. It was the real thing, or rather the gray depressing shadow of it. We stood under the blackness of the actual war

cloud, and the people sensed it. . . . The sight of the men seemed to grip the heart and check the voice—tears lay too near the surface. . . . These volunteers of the victorious Cuban army of the United States, having been furloughed 60 days from Camp Wikoff, were a sad and moving sight. . . . There were a score more men too weak to march, and these were taken in carriages. . . . From the beginning to the end the mustering out of the 2d regiment of United States volunteers from Massachusetts was a sobering spectacle.[23]

With terms such as "sad and moving," "depressing," and marked by "blackness," the editorialist excised the energy, festive spirit, and color from the scene, focusing instead on the "sobering" and "pathetic" sight of the men, many "too weak to march." The condition of the men, according to Sergeant Walter W. Ward of the Massachusetts volunteers, led event planners to conclude that "the occasion would be an ill-timed one for any display of ceremony or pageantry," unlike the "glittering" "spectacle" that had been anticipated and marked their sendoff to war.[24] From manly hero to heartbreaking victim, the new image of the soldier seemed no longer appropriate for pageantry but instead a testament to the solemn and divided mood marking the finale of the war.

Critics of the administration, particularly from the Democratic press, adopted a muckraking style, using factual data in the form of names, dates, statistics, and testifying images to document the alleged negligence. This was evident in the increasing use of statistics comparing the numbers of men killed or wounded in combat to inflated numbers of sick men, many of whom never fought in battle. Although the final tally came to 243 men killed in action, 1,445 wounded, and 771 dead from sickness in Cuba and Montauk, newspapers frequently embellished the numbers of sick and dying to between two to five thousand.[25] In the end, out of an army of 200,000 soldiers, only thirteen men died from malarial diseases.[26] Nevertheless, to legitimate their alleged statistics, press accounts published the testimonials of war surgeons, generals, soldiers, and government officials attesting to the hardships of camp life.

No longer presenting the soldiers as well fed and cared for, graphic artists of the Democratic press in August and September 1898 turned to producing images of wounded and sick men in transport, the burning of the uniforms and baggage of the ill, burials at sea, and soldiers begging for food, sleeping on the ground, or getting "a chance at last to get clean" by washing themselves in the ocean.[27] Press illustrations depicted the returning troops not marching in grand parades but arriving on ambulance stretchers from army hospital units before distraught family members. The caption of one such image in the *Richmond Times* reads, "The most distressing and harrowing incidents of the late war are the greetings at the stations of mothers, wives, and sweethearts to their returning soldiers."[28] Edison's Biograph also began showing motion picture scenes in vaudeville houses of wounded and sick men boarding hospital ships.[29]

The imagery of the war came full circle with the prolific graphic production of sick and emaciated American soldiers marking its conclusion. These representations mirrored the *New York Journal*'s earlier "Human Documents" campaign that pictured starving Cuban *reconcentrados* and helped propel intervention in Cuba in the first place. As the war drew to a close, artists displaced the iconography of Cuban suffering onto American soldiers. In early September the *New York World* printed "before" and "after" sketches of four U.S. soldiers serving in Cuba (figure 5.3); the caption reads: "Not starving reconcentrados in Cuba, but American heroes who went there to fight for them—now wrecks from fever, starvation and incredible neglect at home camps." The "after" sketches, depicting the formerly robust men now with forlorn faces and emaciated bodies, recall the style of imagery utilized earlier in images of the Cubans (see figure 1.11). In late August the *Denver Evening Post* published a similar depiction of the effects of camp life on the average soldier (figure 5.4). The "before" sketch presents the soldier three months earlier bidding his wife and child good-bye with his rifle held upright, his uniform tidy, and his body full of vigor. "Today" he returns a shadow of the man he was, his uniform ripped and torn, his face despondent, his eyes bulging, his fingers thin and bony, and his spirit presumably broken. *Harper's Weekly* contended:

> The country has had its war and its victory, and is now horrified at the consequences of army incompetency and mismanagement. We have had our glory, and are finding out the terrible cost of it. . . . A terrible episode has occurred in the history of the country—an

episode so criminal that the glory of war and victory has been
dimmed by the wrath caused by the wrongs and sufferings of the
soldiers who have fought the war and achieved the glory. We are
seeing the other side of war, and it is even more terrible than it
ought to be.[30]

Such language accusing the government of "criminal" behavior epitomized the exposé style, shattering the romantic imagery and spirit
of celebration of the early war period and instead emphasizing "the
other side of war." Rather than saving the Cubans, critics alleged, the
American soldiers had been degraded to similar dire conditions.

Cartoonists from the Democratic press further borrowed from
the visual vocabulary of the war, appropriating the iconography of
the Black Legend to expose the horrors of military service. Their
reuse of gothic symbols that had previously been used to demon-
ize Spain—such as skeletons, skulls, and graveyards—in association
with the U.S. War Department signified the reformulation of the
war's cast of characters during the final phase of the war. The effect
was to show that the Spanish were not the true enemy, for fewer men
had lost their lives in combat than to disease. Instead critics directed
their indignation at the war's newest villain, Secretary of War Russell
Alger. This was particularly evident in press coverage of the arrival
at Camp Wikoff in August of the transport ships, which they labeled
"horror ships" and "fever ships." In one *New York World* illustration titled "Horror Ships Which Have Brought Dying Soldiers
From Cuba," the artist drew a large skeleton in the sky over the
vessels, symbolizing the death and misery aboard.[31] One of the best-
known cartoons from the final segment of the war, first published
in the *Chicago Tribune,* depicts a robed skeleton, the angel of death
and disease, standing over a gravestone that memorializes the dead,
wrapped in the "red tape" of War Department bureaucracy (figure
5.5). The tombstone reads: "Killed by Spaniards 200. By Official
Negligence and Incompetency 2000." The caption asks, "Shall this
be the national memorial of the Spanish War?"[32] In this way graphic
artists recast in the role of victim not the suffering Cuban but the
triumphant but ill-treated soldier who brought forth U.S. victory.

Although voices of indignation came from both parties, many
Republican editors came to McKinley's defense, labeling the

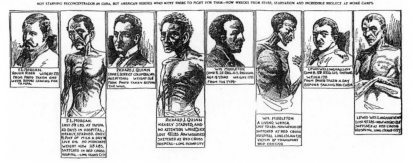

5.3. "Before and After Cuba and Montauk." *New York World,* September 4, 1898, 15.

5.4. Steele, "Three Months Ago and Today." *Denver Evening Post,* August 26, 1898, 1.

5.5. "Shall This Be the National Memorial of the Spanish War?" *Chicago Tribune,* August 27, 1898, 3.

scandal a partisan ploy to discredit victory. According to the Republican *San Francisco Chronicle,* the mudslinging of the yellow press prolonged the war and dishonored the military: "Undoubtedly they have influenced Spanish demands at Paris. To that extent the course of the yellow journals was little less than *treasonable,* saying nothing about the harm done in discouraging enlistments, demoralizing volunteers in other camps and in blighting the prestige of the American military organization."[33]

The presence of returning troops on U.S. soil marked a fundamental change from earlier war coverage and put Republican supporters

THE DARKER SIDE.

The Yellow Editor: "Alas! How Disappointing; the Boys Don't Look Like Living Corpses at All!" (Muffled Sobs.)

5.6. "The Darker Side." *Chicago Inter Ocean,* September 10, 1898, 3.

on the defensive. Returning soldiers were now "visible" to Americans in certain regions of the country, and Republican defenders had a stake in convincing Americans that they did not look neglected or abused. A cartoon from the Republican *Chicago Inter Ocean* criticized the yellow press for falsifying reports of abuse (figure 5.6). It depicts a yellow press editor frustrated by the parade of strong, healthy men returning from war because it undermined the image of debilitated American manpower he had endeavored to create. Scattered on the floor and in the trash are newspapers bearing his fabricated allegations. The editor covering his face in dejection, says with "muffled sobs": "Alas! How Disappointing; the Boys Don't Look Like Living Corpses at All!" Even when Republican defenders conceded that the returning soldiers looked forlorn, they rationalized their appearance as customary after the trials of war. Declared the Republican *Boston Transcript:* "All troops coming off a hard campaign look a great deal more worn out than they really are. The gloss of uniforms has been worn off, the men have lost weight, and they have acquired a look that deceives inexperienced observers into the belief that they are used up."[34]

In the immediate postwar period, publicity over the army scandal made it possible for alternative images of American warfare to emerge. Given the euphoric patriotic spirit during the first two months of the war, few images in any media format had confronted Americans with the harsh realities of war. In the wake of the controversy, some media producers speculated that audiences might be more open to seeing more gruesome battle depictions. Lyman H. Howe's traveling motion picture exhibition before a standing-room-only audience at the Nesbitt Theater in Pennsylvania in September 1898 presented scenes depicting the bloody effects of U.S. naval and land bombardments in Cuba. According to one newspaper account: "Men and officers may be seen shot and falling on all sides. An officer who stands by the side of a cannon grabs the flag and holds it against all, defending himself with pistol and then with sword until all about him are dead and wounded."[35] A review of one of his shows in January 1899 highlighted its violent imagery, describing pictures of the "individual slaughter" of "men, horses and boats going down under the terrible fire," made even more potent by Howe's supplementation of musketry sound effects.[36] Unlike earlier battle reenactments, which suppressed any indications of human casualties, Howe's spectacular visual display of American military actions amplified the devastating effects of war.

The scandals also liberated some theatrical performers from the patriotic stranglehold of the early war period and allowed them to turn images of U.S. military deficiencies into a source of entertainment. Picking up on the controversy in the press, Dumont's Minstrel troupe in September 1898 created a satirical bit called "The Return of Wanamaker's Regiment," which the *Philadelphia Public Ledger* claimed "struck the audience as so irresistibly funny that the performance was stopped for full five minutes while the house roared at the grotesque appearance of the 'army.'"[37] The review in the Republican *Public Ledger* emphasized that rather than take offense, audiences found entertaining the humorous impersonations of afflicted soldiers and scenes making fun of managerial incompetence.

In the wake of the scandal, conflicting images of the American serviceman—as the masculine, martial ideal and as suffering, maltreated victim—competed for media attention. At one end of the spectrum, some photographers invited viewers to enjoy the pleasure of beholding the nation's strong, fit troops. Photographs of American sailors stripped to the waist loading the cannons or sporting on the decks of the ship visually united military success with manly athleticism and bodily performance, promoting the poised, robust male physique as the nation's most powerful weapon. An illustrated children's history

5.7. "Single-Stick Exercise on a War Ship." From Frank T. Wyatt, *Child's History of Our War with Spain: A Fascinating Account of the Spanish-American Contest* (Chicago: W. B. Conkey, 1899), 105.

of the war published in 1899 correlated "play" and "war-making," picturing the precision and skill of U.S. sailors in fencing formation (figure 5.7). Savannah's Eden Musee postwar exhibition celebrated the manly martial ideal with a scene of wax models of sailors manning the guns in "intense heat" (and without shirts) aboard Dewey's ship, the *Olympia*. Describing the sailors as "perfect specimens of manhood," the *Savannah Press* praised the figures as "so real that you can see the perspiration coming from every pore and each muscle and sinew seems taxed to their utmost tension." Indeed, "what has given the United States complete victory in this war with Spain is not wealth, or ships, or superior guns, or overpowering force, but manhood," affirmed the *New York Journal*.[38]

Other postwar depictions of American servicemen, however, reflected the shaken confidence in the U.S. military. Secretary Alger permitted photographer Burr McIntosh to travel with U.S. troops to take photographs of the war, and in 1899 he published an illustrated memoir of his experience titled *The Little I Saw of Cuba*. Despite his official charge, his disillusionment with military mismanagement shaped his presentation of content. He unleashed his anger at the War Department in his opening remarks: "If he who was dearest to you, fought his fight bravely and well, and was then forced to go to the pest-holes of Montauk, instead of to your loving arms, forced to have the last vestige of life choked out of him by strangulating 'red tape,' from whom shall you demand justice?" His book contained snapshots of many U.S. servicemen, including a smiling portrait of a wealthy young Rough Rider from New York, Hamilton Fish Jr. To make the point that many of these brave men did not return alive, he also included a photograph of two fallen Americans. Even though their bodies were covered, this was a sight that had been almost entirely suppressed in wartime photography prior to the military scandal. One of the dead bodies was Fish, who fell at the battle of Las Guasimas on June 24. McIntosh wrote that he had considered lifting the blanket to "steal a picture of the face," but decided against it and was "glad of it." He offered two views of the bodies, one a close-up and the other of the bodies in proximity to a group of officers (figure 5.8). He explained that he had added the wider shot because while standing there, he had overheard the officers laughing; this, he wrote, created "a resentment which I never expect to be able to overcome." By presenting viewers with a progression of U.S. soldiers, from smiling volunteers to covered corpses, McIntosh's photographs and uncompromising text reflected his disenchantment with the military conduct of the war, which he felt had disrespected the memory of those who had perished.[39]

In the fall of 1898, newspaper advertising campaigns, such as for Paine's Celery Compound, also incorporated into their marketing schemes perceptions of the physical and psychological deterioration of the army. "Four Troopers of the Gallant Rough Riders" read the ad promoting the product: "How It Gave Them Back Health and Strength after Their Impoverishment from Disease and Hardship in the Cuban Campaign." Alongside portraits of several cavalrymen were testimonial accounts describing how the patent medicine saved them from the perils of warfare and disease. B. C. Bassage of Jerome, Arizona, attested: "I will say that my complete restoration to health after the trying ordeal of the Santiago campaign is due entirely to its

5.8. Burr McIntosh, "Scene after 'Rough Riders' Battle, July 24th." From McIntosh, *The Little I Saw of Cuba* (London: F. Tennyson Neely, 1899), 107.

use. It is the greatest nerve tonic ever invented."[40] An advertisement for Dr. Flower's "Vigor Tablets" in the *New York Journal* took a similar approach. Titled "Up San Juan Hill," it featured a horrifying graphic image of a bullet striking a Rough Rider, severing his arm entirely from his body and sending his cowboy hat flying off his head. "When Private Henderson fell, robbed of his right arm by a Spanish shell, his first thought was: 'God keep the wife and little ones!' When he came to in the surgeon's arms he moaned out, 'Save me, doctor!' He didn't ask the cause of his misfortune, he asked for help. . . . The right remedy from Dr. R. C. Flower is sure as the health which follows its use."[41] In contrast to earlier war-themed advertisements that clung to ideals of patriotism and manly heroism, this marketing strategy undercut the notion of war as in itself restorative of masculine vitality. Rather, these consumer products promised to restore the mind, body, and spirit of America's wounded and to undo the ill effects of combat and privation.

Frederic Remington's paintings of the Cuban military campaigns perhaps best demonstrate the contested representations of the male body in the postwar period. The well-known artist of the American West went to Cuba in 1898 under contract with *Harper's*, the *New York Journal,* and the *Chicago Tribune.* Like Theodore Roosevelt, Remington was a firm believer in the "strenuous life" as a means to restore the masculine, Anglo-Saxon character of America's youth. He seized the opportunity to go to war, which he called "the greatest thing which men are called on to do."[42] Despite his initial burst of martial spirit, his experience in Cuba was harder than he had anticipated. He took ill with fever from the poor sleeping conditions, heat, and insufficient food and felt demoralized by the sights of war he witnessed. Sick and exhausted, he was present at the battle of San Juan Hill but saw little of it, having taken cover over a thousand yards behind the lines. He wrote: "The sight of that road as I wound my way down it was something I cannot describe. The rear of a battle. All the broken spirits, bloody bodies, hopeless, helpless suffering which drags its weary length to the rear, are so much more appalling than anything else in the world." That night, as he thought about what he had seen, he claimed, "I could not get the white bodies which lay in the moonlight, with the dark spots on them, out of my mind."[43] Shortly after, he left Cuba and returned to New York.

Two paintings he produced of the battle of San Juan Hill after his return depict conflicting representations of the scene. In April 1899, at Roosevelt's request, *Scribner's* commissioned one of Remington's most famous war-related works, titled *The Charge of the Rough Riders at San Juan Hill,* to illustrate Roosevelt's article "The Cavalry at Santiago" (figure 5.9). It replicates the conventions of epic myth-making common to most images of the battle published soon after it was fought (see figure 3.4). On horseback, Roosevelt leads an energetic charge of cavalrymen. Two Spanish soldiers lie dead, about to be trampled by the victorious American ascent up the hill. While Remington does not completely suppress the threat to the American forces (a few men appear to be hit), art historians have characterized the scene as more like a football play than a military campaign. Remington's vision correlated battle and football as mutually constitutive fields for the nourishment of Anglo-Saxon manhood. Despite the presence of a token African American soldier in the pack, the painting largely celebrates the manly white martial spirit of the U.S. forces.[44] Reflecting larger patterns of U.S.-produced war images, Remington recognized only American male bodies for fighting and sacrificing in this war, minimizing, though not totally excluding, the participation of black U.S. servicemen, while Cuban nationalist forces are entirely absent from the scene.

5.9. Frederic Remington, *Charge of the Rough Riders at San Juan Hill.* 1898. Courtesy Frederic Remington Art Museum, Ogdensburg, New York, Public Library Collection.

In a second painting he produced of this battle after returning from Cuba, *The Scream of Shrapnel at San Juan Hill, Cuba,* Remington reveals a less glorious view of war, more in tune with his traumatized descriptions (figure 5.10). The sound of incoming fire causes the soldiers to halt their heroic advance and topple like a row of dominoes. One serviceman, with his bugle and drum, takes off in flight while the others brace for attack. Perilously exposed to an artillery shower invisible to the viewer, the men signal their helplessness and disorientation in their facial expressions and awkward bodily contortions. Their distorted and jarring postures sharply contrast to the vigorous and focused rush of bodies in Remington's *Charge.*[45] Like many other observers of the war, Remington felt more disillusioned by what he had witnessed than assured of U.S. military preparedness, and his paintings convey the internal conflict between his idealization of U.S. military manpower and the realities of what he saw in Cuba.

Scandals + Empire = Manly Imperial Ideal?

During the critical period when the nation pondered the imperial question, mass-circulating images of robust American male bodies coexisted with those picturing weakness and affliction, empowering critics to cast doubt on the nation's capacity for managing an

5.10. Frederic Remington, *The Scream of Shrapnel at San Juan Hill, Cuba*. 1898.
Courtesy Yale University Art Gallery.

overseas empire. As I argued in chapter 4, emerging imperialistic aspirations after the battle of Santiago had the effect of displacing the prior emphasis on securing Cuban independence in prewar media campaigns. The military scandals that broke in July and August, however, complicated this neat shift from liberation to conquest. The iconography of suffering U.S. soldiers overshadowed that of Cuba's former role as victim, diverting attention from the humanitarian crisis that had initially compelled intervention and facilitating the ideological turn toward imperialism. But at the same time, the scandals undermined confidence in the McKinley administration and helped generate the partisan divisions that fostered the emergence of an organized opposition to imperialism.

In their attacks on the War Department, members of the Democratic press called into question U.S. military preparedness just as Americans were contemplating whether the nation should take on new imperial responsibilities. According to the *New York Journal*, "there was no reason . . . why the 1st of September should not find us with an army of 275,000 strong, superior in fighting power to any other of its size in the world. . . . Instead, we find ourselves with the tottering skeleton of an army, wasted by disease and starvation, and less ready in all respects to take the field against an enemy than it was three months ago. Worse yet, the very springs of national military vigor have been sapped."[46] The *Denver Post* shared the *Journal*'s

disillusionment: "This aftermath of the war brings many sad reflections. There is Admiral Dewey, who conquered an empire and
destroyed a fleet with the loss of but few men; there is Commodore
Schley, who destroyed a whole squadron with the loss of but one
man; and there is General Miles, whose campaign in Porto Rico was
almost bloodless. . . . With the surrender of Santiago nearly two
months ago the active operations in Cuba ceased . . . but since then
the death list has kept on increasing. . . . What war abroad failed to
do[,] general incompetency at home has accomplished in a most fearful way."[47] Instead of proclaiming the ascendency of a nation on the
verge of becoming a world imperial power, the Democratic opposition put forward the "wasted" state of the U.S. Army as fearful evidence that American military "vigor" was being "sapped" by an in-
competent leadership.

Whereas earlier in the war cartoonists had pictured a muscular
Uncle Sam to symbolize the nation's newfound military prowess,
postwar depictions of Uncle Sam's physical condition became an
important site for cartoonists to debate the benefits and detriments
of imperialist expansion. The *Dallas News* noted that the figure of
Uncle Sam "must be made to keep pace with the exciting march of
events" and that "he must acquire an air that suggests the deliverer
of slaves from the yoke of the oppressor and possessor of a vast
empire of free and happy people."[48] His new regimen of territorial
ingestion became a popular graphic motif, particularly in the art of
Clifford K. Berryman of the *Washington Post,* Charles Nelan of the
New York Herald, and Grant Hamilton of *Judge.*[49] In a cartoon
from early August 1898, Nelan contrasts Uncle Sam "before and
after taking," depicting his transformation from a tall and lanky
figure, labeled "nothing but skin and bone," to a large, globular
form (figure 5.11). The image of a fattened Uncle Sam on a scale
symbolized the physical effect of incorporating colonies into the
national body, with the names of his new possessions emblazoned
on the stars and stripes of his costume. World leaders nervously
stand before his commanding presence in fearful recognition of his
newfound girth. Uncle Sam writes to his doctor: "After four months
use of your Great Humanitarian-Expansion–Specific, you wouldn't
know me. I am getting fatter and fatter and never felt better in my
life." The caption explains, "Uncle Sam proudly informs his physi-

"BEFORE AND AFTER TAKING."

Uncle Sam Proudly Informs His Physician That the Treatment Has Been a Success.

5.11. Charles Nelan, "Before and After Taking." *New York Herald,* August 7, 1898, 1.

cian that the treatment has been a success." The impact of his growing size, though, is ambiguous; while the caption frames Uncle Sam's weight gain in terms of rising prosperity, his unkempt attire and distended body suggest excessive engorgement. Although Nelan created this cartoon for the independent *New York Herald,* which gen-

erally supported imperial expansion, the Democratic and anticolonialist *Cleveland Plain Dealer* reprinted it, further suggesting the
ambiguity of the cartoon's stance on imperialism.[50]

Clifford Berryman of the *Washington Post* also envisioned the
effects of imperialism on Uncle Sam's body as unhealthy enlargement and physical susceptibility. An editorial articulates the *Post*'s
pro-imperialist position: "If we have a mission in Cuba—and it
now seems that we have—that mission is to protect the masses
of these downtrodden, brutalized, and degraded wretches against
the rapacity and the despotism of their self-appointed leaders."[51]
Berryman's image of Uncle Sam (which appeared in many of his
cartoons) expresses a more cautious viewpoint, however, marking
Uncle Sam's widening girth as a potential source of vulnerability.
In the debates over the peace agreement, he portrayed the leading
political figures of the anti-imperialist movement, including Grover
Cleveland, Andrew Carnegie, William Jennings Bryan, and Senators
Benjamin Tillman and Thomas Reed, indignantly surrounding a
corpulent Uncle Sam (figure 5.12). Despite having popular support,
symbolized by the club of "The People" which seems his only line of
defense, Uncle Sam looks anxious, as these angry combatants prepare to stab him with their pitchforks and burst his balloon-like
sphere of a body. Berryman asks, "Will they succeed in puncturing
Uncle Sam's Expansion System?"

Life magazine, in January 1899, took this visual metaphor one
step further in a sequence of images of Uncle Sam's "progress
toward global ingestion," as Martha Banta aptly put it, from 1776
to the present (figure 5.13).[52] Slender and content in 1776, Uncle
Sam uncomfortably expands his waistline to absorb the Louisiana
Purchase, the Mexican cession, and Alaska, and by 1898 appears dis-
tressingly burdened by the weight of his new acquisitions. The series
culminates with the explosion of his stomach, the bubble bursting
at some imminent point. The pictorial transformation of Uncle Sam
in the postwar period represents the graphic incarnation of anxieties about the impact of imperialism on the future of the nation,
expressed visually by Uncle Sam's bodily engorgement and risk of
self-implosion.

Will They Succeed in Puncturing Uncle Sam's Expansion System?

5.12. Clifford Berryman, "Our Next Conflict." *Washington Post,* December 23, 1898, 1.

Peace Jubilee: The Last Gasp of Wartime Spectacle

Pronouncements of national "disgrace" owing to the state of military affairs cast a shadow over America's swift defeat of Spain and stifled the shouts of jubilation expected to accompany military triumph. An editorialist of the Democratic *Savannah Press* wrote, "Were our soldiers to die on the field of battle there would be some consolation in the manner in which they gave up their lives, but to die in hospitals, camps, transports, and crowded cars, and that, too, from the incompetency of men at the head of the government's department, is a source of disgrace which should cause the country to be ashamed."[53] In the midst of military scandal and growing anticolonialist dissent during the fall of 1898, public celebrations of U.S. victory in the Spanish-American War were held across the nation.

5.13. *Life* 33 (January 26, 1899): 72–73.

Despite their festive spirit, these events illuminate the discordant state of press and public opinion in the immediate postwar period.

The peace celebrations expressed American imperialist ideologies by celebrating U.S. military achievements without acknowledging the contributions of Cuban and Filipino forces. The chairman of the planning committee for the largest of these events, the Philadelphia Jubilee, noted the "absence of applications for positions in the civic parade from Cubans," but no further action was taken to solicit them.[54] Editor Victor F. Lawson of the pro-imperialist *Chicago Record* had a dissenting opinion; he urged planners of the Chicago Peace Jubilee to invite Cuban nationalist leaders, Generals Máximo Gómez, Calixto García, and Demetrio Castillo Duany, in addition to a contingent of revolutionaries. Lawson imagined a protectorate style of imperialism in which local elites would rule and urged inclusion of the Cubans to facilitate U.S. control: "The royal reception which would be given the Cuban generals if some of them could be induced to take part in the Chicago celebration would be flattering to Cuban pride and would help to dispel any feelings of jealousy." Lawson believed that welcoming the Cubans would enable them to express their gratitude, for they were the ones with the "most to be thankful for."[55] The planning committee, as well as other Chicago papers, however, did not endorse Lawson's suggestion, instead opting to make the United States central in the affairs of war and peace.

Newspapers across the country reported on the events of the Philadelphia Peace Jubilee, with President McKinley as its most distinguished guest, in late October 1898.[56] Replicating the opening of the war with Dewey's spectacular naval victory in Manila Bay, the festivities began with a large-scale naval regatta on the Delaware

River. Captain Charles D. Sigsbee, commander of the ill-fated battle-ship *Maine*, directed the pageant. The *Philadelphia Times* noted: "No feature of the Peace Jubilee is likely to efface the impression made by the naval display of yesterday upon all of the many thousands who witnessed it. The scene upon the river, whose broad surface was made brilliant by the movement of innumerable gaily decorated craft, while the shores were black with people, was as stirring as it was picturesque." Claimed the *Philadelphia Inquirer:* "Ushered in by an imposing naval demonstration the display of patriotism was in itself an imposing spectacle. . . . It was a brilliant, bold and splendid entertainment . . . a sublime testimonial to the beauty of patriotism."[57]

The second major event, the Philadelphia civic parade, endeavored to display U.S. imperial gains in the war. The most publicized feature was a series of moving floats representing Puerto Rico and Cuba, the Philippines, and Hawaii designed by the Commercial Museum. Each float accentuated the commercial benefits of colonization, densely packed with sugar, hemp, tobacco, and fruit from the colonies, while featuring "authentic" native representatives. The Hawaiian float exhibited two dark-skinned Hawaiian natives, in Native American garb, who spoke English to the crowds. The Philippine float featured relics from the battle of Manila Bay along with six Negritos, two of whom were dressed in primitive costume and performed as warriors while the remaining four wore contemporary attire. Professor William P. Wilson, overseeing the project for the Commercial Museum, cast the natives in two roles, as exotic peoples in need of guidance and as examples of "uplifted" subjects. He sought to harness the spectacular attraction of showcasing "savage" peoples while also demonstrating America's ability to colonize effectively.[58] Still, few press accounts took note of the "civilized" representatives; what ultimately lent these floats media notoriety was the peculiar and curious depiction of colonial primitivism that they provided.

Not all the floats in the parade offered as clear an imperial vision. One of the floats reproduced a Joseph Keppler cartoon from the illustrated magazine *Puck* titled "A Trifle Embarrassed," published in early August (figure 5.14). Float designers often drew their inspiration from cartoons, and their selection of *Puck* is a revealing choice, for it was known for its highly satirical style. The cartoon and float, both with the same title, depicted Uncle Sam and Columbia receiving a basket of crying infants at the gates of the "U.S. Foundling Asylum" from the arms of Manifest Destiny. Uncle Sam says: "Gosh! I wish they wouldn't come quite so many in a bunch; but if we got to take them, I guess I can do as well by them as I've done by the others!" Whereas Uncle Sam and Columbia seem bewildered by the unexpected arrivals, the children inside the asylum (a Texan, a Mexican, a Californian, and a Native American) gesture toward America's successful history of territorial expansionism. Still, Keppler portrays these children with mischievous expressions and includes a Native American child in the "bunch," suggesting that Uncle Sam may not in fact have done so well by "the others." He also depicts the new colonial additions as screaming, angry babies, conceptualizing empire as an obligation and a sacrifice. Although the float did not overtly denounce empire, the image of unruly colonial subjects with their fists clenched hardly seems the visual symbol to celebrate it. The decision to reproduce this cartoon at the Jubilee was significant, for it spoke to both advocates and opponents of colonial rule and demonstrates how public spectacle can encompass contradiction and avoid a simple partisan stance.

Audience reactions to the civic parade shed light on the divisiveness of the moment. Along a six-mile route bedecked with flags and bunting, the procession featured Lieutenant Hobson and his crew, many leading war generals, and over 25,000 soldiers and sailors returning from the front. The troops marched up Broad Street through the Court of Honor, an arch and colonnade constructed for the Jubilee. According to the *Philadelphia Inquirer,* "it was really not until Hobson came along that the climax of the shouting and yelling was reached." In contrast to the reception of the war celebrities, popular reaction to the ranks of regiments was not what might be expected toward returning heroes. Whenever the soldiers came to a standstill on Broad and Market streets, the crowds pelted them with biscuits, sandwiches, apples, bananas, and other edible missiles, to the point of "demoralizing" the troops.[59] William Rau, the official photographer of the Jubilee, captured this scene on camera (figure 5.15), depicting a group of soldiers in disarray, no longer in line or able to keep marching with food debris littering the ground. Such irreverent treatment of the soldiers was perhaps a means for spectators to express their dissatisfaction with the imperial turn of the war. It may

5.14. Joseph Keppler, "A Trifle Embarrassed." *Puck* 43 (August 3, 1898). Collection of The New-York Historical Society, neg. no. 83572d.

also reflect one of the primary uses of parades, according to Susan G. Davis's study of nineteenth-century street life in Philadelphia: the "mockery of institutions and politics."[60] Despite the intentions of the Jubilee to foster a unified public mood of patriotic and imperial sentiment, the crowds may have participated for their own reasons.

The disjuncture between celebrating the war and its potential imperialist outcome also surfaced in the struggle to put together a Peace Jubilee in Savannah, Georgia. The local government encountered unexpected resistance from citizens who objected to calling the event a "peace jubilee," preferring to disengage it from the politics of the war. It was also rumored that members of the city council opposed inviting President McKinley because of his imperialist agenda. The council ultimately decided to invite the president, but to reassure critics, the Democratic *Savannah Press* overtly depoliticized the event: "There is no politics in the tour of President McKinley. . . . It was not asked and not expected that the people of this state would indorse all the political opinions of the president, nor were they asked to indorse his administration."[61] In an effort to guarantee attendance and cordial treatment of the president, the *Press* preemptively urged

5.15. William Rau, photograph of the Philadelphia Peace Jubilee Military Parade. Courtesy The Historical Society of Pennsylvania.

its readers not to let partisanship impede their participation in the celebration of peace.

During the final phase of the war, unifying visions of U.S. military and moral supremacy fractured amid pressing concerns about army incapacitation and long-term imperial commitments. The findings of the government's investigations into the management of the U.S. Army, made public in the spring of 1899, failed to reunite press and public opinion. The Dodge Commission concluded that the War Department was not intentionally neglectful or corrupt, though it conceded that "there was lacking in the general administration of the War Department . . . that complete grasp of the situation which was essential to the highest efficiency and discipline of the Army."[62] The court of inquiry into the quality of the beef supplied to the military also exonerated the commissary, claiming the meat to be sound and at worst a victim of the tropical climate, and censured General Miles for his accusation. Reactions to these findings divided along party lines; the Republican press felt vindicated by the report, while the Democratic press accused the McKinley administration of whitewashing the scandal.

Although the controversy soon faded from public view, the effects of it did not. At the height of the Spanish-American War, thousands of spectators had attended large-scale reenactments of the battles of Manila Bay, San Juan Hill, and Santiago. Yet, in the immediate postwar period, media producers resisted the temptation to follow in the footsteps of the great European empires and create elaborate displays celebrating U.S. militarism to launch America's new career as a world imperial power. The divisiveness over U.S. military and imperial policies along with the negative response that the soldiers received during the Philadelphia peace celebrations were, perhaps, strong disincentives. In testament to the stultifying effect of political dissension on the war spirit, the *Springfield Republican* noted that that "the rampant spirit of militarism" had "quickly and decisively" dissipated.[63]

It was within this turbulent climate, as the romantic spectacle of war began to fade in the late summer of 1898, that the nation had to address the burning question: What role would the United States play in the future of the Spanish colonies? This would be formally decided at the fall peace conference in Paris. After signing the armistice in August 1898, McKinley sent inquiries to Admiral George Dewey, General Wesley Merritt, General Francis Greene, and others about the commercial prospects of acquisition as well as the desirability of the Philippines and their people.[64] He assembled a group of five men to negotiate the peace settlement on his behalf: Secretary of State William R. Day, who was undecided on the Philippine question; Whitelaw Reid, editor of the *New York Tribune,* a known expansionist; pro-imperialist Republican senators Cushman K. Davis and William P. Frye from Minnesota and Maine, respectively; and anti-colonialist Democratic Senator George Gray from Delaware. In his instructions as they departed for Paris in late September, McKinley ordered them to take the main island of Luzon but left the fate of the rest of the Philippine archipelago unresolved. That October he embarked on a ten-day tour of the Midwest, traveling to Iowa, Omaha, St. Louis, and Chicago, making fifty-seven public appearances.[65] During this whistle-stop tour, McKinley praised the U.S. victory and gestured toward the next step, telling a crowd of nearly 99,000 people at the Trans-Mississippi and International Exposition in Omaha: "The war was no more invited by us than were the questions which are laid at our door by its results. Now, as then, we will do our duty."[66]

While he presented imperial acquisition as a question of "duty," his language was vague and avoided any clear pronouncements, leaving historians to debate exactly when he settled on his course of action. Conventional interpretations of McKinley's presidency accent his indecisiveness and present the whistle-stop tour as his means to gauge public opinion in order to decide what to do about the Philippines and other territories. Supporting this view was his employment of a stenographer to measure the intensity and length of applause at each station stop to statements suggesting the possibility of taking colonies.[67] Historian Robert Hilderbrand compellingly disputes this position, arguing that McKinley had settled on acquisition by late summer at the latest and that his tour aimed to consolidate support for empire. Within minutes after addressing audiences, McKinley's secretary, George Cortelyou, provided reporters with copies of the speech. Already adept at managing public relations, McKinley had been the first president to create a modern political public relations machine to rally popular support, which he successfully mobilized in the presidential campaign of 1896. In his whistle-stop tour McKinley downplayed his imperialist inclinations by styling himself a "follower of the people," as Hilderbrand put it; but in actuality, this was a highly crafted and effective public relations effort intended to give the impression that he was feeling out public sentiment on imperialism. The Republican press took the cues and publicized the positive reception; noted the *Chicago Inter Ocean*, "The enthusiasm with which President McKinley's address was received was significant of the enthusiasm of the people for the whole policy of expansion."[68] McKinley wrote to peace commissioner Whitelaw Reid, "Everywhere there were the most enthusiastic demonstrations and the Government seemed to have the hearty support and encouragement of the people." Upon his return to Washington on October 26, he instructed the commissioners in Paris to demand the entire Philippine archipelago.[69]

McKinley used his speaking tour to reframe the outcome of the war in order to correspond with the humanitarian goals of its beginning. Drawing on the media script compelling intervention on Cuba's behalf in the first place, he spoke of the war as one for "humanity's sake" that was "not invited" and justified American colonial guardianship as the fulfillment of that purpose. He called Americans the "emancipators" of the Filipinos, not the "masters," mimicking the same rhetorical sleight of hand used by imperialists who rejected the term "imperialism" in favor of the softer alternative—"expansionism." McKinley demonstrated his shrewd management of public relations by cementing colonization into the humanitarian premise of the war, despite the fact that many Americans had supported the war as a means to secure Cuban independence, with no expectation of long-term occupation or acquisition of the rest of the Spanish empire.[70] But after defeating Spain, taking responsibility for its colonies was the nation's only viable option, claimed McKinley. He marshaled the humanitarian intent of military intervention to justify colonial acquisition as a self-sacrificial national act, not one rooted in U.S. geopolitical and commercial gain; but the articulation of his goal to replace Spanish rule with a more "benevolent" brand indeed came after the fact.

6

Building an Imperial Iconography
RACE, PATERNALISM, AND THE SYMBOLS OF EMPIRE

Pile on the brown man's burden
To gratify your greed;
Go clear away the "niggers"
Who progress would impede;
Be very stern, for truly
'Tis useless to be mild
With new-caught, sullen peoples,
Half devil and half child.

Pile on the brown man's burden;
And if ye rouse his hate,
Meet his old-fashioned reasons
With Maxims up to date.
With shells and dumdum bullets
A hundred times make plain
The brown man's loss must ever
Imply the white man's gain.

"A Brown Man's Burden" (1899), a parody of
Rudyard Kipling's poem "The White Man's Burden"

In March 1899 a group of New York society women organized a "mid-Lent entertainment" that they called "Uncle Sam's Annexation Party." They asked guests to come to the party in costume as American colonial subjects. Those arriving as Filipinos wore rings in their noses and ears and "primitive-style" clothing, and the *New York Journal* noted that the party caused local costume shops to run out of chocolate-colored greasepaint.[1] "Blacking up" into colonial caricature enabled these society folks to perform the fantasy of dominating nonwhite peoples at home and abroad, revealing how deeply these imperialistic visions were ingraining themselves into the culture.

The United States was an imperial power long before its brief war with Spain, having taken ownership of large tracts of land from Mexico, Britain, and France, waged a war of extermination and land dispossession against Native Americans, and assumed a position of economic and diplomatic ascendancy in the Western Hemisphere. The Spanish-American War of 1898, however, broke new ground insofar as it presented an opportunity for the United States to acquire *overseas* territories without the promise of extending the full rights and privileges of statehood. This sparked a national debate that provoked greater opposition than the initial decision to intervene in the Cuban crisis.

An anticolonialist movement grew with support from prominent American political and intellectual leaders, including ex-presidents Benjamin Harrison and Grover Cleveland; Republican senators Eugene Hale and George F. Hoar and House Speaker Thomas Reed; Democrat William Jennings Bryan; labor leader Samuel Gompers; activists Jane Addams, Josephine Shaw Lowell, and W. E. B. Du Bois; businessmen Andrew Carnegie and George F. Peabody; writers Ambrose Bierce, William Dean Howells, Henry Blake Fuller, and Mark Twain; and Harvard and Yale intellectuals William James, Charles Eliot Norton, and William Graham Sumner. Because such strange bedfellows came together in this anticolonialist coalition, their arguments ranged widely in scope. They expressed concerns over the effects of colonization on American values, republican institutions, labor, and free trade, and the incorporation of subjects who were viewed as racial and cultural inferiors. Still, many of them favored the establishment of permanent coaling stations and extension of U.S. trade and cultural dominion, a policy we now call neoimperialism, but without the burdens of formal occupation.[2]

This chapter identifies the prevailing representations for and against colonial acquisition that appeared in political cartoons and other commercial entertainments during the late war and immediate postwar periods. These images helped Americans to make sense of the shifting meaning of the war and to rationalize an imperialist outcome. In the fall and winter of 1898–99, editorialists, politicians, writers, and other intellectuals produced copious writings and speeches voicing moral, racial, constitutional, political, diplomatic, and economic considerations for and against colonization. Race was a crucial issue in these discussions, but did not necessarily carry the most weight. In the visual distillation of this debate in political cartoons, however, race transcended all others factors. Cartoonists' reliance on certain symbols and stereotypes at the expense of others reduced the stakes of the imperial debate to those idioms that proved most economical for visual expression. As instruments of persuasion, images communicate differently than words do, reach broader audiences, and may or may not be overtly political.[3] Even when cartoonists were attempting to articulate a broader array of relevant issues, the act of representing the colonies inevitably positioned race at the center. Marking the colonies with visual distinctions of "race"—skin color, facial features, and hair type—became a delivery system for imperial ideologies. These attributes of colonial subjects deviated from the visual imagery of normative whiteness, the "race" equated with civilization and the competence to self-govern.[4] The racial tenor of pro- and anticolonialist arguments hindered the ability of anticolonialist cartoonists to challenge imperialist logic; hence, a shared racial vision across the table neutralized anticolonialist dissent.

The racialized spectacle of colonialism arising from the cultural production of empire on both sides of the debate made use of popular imagery that circulated widely in mass entertainments, including the attractions of P. T. Barnum, circus and midway vendors, and minstrel shows. Relying on established visual and popular conventions enabled artists to produce cartoons quickly; *New York Herald* cartoonist Charles Nelan claimed that he was "often called on to make a cartoon in two or three hours and sometimes in less time."[5] The reproduction of stereotypes from familiar social categories in the visual depictions of colonial peoples also enhanced reader comprehension.[6] Racial and ethnic caricature thrived in popular cartoons, comic strips, and prints in the period after the Civil War.[7] By presenting the terms of overseas imperialism through the lens of American popular culture, cultural producers embedded messages of imperialist and racial ideologies in a framework that could be widely recognized and had mass appeal. Consequently, these mass-produced representations bore little relation to the actual demographic composition of the colonies.

The racial grammar of imperial iconography was also compelling because it linked overseas subjects with the foremost "undesirables" within U.S. borders and resonated with wider concerns about the degeneration of American culture, race, and nationhood. The

Spanish-American War came at a tense moment in the history of American race and ethnic relations, occurring in the midst of white supremacist campaigns to institutionalize segregation. 127 lynchings took place in 1898 alone.[8] The success of southern disfranchisement further inspired northern efforts to use exclusionary tactics to amass power through urban ethnic political machines. The racial coding of imperial images, in effect, represented the foreign side of a domestic discourse of racial control.

This process consolidated imagined racial and ethnic ties of whiteness into what became known as "Anglo-Saxonism," an invented racial formation bonding white Americans to their British brethren across the Atlantic while marking their distance from subordinate racial or ethnic groups at home and in acquired territories. Cartoons, popular prints, and sheet music solidifying "Anglo-Saxon" racial ties (figure 6.1) circulated in tandem with racialized images of colonial peoples. Reviving kinship with Britain became politically feasible after the peaceful reconciliation between the United States and Britain following the Venezuela border dispute of 1895. By 1898 the ties had grown so close that the *Baltimore Sun* advocated changing the American flag to a "flag of the future" with the Union Jack and the Stars and Stripes joined in a coat of arms, symbolizing the merger of U.S. and British imperial histories into a shared venture of enlightened colonialism. "Our British cousins have shown us the models of a colonial service that is practically perfect," claimed the *San Francisco Examiner*. "The world's destiny, in a large measure, lies within the keeping of the two great branches of the Anglo-Saxon race," declared the *Atlanta Constitution*.[9]

Still, this process cannot simply be described as one of historical "export" or "projection" of American domestic racial visions, particularly of Native and African Americans, onto a colonial context.[10] Instead of merely reproducing generic racial or colonial images used elsewhere, cartoonists created an amalgamated racial-imperial type that infused new and often contingent meanings into a shared imperialist vocabulary at home. In creating and disseminating mass-produced visions of America's new colonies, the nation's image makers relied on the visual as a way to argue for, critique, and at times equivocate about empire.

IF THE WAR BRING NOTHING ELSE, FOR THIS WE ARE THANKFUL.

6.1. Charles Nelan, "If the War Bring Nothing Else, for This We Are Thankful." *New York Herald*, May 28, 1898, 5.

The Visual Road Not Taken: The "Imperial" Image of the Indian

Continental expansion and the pacification of the Native Americans provided a potential framework for imperialists to justify a national progression toward overseas colonization. In the last decades of the nineteenth century, U.S. foreign affairs received greater priority in policymaking, as politicians, industrialists, and financiers set their sights overseas as a source for expanding U.S. capital and markets. Frederick Jackson Turner's famous speech in 1893 declared the continent "closed" to expanding settlement and became a handy rationale for seeking international frontiers. Many advocates for imperialism upheld colonial acquisition as an extension of America's manifest destiny, the next step after continental expansion. In turn they interpreted the pacification of Native Americans as vital experience in the work of colonization. McKinley reinforced this logic by recruiting commanders with records in the Native American wars to serve in the Philippines, including General Samuel Young, Colonel Jacob Smith, and Brigadier General Henry W. Lawton, who advocated using the same methods against the Filipinos that they had learned fighting the "savages" of the American West.[11]

Politicians, writers, and editorialists often employed this history of internal colonization to lay a groundwork for colonial possession overseas. The defeat of the Lakota at Wounded Knee in 1890, largely conceived as the last of the significant Indian wars, was still fresh in public memory. This view enabled imperialists to argue that the United States was already accustomed to managing imperial subjects, having successfully completed the conquest of its domestic native populations.[12] The pro-imperialist *New York Herald* was one of many voices forging this comparison: "The United States is not entirely inexperienced in the handling of native tribes, and it is to be hoped that the lessons which we have learned in dealing with the North American Indians may bear their full fruit in deciding as to what is best for our oceanic possessions."[13]

Cartoonists for newspapers across the country, however, largely resisted this strain of argument; in fact only a handful of cartoons were published that framed continental expansion as a precedent for colonialism abroad. Still, the existence of a few instances of this argument in prominent news sources demonstrates that the relevance of the Native American conquest was at least considered. Giving them a brief look brings to light the conceptual problems that ultimately led graphic artists to opt for other ways of visualizing the work of colonization.

Most of these anomalies appeared in political cartoons from anti-colonialist sources. Graphic artists in these cases drew on the turbulent history of Native American dispossession in order to question the civilizing mission of pacification through violence. On a January 1899 cover of *Life*, a journal that consistently opposed imperialism, cartoonist William H. Walker depicts an American Indian prophesying the future of Filipino and Hawaiian subjects (figure 6.2). With hostilities imminent, the "Big Injun," as Walker calls him, stands before a Filipino and a Hawaiian; he is wrapped in blankets with a feather in his hat and the elixir of "civilization" in his pocket. This

VOLUME XXXIII.   NEW YORK, JANUARY 12, 1899.   NUMBER 841.

Entered at the New York Post Office as Second-Class Mail Matter.
Copyright, 1899, by LIFE PUBLISHING COMPANY.

PROPHETIC.

Big Injun: I SEE YOUR FINISH.

6.2. William H. Walker, "Prophetic." *Life* 33 (January 12, 1899): 1.

flask of "civilization" refers to the tactic of promoting alcohol addition to subdue native populations, an argument that explicitly defies
the imperialist logic of the "white man's burden." "Prophetic" as
he is, he warns them, "I see your finish" (signified by a gun-toting
American sentry on patrol). A political cartoon in the anticolonialist *Houston Post* conveyed a similar message, illuminating the false
pretense of imperialist claims to "educate" others through the use of

force. Appearing after the exchange of fire between U.S. and Filipino troops, the cartoon depicts a bitter American Indian, cloaked in the same stereotypical symbols that Walker employs, watching the Philippine-American War unfold. As he observes U.S. soldiers shooting Filipino subjects, who flee in terror, he says: "Ugh! Educatin' Filipinos! Injin Already Educated!"[14]

While Walker questions the morality of imperial warfare, his "prophetic" Indian could also be foreseeing the inevitability of U.S. expansion. A viewer could find confirmation in this cartoon that Native Americans, held back by their primitive lifestyle, could not (and should not) compete with U.S. power. This reading was compatible with imperialist arguments; in the words of one writer of the period, the U.S. government had justifiably pacified Indians "in flagrant disregard of the principle of consent" because "the overmastering spirit of moral and material advancement, actuating the progressive nations of the globe, has found its justification for aggression in the ultimate enlightenment and betterment of those whom it has assumed to dominate." This strand of imperialist ideology deemed "barbarism, heathenism, ignorance and sloth" necessary casualties in order to uplift "lower" races.[15] With this view, these cartoons could be forecasting the triumph of the "higher" civilization, but at a heavy cost.

A rare example of a pro-imperialist cartoon that incorporated the Native American conquest reflects the tensions embedded in this iconographic argument. Artist Victor Gillam of *Judge* presented a two-page spread depicting an American Indian, "the last of a once powerful race," sending a telegraph message to a primitive Filipino (figure 6.3). "Speaking from experience," says the old Indian, "Be good, or you will be dead!" This ominous warning, coming from a worthy, but defeated, adversary, accentuates the belief that American civilization would prevail. Casting the Filipino comparatively as black-faced may have been an intentional jeer at the capability of the Filipinos to persevere against U.S. military might. Cultural attitudes often characterized the African American as more acquiescent than the Native American, who had at least resisted, though unsuccessfully.[16] Through the Indian's message, Gillam confirms the ascendancy of Anglo-Saxon expansion. At the same time, from one victim of U.S. aggression to another, the Indian's warning also highlights

6.3. Victor Gillam, "Speaking from Experience." *Judge* 36 (April 22, 1899): 248–49. Courtesy New York State Library, Manuscripts and Special Collections.

American dependence on violence in schemes of pacification, signified by the pile of dead Filipinos on the ground.

The deeply rooted associations between Native Americans and prolonged campaigns of resistance in American popular culture made it a problematic analogy for the imperial context of 1898–99. Some pro-imperialist editors invoked Wounded Knee, such as one who advised the U.S. government to "treat the Filipinos as we had to treat our Western Indians in their outbreaks a few years ago." After "a severe lesson," claimed an editorialist of the *Louisville Courier-Journal*, "they will quickly surrender."[17] Yet despite the widespread belief that Native American resistance had finally been stifled, not a single cartoonist presented American Indians as a symbol of successful incorporation. Their representation could not be disengaged from the history of their violent conquest, which, as Richard Slotkin has shown, was central to constructions of American national ideology and circulated broadly in Wild West shows, dime novels, and popular art.[18] In light of growing Philippine dissent, imperialist image makers turned to other racial motifs to represent the politics of empire, perhaps in a conscious attempt to avoid unwelcome associations with a protracted struggle of conquest and pacification.

Contingencies of Empire: The Shifting Image of Aguinaldo

Even though graphic artists most typically refrained from depicting Filipinos as "Indians," they nonetheless experimented with several permutations before settling into the pattern of caricaturing them as "Africanized" savages. These changes stemmed from the changing political circumstances surrounding U.S. interests in the Philippines. Prior to the declaration of war, Philippine resistance to Spanish colonization was merely a footnote, if that, to Cuba's story of oppression. After the war began in Manila Bay, many news editors hastened to educate their readers about the Philippines and the leader of its nationalist movement, Emilio Aguinaldo, a middle-class Filipino from Cavite of mixed Tagalog and Chinese ancestry. In 1898, Aguinaldo was the recognized head of the Katipunan, an organization dedicated to bringing independence to the Philippines after centuries of Spanish colonial rule. Inspired by the writings of José Rizal, Andrés Bonifacio launched this movement in 1892 after Spain failed to institute reform. Spanish authorities cracked down on Katipunan resistance in 1896, declaring martial law and executing some rebel leaders, including Rizal. By 1897 a growing divide between the factions of Bonifacio and Aguinaldo resulted in Aguinaldo's seizure of power within the organization, sealed by ordering Bonifacio's death. Still, Aguinaldo was unable to forestall further Spanish repression; he agreed in the Pact of Biak-na-Bato with Spain to surrender and go into exile in Hong Kong in exchange for a few reforms and a large cash payment. From abroad, Aguinaldo resumed his efforts to amass financial and military resources for revolution. After the United States declared war against Spain, American officials approached him to see if he would return to the Philippines to take up the fight. He agreed, claiming that he had been assured that independence would follow Spain's defeat. Dewey supplied him with arms upon his landing in Cavite on May 19, but Secretary Long of the navy urged Dewey to avoid making any "political alliances," a request with which Dewey said to have "complied." The misunderstandings, or perhaps manipulations, that emerged from these meetings laid the groundwork for later tensions.[19] At the outset, McKinley did not clarify his intentions in the Philippines to Aguinaldo or to his constituents at home, and this uncertainty underscores the instabilities of Aguinaldo's image in the American press.

On the basis of preliminary expectations that Aguinaldo welcomed U.S. involvement and would collaborate with the U.S. military, initial accounts in the American press lauded Aguinaldo's charisma, bravery, and leadership. Graphic artists presented him in Western clothing, neatly groomed, resolute, and often with "white," Westernized facial features. In July 1898 the *Rocky Mountain News,* which later advocated for taking the Philippines, published a front-page cartoon showing Aguinaldo relaxing with Uncle Sam in a bed labeled "Philippines" (figure 6.4). "Two's Company," reads the caption, as "Emperor William" of Germany and Spain (hiding under the bed) find themselves unwelcome. The cartoonist constructs Aguinaldo and Uncle Sam as allies, even if not on equal terms. Aguinaldo is rendered as a Caucasian male, smaller in stature but of the same facial construction and skin color as Uncle Sam. Other published portraits depicted Aguinaldo as a "brainy leader" worthy of directing the future of the Philippines (see figure 6.5, from the *Minneapolis Journal*). One caption described a heroic Aguinaldo as "young, handsome, brave as a lion, patriotic and self-sacrificing."[20] The *San Francisco Examiner,* which would also take a pro-imperialist stance, published a similar portrait with a caption that read, "The rebel chief has been complimented by the American Admiral for his bravery and excellent military qualities, and bids fair to be proclaimed the emancipator of his people."[21]

The image of Aguinaldo as an authoritative leader disappeared after reports were published of a ceremony held on July 12, 1898, in which he proclaimed the independence of the Philippine Republic and declared himself dictator. This sent a clear signal that he would not readily yield to U.S. directives. Still, U.S. interests in the Philippines were yet unclear, and it would be months before McKinley publicly announced his decision to take the Philippines as an American colony. His policy was not made explicit until the November peace talks, when he excluded the Filipino nationalists from participating and demanded that Spain relinquish all of its remaining colonies, including Cuba, Guam, Puerto Rico, and the Philippines, to the United States in exchange for a $20 million payment. In December 1898 McKinley proclaimed his intention to claim sovereignty over

"TWO'S COMPANY ———."

Uncle Sam—"Sorry, Willie, don't see how me and Aggy can make room for another'n."

6.4. Smith, "Two's Company." *Rocky Mountain News,* July 12, 1898, 1.

the entire archipelago and defined "the mission of the United States" as "one of benevolent assimilation, substituting the mild sway of justice and right for arbitrary rule."[22] Aguinaldo and his followers, not surprisingly, did not readily cooperate; as the Senate debated ratification of the peace treaty, tensions flared in the Philippines. On February 4, 1899, U.S. soldiers opened fire on Filipino troops. U.S. military and press accounts blamed the Filipinos for triggering the outbreak and began representing them as "rebels" or "insurrectionists" rather than "nationalists" or "revolutionaries." Two days later the Senate passed the peace treaty by a vote of 57 to 27, and the United States staked its claim to an overseas empire in the Eastern and Western hemispheres.

Visual constructions of Aguinaldo's physical appearance, from his skin color to his facial structure, underwent a transformation as U.S. imperial designs on the Philippines came to light. The graphic improvisation with his image exemplifies the fluidity of visual constructions of race and illustrates a conception of race as an effect or

GEN EMILIO AGUINALDO

The Brainy Leader of the Philippine Insurgents.

He is the president of the republic of the islands, the leader of the insurgents, the idol of the natives and the terror of the Spanish. He is the Antonio Maceo of Spain's Asiatic colonies. Young, handsome, brave as a lion, patriotic and self-sacrificing, this native Malay is the type of the insurrectionists who, like the Cubans, have fought the tyranny of Spain through blood and death and destruction until they now seem assured of victory. Aguinaldo was betrayed by the Spaniards with promises of reform which were never kept and promises of pardon which were made to be broken. He saw his brothers butchered and his country robbed and raked and combed into poverty by the enemy. On Dec. 14, Governor General Rivera made peace with Aguinaldo and betrayed him. The rebel chief left the islands to return with Commodore Dewey's victorious squadron and to again take his place at the head of the army of revolution, which was waiting for him. From Singapore to Hongkong, Aguinaldo traveled in disguise, and was assisted on his mission by Spencer Pratt, the American consul-general at Singapore. Aguinaldo will be a powerful help to the United States in the making of oriental history that will go on in the Philippines for some time in the near future. The daring Malay has pledged himself to maintain order, prevent massacre and in other ways assist the United States in putting things to rights in the Philippines.

6.5. "Gen. Emilio Aguinaldo." *Minneapolis Journal,* May 6, 1898, 6.

argument rather than a fixed biological or sociological category. The use of hand-drawn portraits as opposed to photographs facilitated this flexibility. To revise Aguinaldo's image from heroic revolutionary to degenerate rebel, some artists integrated stereotypical "Asian" features into his caricature. Thomas Nast, the famed cartoonist for *Harper's Weekly,* helped to establish the basis for this "Asian" portrait in American graphic art during the post–Civil War period. In September 1898, an advertisement for Work Bros. & Company wholesale clothing, for example, depicted Aguinaldo with slanted eyes and a mustache, adding hot pepper to his cauldron in a sinister attempt to "brew trouble" in the Philippines, just as the wholesalers imagined their "high-grade clothing" to "brew fame" with its customers (figure 6.6). Many advertisements of the period, as we have seen, borrowed themes from news reports to draw customers, regardless of their relevance to the products sold. In this advertisement as in other graphic depictions, cartoonists denigrated Aguinaldo's capacity for leadership by accentuating his part-Chinese ancestry and employing an "Asian" racial casting.[23] The usage of "Asian" caricature in depicting Filipinos likely stemmed from estimates of the growing Chinese and Japanese populations in the Philippines.[24] In this period, rampant cultural prejudice against Chinese and Japanese immigrants in the United States resulted in exclusionary labor practices and rigid immigration restrictions. Even so, as McKinley solidified his imperial position in the fall of 1898, graphic artists employed the "Asian" racial categorization much less frequently, opting more often to represent the Filipino as "Africanized." Why cartoonists preferred the "Africanized" image is not clear, but perhaps they found the "Asian" construction less adaptable or provocative than other racial types.[25]

By the time McKinley clarified his intent to take the Philippines, the "Africanized" image of the Filipino had become predominant in cartoon art across the country. An editorialist of the pro-imperialist *Los Angeles Times* called this racial transformation "the most absurd fake," arguing that "the natives of the Philippine Islands come from Malay-Chinese stock and bear no resemblance either in feature or in color of the skin to the native African."[26] Shortly after U.S. and Filipino troops first engaged in combat in early February 1899, cartoonist Fred Morgan of the pro-imperialist *Philadelphia Inquirer* rendered Aguinaldo in his most typical racialized expression, with black

6.6. "Aguinaldo Brews Trouble in the Philippines." *Chicago Tribune,* September 18, 1898, 13.

skin, large lips, hoop earrings, and kinked hair, demeaned as a black child in a diaper (figure 6.7). He wears bandages on his head bearing the names of the Filipino cities of Manila, Caloocan, and Iloilo, which U.S. troops had already pacified in the first two weeks of the campaigns. "Such a Headache!" reads the caption. "Yes! It all comes back to me now, too late! I distinctly 'Remember the *Maine.*'"

The cartoon is a composite medium, and its power to articulate its message lies in the balance between image and text. Imperialist cartoons like Morgan's not only represented the colonial subject visually but also used words to describe his feelings and actions. In this sense the violence of pro-imperialist cartoons went beyond the silencing of U.S. imperial subjects; rather they spoke for them, claiming their "inferior" perceptions, beliefs, and expectations. In this case Aguinaldo says he has learned the lesson of the Spanish-American War, that is, that opposing the United States only leads to defeat. This pattern of representing Aguinaldo as a black child became even more entrenched in pro-imperialist iconography with

SUCH A HEADACHE!
*Aguinaldo—Yes! It al comes back to me now, too late!
I distinctly "REMEMBER THE MAINE."*

6.7. Fred Morgan, "Such a Headache." *Philadelphia Inquirer,* February 16, 1899, 1.

the onset of U.S. occupation. For pro-imperialists, this racialized image confirmed the moral, political, and economic necessity of U.S. dominion over the islands.

From Seduction to Paternalism: Deploying the Parent-Child Analogy

After the war began in Manila Bay, press coverage in May–June 1898 initially sensationalized the sexual availability of Filipina women in order to awaken popular interest in the Philippines. "The native women of the Philippines are, as a rule, excessively pretty and engaging creatures, with supple figures accentuated by the thinness of their garments, beautiful, languishing eyes, shaded with long lashes, and luxuriant blue-black hair," declared the *Chicago Record* alongside a drawing of "A Manila Beauty" lounging in a hammock with her hair "loose" and "unbound," her dainty hands stroking her long bare legs.[27] The *Boston Globe* similarly claimed that "travelers" described Filipinas "as handsome, vigorous and intelligent, with large black eyes, clear olive complexions, perfect teeth, and satiny black hair."[28] Because U.S. intervention in the Philippines occurred unexpectedly and had already begun, there was no need for press accounts to frame the sexual objectification of the Filipina within a narrative of chivalric rescue, as they had in the case of Cuba. The Filipina merely appeared ripe for American sexual advances.

With the rise of the imperial debates toward the end of the war, however, the erotic images of the Cuban and the Filipina that had prevailed in the early war period disappeared because they tapped into contemporary preoccupations with preserving "Anglo-Saxon" racial purity in view of long-term possession. Using testimonial accounts of soldiers, reporters, and observers, postwar press reports delighted in shattering the "fantasy" of seduction with a new racialized "reality" of debased and unsightly womanhood. A *Chicago Record* reporter wrote that the troops aboard a transport ship to Cuba were prone to "fancy" dreaming of the "delicate oval faces" and "voluptuous grace" of Cuban women; but after they landed, their expectations were met with "disillusionment" at finding women of a "dingy yellow hue," "fat with an oily fatness," and smoking cigarettes as they nursed their "naked brown" babies. A similar reversal occurred in the case of the Philippines; the press published statements such as that of Dr. Frank H. Titus, surgeon of the Twentieth Kansas Volunteers, who told the *Cleveland Plain Dealer:* "The Tagalo woman is generally old and thin and brown and scrawny. She is amiable and friendly and all that, but she don't pretty worth a cent."[29]

The possibilities of indefinite territorial occupation complicated the romantic script by raising the disturbing question of longer-term racial amalgamation.[30] Image makers had initially shaped the scenario of seduction as a temporary military fling, not the beginning of a long-

ENGAGED.

—New York Evening Journal.

6.8. "Engaged." *Houston Post,* August 1, 1898, 3.

lasting relationship. The *Houston Post,* one of many newspapers that initially promoted McKinley's imperial agenda and then gradually retracted its support, manifested this emerging threat in the political cartoon "Engaged" (figure 6.8).[31] The figure of "Europe" interrupts Uncle Sam's courtship of a Filipina, racialized with black skin, kinked hair, and muscular appendages that hardly seem feminine. He sits at her side paralyzed with fear, particularly at the implication of marriage and procreation. This cartoon typifies the satirical feminization of European and Anglo-Saxon male characters, depicting a swaggering Europe whose helmet spouts a large plume (for another example, see figure 1.4). Even as these cartoons reinforced imperial ideologies, they also played on cultural anxieties about the "manliness" of Euro-

VOLUME XXXIV. NEW YORK, AUGUST 31, 1899. NUMBER 875.

Entered at the New York Post Office as Second-Class Mail Matter.
Copyright, 1899, by LIFE PUBLISHING COMPANY.

THREE YEARS AFTER.

CORPORAL O'TOOLE, AFTER LEAVING THE ARMY, DECIDED TO REMAIN IN THE PHILIPPINES.

6.9. William H. Walker, "Three Years After." *Life* 34 (August 31, 1899): 1.

American civilization, warning that the temptations of colonial sexuality held the power to weaken racial purity and virility.[32]

For critics of empire, "blackening" the female colonial type and heightening the threat of interracial sexual contact became a partisan tactic to deter acquisition. William H. Walker exemplified this visual argument in a cartoon titled "Three Years After: Corporal O'Toole, after Leaving the Army, Decided to Remain in the Philippines," published on the cover of *Life* magazine in August 1899 (figure 6.9).

Founded by John Ames Mitchell, a well-to-do Harvard graduate, *Life* offered its white middle- to upper-class readership a conservative and nativist social and political critique. Mitchell, who selected every illustration published in *Life* between 1883 and 1920, shaped a nostalgic vision of an English Protestant America prior to the immigrant invasion of Irish Catholics, Germans, and Jews. Walker represents *Life*'s worldview and the white Anglo-Saxon critique of the imperial project by sending an Irishman to do the work of civilization.[33] He pictures an Irish American soldier who has "gone native," whose unseemly sexual union with a racialized and primitive Filipina has produced a baboon-like child of mixed race.

Because of the complicated sexual politics of empire, pro-imperialist artists largely discontinued representing the colonial dependent in adult female form and instead revived the native-as-child image already familiar in the colonial vernacular of European imperialism.[34] Denoting political immaturity, the "child" image confirmed the up-and-coming geopolitical role of the United States as protector of the developing nations of Latin America and the Philippines in the American cultural imagination. The childlike image also reinforced the deference and gratitude expected of America's new subjects, now freed from Spanish oppression. By imagining them as children, image makers maintained the hierarchy of power that justified imperial dominance while emphasizing the bonds developing between the United States and its new dependents. The image of the native-as-child rationalized denying the colonial subject the rights of full-fledged citizenship while also implying that the colonies would someday grow to adulthood, an implication that complemented McKinley's stated aim of preparing them for self-government. Complicating these intended meanings, however, was the common practice of picturing the child as black, which pitted theories of scientific racism and assumptions of the colonies' inherent inferiority against expectations of eventual maturity.

The metaphor of imperial rule as parental discipline was more than a graphic symbol; it became a widely shared political and military strategy. Admiral George Dewey advised policymakers in January 1899 that the Filipino natives "should be treated kindly, exactly as you would treat children, for they are little else, and should be coerced only after gentler means of bringing them to reason have failed."[35]

The child image encapsulated a view of the colonies as politically immature, deficient in education and religion, economically under-privileged, and militarily insignificant. The image helped rationalize McKinley's proclaimed policy of "benevolent assimilation" in the Philippines and his project of political and social restructuring.

One might expect to see representations of America's maternal icon, Columbia, comforting America's new colonial dependents. Deployment of an imperial "mother" figure was not unprecedented, for British cartoonists during the Revolutionary War most often pic-tured the female Britannia, as opposed to John Bull, as parent of the American colonies.[36] In the imperial aftermath of the Spanish-American War, however, cartoonists almost exclusively assigned Uncle Sam the role of colonial caregiver, pioneering an alternative vision of him as benevolent, nurturing, and paternal. He was often portrayed holding or soothing a crying baby, rocking a baby to sleep, caring for a sick infant, teaching a child, or meting out discipline.[37] Representing imperialism as a paternal responsibility thus retained empire within the realm of manly authority. In the pro-imperialist *Boston Globe,* a front-page cartoon in late July 1898 depicted Uncle Sam looking fondly upon a contented white baby (labeled the Philippines) bundled in his arms. The caption reads: "Left on His Hands! What Will He Do With It?" A follow-up cartoon a few days later depicted an exas-perated Uncle Sam in his bedclothes fruitlessly trying to soothe that screaming Filipino baby in the late-night hours.[38] The bittersweet joys of parenting, with its rewards and sacrifices, became symbolic of imperial duty.

The parenting analogy enabled imperialist cartoonists to set the expectation that managing colonial subjects can be arduous work. Correlating the tensions of colonial pacification to the difficulties of parenthood rationalized ongoing military efforts to subdue unrest by making the point that the frustrations of child rearing never war-rant abandonment. Uncle Sam therefore often appeared uncomfort-able and overwrought as he fulfilled his fatherly responsibilities in many cartoons. The pro-imperialist *Boston Herald,* for example, pictured Uncle Sam holding two crying black babies (Cuba and the Philippines) while another ("Porto Rico") throws a tantrum on the floor (figure 6.10). Uncle Sam grumbles, "Who Said Peace with These Two Kickers." Despite holding the babies awkwardly away

"WHO SAID PEACE WITH THESE TWO KICKERS."

6.10. Lee, "Who Said Peace with These Two Kickers." *Boston Herald,* August 8, 1898, 8.

from his body and seeming hassled by their outbursts, he nonetheless rises to the challenge. Similarly, just after the fighting began in the Philippines, a *Minneapolis Journal* cartoon pictured Uncle Sam trying to soothe two hysterical Filipino babies while claiming, "This isn't exactly pleasant, but these children have got to be brought up right and I'm not backing out on the job."[39]

Along the same lines, pro-imperialist cartoons often depicted Uncle

Sam spanking the native-as-child, usually Aguinaldo, to demonstrate that a certain degree of force can be constructive when implemented in the context of good parenting.[40] After Aguinaldo's diplomatic representative Felipe Agoncillo threatened in February 1899 that resistance would not abate until the United States yielded, Fred Morgan of the pro-imperialist *Philadelphia Inquirer* graphically depicted Uncle Sam's response: smacking the rear end of an anguished black Aguinaldo, who is wearing only a diaper. "Say When," Uncle Sam responds firmly to his child's defiance.[41] The prevalence of the spanking motif became another means for image makers to frame colonial resistance as a parent-child power struggle and reduce Aguinaldo's leadership to a juvenile tantrum.

Picturing the native-as-child required a departure from depictions of other recognizable child types in American popular culture. The selection of certain images, such as the pickaninny, and the suppression of others, such as the hard-bitten street Arab, reflects a collective stylization of the child symbol to substantiate imperial ideologies. The native-as-child, for instance, had nothing in common with the familiar street-savvy, independent-minded urban child of the slums circulating in fiction, popular prints, photography, and the literature of reform. Late-nineteenth-century reformer Jacob Riis documented the street Arab type in photographs and described him as "bright and sharp as the weasel." Though noting the street Arabs' penchant for petty crime, Riis also acknowledged their "rude sense of justice" and claimed "the great mass, with this start given them, become useful citizens."[42] Likewise, in novels such as *Ragged Dick* and *Adrift in New York,* Horatio Alger populated the juvenile underworld of the streets with heroic and spirited young boys (and girls) who were ultimately good-hearted, despite their grimy fists and rough exteriors. Conventionally, popular culture envisioned these children as white, though often from the lower or immigrant classes, and recognized their sharp wit, moral virtue, and acute survival instincts, but these traits were not typically ascribed to "inferior" races.

Instead, cartoonists represented colonial subjects through the classic character of the pickaninny, the child minstrel "darky," known for uncontrollable whims of frivolity and mischievousness. On the cover of *Judge* on February 11, 1899, Victor Gillam depicts Aguinaldo as "Our New Topsy" (figure 6.11). She says, "I's so awful wicked there cain't nobody do nothin' with me. I keeps Miss Feeley [Uncle Sam] a-swearin' at me half de time, 'cause I's mighty wicked, I is." The illustrated weekly *Judge* supported McKinley's agenda; in fact, *Judge's* art director and fellow cartoonist, Grant Hamilton, had been a friend of McKinley's since boyhood.[43] Imagining the colonial subject as "Topsy" helped to rationalize McKinley's policy of "benevolent assimilation." Making reference to Harriet Beecher Stowe's *Uncle Tom's Cabin,* the cartoon directly tied into ideologies of abolitionism and slavery. Relocating "Topsy" within the imperial context at first seems an ideal choice, given that the trajectory of her character in the novel legitimates the progressive intentions of colonial rule. From an unmanageable child, she becomes a genteel Christian dedicated to the Christianization of Africa. Appropriating "Topsy" in imperial graphic art stopped short, however, with the image of the naughty pickaninny lacking female graces and self-control. Depicting Aguinaldo as "Topsy" prior to uplift diminished his grievances to a fit of female hysterics and justified harsh disciplinary action. Image makers had no use for a mature, assimilated "Topsy." The prospect of adulthood, with its connotations of maturity and readiness for self-government, required a sensibility that was inherently redeemable and respectable. Popular representations affirmed that the self-reliant street urchin possessed the necessary qualities to develop into an independent, reliable citizen, but not the impish pickaninny. Declared the pro-imperialist *Philadelphia Inquirer,* "The Filipinos are like children who need to be ruled with a firm hand, and if there are any who entertain the idea that they will sooner or later acquire the ability to stand alone they had better dismiss that illusion."[44]

Although cartoonists often homogenized representations of the peoples of Cuba, the Philippines, Puerto Rico, and Hawaii into the child type, they also used racial and gender stereotyping to differentiate them. These variations reflected perceptions not only of the colonies but also *among* them, to denote expectations of their competence for self-rule, their cultural or racial foreignness, and their degree of resistance.[45] As a general rule, pro-imperialist artists coded obedient subjects "white" and disobedient ones "black."[46] In August 1898 Boz, the cartoonist of the *Boston Globe,* depicted the new colonies (of "Porto Rico," Hawaii, Cuba, the Philippines, and the Ladrones) as "white" youngsters under Uncle Sam's tutelage, ready to learn in an

OUR NEW TOPSY.

Topsy (Aguinaldo)—"I's so awful wicked there cain't nobody do nothin' with me. I keeps Miss Feeley (Uncle Sam) a-swearin' at me half de time, 'cause I's mighty wicked, I is."

— *Uncle Tom's Cabin.*

6.11. Victor Gillam, "Our New Topsy." *Judge* 36 (February 11, 1899): 81.

UNCLE SAM'S KINDERGARTEN FOR THE PROPAGATION OF LIBERTY.

6.12. Boz, "Uncle Sam's Kindergarten for the Propagation of Liberty." *Boston Globe,* August 23, 1898, 1.

American kindergarten (figure 6.12). Boz surrounds them with images of U.S. power: the eagle in flight and a globe picturing America's new sphere of influence, the Western Hemisphere. He was careful to use "whiteness" to suggest the capacity for obedience, not racial equality; although their skin color is white, their facial features and hairstyles remain of the "African" type. Especially after the Philippine war began, artists most often differentiated Puerto Ricans, Hawaiians, or Cubans as "white" subjects from "black" Filipinos. In a period when American intellectual and popular thought was busy disaggregating humankind into a hierarchy of races, image makers ultimately grafted colonial subjects onto that hierarchy according to their degree of resistance to U.S. imperial objectives.

Imperial and Popular Culture Merge: The Making of the Filipino Savage

In spite of the geographic and cultural diversity of the Philippines, by early 1899 the principal image of the "Filipino" in American cartoon art was as a primitive "Africanized" savage. The Philippine archipelago contains over seven thousand islands and spans more than 500,000 square miles. McKinley initially sought only Luzon, the largest of the islands and home of the capital city, Manila, but later ordered U.S. peace commissioners to demand the other island groups as well: the Visayans, Mindanao Island, and the Sulu archipelago. These islands varied widely in terrain, and their inhabitants spoke different languages. Internal division within the Philippine independence movement was in part due to political, military, and cultural differences among island groups.[47] Particularly in the immediate postwar period, editorialists and cartoonists of the American press paid little attention to the complexity of colonial populations, if they were even aware of it at all.

The "Africanization" of the Filipino turned the imperial project into an extension of domestic conversations about race relations. "Can We Govern New Colonies?" asked the pro-imperialist *Chicago Times-Herald*. To justify taking control of nonwhite foreign subjects, the editorialist answered, "Having abolished slavery we have admitted the negro to full privileges of American citizenship," adding that "the condition of the black race, measured by its possession of property and its approach to industrial independence" was "far better than twenty-five years ago."[48]

Anticolonialists, by contrast, pointed to the ever present racial instability of American society to forestall incorporating additional "inferior" peoples. The *New York Evening Post* urged, "When the United States ask us to support them in taking charge of 10,000,000 or 12,000,000 of people, mainly ignorant colored barbarians, we, if prudent men, ask at once: How did you succeed with the last colored barbarians you had charge of?"[49] In one of C. G. Bush's cartoons in the *New York World,* McKinley ponders annexation as he studies a map of the Philippines (figure 6.13). The process of mapping in itself was a visual exercise in defining the boundaries of power. McKinley claimed publicly that his decision to take the Philippines had been inspired by divine guidance while praying late one night. Upon waking the next morning, he said, he immediately called to ask the War Department to prepare him a new U.S. map that included the Philippines, an act to codify his new vision of national territorial growth. In Bush's anticolonialist cartoon, McKinley examines

"CIVILIZATION BEGINS AT HOME."

6.13. Charles G. Bush, "Civilization Begins at Home." *New York World,* November 14, 1898, 4.

this map as Lady Justice counsels him that "civilization begins at home," drawing back the curtain on a scene of America's racist terrorism. Bush reminds viewers that with the prevalence of racial violence around the country, the nation needed to attend to its own race problem before acquiring a new one.

One backdrop to the imperial debates was the race riots that broke out in Wilmington, North Carolina, in November 1898 in a bid to retake political power from the Republicans. A group of angry white citizens demanded the closure of a local African American newspaper, prompting a riot that left eight African Americans dead and many wounded. Alluding to the violence in Wilmington, the anticolonialist *St. Louis Post-Dispatch* insisted: "One race question at a time is quite enough. To multiply it by indiscriminate and whole-sale annexation of inferior peoples is not calculated to make political problems any easier to deal with."[50] The timing of the riots, which revealed ongoing domestic racial tensions just as the peace process was beginning in Paris, allowed editorialists to marshal the imperial question to debate domestic issues such as race relations, class conflict, and immigration in coded form.

Racial representation became the primary pictorial strategy for arguing the merits and drawbacks of imperialism. Imperialist cartoonists sentimentalized images of colonial subjects as inferior but impressionable savages and/or children in need of uplift. If Spanish oppression had compelled the United States into war, imperialists argued, then adopting Spain's former wards and offering them the chance to assimilate and prosper under a "benevolent" guardian was a moral necessity in line with the war's noble purpose. Otherwise, they claimed, the colonies would fall prey to barbaric or corrupt native rulers, or more likely the foreign aggression of Germany or Japan.

Anticolonialists were in a more difficult position in the debate, having to counter the wave of patriotic and militaristic sentiments propelling postwar imperialist desires. Although they did not embrace the shift from liberation to conquest, their views did not neccessarily stem from a position of liberal racial thought. As Christopher Lasch has argued, the anticolonialists utilized arguments just as racist as the imperialists', if not more so.[51] In opposition to the peace treaty, Senator George Vest, a Democrat from Missouri, backed by Senators George Frisbie Hoar (Republican of Massachusetts) and Benjamin Tillman (Democrat of South Carolina), offered a resolution that declared it unconstitutional for the U.S. government to acquire territory without the intent of conferring eventual statehood. Because most anticolonialists held the same racial views of the colonies as those arguing for acquisition, this effort was intended to deter the taking of colonies in order to avoid the extension of statehood to "inferior" peoples broadly deemed unworthy of U.S. citizenship.

Anticolonialists' visual representations of colonial subjects as sub-human, leprous degenerates placed them on the defensive, for if the racial inferiority of the natives made them unfit to govern themselves, who would take on the moral responsibility to lead and protect them?

Anticolonialists thus undercut their own mobilizing power by focusing on protecting U.S. interests from an external racialized threat,
whereas imperialists skillfully claimed the moral high ground with
their willingness to accept the burdens of occupation while at the same
time reaping the gains. Had the anticolonialists chosen to represent
the colonies as capable of self-government, they could have drawn
from the rallying power of Cuba Libre to argue that the only honorable course was independence. The anticolonialist *Boston Transcript*
recognized the political opportunism in the tactic of blackening the
Cuban image: "The American caricaturist appears to enjoy a peculiar pleasure in representing the Cuban as a negro dwarf, wearing an
old hat and a pair of sandals, and not much of anything else. . . . Now
as a matter of fact the Cubans of white blood outnumber the colored
islanders two to one."[52] The *Transcript*'s attempt to place Cubans on
the white side of the color line was submerged, however, in a sea of
racist anticolonialist images. The failure of the anticolonialist opposition was in part a visual one. Anticolonialist artists were trapped by
their own racialized vision, because visualizing a morally acceptable
alternative to acquisition would have required imagining colonial
subjects as self-governing citizens.

Because a shared racial vision blurred political positions in these
debates, political cartoons relied on captions and editorial commentary to make their politics on empire known. Both sides of the debate
had a stake in portraying the native as dark-skinned and primitive;
to imperialists, blackness signaled inferiority and justified uplift and
guidance. For anticolonialists, the exotic native served as visual shorthand for the cultural, racial, and political perils of empire. In the anticolonialist *Life* magazine in April 1899, cartoonist William H. Walker
depicts the native in a state of primitive racial and cultural development (figure 6.14). The sarcastic caption derides the native figure: "A
being who will shoot arrows at a rapid fire gun will make an intelligent
citizen." Walker mobilizes the Africanized savage type to distinguish
a "subject" from a "citizen" by representing the deficiencies he would
bring if absorbed into American society. He is skinny and apelike, has
big lips and earrings, and wears only a loincloth. Rather than standing next to Uncle Sam on equal footing, he is significantly shorter
than Uncle Sam, who reaches out to pet him like an animal. On the
cover of *Judge* in March 1899, Victor Gillam advocates for U.S. impe-

U. S.: A BEING WHO WILL SHOOT ARROWS AT A RAPID FIRE GUN WILL MAKE AN INTELLIGENT CITIZEN.

6.14. William H. Walker, "A Being Who Will Shoot Arrows at a Rapid Fire Gun Will Make an Intelligent Citizen." *Life* 33 (April 20, 1899): 337.

rialism with a similar racialized depiction of the primitive Filipino, helplessly backed against a rock with Uncle Sam's bayonet pointed at him (figure 6.15). Attached to this weapon is a proclamation of "Liberty and Civilization." Gillam notes, "He wouldn't take it any other way." Here Gillam employs the same reasoning as the parental spanking analogy; he justifies using force to bestow the blessings of lib-

VOL. 36 NO. 907   MARCH 4 1899.   PRICE 10 CENTS

ENTERED AT THE POST OFFICE AT NEW YORK AS SECOND CLASS MATTER, COPYRIGHT 1899   BY ARKELL PUBLISHING COMPANY. TITLE REGISTERED AS A TRADE MARK

HE WOULDN'T TAKE IT ANY OTHER WAY.

6.15. Victor Gillam, "He Wouldn't Take It Any Other Way." *Judge* 36 (March 4, 1899):
129. Courtesy New York State Library, Manuscripts and Special Collections.

erty and civilization on the colonies. The Filipino's appearance affirms the necessity of U.S. intervention on his behalf, even if he does not realize it. While offering opposing viewpoints, Walker and Gillam's colonial depictions contained only subtle degrees of visual difference. This placed the burden of argument on the surrounding text to help the viewer parse an imperialist versus an anticolonialist message. At a quick glance, viewers who did not stop to consider the text could easily project their own meanings into these cartoons, finding confirmation for or against U.S. imperial policies.

Pro- and anticolonialist representations inscribed new meanings onto existing racial and ethnic types, resulting in the pictorial fusion of ideologies of race and empire applied domestically and overseas. Image makers started with identifiable stereotypical types that had appeared in cartoons and comic strips and on the minstrel stage for decades and gave them a distinctly imperial flavor. In newspapers across the nation, there was a proliferation of political cartoons picturing U.S. imperial subjects in characteristic blackface, with white lips, gleaming teeth, and kinked hair along with added signifiers of colonial primitivism, including loincloths, big hoop earrings, bones through their nose and ears, and bow and arrow accessories.[53] The pro-imperialist *Boston Globe* illustrates the Filipino as this racial-imperial type "before" and "after" imperial expansion (figure 6.16). In a two-act production, the Filipino begins as a dark-skinned primitive and is transformed into the principal minstrel type of Zip Coon, the northern urban dandy, with top hat, cane, suit, ruffled shirt, and grinning expression. "From the war dance to the cake walk is but a step," reads the final caption. Not only does he partake in American cultural activities such as baseball and football, but also he has learned the "cakewalk," a dance invented by African Americans and widely popular on the minstrel stage. He is the exemplar of a candidate for uplift; as the cartoon demonstrates, "he could exchange the war club for the baseball bat readily."

Not only did minstrelsy inspire how cartoon depictions envisioned the new colonies, but also, in return, these representations were integrated into minstrel shows. In the late nineteenth century, minstrelsy itself was changing as pieces of it spun off into vaudeville, black theater, and plantation shows. Part of minstrelsy's formula for success was its adaptability and manipulation of the latest events to maintain

6.16. Boz, "Expansion, Before and After." *Boston Globe Magazine of Humor and Stories,* March 5, 1899, 1.

currency.[54] Minstrel theater productions in the fall and winter of 1898 incorporated imperial themes into their music, dance, and comedy, such as the musical number "Life in the Philippine Islands," performed by the traveling Dumont Minstrels, which "met with a rousing reception," or the closing burlesque that the Big Sensation Burlesquers performed in many cities, titled "Who Owns the Philippines?"[55] In December 1898, moreover, a group of fraternity brothers performed in blackface a skit they called "Congressman from Cuba, Porto Rico, and the Philippines" at the University of Vermont's Kake Walk campus event.[56] Performers of "Filipino" roles reproduced the visual conventions of graphic art by blacking up and/or appearing as children. A Boston minstrel show in April 1899 ended with a tableau of three little children, representing Cuba, Puerto Rico, and the Philippines, sitting at the feet of Lady Liberty.[57] Serving to entertain, not politically mobilize, none of these shows made its stance on U.S. imperialism explicit, but these performances encouraged audiences to laugh at and think themselves superior to dark-skinned colonial peoples, a frame of mind mobilized by both sides of the debate.

In addition to drawing on conventions of minstrelsy, cartoonists borrowed conventions from popular comic strips to create images and scenarios for "native" characters. The comic strip was still in its infancy when the United States acquired Spain's empire, but in its short history it thrived on the use of racial and ethnic caricature. Black images in the comics initially appeared in British, German, and French humor magazines, and in the 1880s and 1890s a few American artists brought black comic strip characters from illustrated humor magazines into the mainstream press. The *New York World*'s Richard Outcault in 1895 introduced a "tough black boy" character that fit the "buck" stereotype of the strong, defiant, and wayward black youth in his series "Here's the New Bully." Also in the *World,* Rudolph Dirks created in 1897 the long-running series "The Katzenjammer Kids," set in Africa and depicting African characters as cannibalistic, lazy, and dimwitted.[58] Although comic strips had not yet spoken directly to political issues prior to the war with Spain, the novelty of the graphic medium made it a compelling frame of reference for artists seeking a visual racial scheme to represent the colonies in the imperial debates. In turn the proliferation of racial caricature in graphic commentaries on imperialism spurred the rise of the comic arts more generally.

Some newspapers, like the pro-imperialist *Boston Herald,* created imperialist cartoon serials that integrated the comic strip form into freestanding political cartoons. The first of these series in the *Herald,* titled "Society in Our New Possessions," was published in December 1898. Akin to Thomas Worth's "Darktown" comic series of the 1880s and 1890s which lampooned African American life, they featured burlesque views of the same colonial characters dabbling like inept buffoons in the everyday activities of American cultural and political life.[59] The central actors conform to the recognizable minstrel type of the "plantation darky," struggling to comprehend the ways of urban culture. In one instance the subjects attempt to play golf (figure 6.17). In their tattered overalls, golf hats, and checkered socks, they appear as misfits on the golf course, bewildered about what to do with their clubs. Despite the episodic quality of the serials, which enabled viewers to see the same characters in multiple installments, there is no sense of cultural or moral progression over time. The message is always the same; while "they" can pretend to be like "us," they remain permanently fixed in a state of comical absurdity.

GOLF.

6.17. Gardner, "Society in Our New Possessions, No. 7." *Boston Herald,* December 10, 1898, 3.

Pro-imperialists also borrowed the "coon" image from popular comic strips and minstrel shows as a means of deriding the Filipinos' quest for independence. Pro-imperialists utilized the symbol to mock the Filipino nationalists' flag of independence, first formally displayed when Aguinaldo proclaimed independence for the Philippines on June 12, 1898. The actual flag, which consisted of red, white, and blue divisions with a yellow insignia of sun and stars, rarely appeared in U.S. media accounts. American artists designed their own version, which circulated so widely in the postwar period that many viewers may have presumed it to be the genuine article.[60] In February 1899 a *New York Herald* cartoon denigrates Aguinaldo, holding this lampooned flag, as the traditional coon stereotype (figure 6.18). The flag, which mirrors his caricatured facial expression, reduces the cause of Filipino nationhood to a foolish quest for dictatorship. It signals the end of his reign, with his flag, crown, and cause in tatters. It was not

"ALL COONS LOOK ALIKE TO ME!"

6.18. "All Coons Look Alike to Me." *New York Herald,* February 9, 1899, 4.

coincidental that this cartoon first appeared in New York, the seat of black musical theater in this period. The caption, "All Coons Look Alike to Me," refers to a popular "coon" song in the late 1890s of the same title, written by African American composer Ernest Hogan for the New York stage.[61]

Moreover, imperialist representations played on the racial classification of colonial subjects in ways that would have been familiar to patrons of popular museum exhibits. "The most famous freak of its era," claims a P. T. Barnum biography, was the "What Is It?" exhibit at Barnum's American Museum.[62] The African American performer William Henry Johnson, also known as "Zip," was one of several actors to play this role. With his cone-shaped head, big grin, and crooked physique, Johnson captivated audiences as the "missing link" of evolution between gorilla and man, entreating the spectator to determine if he was in fact man or animal. The exhibit opened during the election of 1860 and continued until Johnson's death in 1926, making it well known to audiences at the turn of the century.[63] Representing the first of many exhibits depicting African Americans as animalistic, the "What Is It?" image circulated widely in guidebooks, photographs, and lithographs and brought questions of scientific authority and evolutionary development to bear on racial classification and social order.[64]

To justify U.S. guardianship in the colonies, pro-imperialist editorialists and illustrators applied the same fundamental question raised by these exhibits to the colonial context: Were the Filipinos human or animal? The *Louisville Courier-Journal* described Filipinos as belonging "to a race that is considered the most apelike on earth," adding that "they are savages, eating raw meat cut from the animals they kill with their poisoned arrows and living a semi-simious life in the densest forest." The *Philadelphia Inquirer* similarly compared the skull of an "every-day Malay seen in Manila" with the skulls of apes and gorillas. Applying popular theories of scientific racism and eugenics to colonial visions, the *Inquirer* attempted to persuade viewers that the cranial-facial angles, particularly the inclined jaw and the convex bones in the nose, demonstrated that "some of our new citizens in the Philippines may be genuine missing links."[65]

Pro-imperialist artists further exploited popular fascination with cannibalism, witchcraft, idol worship, and devil dances to legitimate the white supremacist assumptions of imperial rule. A portrait of a Filipino "witch" in the pro-imperialist *Philadelphia Inquirer* accompanied this statement: "With the acquisition of Manila and the extensive Philippine Islands Uncle Sam acquires a people who are given over to some of the most hideous practices the mind can imagine." The *New York Journal* published images of Filipinos' "barbarous pagan ceremonies," including witch killing orgies and human sacrifices. The *Richmond Times* printed illustrations of Philippine idols and weapons along with salacious descriptions of primitive torture methods.[66] Images of gruesome killings, orgies, war dances, and cannibalism validated the need for U.S. guardianship to end colonial backwardness, violence, and superstitious behaviors while also tantalizing readers with sensationalistic visions of the macabre and exotic.

In comparison, caricaturing the natives as animalistic enabled anticolonialist artists to magnify the disastrous consequences of imperial incorporation on American politics, race, and culture. This argument was exemplified on the cover of the anticolonialist *St. Louis Post Dispatch Comic Weekly,* as the artist presents "A Glimpse into the Halls of Congress a Few Years Hence (If We Go On Annexing Islands)." The cartoon depicts Congress swarming with baboon-like, demonic-looking characters with simian expressions and curling tails (figure 6.19). The ape-like "Speeker," the "Honorable Representative from the Ladrones," wears big hoop earrings as he presides over a crowd of menacing legislators eager to "abolish work" and investigate cannibalism. The discipline of the House has deteriorated into a chaotic circus. Cartoons such as this one that characterized the inclusion of racialized subjects as a threat to American democracy were reminiscent of parodies of black legislators during Reconstruction. They also echoed one of Barnum's well-known exhibits in the late nineteenth century, the "Ethnological Congress of Savage and Barbarous Tribes," which presented a "human menagerie" of what Barnum billed as "100 Uncivilized, Superstitious and Savage People" from around the world.[67]

Postwar image makers did more than reproduce popular conventions of theatrical and graphic expression; they constructed the work of colonization as popular amusement. To maintain the titillation of empire without the narrative of seduction, pro-imperialist cartoonists recalibrated the appeal of the colonies from sexual object to freak attraction. The pro-imperialist *Boston Herald* published a cartoon in December 1898 playing on the success of imperial-themed circus attractions, advertising the "monstrous aggregation" named "Phillipina" sitting on a box of U.S. Army hardtack as well as other racialized "tropical beauties" (figure 6.20). The cartoon amplifies the allure of colonial exoticism by turning "Phillipina" into a grotesque spectacle, with her black skin, hulking feet, big white lips, kinked

6.19. "A Glimpse into the Halls of Congress a Few Years Hence." *St. Louis Post Dispatch,* Sunday Comic Weekly, September 18, 1898, 1.

hair, and large mannish body. "You Can't *Luz On* Me," reads her fan (a play on the largest of the Philippine islands, Luzon). In another *Herald* cartoon published two months later, titled "The Great and Only Aguinaldo," the artist again reduces the Philippine nationalist struggle to a circus sideshow. Aguinaldo appears onstage as a human curiosity next to the fat lady, allowing spectators to gaze upon him as they would any other freak, with astonishment and revulsion.[68] Objectifying Filipinos as objects of amusement reflects the commercialization of empire as popular spectacle, and indeed, Wild West

6.20. Robbins, "Phillipina." *Boston Herald,* December 4, 1898, 35.

shows, world's fair attractions, circus acts, vaudeville and minstrel skits capitalized on exotic displays of U.S. imperial subjects as an audience draw.

The making and remaking of colonial peoples in the cultural productions surrounding the imperial debates helped forge expectations of U.S. racial, cultural, and military ascendancy. According to a *Boston Globe* editorialist in July 1898:

> The unbounded ramifications of this war continue to amaze all who innocently limited the conflict in the beginning to a campaign in Cuba, only 100 miles from our shores. As a means of introducing the American public to strange peoples and obscure places it outruns every expectation and is far superior even to a stroll along the midway plaisance. But a newspaper reader is helpless unless he has a map of the world and an ethnological history constantly before him while perusing his daily paper. One day we are led through the dark chaparral of Santiago province and the next

goaded over the mountains of Porto Rico, while swimming before
our eyes intermittently are those heretofore unheard of specks on
the western ocean, the Ladrones, the Carolines, the Sulus, and like
a barbaric pageant in a spectacular melodrama the various tribes
of the Philippine Islands, the Tagalogs, the Visayas and the Moros,
wind about in an unending and bewildering procession.[69]

This editorialist describes the popular "amazement" at the imperial
turn of the war, which came as a shock to a nation that had "inno-
cently" supported war for the purpose of freeing Cuba. As U.S. foreign policy branched outward to Hawaii, Puerto Rico, Guam, and
the Philippines, cartoonists paraded images of primitive and exotic
peoples before their viewers, a "barbaric pageant in a spectacular
melodrama," as the *Globe* put it. Merging popular visual conceptions of "domestic" and "foreign" stereotypes helped to integrate
imperial ways of thinking and seeing into everyday cultural life. The
press and the popular stage extended the midway plaisance of the
world's fair, which had the effect of reinforcing domestic social tax-
onomies, validating the legitimacy of popular theories of scientific
racism, Social Darwinism, and eugenics, and substantiating the need
for exclusionary policies at home.

The prevalence of racial imagery on both sides of the imperial
debate demonstrates that racial thinking was central to justifying
the changing purpose of the war. It explains, as historian Paul T.
McCartney puts it, how "Americans could act as conquerors while
believing themselves to be liberators."[70] Just as the circulation of
derogatory racial representations supported the domestic politics of
exclusion, these images also shaped the moral belief that granting
independence to Spain's former colonies was neither feasible nor
responsible. In short, these images helped construct the belief that
the necessity for imperial expansion was self-evident when in actuality it was a strategic direction that brought substantial political and
economic gains for the United States.

Even without record of the professed intentions of graphic artists,
the range of available images in the cultural repertoire and their
revealing selections bring to light the efforts of artists to shape a
collective visual vocabulary of empire. Cartoonists of the Gilded Age

THE WHITE MAN'S BURDEN.—*The Journal, Detroit.*

6.21. "The White Man's Burden." *Literary Digest* 18 (February 18, 1899): 180.

often took shots at opposing political factions by reducing them to bratty and ungrateful children. But pro-imperialist cartoonists refrained from using this infantilized image to caricature anticolonialist agitators, instead reserving it for the colonies. They emasculated the "anti" colonialists by depicting them in the form of a crotchety old "Auntie" whose shameless indulgence of her newfound nieces and nephews, they alleged, accounted for the persistence of colonial unrest.[71] It then became the "white man's burden" (a phrase Rudyard Kipling's poem made famous in reaction to U.S. involvement in the Philippines) not only to carry the dark-skinned colonial savage up the slope of progress and over the corpses of American soldiers to the schoolhouse, but also to bear the weight of his irksome "Auntie" on his back (see figures 6.21 and 6.22). In this way, America's leading cartoonists constituted a white "Anglo-Saxon" male figure of empire and subordinated his counterparts through visual gradations of age, gender, and color.

Cartoonists settled into these patterns of representation by the spring and summer of 1899. By then, imperial themes in American graphic art had sharply decreased, even as fighting in the Philippines

THE WHITE MAN'S BURDEN.

6.22. "The White Man's Burden." *New York Herald,* February 11, 1899, 6.

escalated. The dramatic appeal of the spectacle was in the story of emerging victorious and stripping Spain of its empire, despite the controversies. The long, arduous task of occupation, with its high casualties and extensive financial and military commitments, proved much less interesting.

7

The Spectacular Wrap-Up in Three Postwar Moments

> The idea of imperialism as a national experience and condition is new to the American people. Probably the charm of novelty is one reason so many are attracted by it. It has a sonorous sound. It suggests purple and gold, pomp and spectacle. It promises collective distinction. . . . It carries with it a vague association of largeness and power. Still it is wise to seek all the light on the matter we can find before taking the final plunge, darkness not being particularly favorable to such ventures.
>
> *Boston Evening Transcript,* September 29, 1898

After Filipino nationalist leader Emilio Aguinaldo was captured in 1901, the U.S. military held him prisoner in Manila. In 1902 American photographer William Dinwiddie for the *New York World* visited him during his captivity and was struck by the "quiet dignity" and "calm, judicial air" of the man. Dinwiddie recalled Aguinaldo's transformation in the eyes of Americans from "a man blazoned as a hero one day and ridiculed into the mire the next." For Dinwiddie, the explanation for his descent lay not in his politics but in his face. He marveled at the strength of Aguinaldo's facial features—his "high and straight" forehead, straight nose, and heavy, square jaw—which he concluded were "far stronger than those of the average representative of his race." He photographed Aguinaldo alongside his American guard, a Lieutenant Johnson, to illustrate their "general similarity of head." But he was particular to note Aguinaldo's short stature, broad nostrils, and full lips and the Chinese cast of his slanted eyebrows. Dinwiddie's descriptive blend of presumed

Anglo, African, and Asian physical characteristics provided a basis
to explain the contradiction between Aguinaldo's stunning rise to
leadership, which Dinwiddie could not help but admire, and the
"indelible mark of failure upon his brow." In drawing this complex
racial portrait of the Philippine leader, Dinwiddie rationalized the
shift in American policy from liberation to conquest, acknowledging his "truly aristocratic" demeanor and "great executive capacity"
while also justifying his removal from power.[1]

In 1898 war and imperial themes infiltrated nearly every form
of cultural expression, including the press, graphic art, fair exhibits, theatrical performance, popular literature, advertisements, film,
and public celebrations. The result was mutually reinforcing; these
cultural productions helped to generate and sustain interest in U.S.
actions abroad, while at the same time, war themes boosted the sales
of news publications, commercial entertainments, consumer products, and more. Popular interest in war-related media may have been
short-lived, but it had profound and long-lasting implications not
only for America's national and imperial consciousness but also for
Spain, Cuba, Puerto Rico, Hawaii, Guam, and the Philippines.

In many cases, cultural producers adopted war and imperialist themes without explicit consideration of the politics surrounding them. Many viewers, in all likelihood, consumed these amusements with the same political ambivalence. In his pathbreaking study
Understanding Media, Marshall McLuhan's insight—"the medium is
the message"—encapsulates why "messages" of war and empire in
mass-cultural productions must not be taken at face value. McLuhan
explained, "The owners of media always endeavor to give the public
what it wants, because they sense that their power is in the *medium*
and not in the *message* or the program."[2] The success of the Cuban
rescue narrative in propelling intervention tells us more about public fascination with melodrama and the excitement of "playing savior" than about any serious popular reflection on Cuba's struggle
for independence, a point reinforced by how quickly sympathy for
Cuban nationalism evaporated once American guns began shooting.
The media spotlight then shifted to an equally captivating theme:
U.S. military heroics and sacrifice. The invigoration of patriotic sentiment was not due to "hysteria" or a "psychic crisis," but instead
suggested the programmatic effect of a successful apparatus of print,

popular, and visual culture serving the perceived needs of its audience. President McKinley did not have to convince his constituents that war would facilitate commercial access to the Caribbean or the Pacific; the romantic script of the swashbuckling American coming to the rescue of the Cuban damsel in distress was far more appealing, and it sustained the self-perception of a nation acting out of moral righteousness, not materialistic greed.

By way of conclusion, this chapter sketches some of the effects of the Philippine pacification campaigns on the spectacular constructions of war and empire in mass media. In February 1899 the Treaty of Paris formalized U.S. possession of the Philippines. Two days before the Senate ratified the treaty, fighting first broke out between Filipino nationals and U.S. troops. While it is now believed that the Americans initiated this confrontation, at the time U.S. military and press accounts related the incident to the American public as an act of Filipino aggression, confirming the narrative of "necessity" rationalizing U.S. guardianship. McKinley and pro-administration newspapers framed the outbreak as an act of "insurrection," which immediately differentiated the conflict from its predecessor.[3] This was not a war against another nation; it was suppression of an illegitimate rebel force.

This understanding profoundly affected how media makers represented U.S. actions in the Philippines to home audiences. National headlines reported on the U.S. advance into Iloilo, Malolos, Panay, Santa Cruz, Calumpit, and Caloocan in the early months of pacification, but none of these campaigns was imagined on the scale of the battles of Manila Bay, San Juan Hill, or Santiago Bay. *New York Evening Post* correspondent Albert G. Robinson, stationed in the Philippines, claimed that there was "a skirmish here and a skirmish there," making it difficult for correspondents to cover the scattered "scraps" of conflict or package them into a well-defined confrontation. By March, the pro-imperialist *Louisville Courier-Journal* could report: "the engagement has now shaped itself so that it is looked upon as more of a chase than the execution of a strategic movement. . . . There was no excitement and none of that anxiety and tension shown during the memorable days of last summer when the decisive blows were being struck at Santiago."[4] Expecting to suppress the rebellion swiftly, the McKinley administration did not attempt to mobilize the nation for full-scale war. General Wesley Merritt, who took command at Manila as of July 25, gave McKinley the assessment that "if a few ambitious insurgent chieftains could be disposed of, [then the] masses of natives could be managed by the United States."[5] The nature of the pacification campaigns, as well as the belief that they would be expeditiously handled, did not lend itself to the elaboration of military fanfare that media makers had so effectively manufactured the previous year.

Hence audiences viewing a Thomas Edison film titled "Filipinos Retreat from the Trenches" (produced by James H. White) saw a different vision of warfare in the Philippines from that presented by motion picture footage of the conflict with Spain. Spanish-American War films had celebrated U.S. military and naval accomplishments, whereas motion picture views of the Philippine campaigns were less clear-cut. White's film opens in a smoky Filipino trench as the insurgents shoot and reload their weapons. As some Filipinos fall, a company of U.S. infantry arrives to make an advance as the remaining rebels flee. A lone U.S. general on horseback remains, circling the fallen Filipino bodies. White reenacted the scene in May 1899 using members of the New Jersey National Guard near West Orange. His scenes of trench warfare are action-packed, but the central plot revolves around the retreat of an elusive enemy. Even at the end of the film the chase continues, and the objective of capturing the insurgents is not met. As in many Spanish-American War films, the camera fixes the vantage point of the viewer in the line of action, but the untitled battle scenes deny the spectator the ability to "witness" and participate in a specifically defined moment of history.[6]

Photographic views of U.S.-Philippine confrontations also provided a less glorified view of warfare. During the campaigns against Spain, there were very few published photographs of dead bodies, either Spanish or U.S. casualties. In the rare instances when photographers took pictures of the dead, the bodies were covered. Present in their memory were the photographs of dead American soldiers at Gettysburg and Antietam during the Civil War, taken by Matthew Brady, Alexander Gardner, and others, and their sustained impact on the nation.[7] Spanish-American War photographers, by contrast, deliberately photographed the wounded and dead at a respectful distance. This changed in the pictures taken of the Philippine resistance.

7.1. Lieut. C. F. O'Keefe, "Dead Filipinos in Trench of Bastion Fort before Santa Ana." From *Harper's Pictorial History of the War with Spain* (New York, Harper & Brothers, 1899), 463.

Photographers conveyed imperial warfare to Americans through images of mutilated Filipino bodies lying on roads or in trenches (see figure 7.1). F. Tennyson Neely published a collection of photographs in 1899 of the Philippines that included numerous pictures of Filipino casualties. One such image, taken near the Pasig River,

The illustration was taken not far from the water works toward the river Pasig.

7.2. F. Tennyson Neely, "The illustration was taken not far from the water works toward the river Pasig." From Neely, *Fighting in the Philippines: Authentic Original Photographs* (London: F. Tennyson Neely, 1899).

clearly differentiates between the rebellious Filipinos (who lie dead on the grass) and the loyal ones, who pose no threat and engage in their agricultural labors (figure 7.2). Neely reinforced the visual expression of power by positioning American soldiers adjacent to the dead Filipino bodies, presented as trophies of war.

As the Philippine-American War dragged on, America's struggle to defeat the guerrilla tactics of the Filipino army led to allegations and subsequent investigations of U.S. military atrocities, including Brigadier General Jacob H. Smith's "kill and burn" campaign in Samar and the employment of torture, such as the infamous "water cure," on captured prisoners. Although the U.S. government denied officially sanctioning these acts, the accusations seemed disturbingly similar to the ones leveled against Spain which had provoked U.S. intervention in Cuba in the first place. The United States even utilized the infamous policy of reconcentration which had earned Spanish governor-general Weyler the title of "butcher" in the American press. And in fact Congress in 1902 officially absolved Weyler of blame for his actions in Cuba—a telltale sign that the United States had crossed sides at the table.[8] To rationalize the military actions required to suppress the Philippine insurgency, it was crucial that the American court of public opinion accept the official story that Filipino "rebels" had initiated hostilities, thus making the U.S. military defenders, not offenders. Still, it is striking that it was presumed acceptable for Americans to gaze at Filipino but not Spanish dead, and that there wasn't greater concern that these images would empower anti-colonialist critics. The racial degradation of the Filipino across both camps of the imperial debate enabled these images to proliferate. Image makers rendered Filipinos as less than human, and their death, no matter how brutal or bloody, was therefore tolerable for Americans to see. The guerrilla tactics of the Philippine army became proof of Filipinos' racial inferiority, framed as the war-making method of the noncivilized, and justified the policy of a race war in which no distinction was drawn between military and civilian targets.[9] Especially early on in the campaigns, pictures of dead Filipino bodies expressed the legitimacy and effectiveness of U.S. militarism.

As pacification efforts intensified in the spring of 1899, more stringent rules of government censorship shaped the portrait of U.S.-Philippine warfare on the home front. There had been minimal government censorship of the press during the conflict with Spain, and what there was aimed primarily at restricting strategic information from reaching the enemy, not withholding information from the American public. This changed in the early months of the Philippine occupation, when General Elwell S. Otis, commander of the U.S. military regime, ordered much more rigid censorship in order to regulate public perceptions of U.S. actions in the Philippines.[10] After only a month of fighting, a frustrated correspondent of the pro-imperialist *Dallas News* stationed in Manila sent a special dispatch from Hong Kong to evade the censor. He wrote:

> The movement of Gen. Wheaton's flying brigade around Pasig during the past week has been largely exaggerated. The censor has refused to allow correspondents to cable the plain fact that the insurgents simply ran away before the advance of the American troops. He seemed to wish that all dispatches sent out should represent the small skirmishes as serious battles with the natives resisting furiously. Complaisant correspondents were made to represent the insurgents' losses as enormous. Gen. Otis' advances, however,

actually consist of elaborate skirmishes, with few losses, with no determined forward movement.[11]

According to this reporter, the censors sought to amplify military hype by transforming "small skirmishes" into "serious battles" and proclaiming the heroism of U.S. troops against a significant show of native resistance. Otis's push to embellish native losses suggests that rather than downplaying U.S. military efforts, he hoped to rally pride in the enormity of the undertaking while also reassuring Americans that the restoration of order would be forthcoming. Correspondent Albert Robinson of the *New York Evening Post* later wrote that "no secret was made of the distinct intention to give a certain color to all matter sent by telegraph from the Philippine Islands. Such matter *must* support the local and Washington administration, right or wrong, in all their acts."[12]

Many war correspondents, however, resisted U.S. censors rather than be complicit with them. The situation came to a crisis in July 1899 when Robinson along with other discontented correspondents in Manila signed a "round-robin" petition and submitted it for transmission via telegraph to U.S. press outlets. It began:

> The undersigned, being all staff correspondents of American newspapers stationed at Manila, unite in the following statement: We believe that from official dispatches made public in Washington the people of the United States have not received a correct impression of the situation in the Philippines, but that these dispatches have presented an ultra optimistic view that is not shared by the general officers in the field. . . . The censorship has compelled us to participate in this misrepresentation by excising or altering uncontroverted statements of facts on the plea, as General Otis stated, "that they would alarm the people at home," or "have the people of the United States by the ears."[13]

Otis denied their request to transmit the petition and threatened to court-martial them for conspiracy. But they bypassed him by sending it through Hong Kong (a practice that Otis unsuccessfully tried to outlaw), and newspapers across the nation published it. To alleviate the tensions, Otis promised to institute censorship reforms, but the petition had already aroused public indignation and provided ammunition to the anticolonialist opposition. Even pro-administration newspapers castigated Otis; declared the pro-imperialist *New York Journal*: "For six months General Otis has been sending dispatches from Manila reporting 'imminent success' over the Philippine insurgents and the constant disintegration of Aguinaldo's army. After many months of campaigning against the half-armed natives with the best army the United States ever put into the field, General Otis is no further advanced in the pacification of the Philippine Islands than he was at the beginning."[14]

Otis became the target of a variety of charges, including incompetence and deliberate falsification of reports. "There is no doubt that the Administration entered upon the necessary work of restoring order in the Philippines without a full realization of the difficulties to be overcome. It seems to have placed implicit confidence in Gen. Otis; and in that it blundered," insisted the *Louisville Courier-Journal*.[15] Critics further blamed Otis for failing to ask for more troops out of concern that it might alarm the public, crippling his ability to end the rebellion quickly and decisively. *New York Herald* correspondent John T. McCutcheon, who was the first to sign his name on the famous "round robin," later wrote that the exposé had an immediate effect; it created a public sensation over U.S. actions abroad, contributed to the resignation of Secretary of War Russell Alger in July 1899, and induced McKinley to order more troops to the Philippines. Still, Robinson later wrote that despite Otis's decrees abolishing censorship, very little changed in practice.[16] The controversy nonetheless had important repercussions on the relationship between the press and the administration. War correspondents did little to sell the Philippine war to the American public. The vivid language of drama, heroism, and action that had so punctuated the war correspondence of the Spanish-American conflict largely disappeared.

Even if most journalists were unwilling to sensationalize U.S. imperial conquest, leisure entrepreneurs embraced the tourism potential of the new possessions, providing an alternative means to acclimate Americans to imperial culture. Many cruise lines exploited popular interest in Cuba and the Philippines as they designed their winter and spring tours of 1899. Steamship tours offered Americans the opportunity to vacation in the new colonies and at the same time visit the sites of actual Spanish-American War battles.[17] A *Chicago Record* cartoon called attention to this new orientation in leisure. A man in a heavy winter coat, suffering from the cold weather, looks at the store window of a travel agency offering excursions to Cuba, Puerto Rico, and the Philippines. The posters tantalize with tropical images of scantily clad natives, summer fruit and flowers, and warm beaches. The caption states, "Another Convert to Expansion."[18]

Throughout 1899 a range of popular entertainments found ways to turn imperialism into a form of pleasure. Vaudeville acts depicted dancing Hawaiian hula girls, minstrel shows featured entertaining Filipinos in blackface, and melodramas recapitulated the romantic imperial encounter between American men and colonial women. The Washington zoo in November 1899 offered a new exhibit, titled "Uncle Sam's Congress of Animals around the World," purporting to display the "wild" animals of the Philippines, including the "'spectre,' carabao, tamarau, flying-lemur, biuturong and many other *freaks*."[19] The imperial fantasy, with its penchant for romance, exoticism, and novelty, became a popular theme in American mass entertainment.

The multifaceted promotion of American imperialism in different forms of mass culture stemmed from a combination of factors, including popular fascination with the exotic locales and populations of the new colonies, uncertainties about the nature and duration of Philippine resistance, censorship regulations, and vocal domestic opposition. I end with a brief look at three subsequent events of spectacular magnitude in the post–Spanish-American War period: the Greater America Exposition of 1899, George Dewey's homecoming celebration in the fall of 1899, and the capture of Emilio Aguinaldo in March 1901. These episodes pinpoint the strengths and limitations of this new media politics that amalgamated spectacle, celebrity, and popular amusement with the extension of U.S. policy abroad.

America's First Colonial World's Fair: The Greater America Exposition, 1899

In the spirit of Europe's colonial fair tradition, fair organizers proclaimed the Greater America Exposition (GAE) of 1899 America's first colonial exposition, counterpart to London's Greater Britain

Exhibition of 1899. Largely overlooked in histories of U.S. imperialism, the GAE emerged as an idea after the great success of the Trans-Mississippi and International Exposition in Omaha in the summer of 1898. Its very title encapsulated its imperial theme; as the *Omaha Bee* explained, "the two words 'Greater America' mean that we propose to represent in the coming exposition all new acquisitions of territory we have made through the war with Spain and by annexation."[20] To create a colonial atmosphere, the Omaha fairgrounds from the previous summer were "transformed into veritable tropical gardens," stated the fair's prospectus.[21]

The GAE immersed the spectator in celebration of the Spanish-American War. The Grand Court displayed captured Spanish cannon. The Government Building offered an extensive war exhibit, including uniforms, medals, rifles, pennants, military photographs, and views of the new colonies. It also displayed photographs of the graves of *Maine* victims.[22] The Fine Arts Building featured the *Chicago Record*'s war exhibit, consisting of over two hundred original drawings and war sketches along with hundreds of souvenirs that correspondents had brought home from the colonies.[23] On the midway, Edison's kinetograph (dubbed the "War-graph") presented daily showings of motion picture scenes of the battles of Manila Bay, El Caney, San Juan Hill, and Santiago. Other exhibits included a great painting, designed with electrical effects, retelling the story of Hobson and the *Merrimac*, a series of panoramas titled the "Great Sea Fight Fought by Admiral Dewey in Manila Bay," and the "Living Wounded Heroes," featuring actual Spanish-American War veterans.[24] Evening entertainment dazzled spectators with an explosive reenactment of the battle of Manila followed by fireworks over the lagoon.

The professed purpose of the fair made it an ideal space to rally support for U.S. imperialism.[25] Celebrating the return of U.S. servicemen from the Philippines presented just such an opportunity. One year earlier the Trans-Mississippi and International Exposition had promoted national pride in American armed services with a number of elaborate parades of soldiers marching in formation. The military parades at the GAE's opening day festivities, however, failed in their efforts to glorify imperial warfare; the pro-imperialist *Chicago Times-Herald* noted:

The last military organization in the line was a detachment of the First Nebraska. The passing of these boys was greeted with many cheers and handclapping, yet there was something pathetic about their appearance. . . .

They were the men who have been wounded in the engagements with the Filipinos, or who have been sent home after struggling with the enemy and fevers of the swamps and jungles of the islands. They were all in uniform, but their uniforms were tattered and torn and cut by the bullets of the treacherous natives whom they originally went abroad to assist, and who later on turned against them.[26]

After five months of fighting in the Philippines, the GAE opened with the "pathetic" and "tattered" march of the wounded soldiers who had advanced into the "swamps" and "jungles" of this foreign land to pave the way for U.S. occupation. Their torn, bullet-riddled uniforms offered a less than confident picture of U.S. military and imperial ascendancy.

But this march was just one imperial image offered on the fairgrounds; GAE publicity marketed a range of exhibits and attractions to introduce Americans to their newest acquisitions. The prospectus stated: "The dominant note of the Greater America Exposition of 1899 will be novel and attractive exhibits of the material resources, products, industries, manufactures, architecture, art, types of native people, and illustrations of the present state of civilization of the islands of the sea recently acquired by the United States. . . . Hence Omaha will be the first American city to exploit the wonders of the colonial possessions."[27] Fair president George Miller told the crowds on opening day, "The characteristics of our new possessions can be more intelligently understood in these grounds than by a trip to the islands themselves. Here the children, as well as their elders, can learn much that could never be acquired in schools and at the same time enjoy a recreation that will be at once healthful and enjoyable."[28]

The local press played an integral role in fair publicity. Edward Rosewater and Gilbert Hitchcock, the editors of the two largest Omaha newspapers, the *Omaha Bee* and *Omaha World-Herald*, respectively, held official positions in fair management. Initially, Rosewater headed the Department of Publicity and Hitchcock directed the Department of Promotion, though Hitchcock later resigned, and the two departments merged under Rosewater's direction. Although newspapers nationwide reported on the fair, these two Omaha papers had a stake in boosting attendance, and in turn, their press coverage sensationalized fair exhibits, especially the colonial displays.

The *Springfield Republican* idealized the colonial exhibits as "an ethnological exhibition, accurate and complete as possible in all respects, with the 'circus' element omitted," but concessionaires, striving for profit, did not share the same mandate.[29] Recruiters selected "living exhibits" to conform to imagined conceptions of savage and exotic peoples. Management reinforced this vision by following the traditional practice of relegating the colonial villages to the midway, the amusement section of the fair, apart from the White City, the zone of "civilization" and "progress." The one exception that broke convention was the erection of a Colonial Building inside the White City, displaying native fruits and vegetables from the colonies along with collections of paintings and photographs of Hawaii and the Philippines.[30]

The GAE was the first of its kind to display "living" subjects from U.S.-controlled territories, in three large colonial displays positioned on the midway. The first was the Hawaiian Village. Special Commissioner W. W. Umsted arranged for native Hawaiians to be "selected with a view to the best amusement," claimed the *Omaha Bee*. The hula-dancing girls were one of its most popular attractions, along with exhibitions of poi making, luaus, and great feasts. "To see these natives kill and dress a pig and cover it with red hot stones, picking them up at will with their bare hands, is a sight that is seldom to be seen," claimed the *Omaha World-Herald* in an effort to drum up interest.[31]

Fair publicity for the Cuban Village emphasized the exoticism of its native participants and natural surroundings. C. E. Llewellyn, special commissioner to Cuba and Puerto Rico, arranged for fifty-five Cubans to travel to the fair, a dozen of whom were well-known dancing girls. To attract patrons, fair planners strategically placed the Cuban women at the entrance to "flirt with the passerby, as is the custom in Havana and the other cities of the island," explained the *Omaha Bee*. Inside, fairgoers could enter into the spectacle of the tropical wild, viewing a large den with hundreds of snakes and electric eels of varying kinds and sizes. The *Bee* noted that "these snakes are not trained, but instead are in the same condition as those which move about in the mountains and jungles of the island."[32]

The main thrill of the Cuban Village, and one of the greatest attractions on the fairgrounds, was the performance of Valentine Ruiz, General Weyler's executioner in Cuba. Known as "the strangler" and "the hangman," Valentine allegedly put to death hundreds of political prisoners. Valentine reproduced Black Legend depictions of Spanish oppression that had circulated in media representations of Spain. He performed daily reenactments of executions, featuring the authentic garrote used to break the necks of victims as well as the "famous chair" that came directly from Cuba. The *Omaha World-Herald* described Valentine's chilling exhibition as a spectacle of horror: "Great excitement prevailed at the Cuban Village for a few seconds last evening. Valentine was giving an exhibition with the garrote, and by mistake the throat-piece of the machine was set in place, something which is never done during an exhibition. Had it not been noticed by one of the guards just in the nick of time, the man would have been killed." The *Omaha World-Herald* called Valentine an "inhuman monster, whose delight is the shedding of human blood," and urged audiences to enjoy the sensational pleasures of his gruesome display.[33]

For the third of the "living exhibits," the Philippine Village, Special Commissioner Henry F. Daily transported fifty natives to Omaha with a collection of relics, weapons, animals, and other native goods along with twenty tons of materials to construct thatched grass and bamboo huts to house the subjects on display.[34] Despite its own interest in promoting the Philippine Village, even the *Omaha World-Herald* had to concede that the Filipino participants were unwilling to perform as objects of colonial amusement. The *World-Herald* claimed that initially audience interest "warmed their hearts," but soon after, "the novelty wore off, and the flattery and attentions grew stale." In time "they began to shrink from the cold calculating stare of the ever curious visitors." The concurrent war in the Philippines also cast a shadow on the village. According to the *World-Herald,* "when the Filipinos saw the First Nebraska marching in to the street they were told that that was the regiment that had won so much fame in the

Philippine islands, and they started to run for their lives, thinking the regiment had come to take them prisoners."[35]

In the end, the colonial villages may not have turned fairgoers into champions of empire. The logic behind these consciously constructed exhibitions was to give visitors a privileged gaze as they looked upon "real" native subjects, not an imitation of imperial display. The GAE prospectus set forth: "While Americans are heatedly discussing the capacity of the Filipino for self-government, or his adaptability to enlightened citizenship, none of us, with the exception of the few returning and heroic promoters of American arms and valor on far shores, have ever seen a Filipino. Fourteen months ago most of us had never heard the name."[36] Fair publicity claimed that meeting actual natives of the various colonies would provide visitors with new insights into U.S. imperial responsibilities, but the organizers could not necessarily dictate what those insights would be. Human subjects could not be easily controlled, and unscripted exchanges inevitably transpired between subjects and fairgoers.[37] On Children's Day, some young visitors failed to react with shock, disgust, or pity toward the Cuban natives. According to the *Omaha Bee,* the children "had read or had heard their parents tell of the Cubans and were anxious to see what to them seemed a queer people. After looking them over the children came to the conclusion that the residents of the islands are flesh and blood, the same as those who reside in the states." Observing the Cubans humanized them in the children's eyes, for they did not conform to exotic depictions. Many visitors expressed a similar impression of the Filipinos: "People who expected to find the Filipinos representatives of a race of savages are disappointed. . . . They are stylish dressers, wear good clothes, derby hats, carry canes and clothe themselves in coats and trousers that are as white as snow," claimed the *Bee.*[38]

The GAE was not successful as a moneymaking venture; attendance was lower than expected, and investors did not turn a profit.[39] The GAE epitomized the failure to commercialize imperial culture in a way that could generate pleasure for spectators while also coming across as didactic and respectable. Fair management had composed a list of articles to assemble in the colonies and sent commissioners with no practical or academic knowledge of the native societies. As expected, they acted in the interest of maximizing public appeal, making choices that emphasized exoticism and spectacle without even a pretense of ethnographic concern.[40] According to the *Nebraska State Journal,* "one of the directors admits that instead of a colonial exposition, with its educational features, it is a rotten, immoral midway, liable to cause the ruination of hundreds of young men and women."[41] A writer in a local newspaper agreed: "The only true good colonial exhibit is one from Hawaii. . . . Without this exhibit, the exposition could not deserve the name 'colonial.' Natives from Hawaii, the Philippines, Cuba and Porto Rico, are to be found only in shows along the midway."[42] The only concessions that profited were the Giant See-Saw, the Old Plantation, the Scenic Railway, the Chutes, Hagenback's Animal Show, and Edison's War-graph. The Cuban and Hawaiian villages lost money, and the heaviest loser on the grounds was the Philippine Village.[43]

Contributing to the disarray of the Philippine Village was the fact that the metropolitan and colonial governments did not agree on the wisdom of placing "living exhibits" on display.[44] Assistant Secretary of War George Meiklejohn approved the transport of Filipino natives to Omaha, but General Otis in the Philippines did not support the proposal. Otis initially forbade exposition agents to assemble any participants while he protested to the War Department that Filipinos' involvement would be detrimental to his mission. Meiklejohn took the matter to President McKinley, who ordered Otis to comply, and Meiklejohn finally arranged for their transportation to the United States. Even so, this procedure proved more complicated than expected. After arriving in San Francisco, the Filipino participants were denied entrance by immigration authorities, who were unaware of the special provisions made for the Omaha fair. Again Meiklejohn stepped in to reassure authorities that the War Department would take responsibility for transporting them home after the exposition closed.[45] These glitches delayed the arrival of the Filipinos at the fairgrounds, causing the village to open two months late.

The experiment of the GAE of 1899 suggests the complexities of using empire as a commercial draw in turn-of-the-century popular amusements. Despite the initial impulse to attract visitors by glorifying U.S. imperialism, fair planners failed to promote empire with the pomp and circumstance that had consumed the nation in its campaigns against Spain. The planners' inability to generate mass demonstrations of imperial pride was especially noteworthy in contrast to the success of London's Greater Britain Exhibition of 1899. Still, the fair encouraged inclusion of exhibits from America's new colonies at world's fairs, and these would be developed more effectively in later expositions, such as the St. Louis world's fair of 1904. For fairgoers, the experience of seeing "living exhibits" helped foster an illusion of familiarity with colonial peoples, who could now be seen and observed firsthand. The living exhibits naturalized the place of colonial peoples in American popular culture and reinforced a worldview that cast the peoples of the new U.S. territories as exotic novelty acts.

George Dewey: America's "Fallen Idol"

When Admiral George Dewey defeated the Spanish navy at Manila Bay in early May 1898, he became the "Idol of the American Nation," as the *Chicago Tribune* put it. The *New York World* called him the "most popular American living." The *Boston Herald* went so far as to credit Dewey with "being of royal descent."[46] Dewey's public image faltered, however, in the wake of controversies surrounding the nation's attempt to honor him in the fall of 1899. Claimed the *Dallas News:* "Admiral Dewey awakens to the fact that in his country it is 'off with the old love and on with the new.' The hero of one hour may be the laughing stock of the next hour." Dewey told the press, "If it were not for my country I would wish that I had never fought the battle of Manila."[47] Dewey fell victim to the culture of celebrity, which catapulted him beyond expectation to the heights of popular adulation and even more quickly abandoned him.

At the height of his acclaim, press reports called Dewey "the highest type of our naval and military spirit" and "the ideal American in war." He embodied "the value of manliness . . . united with great modesty," according to the *New York Journal.* Particular emphasis was placed on his "Anglo Saxon strain of blood" to explain his heroism, moral fiber, and military talent. The *Chicago Times-Herald* reported that a New York doctor had read Dewey's palm and found evidence of his "physical endurance," "energy and industry," and "great independence of character." The article also claimed that Dewey's brain was "more than ordinary size and strength," a reflection of the popular "science" of phrenology, which maintained that the size of the brain was an indicator of intelligence and racial advancement. Dr. John Capen of Philadelphia, who also made a phrenological assessment of Dewey, contended that his head was "remarkably developed" and indicated that he possessed the qualities of "physical courage, firmness, prudence in planning and great decision in action."[48] Cultural producers enlisted pseudoscientific racial theories to transform Dewey into the embodiment of superior manhood, race, and civilization.[49]

Dewey, however, found it difficult to play the part of a conquering hero. While he was consistently praised for bearing his deeds like a true gentleman, he did not open himself up to media promotion with the same enthusiasm as other war celebrities, such as Theodore Roosevelt, Richmond P. Hobson, and Frederick Funston. John Rathom in the *San Francisco Chronicle* argued that "the real heroes" of war "deny their own deeds and shrink from popular adulation." He wrote: "One need not search farther than Admiral George Dewey for the true type. Modesty, combined with bravery, tact and great achievement find their real proportions in this American sailor." But Dewey's aversion to the spotlight hampered attempts to mass-market him. Alan Dale, theater critic of the *New York Journal,* noted: "If Dewey were staged he would be found lacking in 'human interest.' A Sydney Rosenfeld, or a Henry Guy Carleton would be employed to write in some little incident, such as the rescue of a Philippine maiden from demon Spaniards, or the discovery made by the hero that he had just killed his long-lost brother at the battle of Manila."[50]

Dewey initially refused to attend the honorary celebrations planned for his return to the United States, which spawned a wave of speculation in the press regarding his emotional and physical state. Explained the *Atlanta Constitution,* "Admiral Dewey's hair has turned white and he shows the severe effects of the strain he has been under." J. J. Ingalls of the *New York Journal* wrote, "He is sensitive and retiring, of nervous temperament, in delicate health, worn down with immense strain and responsibility in a tropical climate, and needs the medicine of rest and quiet." When photographer J. C. Hemment interviewed him in September 1899, he reportedly told Dewey, "The American public has an idea that you are a sick man." According to Hemment, "The Admiral sprang to his feet with a laugh, and standing as straight as a ramrod taking his cap off and said: 'Now, really, do I look like a sick man?'" Hemment observed: "In truth he did not. His face was bronzed and healthy, his eyes clear and bright and his step elastic."[51]

After Dewey changed his mind and agreed to attend the celebrations, public officials and volunteers turned his homecoming from the Philippines in the fall of 1899 into the grandest spectacle yet of the Spanish-American War. The city of New York offered a weeklong festival of events, organized by a committee of over one thousand members; it included a seven-mile naval parade and amassed a crowd of over 2 million spectators. The *Houston Post* reported, "New York has never witnessed before anything approaching this wonderful and remarkable demonstration," further noting "the mass of humanity that crowded the water front of Manhattan Island and filled every point of vantage along the Jersey coast." After New York, Dewey moved on to another extravagant reception in Washington, D.C. Secretary Long presented Dewey with a $10,000 jeweled sword, paid for by congressional appropriation. "No living man ever saw anything approaching in magnitude and enthusiasm the tribute that was laid at the feet of Dewey," observed the *Boston Herald*.[52]

Dewey mania knew no bounds. Spectators gathered in cities across the United States to pay homage, as in Keene, New Hampshire, where a large group of citizens created a huge bonfire in Dewey's honor. Local authorities warned them that the strong winds could spread the fire, but they persisted. The ensuing blaze caused considerable damage. Calling them "patriotic idiots," the *Chicago Tribune* remarked, "The sober, slow-going old State of New Hampshire is about the last place in the country where one would expect to find patriotism so enthusiastic as cheerfully to consent to burn a town for the glorification of a naval hero."[53] In a very different form of hero worship, the *New York Journal* collected seventy thousand nickels from subscribers and had them melted down and fashioned into a "Loving Cup" as a gift for the Admiral. "The shop girl, the laborer, the mechanic, the farmer—all classes of people are amalgamated in this grand testimonial," proclaimed the *Journal*. What is more, 1,500 New York schoolgirls volunteered to spell out Dewey's name in "human letters" on a stand at Seventy-second Street and Central Park West during his homecoming parade.[54] Dewey's portrait was also reproduced on countless souvenirs, including spoons, plates, and buttons.[55] The Metropolitan Opera House staged a special performance of "The White Squadron," reenacting the battle of Manila Bay with materials borrowed from the Brooklyn naval shipyards.[56] Cinematograph exhibitions at the Eden Musee and vaudeville houses in many cities featured film footage of Manila Bay and the parades celebrating the admiral's return.[57] During those six festive days, the nation came together to celebrate Dewey.

Over twenty sculptors from the National Sculpture Society volunteered to erect a "Dewey Arch" in Manhattan in honor of his homecoming. In order to have it ready in time, the sculptors built the arch of staff, a temporary material also used to construct the buildings at world's fairs, with the intention that it would later be made permanent. But to the disappointment of the sculptors, nobody saw Dewey pass through the arch at any time during the celebrations.[58] Nonetheless, following the festivities, the citizens' committees launched a campaign to make the arch a permanent part of the New York landscape. "So much headway has already been made in the project of perpetuating the Dewey arch in marble that the promoters announced yesterday the absolute success of the movement," announced the *New York World* on October 8.[59]

The arch itself was an artistic testament to the military, naval, and imperialistic spirit engendered by the Spanish-American War. Its sculptures represented the "four great steps in patriotism": on the northeast face was *The Call to Arms* (representing patriotism) by Philip Martiny; on the southeast, *The Combat* (war) by Karl Bitter; on the southwest was *The Victors Returning* (triumph) by Charles Niehaus; and on the northwest was *The Warriors Resuming Their Occupations* (peace) by Daniel Chester French. On the tops of the large Corinthian columns were sculptures of U.S. naval heroes, and terminating the colonnade were sculptural groups representing the U.S. Army and Navy and the East and West Indies. Despite inclusion of these island groups, the sculptural design made a subtle distinction in celebrating the United States as a "maritime" nation, as one writer in 1899 described it, not an imperialist one.[60] The visual representation of the war ending in "peace" and a resumption of normalcy ignored the ongoing battles for pacification in the Philippines. Beyond venerating Dewey's naval triumph as exemplary of the military strength that could thrust the United States onto the world stage, the arch, as with the festivities as a whole, did not explicitly connect Dewey to the nation's new venture into overseas colonialism.

Given that Dewey's victory in Manila Bay had initiated the entry of the United States into the Philippines, one might expect his name to have been synonymous with U.S. imperialism. But when he first came to public acclaim after defeating the Spanish squadron at Manila, press and public opinion had not yet realized the imperial ramifications of the war. It was thus that the festivities honored Dewey as the epitome of U.S. military and naval prowess without the imperialist subtext. Even though he remained in the Philippines during the early months of the U.S. occupation, much of the press coverage detached him from the escalation of hostilities. "As long as Dewey was left to deal with Aguinaldo after his own manner there was no trouble," wrote the *Boston Herald*. "It was not until a different class of the nation's agents took up the subject of adjusting national affairs . . . that trouble arose."[61] By a "different class" of agent, the *Herald* meant General Otis. Turning Otis into a scapegoat for the Philippine situation freed Dewey from any association with the ongoing struggle. Because the Dewey celebrations focused attention on the military might of the United States without overtly acknowledging its imperial claims, mass participation in the festivities cannot be read as a referendum on popular commitments to U.S. occupation of the Philippines.

After Dewey's homecoming, the press continued to seek out ways to honor him. A Boston newspaper proposed renaming the Philippines the "Dewey Islands," but the idea didn't take hold. Instead the *Chicago Tribune, New York Journal,* and other large urban dailies organized a national subscription drive to present Admiral Dewey with a house in Washington, D.C.[62] Dewey initially declined the offer but later accepted it out of respect for those honoring him. The committee purchased a $50,000 house on Rhode Island Avenue, fully furnished. Shortly afterwards, the press announced that Dewey had wed Mildred M. Hazen. A convert to Catholicism with a reputation for snootiness, Hazen did not inspire public affection, which may at least partly account for the scandal that was about to erupt.[63]

Controversy arose when Dewey signed over ownership of his new house to his bride. A reader wrote to the *Washington Star:* "As one of the contributors, in a small way, to the Dewey home fund, I have read with surprise, pain and indignation your statement in tonight's issue concerning the transfer of the home to the admiral's new wife. I have the feelings of a man who has been imposed upon, swindled. . . . But our idol has fallen, and by this one act, almost an insult to thousands of his countrymen, he will lose in the esteem of the people what it took him years to win."[64] A surge of letters denouncing Dewey's action poured into editors' offices around the country. Banker Emerson McMillan offered to refund subscribers the money they had contributed to the fund.[65] Audiences in many cities withheld applause in theaters when motion pictures of Dewey appeared on the screen.[66] Dewey's wife signed over the title of the house to Dewey's son George Goodwin Dewey in an attempt to restore public favor. According to the *Chicago Tribune,* "this disposition of the property seems to prove entirely satisfactory, even to the most captious critic, and the sudden outburst from the public has subsided as quickly as it arose."[67] Still, the damage was done. Dewey later wrote in his memoirs, "It seemed impossible to live up to all that was expected of me as a returning hero."[68]

Perhaps best exemplifying the turn against Dewey was the fate of the Dewey Arch. A dramatic decline in subscriptions in subsequent months made it difficult for the committee to raise the rest of the money needed to set the arch in marble. The chairman of the executive committee claimed, "Our subscription list has fallen off owing to the apathy of New Yorkers."[69] Ultimately the committee dropped the project entirely. The press reported that in the arch's final hours, "vandals" hacked away at it, perhaps as an expression of anticolonialist protest, or more likely to obtain a material reminder of the celebrations prior to its destruction.[70] In April 1900 Dewey's attempt to secure a nomination for the presidency failed. It seemed that the shelf life of Dewey's popularity matched that of the material used to construct the provisional arch in the first place. Popular news satirist Finley Peter Dunne, speaking as his fictional alter ego Mr. Dooley, said it best: "When a grateful republic, Mr. Hinnessy, builds an ar'rch to its conquering hero, it should be made of brick, so that we have something convenient to hurl after him when he has passed by."[71]

Dewey's cautionary tale of the perils of fame highlights the fleeting quality of spectacle. The quick dissipation of Dewey's celebrity in late 1899 was an indication of a wider evaporation of popular interest in the Spanish-American War. Reenactments of the destruction of the *Maine* and the war's major battles ceased to be as commercially viable. Theaters discontinued showing motion picture footage of the war and even views of the ongoing Philippine campaigns. The *Chicago Tribune* noted in the spring of 1899, "The camp and field scenes which were so popular while the martial spirit ruled the nation have been relegated to the rear, and the pictures offered this time reflect the lighter humors of peace."[72] Whether a consequence of public disinterest or the limitations imposed by censorship, this perception of a nation at peace is a striking commentary, considering that there were more U.S. troops committed abroad and higher casualty rates than in the brief war against Spain and that the ensuing struggle would take more Filipino lives than the three centuries of authoritarian Spanish rule that preceded it.[73]

After 1900 political cartoonists subjected U.S.-occupied territories to visual comment with much less frequency. At the same time, military officials, anthropologists, and social scientists produced an array of ethnographic and cartographic imagery that reinforced the racialized vision of U.S.-colonized peoples. While more sophisticated and steeped in the legitimacy of pseudoscientific authority, these government-commissioned images contained the same imperial logic of cultural and racial difference as imperialist cartoons.[74] But despite the overall decline of colonial imagery in the press, on stage, and in motion pictures, the capture of Emilio Aguinaldo in 1901 once again thrust the Spanish-American War and its imperial legacy into the spotlight.

From Military Enemy to Pop Culture Icon: The Exit of Aguinaldo

The capture of Emilio Aguinaldo in 1901 provided a media moment unlike anything in news coverage of the prior pacification campaigns, epitomizing how newsmakers conveyed content to readers through literary and theatrical ways of thinking and seeing. When U.S. and Filipino forces first clashed in February 1899, newsmakers mistakenly projected that Aguinaldo would be caught and punished quickly, but it was not until late March 1901 that General Frederick Funston achieved his capture. According to General Arthur MacArthur's report to the War Department on February 28, 1901, General Funston received intelligence of Aguinaldo's location in Palanan from a deserting Filipino national. Funston led an expedition consisting of U.S. cavalrymen, Tagalo-speaking natives, and four former insurgent officers. He dressed his cavalrymen to appear to be prisoners of the natives, who were armed and dressed as Filipino insurgents. On March 23 they reached Palanan, where they misled Aguinaldo's men into believing they were a detachment of his forces. Shortly before approaching Aguinaldo's quarters, they shed their disguises and attacked; two Filipinos were killed but no Americans. The successful mission ended with the capture of Aguinaldo and two of his highest-ranking officers.[75]

Remarkably, a fiction writer anticipated, or perhaps even helped formulate, this military strategy. Over a year before the actual deed, *Harper's Weekly* published a fictional account of Aguinaldo's capture that eerily resembles the details of MacArthur's report, although we do not know for sure if Funston had prior knowledge of it.[76] In Duffield Osborne's short story, titled "The Capture of Aguinaldo," Lieutenant Farley of the U.S. Marine Corps assembles four Malays and disguises them as insurgents, with Farley as their prisoner. Having gained knowledge that Aguinaldo is in Tarlac, they make their way to his headquarters, use their false identities to gain access, and seize him. Although two natives are killed in the process, Aguinaldo concedes with dignity. The mission is a success, despite, unlike in Funston's case, one American casualty. The similarities between the two accounts are striking: the use of disguise, the method of capture, the number of rebels killed, and the taking of Aguinaldo alive. Osborne did not accurately predict the end of the real story, however. In his version the mission results in "the sudden melting away of an organized rebellion," whereas the actual Filipino nationals did not surrender until May 1902, and Moro resistance continued sporadically for more than a decade, with two of the bloodiest battles occurring at Bud Daho in 1906 and Bud Bagsak in 1913.[77]

Osborne integrated journalistic conventions into his fictionalized account, employing the form of news dispatches to give it the semblance of a breaking news report; conversely, press reports framed the actual event with the literary flair of Osborne's heroic tale. The *Chicago Inter Ocean* reported, "General Funston's success in carrying out a plan of capture as romantic as it was daring comes as a fitting climax to the long-drawn-out rebellion in the Philippines." Nevertheless, "the parallel between the fiction of sixteen months ago and the fact of last week is so close as to suggest that General Funston got the idea that resulted in signal success from the tale of the story writer. If this is not so the coincidence is all the more remarkable," commented the *New York Journal*. The *Boston Herald* also found it suspicious that Funston's dramatic plan of capture was made public prior to the accomplishment of the deed, further evidence of its construction as a media spectacle.[78] Despite MacArthur's order to keep the mission a secret, Funston's staff leaked the story before Aguinaldo's capture.[79]

It was also opportune that Funston led the mission, because even prior to Aguinaldo's capture, the press singled out Funston more than any other U.S. general serving in the Philippines as the turn-of-the-century manly martial ideal. Known as the "fighting Kansan," Funston led one of the best-known regiments in the Philippines, the Twentieth Kansas Volunteers, also known as the "Kansas Demons." Even before Aguinaldo's capture, the press featured illustrated accounts of Funston's brave exploits, reporting how he had led his men across the river at Malolos in order to capture seventy Filipinos. The charge he led at Calumpit, according to one account, "will live in history along with the charge of the Rough Riders at San Juan Hill as one of the bravest feats" for "driving them [the insurgents] from their fortifications and breaking the backbone of the insurrection in the Philippines."[80] The charge achieved such notoriety that Wichita State Fair organizers offered Funston $2,000 to attend the fair and participate in a mock battle with "colored" cavalrymen acting as Filipino nationals. They arranged for Funston and his men to swim across a section of the Arkansas River to reenact the infamous crossing in May 1899. The *Los Angeles Times* exclaimed: "The boys from Kansas are all right, and the little colonel who leads them has won not one star upon an epaulet, but two of them. Glorious Fred Funston of Kansas, you do us mighty proud!"[81] The "fighting Kansan" was a war hero even before the capture took place, and once it did, media accounts attributed full credit to him for single-handedly putting down the rebellion and bringing Aguinaldo to justice.

To foster the profitability of reenactments of the capture, cultural

Why Not Bring Them Over on a Lecturing Tour?

7.3. "Why Not Bring Them Over on a Lecturing Tour?" *Cleveland Plain Dealer*, April 6, 1901, 1.

producers continued to stoke the fierce rivalry between Funston and Aguinaldo. The U.S. military regime in the Philippines, by contrast, sought to promote a softer image of the Filipino leader, requiring him to swear allegiance to the United States upon his capture and urge his followers to surrender. One pro-administration newspaper recognized that for his message to be heard, Aguinaldo's image had to change from a "blood-thirsty tyrant" to an "honest, sincere . . . natural leader of men with considerable shrewdness and ability . . . highly respected by all."[82] But from a commercial perspective, the image of Aguinaldo as enemy was more compelling. The *Cleveland Plain Dealer* suggested: "Why not send him to this country, on a contract with Major Pond, to go on a lecture tour, or engage him to 'do stunts' for the vaudeville trust? That would keep him busy, flatter his vanity and fill his pockets so full that he would have no temptation to go into hiding again in the Philippine wilds."[83] In a front-page cartoon, the *Plain Dealer* asked, "Why Not Bring Them Over on a Lecturing Tour?" It depicts Uncle Sam painting a billboard advertising the "special engagement" of "Aggy & Funston in their joint act," a spectacle "billed for America" (figure 7.3). The title of their act, "Life in the Philippines and Its Strenuousness," accents the stylization of Funston as a rugged cowboy, complete with hat, full beard,

and broad chest, in contrast to a ragged-looking Aguinaldo. Teddy
Roosevelt, a man adept at turning "strenuous" military performance
into an opportunity for self-promotion, observes with vigilance.
While the tone of the proposal is clearly satirical, the cartoonist calls
attention to an actual movement on the part of American cultural
producers to commercialize Aguinaldo. Within a month of his capture, the War Department received numerous requests from muse-
ums, athletic clubs, and theaters for permission to offer Aguinaldo a
contract.[84] The act of soliciting Aguinaldo for the popular stage,
whether in earnest or in jest, trivialized his cause, his political and
military leadership, and his role in history.

After Aguinaldo's capture, Wallace Irwin encapsulated Aguinaldo's
transformation into a pop icon in a humorous poem published in the
San Francisco Examiner titled "A Job for Aguinaldo." Irwin offers him
"a suggestion or two of jobs you might get or things you might do" now
that Funston had cut short his leadership career in the Philippines:

> First of all there's the stage, that dear refuge so easy,
> That home for all has-beens both tuneful and wheezy.
> It's no trick at all just to master the trade,
> Since you'd travel with ease on the name you have made.
> Were your stunt comic opera, clown or comedian,
> Dark villain, light hero, or heavy tragedian.
> Just get a good manager, much as they all do.
> And post on each bill board the sign:

> AGUINALDO!!
> Presents the Great War Drama,
> 'Hiding in Luzon.'
> A Thrill for Your Money!—
> A Play to Enthuse On!!
> Real Water! Real Gu-Gus! Real
> Swamps! And in Fact
> A Bonafide Otis to Every Act.
> Don't Miss the Great Hide and Seek
> Game on the Stage,
> The Biggest Sensational Act of the Age . . .

> Give rates to schoolchildren; look wise and explain
> The things you have done in a discussive vein.
> While all of your hair-breadth escapes, scene by scene,
> Are duly depicted when flashed on a screen . . .
> You needn't feel hurt if the people who pay
> Don't like your remarks or can't hear what you say.
> It won't be to hear your discourse that they fee you—
> 'Twill be worth the price of admission to see you.[85]

What Aguinaldo had to say or could do was irrelevant; his "message" of Filipino resistance to Western imperial domination was subordinated, if not lost altogether, in his exile into U.S. popular culture.

The Cuban crisis and Spanish-American War were moneymakers. The press conveyed war news as entertainment, and in turn the entertainment industries raided the news for popular topics. The combined effect of this synergy between popular, print, and visual media was the mass production of war and empire as spectacle, which, intentionally or not, fostered support for military and imperial policies with significant consequences for the United States and the territories it acquired. Applying theatrical, graphic, and literary conventions to international politics had the effect of turning political decisions into simple moral questions of good and evil. Framing military action as liberation and nonintervention as selfish neglect thus diverted attention from the substantive political, diplomatic, and economic considerations underlying those choices. The line between foreign policy and popular spectacle was a blurry one when colonial acquisition served as popular amusement, military heroes became celebrities, and hunted enemies were turned into pop stars.

Whatever their means and motivations, American cultural producers were on the front lines of advocating U.S. foreign policy decisions in 1898–99. American imperial expansion at the turn of the century did more than foster a military and naval buildup or place the United States on the map of world imperial powers; war-related themes suffused the media environment and reinforced a cognitive map that defined American manhood and national purpose in relation to allegedly inferior races at home and abroad. Even so, the system of delivering military and imperial ideologies across a broad spectrum of media did not have a totalizing or coherent effect. As cultural producers strove to create profitable attractions, the spectacular packaging of their productions at times clouded messages for and against war and empire. Americans shared in their consumption of war-related media, from reading newspapers and viewing cartoons, photographs, and moving images to attending theatrical performances, battle reenactments, and fair exhibits. This bonding experience not only inspired patriotic unity and imperialist desires but also, perhaps of equal importance, functioned to secure the foothold of image, spectacle, and drama in American media during a period of unprecedented expansion of mass cultural production.

The fact is, for a very brief period of time, the greatest show in town was War and Empire.

APPENDIX:

ASSESSMENT OF NEWSPAPERS AND PERIODICALS
IN THE SAMPLE

NEWSPAPER OR PERIODICAL	AVERAGE DAILY CIRCULATION FOR 1898*	PRO-WAR?	POLITICAL PARTY AFFILIATION	PRO-IMPERIALIST OR ANTICOLONIALIST?
Atlanta Constitution		Yes	Independent Democratic	Pro
Baltimore Sun		No	Independent	Anti
Boston Globe	230,515	Yes	Independent Democratic	Pro
Boston Herald	250,000	No	Independent	Pro
Boston Transcript		Yes (reluctantly)	Independent Republican	Anti
Charleston News & Courier		Yes	Democratic	First pro, then anti
Chicago Inter-Ocean	20–40,000	Yes	Republican	Pro
Chicago Record	240,000	Yes	Independent–Republican	Pro (reluctantly)
Chicago Times-Herald		Yes	Republican	Pro
Chicago Tribune	70,000[1]	Yes	Republican	Pro
Cleveland Plain Dealer	22,000	Yes	Democratic	Anti
Collier's Weekly				
Dallas Morning News		Yes (reluctantly)	Independent	Pro
Denver Post	23,000	Yes	Silverite–Independent	Anti
Frank Leslie's Weekly	75,000	Yes		Pro
Harper's Monthly	150,000–200,000			
Houston Post		Yes	Democratic	First pro, then anti
Indianapolis Freeman ("An illustrated Colored Newspaper")	80,000	Yes (reluctantly)	Republican (called itself "a race paper")	Anti
Indianapolis Sentinel		Yes	Democratic	Anti
Judge	114,000[2]	Yes	Republican	Pro
Life			Independent Democratic	Anti
Los Angeles Times		Yes	Independent Republican	Pro

NEWSPAPER OR PERIODICAL	AVERAGE DAILY CIRCULATION FOR 1898*	PRO-WAR?	POLITICAL PARTY AFFILIATION	PRO-IMPERIALIST OR ANTICOLONIALIST?
Louisville Courier-Journal		Yes	Democratic	Pro
Memphis Commercial Appeal		Yes	Democratic	Pro
Minneapolis Journal	50,000	Yes	Republican	Pro
New Orleans Picayune		Yes (reluctantly)	Democratic	Pro
New York Evening Post		No	Independent	Anti
New York Herald	500,000	Yes	Independent	Pro
New York Journal	1,250,000	Yes	Democratic	Pro
New York Times Illustrated Magazine	25,000–75,000[3]	Yes	Independent Democratic	Pro
New York World	1,010,000	Yes	Democratic	Anti
Omaha Bee		Yes	Republican	
Omaha World-Herald		Yes	Democratic	
Philadelphia Inquirer	175,000	Yes (reluctantly)	Republican	Pro
Puck	90,000[4]	Yes	Independent Democratic	Pro
Richmond Daily Times		Yes	Democratic	First pro, then anti
Rocky Mountain News	25,000	Yes	Independent Silver Fusion	Pro
San Francisco Chronicle	78,000	Yes	Republican	Pro
San Francisco Examiner	80,000	Yes	Democratic	Pro
St. Louis Post-Dispatch	93,537	Yes	Democratic	Anti
Savannah Press	5,000	Yes	Democratic	First pro, then anti
Springfield Republican		Yes	Independent	Anti
Washington Post		Yes	Independent	Pro

NOTES

*In most cases the circulation figures are estimates based on the average of a few months of circulation data throughout the year provided by the newspapers themselves. In some cases the newspapers or periodicals did not supply this information.

1. The *Tribune*'s circulation was 70,000 in 1900, according to Richard A. Matré, "The Chicago Press and Imperialism, 1899–1902" (Ph.D. diss., Northwestern University, 1961), 13.

2. James H. Dorman claims that *Judge* had a subscription list by the year 1901 of 114,000; see his "Ethnic Stereotyping in American Popular Culture: The Depiction of American Ethnics in the Cartoon Periodicals of the Gilded Age," *Amerikastudien* 30 (1985): 490.

3. In October 1898 *New York Times* owner Adolph Ochs lowered the price of the paper from three cents to a penny, and over the course of the next year the circulation rose from 25,000 to 75,000. It reached 82,000 by 1900. See Michael Schudson, *Discovering the News: A Social History of American Newspapers* (New York: Basic Books, 1967), 114.

4. John J. Appel, "From Shanties to Lace Curtains: The Irish Image in *Puck*, 1876–1910" *Comparative Studies in Society and History* 13 (October 1971): 365.

NOTES

Introduction

1. Richard A. Matré, "The Chicago Press and Imperialism, 1899–1902" (Ph.D. diss., Northwestern University, 1961), 20.

2. Scholars have begun to explore the mediating role of visual and popular culture surrounding the Spanish-American War. See Janet M. Davis, *The Circus Age: Culture and Society under the American Big Top* (Chapel Hill: University of North Carolina Press, 2002), 192–226; Raymond B. Craib and D. Graham Burnett, "Insular Visions: Cartographic Imagery and the Spanish-American War," *Historian* 61.1 (Fall 1998): 100–118; Jill DeTemple, "Singing the *Maine*: The Popular Image of Cuba in Sheet Music of the Spanish-American War," *Historian* 63 (Summer 2001): 715–29; Kristen Whissel, "The Gender of Empire: American Modernity, Masculinity, and Edison's War Actualities," in *A Feminist Reader in Early Cinema*, ed. Jennifer M. Bean and Diana Negra (Durham: Duke University Press, 2002), 141–65; Kristen Whissel, "Placing the Spectator on the Scene of History: The Battle Re-enactment at the Turn of the Century, from Buffalo Bill's Wild West to the Early Cinema," *Historical Journal of Film, Radio and Television* 22 (2002): 225–43; Christine Bold, "The Rough Riders at Home and Abroad: Cody, Roosevelt, Remington and the Imperialist Hero," *Canadian Review of American Studies* 18.3 (Fall 1987): 321–50. The most all-inclusive work on Spanish-American War–related media is James Castonguay's Web site "The Spanish-American War in U.S. Media Culture," http://chnm.gmu.edu/aq/war/index.html.

3. I focus primarily on mainstream, mass-circulation papers because they had the resources to afford the production of visual representations. See the appendix for a complete list of the newspapers and periodicals in my sample.

4. It is my hope that this book will spawn further study into how minority groups in the United States, such as the Spanish, Cuban, or Filipino American communities, or media producers from the colonies themselves co-opted, reframed, or challenged the mainstream media representations outlined here. I have written elsewhere on the representations of the Spanish-American War from the perspective of the Spanish press; see Bonnie Goldenberg, "Imperial Culture and National Conscience: The Role of the Press in the United States and Spain during the Crisis of 1898," *Bulletin of Hispanic Studies* 77 (2000): 169–91. Scholars who have worked on cultural production in the colonies include Clodualdo del Mundo Jr., *Native Resistance: Philippine Cinema and*

Colonialism, 1898–1941 (Manila: De La Salle University Press, 1998), and Vicente L. Rafael, *White Love and Other Events in Filipino History* (Durham: Duke University Press, 2000).

5. Pamela J. Shoemaker and Stephen D. Reese, *Mediating the Message: Theories of Influence on Mass Media Content* (New York: Longman, 1991), 186. On media framing and agenda-setting research, see also Stuart Hall, Chas Critcher, Tony Jefferson, John Clarke, and Brian Roberts, *Policing the Crisis: Mugging, the State, and Law and Order* (New York: Holmes & Meier Publishers, 1978), 60–62; Walter Lippman, *Public Opinion* (1922; repr., Sioux Falls, S.D.: NuVision Publications, 2007), 203–4; Todd Gitlin, *The Whole World Is Watching: Mass Media in the Making and Unmaking of the New Left* (Berkeley: University of California Press, 1980); Doris A. Graber, *Processing the News: How People Tame the Information Tide*, 2nd ed. (New York: Longman, 1988); Dietram A. Scheufele, "Framing as a Theory of Media Effects," *Journal of Communication* 49.1 (1999): 103–22; David L. Protess and Maxwell McCombs, eds., *Agenda Setting: Readings on Media, Public Opinion, and Policymaking* (Hillsdale, N.J.: Lawrence Erlbaum Associates, 1991); Maxwell E. McCombs and Donald L. Shaw, "The Evolution of Agenda-Setting Research: Twenty-five Years in the Marketplace of Ideas," *Journal of Communication* 43.2 (Spring 1993): 58–67; Donald L. Shaw and Shannon E. Martin, "The Function of Mass Media Agenda Setting," *Journalism Quarterly* 69.4 (Winter 1992): 902–20.

6. Of the 75 million people living in the United States at the time, many had different kinds of social relationships to the war. Some noncombatants were directly involved, whether as volunteers, government workers, or families and friends of servicemen, while others had ethnic ties or financial or other interests abroad, further individualizing the experience of the war and its media production. There is a vast literature on reader reception. A few key texts include Janice Radway, *Reading the Romance: Women, Patriarchy, and Popular Literature* (Chapel Hill: University of North Carolina Press, 1984); Henry Jenkins, *Textual Poachers: Television Fans and Participatory Culture* (New York: Routledge, 1992); Linda Williams, ed., *Viewing Positions: Ways of Seeing Film* (New Brunswick: Rutgers University Press, 1994); Jim McGuigan, *Cultural Populism* (London: Routledge, 1992); John Fiske, *Understanding Popular Culture* (London: Routledge, 1989); Ien Ang, *Desperately Seeking the Audience* (London: Routledge, 1991).

7. My understanding of "spectacle" derives from Jonathan Crary's insightful assessment that the concept eludes a singular definition and must not be seen as a "single and seamless global system of relations." Jonathan Crary, "Spectacle, Attention, Counter-memory," in *Guy Debord and the Situationist International: Texts and Documents*, ed. Tom McDonough (Cambridge: MIT Press, 2002), 455. Vanessa Schwartz demonstrates a similar cultural affinity for "spectacular realities" in fin-de-siècle Paris that materialized in a number of mass-cultural forms, including popular journalism, wax museum art, and cinema. The Spanish-American War took shape in this transatlantic Western culture of spectacle. Vanessa Schwartz, *Spectacular Realities: Early Mass Culture in Fin-de-Siècle Paris* (Berkeley: University of California Press, 1998). See also Susan Glenn, *Female Spectacle: The Theatrical Roots of Modern Feminism* (Cambridge: Harvard University Press, 2000), 12; Greil Mar-

cus, *Lipstick Traces: A Secret History of the Twentieth Century* (Cambridge: Harvard University Press, 1989), 104–5.

8. I am borrowing Marshall McLuhan's phrase here, which is central to this book's argument; see his *Understanding Media: The Extensions of Man* (New York: McGraw-Hill, 1964), 7. This approach is also inspired by Melani McAlister, *Epic Encounters: Culture, Media, and U.S. Interests in the Middle East, 1945–2000* (Berkeley: University of California Press, 2001), and Neil Postman, *Amusing Ourselves to Death: Public Discourse in the Age of Show Business* (New York: Viking, 1985), 3–15.

9. John Lawrence Tone, *War and Genocide in Cuba, 1895–1898* (Chapel Hill: University of North Carolina Press, 2006), 61, 193.

10. Quotes from Louis A. Pérez Jr., *Cuba in the American Imagination: Metaphor and the Imperial Ethos* (Chapel Hill: University of North Carolina Press, 2008), 230; Tone, *War and Genocide in Cuba,* 246.

11. Alfred T. Mahan, *The Influence of Sea Power upon History, 1660–1783* (London: Sampson Low, Marston & Co., 1889).

12. Thomas Schoonover, *Uncle Sam's War of 1898 and the Origins of Globalization* (Lexington: University Press of Kentucky, 2003), 65–66, 77–79; Walter LaFeber, *The American Age: United States Foreign Policy at Home and Abroad since 1750* (New York: W. W. Norton, 1989), 189; R. W. Van Alstyne, *The Rising American Empire* (New York: W. W. Norton, 1960), 166; Thomas J. McCormick, *China Market: America's Quest for Informal Empire, 1893–1901* (Chicago: Ivan R. Dee, 1967).

13. The most prominent studies of Spanish-American War journalism credit the "yellow" press for rousing public opinion and bringing the nation to war. See Joseph Wisan, *The Cuban Crisis as Reflected in the New York Press* (New York: Columbia University Press, 1934); Marcus Wilkerson, *Public Opinion and the Spanish-American War: A Study in War Propaganda* (New York: Russell & Russell, 1967); Charles H. Brown, *The Correspondents' War: Journalists in the Spanish-American War* (New York: Charles Scribner's Sons, 1967); Joyce Milton, *The Yellow Kids: Foreign Correspondents in the Heyday of Yellow Journalism* (New York: Harper & Row, 1989); Sydney Kobre, *The Yellow Press and Gilded Age Journalism* (Tallahassee: Florida State University, 1964). John Tebbel labels the period the "Age of Hysteria" and calls the war correspondents of the "yellow" press "the makers of public opinion" in *America's Great Patriotic War with Spain: Mixed Motives, Lies and Racism in Cuba and the Philippines, 1898–1915* (Manchester Center, Vt.: Marshall Jones Company, 1996), 4, 65. To demonstrate the dominance of this particular theory in general histories of the war, Louis A. Pérez Jr. lists a number of historians who subscribe to this view: Samuel Flagg Bemis, James P. Warburg, Louis Martin Sears, James Ford Rhodes, W. E. Woodward, Roger Burlingame, Richard W. Leopold, and H. Wayne Morgan. See Louis A. Pérez Jr., *The War of 1898: The United States and Cuba in History and Historiography* (Chapel Hill: University of North Carolina Press, 1998), 72–73. More recent accounts that make this argument include Daniel Cohen, *Yellow Journalism: Scandal, Sensationalism, and Gossip in the Media* (Brookfield, Conn.: Twenty-first Century Books, 2000), 30–34; Bruce W. Sanford, *Don't Shoot the Messenger: How Our Hatred of the Media Threatens Free Speech for All of Us* (New York: Free Press, 1999); Gene Wiggins, "Journey to Cuba:

The Yellow Crisis," in *The Press in Times of Crisis,* ed. Lloyd Chiasson Jr. (Westport: Greenwood Press, 1995), 105–6, 117.

14. George F. Pearce articulates this critique of the yellow press theory in "Assessing Public Opinion: Editorial Comment and the Annexation of Hawaii: A Case Study," *Pacific Historical Review* 43 (August 1974): 325–27. See also W. Joseph Campbell, *Yellow Journalism: Puncturing the Myths, Defining the Legacies* (Westport, Conn.: Praeger, 2003), 97–123; Ted Curtis Smythe, *The Gilded Age Press, 1865–1900* (Westport, Conn.: Praeger, 2003), 191–93.

15. This critique is best expressed in Pérez, *The War of 1898,* 64–80.

16. The term "yellow" journalism drew its inspiration from the graphic arts. According to W. Joseph Campbell, Ervin Wardman, editor of the *New York Press,* coined the term in late 1896 or early 1897 as a means of denigrating the *Journal* and the *World.* Wardman came up with the term in response to Pulitzer's and Hearst's struggle over the graphic series the "Yellow Kid," which originated in the *New York World* in R. F. Outcault's comic series "Hogan's Alley." According to the myth, Charles W. Saalberg was trying to devise a nonsmearing yellow ink and needed to test his formula, so he used the ink to color Outcault's newest character in "Hogan's Alley" in solid yellow. In turn, Outcault gave the character a hint of Asian physiognomy to lampoon the "yellow peril" craze emerging from the Sino-Japanese War; hence the "Yellow Kid" was born. This color came to symbolize the competition between Pulitzer and Hearst, and by the end of 1897, the term "yellow" journalism or "yellow kid" journalism became synonymous with their journalistic styles. See discussion in Campbell, *Yellow Journalism,* 7–8, 25–41; Don C. Seitz, *Joseph Pulitzer: His Life and Letters* (New York: Simon & Schuster, 1924), 231–32; Milton, *The Yellow Kids,* 41–43. On the genealogy of the phrase, see Mark Winchester, "Hully Gee, It's a War!!! The Yellow Kid and the Coining of 'Yellow Journalism,'" *Inks: Cartoon and Comic Art Studies* 2 (November 1995): 22–37.

17. W. Joseph Campbell has called attention to the many "shades of yellow journalism" arising from the widespread use of these practices outside the *Journal* and the *World;* see Campbell, *Yellow Journalism,* 5–6. Because of its central role in the historiography, I feel compelled to engage the terminology of the "yellow" press, but I do so hesitantly (hence the quotation marks around it, which hereafter will be implied) because the term is often used pejoratively and imprecisely.

18. See statistics on population and print output in 1898 in Richard F. Hamilton, *President McKinley, War and Empire,* vol. 1, *President McKinley and the Coming of War, 1898* (New Brunswick: Transaction Publishing, 2006), 241–42.

19. A series of local case studies of American press and public opinion in North Carolina, Texas, Minnesota, Florida, New Jersey, Indiana, Oklahoma, Ohio, and Kansas portray a less homogeneous and more measured popular response than traditional histories suggest. See Hamilton, *President McKinley, War and Empire,* 1:171–211; George W. Auxier, "Middle Western Newspapers and the Spanish-American War, 1895–1898," *Mississippi Valley Historical Review* 26 (March 1940): 523–34; Peter Mickelson, "Nationalism in Minnesota during the Spanish-American War," *Minnesota History* 41 (Spring 1968): 1–12; Harold J. Sylwester, "The Kan-

sas Press and the Coming of the Spanish-American War," *Historian* 31.2 (February 1969): 251–67; Mark M. Welter, "The 1895–98 Cuban Crisis in Minnesota Newspapers: Testing the 'Yellow Journalism' Theory," *Journalism Quarterly* 47 (1970): 719–24; David C. Boles, "Editorial Opinion in Oklahoma and Indian Territories on the Cuban Insurrection, 1895–1898," *Chronicles of Oklahoma* 47 (Autumn 1969): 258–67; John J. Leffler, "The Paradox of Patriotism: Texans in the Spanish-American War," *Hayes Historical Journal* 8 (1989): 24–48; William J. Schellings, "The Advent of the Spanish-American War in Florida, 1895–1898," *Florida Historical Quarterly* 39.4 (1961): 311–29; Edward M. McNulty, "The Cuban Crisis as Reflected in the New Jersey Press, 1895–98" (Ph.D. diss., Rutgers University, 1970); Joseph A. Fry, "Silver and Sentiment: The Nevada Press and the Coming of the Spanish-American War," *Nevada Historical Society Quarterly* 20.4 (1977): 223–39; George H. Gipson, "Attitudes in North Carolina Regarding the Independence of Cuba," *North Carolina Historical Review* 43 (1966): 43–65; Morton M. Rosenberg and Thomas P. Ruff, *Indiana and the Coming of the Spanish-American War*, Ball State Monograph Number 26 (Muncie, Ind.: Publications in History, no. 4, 1976).

20. "Telepathic Journalism," *Baltimore Sun,* May 3, 1898, 4.

21. Quoted in Milton, *The Yellow Kids*, 241.

22. Quoted in John Dobson, *Reticent Expansionism: The Foreign Policy of William McKinley* (Pittsburgh: Duquesne University Press, 1988), 26.

23. Quoted in Richard F. Hamilton, "McKinley's Backbone," *Presidential Studies Quarterly* 36.3 (September 2006): 491.

24. On one side of the debate, historians such as Philip Foner, Walter LaFeber, William A. Williams, Fareed Zakaria, David Haward Bain, Thomas J. McCormick, and Daniel Schirmer argue that McKinley had an imperial design in advocating war against Spain which followed the expansionist trends of late-nineteenth-century foreign policy. Others, such as John Dobson, David Healy, Margaret Leech, G. J. A. O'Toole, William Leuchtenburg, Stanley Karnow, and David Trask, claim that McKinley made the decision to take the Philippines reluctantly and after much indecision. McKinley left little written record of his intentions, making it difficult to know his mind as he led the nation to war with Spain. See Philip S. Foner, *The Spanish-Cuban-American War and the Birth of American Imperialism,* 2 vols. (New York: Monthly Review Press, 1972); Walter LaFeber, *The New Empire: An Interpretation of American Expansion, 1860–1898* (Ithaca: Cornell University Press, 1963); William A. Williams, *The Roots of the Modern American Empire* (New York: Random House, 1969); Fareed Zakaria, *From Wealth to Power: The Unusual Origins of America's World Role* (Princeton: Princeton University Press, 1998), 158; David Haward Bain, *Sitting in the Darkness: Americans in the Philippines* (Boston: Houghton Mifflin, 1984); McCormick, *China Market,* 7–9; Daniel B. Schirmer, *Republic or Empire: American Opposition to the Philippine-American War* (Cambridge: Schenkman, 1972); Dobson, *Reticent Expansionism;* David Healy, *U.S. Expansionism: The Imperialist Urge in the 1890s* (Madison: University of Wisconsin Press, 1970); Margaret Leech, *In the Days of McKinley* (New York: Harper & Brothers, 1959); G. J. A. O'Toole, *The Spanish War: An American Epic—1898* (New York: W. W. Norton, 1984); William E. Leuchtenburg, "The People's War," in *American*

Imperialism and Anti-imperialism: Problem Studies in American History, ed. Thomas G. Paterson (New York: Thomas Y. Crowell, 1973), 19–28; Stanley Karnow, *In Our Image: America's Empire in the Philippines* (New York: Random House, 1989), 99–105; David Trask, *The War with Spain in 1898* (New York: Macmillan, 1981).

25. H. H. Kohlsaat, *From McKinley to Harding: Personal Recollections of Our Presidents* (New York: Charles Scribner's Sons, 1923), 67–68.

26. Quoted in David Traxel, *1898: The Birth of the American Century* (New York: Alfred A. Knopf, 1998), 284.

27. Ibid., 284.

28. Richard Hofstadter, "Cuba, the Philippines, and Manifest Destiny," in *The Paranoid Style in American Politics and Other Essays* (New York: Alfred A. Knopf, 1965), 145–87.

29. George Kennan, *American Diplomacy* (Chicago: University of Chicago Press, 1951), 20.

30. Orvell brings to light an important shift in the conventions governing cultural production in the late nineteenth century "from a culture in which the arts of imitation and illusion were valorized to a culture in which the notion of authenticity became of primary value." Miles Orvell, *The Real Thing: Imitation and Authenticity in American Culture, 1880–1940* (Chapel Hill: University of North Carolina Press, 1989), xv.

31. Charles H. Ames, "An Unjustifiable War," *Boston Transcript*, September 7, 1898, 16.

32. This interpretation is inspired by Benedict Anderson's landmark study *Imagined Communities: Reflections on the Origin and Spread of Nationalism*, rev. ed. (London: Verso, 1991).

33. Gerald Baldasty, *The Commercialization of News in the Nineteenth Century* (Madison: University of Wisconsin Press, 1992), 5.

34. Alice Fahs, *The Imagined Civil War: Popular Literature of the North and South, 1861–1865* (Chapel Hill: University of North Carolina Press, 2001), 19.

35. Roger Butterfield, "Pictures in the Papers," *American Heritage* 13 (June 1962): 97, 99. See also Neil Harris, introduction to *The Land of Contrasts, 1880–1901*, ed. Neil Harris (New York: George Braziller, 1970), 1–28.

36. Alan Trachtenberg, *The Incorporation of America: Culture and Society in the Gilded Age* (New York: Hill and Wang, 1982), 122; Neil Harris, "Iconography and Intellectual History: The Half-Tone Effect," in *New Directions in American Intellectual History*, ed. John Higham and Paul K. Conklin (Baltimore: Johns Hopkins University Press, 1979), 199. On the history of pictorial journalism or photojournalism and its technologies in the nineteenth century, see Joshua Brown, *Beyond the Lines: Pictorial Reporting, Everyday Life, and the Crisis of Gilded Age America* (Berkeley: University of California Press, 2002); Christopher P. Wilson, "The Rhetoric of Consumption: Mass-Market Magazines and the Demise of the Gentle Reader, 1880–1920," in *The Culture of Consumption: Critical Essays in American History, 1880–1980*, ed. Richard Wightman Fox and T. J. Jackson Lears (New York: Pantheon Books, 1983), 40–64; Estelle Jussim, *Visual Communication and the Graphic Arts: Photographic Technologies in the Nineteenth Century* (New York: R. R. Bowker Company, 1974);

Ulrich Keller, "Photojournalism around 1900: The Institutionalization of a Mass Medium," in *Shadow and Substance: Essays on the History of Photography,* ed. Kathleen Collins (Bloomfield Hills, Mich.: Amorphous Institute Press, 1990), 283–303; Frank Luther Mott, *A History of American Magazines,* vol. 4, *1885–1905* (Cambridge: Harvard University Press, 1957), 144–54; Michael L. Carlebach, *American Photojournalism Comes of Age* (Washington, D.C.: Smithsonian Institution Press, 1997).

37. Theodore P. Greene, *America's Heroes: The Changing Models of Success in American Magazines* (New York: Oxford University Press, 1970), 60–61; John Tebbel and Mary Ellen Zuckerman, *The Magazine in America, 1741–1990* (New York: Oxford University Press, 1991), 75–76; Richard Ohmann, *Selling Culture: Magazines, Markets, and Class at the Turn of the Century* (London: Verso, 1996), 223–39.

38. Katherine Louise Smith, "Newspaper Art and Artists," *The Bookman* 13 (August 1901): 550. There is an extensive literature on the history and rhetorical analysis of editorial cartoons. A few key texts include Martin J. Medhurst and Michael A. Desousa, "Political Cartoons as Rhetorical Form: A Taxonomy of Graphic Discourse," *Communication Monographs* 48 (September 1981): 197–236; Matthew C. Morrison, "The Role of the Political Cartoonist in Image Making," *Central States Speech Journal* 20 (Winter 1969): 252–60; Lucy Shelton Caswell, "Drawing Swords: War in American Editorial Cartoons," *American Journalism* 21.2 (2004): 13–45; LeRoy M. Carl, "Political Cartoons: 'Ink Blots' of the Editorial Page," *Journal of Popular Culture* 4 (1970): 39–45; Lawrence H. Streicher, "On a Theory of Political Caricature," *Comparative Studies in Society and History* 9.4 (1967): 427–45; Robert Philippe, *Political Graphics: Art as a Weapon* (New York: Abbeville Press, 1980); Charles Press, *The Political Cartoon* (Toronto: Associated University Presses, 1981); Stephen Hess and Sandy Northrop, *Drawn and Quartered: The History of American Political Cartoons* (Montgomery: Elliot & Clark Publishing, 1996); W. G. Rogers, *Mightier Than the Sword: Cartoon, Caricature, Social Comment* (New York: Harcourt, Brace & World, 1969); Mary Campbell and Gordon Campbell, *The Pen, Not the Sword* (Nashville: Aurora Publishers, 1970).

39. Earl W. Mayo, "Cartoons and Cartoonists," *Los Angeles Sunday Times,* March 27, 1898, 12.

40. Lippman, *Public Opinion,* 96–97.

41. Eugene Secunda and Terence P. Moran, *Selling War to America: From the Spanish-American War to the Global War on Terror* (Westport, Conn.: Praeger Security International, 2007), 3.

1. The Spectacle of Endangered Bodies

1. See Ben Singer, *Melodrama and Modernity: Early Sensational Cinema and Its Contexts* (New York: Cambridge University Press, 2001), 45–49; David Grimsted, *Melodrama Unveiled: American Theatre and Culture, 1800–1850* (Chicago: University of Chicago Press, 1968), 16, 171–81; Steve Neale, "Melo Talk: On the Meaning and Use of the Term 'Melodrama' in the American Trade Press," *Velvet Light Trap* 32 (Fall 1993): 66–89; Martin Meisel, *Realizations: Narrative, Pictorial, and Theatrical Arts in Nineteenth-Century*

England (Princeton: Princeton University Press, 1983), 97, 98, 120–21.

2. Singer, *Melodrama and Modernity,* 41–44, 48–49, 53–56.

3. James D. Hart, *The Popular Book: A History of America's Literary Taste* (New York: Oxford University Press, 1950), 183–86.

4. See Lawrence W. Levine, *Highbrow/Lowbrow: The Emergence of Cultural Hierarchy in America* (Cambridge: Harvard University Press, 1988), 184–231.

5. John Lawrence Tone, *War and Genocide in Cuba, 1895–1898* (Chapel Hill: University of North Carolina Press, 2006), 60.

6. "Gomez," *New York World,* February 11, 1897, 8.

7. *Boston Sunday Globe,* January 31, 1897, 1; *New York Journal,* March 14, 1898, 4–5; *Cleveland Plain Dealer,* January 18, 1897, 1; "Weyler Spreads Woe," *New York World,* May 9, 1897, 5.

8. The War of 1898 helped secure the foothold of the Associated Press as a national organization. In 1897 the regional offices of the AP were unified, driving its main competition, the United Press, out of the news market. Placing correspondents in Cuba as early as 1896, the AP set up a flotilla of dispatch boats to carry news to the mainland. Once war was declared, McKinley approved the AP's request to board U.S. flagships. This privileged access enabled the AP to provide detailed reports to press bureaus in the United States as well as London, Paris, Berlin, and other international sites. Charles Sanford Diehl, *The Staff Correspondent: The Beginning and Growth of the Worldwide Associated Press News Service* (San Antonio: Clegg, 1931), 239–53; Oliver Gramling, *AP: The Story of News* (New York: Farrar and Rinehart, 1940), 137–39.

9. W. Joseph Campbell, *The Year That Defined American Journalism: 1897 and the Clash of Paradigms* (New York: Routledge, 2006), 109.

10. See *War Extra: Catalogue of Edison's Films,* supplement no. 4, May 20, 1898, Thomas Edison Papers, Library of Congress.

11. Charles H. Brown called them "romantic adventurers" in *The Correspondents' War: Journalists in the Spanish-American War* (New York: Charles Scribner's Sons, 1967), 63. See also John Seelye, *War Games: Richard Harding Davis and the New Imperialism* (Amherst: University of Massachusetts Press, 2003), 37–41; Joyce Milton, *The Yellow Kids: Correspondents in the Heyday of Yellow Journalism* (New York: Harpers, 1989).

12. Popular songs also propagated this narrative of Cuban suffering. See Jill DeTemple, "Singing the *Maine:* The Popular Image of Cuba in Sheet Music of the Spanish-American War," *Historian* 63 (Summer 2001): 715–29.

13. Roger A. Fischer, "Political Cartoon Symbols and the Divergence of Popular and Traditional Cultures in the United States," in *Dominant Symbols in Popular Culture,* ed. Ray B. Browne, Marshall W. Fishwick, and Kevin O. Browne (Bowling Green: Bowling Green State University Popular Press, 1990), 182, 189; Thomas Milton Kemnitz, "The Cartoon as a Historical Source," *Journal of Interdisciplinary History* 4 (Summer 1973): 85; Alton Ketchum, *Uncle Sam: The Man and the Legend* (New York: Hill and Wang, 1969), 121.

14. Walt McDougall, *This Is the Life!* (New York: Alfred A. Knopf, 1926), 40, 181.

15. *New York Herald,* May 15, 1897, 3, reprinted in the *Chicago Tribune,* May 17, 1897, 1; *Houston Post,* February 13, 1897, 1.

16. See "Starvation and Suffering in Devastated Cuba," *New York Herald,* May 14, 1897, 3; *Chicago Tribune,* May 16, 1897, 2.

17. Crittenden Marriott, "Laid Waste by Fire," *Chicago Record,* February 3, 1897, 1.

18. See Joseph Smith, "The American Image of the Cuban Insurgents in 1898," *Zeitschrift für Anglistik und Amerikanistik* 40.4 (1992): 319–29.

19. "Cuban Patriots These," *New York World,* April 3, 1898, 10. See also "Battle-Scarred Cuban Soldiers the Feature of the Wild West Show," *New York World,* March 31, 1898, 8; "Rousing Reception to Buffalo Bill's Cavalcade as It Passed through the Streets," *New York Journal,* March 30, 1898, 16.

20. Kristin L. Hoganson, *Fighting for American Manhood: How Gender Politics Provoked the Spanish-American and Philippine-American Wars* (New Haven: Yale University Press, 1998), 43–67.

21. Although several scholars have noted the tendency to depict Cuba in female form, they have not acknowledged her sexual agency. Kristin Hoganson argues, "American correspondents frequently depicted Cuban women as pure and virtuous victims of Spanish lust." Hoganson, *Fighting for American Manhood,* 11. Michael Hunt claims that the press "liked to picture the Latino as a white maiden passively awaiting salvation or seduction." Hunt, *Ideology and U.S. Foreign Policy* (New Haven: Yale University Press, 1987), 60. Amy Kaplan shows that romance novelists of the period typically depicted Cuba as "a maiden awaiting rescue from an evil, decadent despot by the young virile hero, America," in "Romancing the Empire," *Culturefront: A Magazine of the Humanities* 7.1 (Spring 1998): 77. See also John J. Johnson, *Latin America in Caricature* (Austin: University of Texas Press, 1980), 72–115.

22. Frederick Pike argues that Latin women, cast "in the role of primitive sensualist," were excluded from the boundaries of civilization through the assumed link between unrestrained sexuality and natural/savage instincts. Pike, *The United States and Latin America: Myths and Stereotypes of Civilization and Nature* (Austin: University of Texas Press, 1992), 6, 8.

23. For examples of the female Cuban victim in graphic form, see *Minneapolis Journal,* March 2, 1896, 9; *Houston Post,* March 24, 1898, 1; *Chicago Tribune,* February 24, 1897, 1; *Boston Herald,* June 5, 1898, 17; *Collier's Weekly* 19.7 (May 20, 1897): 1; *Rocky Mountain News,* March 31, 1898, 1; *Boston Globe,* April 21, 1898, 1; *Denver Post,* May 24, 1897, 1; *Washington Post,* July 24, 1898, 1; *Cleveland Plain Dealer,* January 23, 1897, 22; *Chicago Inter Ocean,* February 12, 1898, 1; *Philadelphia Inquirer,* March 20, 1898, 1.

24. For an extended discussion of this abolitionist emblem, see Jean Fagan Yellin, *Women and Sisters: The Antislavery Feminists in American Culture* (New Haven: Yale University Press, 1989).

25. The yellow press mobilized images of warlike Cuban women, called Amazons, to sexualize the rebellion. *New York Herald* correspondent George Bronson Rea denounced this as fabrication: "From my experience in the field, I feel entirely justified in asserting that all the stories regarding the existence of Amazons with the Cuban insurgent army are downright 'fakes,' and

have been invented by unscrupulous correspondents, or inspired by Cubans, who have nothing else to occupy themselves with." George Bronson Rea, *Facts and Fakes about Cuba: A Review of the Various Stories Circulated in the United States Concerning the Present Insurrection* (New York: George Munro's Sons, 1897), 139. On the Amazon visual type, see Martha Banta, *Barbaric Intercourse: Caricature and the Culture of Conduct, 1841–1936* (Chicago: University of Chicago Press, 2003), 485–92.

26. "War Scenes in Cuba's Isle," *Richmond Times,* April 25, 1897, 18.

27. See Gayatri Spivak, "Can the Subaltern Speak?" in *Marxism and the Interpretation of Culture,* ed. Cary Nelson and Lawrence Grossberg (Urbana: University of Illinois Press, 1988), 271–313.

28. Lois W. Banner, *American Beauty* (New York: Alfred A. Knopf, 1983), 154–66; Singer, *Melodrama and Modernity,* 221–62. On the liberated heroine in historical romance novels of the late nineteenth century, see Amy Kaplan, *The Anarchy of Empire in the Making of U.S. Culture* (Cambridge: Harvard University Press, 2002), 107–11. On the expressive possibilities for women in theater in this period, see Susan A. Glenn, *Female Spectacle: The Theatrical Roots of Modern Feminism* (Cambridge: Harvard University Press, 2000); M. Alison Kibler, *Rank Ladies: Gender and Cultural Hierarchy in American Vaudeville* (Chapel Hill: University of North Carolina Press, 1999); Robert C. Allen, *Horrible Prettiness: Burlesque and American Culture* (Chapel Hill: University of North Carolina Press, 1991).

29. "Jessie Wood on 'Cuba's Vow' and Other Plays," *New York World,* February 14, 1897, 35.

30. "Plays and Players," *Boston Herald,* February 6, 1898, 10. For other reviews, see "Plays and Players," *Boston Globe,* April 4, 1897, 18; "Drama and Music," *Boston Morning Globe,* April 6, 1897, 4.

31. See Emily S. Rosenberg, "Rescuing Women and Children," in *History and September 11th,* ed. Joanne Meyerowitz (Philadelphia: Temple University Press, 2003), 81–93.

32. On enemy imagery, see Murray Edelman, *Constructing the Political Spectacle* (Chicago: University of Chicago Press, 1988), 66–89; Ragnhild Fiebig-von Hase and Ursula Lehmkuhl, *Enemy Images in American History* (Providence: Berghahn Books, 1997).

33. Richard Kagan notes that American historians such as William Hickling Prescott wrote of Spain as America's antithesis earlier in the nineteenth century using Black Legend rhetoric, possibly setting the precedent for later stereotypes that emerged during the war. Richard Kagan, "Prescott's Paradigm: American Historical Scholarship and the Decline of Spain," *American Historical Review* 101 (April 1996): 423–46. On the Black Legend, see Julián Juderías, *La Leyenda Negra: Estudios acerca del Concepto de España en el Extranjero,* 9th ed. (Barcelona: Araluce, 1943); Philip Wayne Powell, *Tree of Hate: Propaganda and Prejudices Affecting United States Relations with the Hispanic World* (New York: Basic Books, 1971); Charles Gibson, ed., *The Black Legend: Anti-Spanish Attitudes in the Old World and New* (New York: Knopf, 1971); Joseph P. Sanchez, *The Spanish Black Legend: Origins of Anti-Hispanic Stereotypes* (New Mexico: Spanish Colonial Research Center, 1990); Hunt, *Ideology and U.S. Foreign Policy,* 58–60.

34. "Amusements," *Chicago Record,* April 1, 1897, 3.

35. For examples of graphic depictions of Spain displaying gothic symbolism, see *Houston Post*, March 27, 1898, 5; *Chicago Tribune*, October 6, 1897, 1; *Rocky Mountain News*, February 20, 1898, 1; *Cleveland Plain Dealer*, March 16, 1898, 1; *San Francisco Examiner*, July 3, 1898, 12; *Judge* 34 (May 21, 1898): 346; *Denver Post*, April 11, 1898, 1.

36. "The Way of Spain," *New York Times*, April 11, 1898, 6.

37. "Cuba a Hell on Earth," *Tennessee Commercial Appeal*, March 4, 1898, 4.

38. "Julian Hawthorne Visits and . . . the Horrors of Starving Cuba," *New York Journal*, February 13, 1898, 34–35; Fannie B. Ward, "In Havana Cemetery," *Chicago Inter Ocean*, April 20, 1898, 2. For analogous images, see *Minneapolis Journal*, March 25, 1899, 7; *New York World*, January 15, 1899, 28; *Chicago Record*, January 16, 1899, 8; *San Francisco Chronicle*, May 22, 1898, 3; *Dallas News*, February 5, 1899, 21.

39. Marion Marzolf, *Up from the Footnote* (New York: Hastings House, 1978), 26. See also Barbara Freeman, "'An Impertinent Fly': The Canadian Journalist Kathleen Blake Watkins Covers the Spanish-American War," *Journalism History* 15 (Winter 1988): 132–40; Charles B. Brown, "A Woman's Odyssey: The War Correspondence of Anna Benjamin," *Journalism Quarterly* 46.3 (Autumn 1969): 522–30.

40. The Cuban War," *Cleveland Plain Dealer*, September 21, 1897, 6; "The War with Spain, and After," *Atlantic Monthly* 81 (June 1898): 723.

41. "'Beats' and 'Fakes,'" *New York Times*, February 16, 1897, 6.

42. "Mr. Davis Explains," *New York World*, February 17, 1897, 2.

43. "All the Correspondence Relating to American Citizens in Cuban Prisons Should Be Laid before Congress at Once," *New York Herald*, February 22, 1897, 8.

44. "Ruiz' Wounds Speak," *Chicago Inter Ocean*, February 23, 1897, 1.

45. "How Dr. Ruiz Was Assassinated," *Chicago Tribune*, February 25, 1897, 6.

46. See *New York Journal*, March 10, 1897, 1; March 13, 1897, 1, 6; March 15, 1897, 9; and March 26, 1897, 3; *New York World*, March 10, 1897, 7; *Chicago Times-Herald*, February 27, 1897, 5.

47. "Strange Light on Ruiz' Death," *New York Herald*, February 25, 1897, 3; "Ruiz's Widow Here," *New York Herald*, March 10, 1897, 11; *San Francisco Examiner*, April 11, 1897, 24.

48. "Dying Words of Dr. Ruiz," *Chicago Tribune*, February 25, 1897, 1.

49. "The Ruiz Case," *San Francisco Chronicle*, March 4, 1897, 6.

50. "Mrs. Ruiz Now Hopes for Vengeance on Fondesveila," *New York Journal*, June 12, 1897, 3.

51. Dazie Noel, *A Spaniard's Revenge or The Death of Ricardo Ruiz*, Stock-Farm and Irrigation Print, 1898, collection of the New-York Historical Society, E714, Box N.

52. See "Sanguilly's Reception at Broad Street Station," *Philadelphia Inquirer*, March 26, 1897, 1; "Julio Sanguilly and His Family at Home," *New York Herald*, February 28, 1897, 5.

53. Robert C. Hilderbrand, *Power and the People: Executive Management of Public Opinion in Foreign Affairs, 1897–1921* (Chapel Hill: University of North Carolina Press, 1981), 8–13.

54. Brown, *The Correspondents' War*, 95. Hearst broke the Cisneros story that August, but the *Journal* was not the first to report the story to the American

public. See *New York Herald,* section 6, April 25, 1897, 9; *Houston Post,* June 6, 1897, 5. These articles, though, went unnoticed, demonstrating that the Cisneros affair did not function as a cause célèbre on its own but required skillful marketing and repetitive promotion.

55. "The Cuban Girl Martyr," *New York Journal,* August 17, 1897, 1.

56. After her arrival in the United States, Evangelina Cisneros published her own account of events. In the photograph illustrating her escape, Cisneros stands before her viewer at a window with long flowing hair, seductive brown eyes, and a face flushed with emotional intensity. Her dress is unadorned and her expression stern; she presents herself as a fighter, suggesting a tension between her self-presentation and public perceptions of her as victim. Even so, the writing and illustrations by *New York Journal* staff frame her text, again usurping her voice and independence from the dominant narrative. Evangelina Betancourt Cosio y Cisneros, *The Story of Evangelina Cisneros, Told by Herself* (New York: Continental Publishing Co., 1897), 97.

57. "Evangelina Cisneros Will Soon Be Free," *New York Journal,* August 26, 1897, 6.

58. "A Victim of the Yellow Kid," *San Francisco Chronicle,* September 9, 1897, 6. For additional examples of skepticism in newspapers nationwide, see "Pleads with Weyler," *Chicago Times-Herald,* September 2, 1897, 2; "Fitzhugh Lee on War Racked Cuba," *New York Herald,* September 9, 1897, 9; "Miss Cisneros's Case Exaggerated," *New York Times,* August 27, 1897, 3.

59. "Cisneros' Latest Conquest," *Richmond Times* (reprinted from the *Washington Star*), October 23, 1897, 2; "The Fair Victim of Weyler's Barbarous Methods," *Chicago Times-Herald,* August 20, 1897, 1; "Karl Decker Is Here," *Washington Post,* October 22, 1897, 3.

60. *New York Journal,* August 23, 1897, 1.

61. "Infamy of Weyler Stirs the Nations," *San Francisco Examiner,* August 23, 1897, 3.

62. For a historiographical overview of maternal politics, see Linda Brush, "Love, Toil, and Trouble: Motherhood and Feminist Politics," *Signs* 21 (Winter 1996): 429–54; Seth Koven and Sonya Michel, eds., *Mothers of a New World: Maternalist Politics and the Origins of Welfare States* (New York: Routledge, 1993); Linda Gordon, *Pitied but Not Entitled: Single Mothers and the History of Welfare, 1890–1935* (New York: Free Press, 1994); Theda Skocpol, *Protecting Soldiers and Mothers: The Political Origins of Social Policy in the United States* (Cambridge: Harvard University Press, 1990).

63. Cisneros, *The Story of Evangelina Cisneros,* 47, 53; "American Women Unite to Save Miss Cisneros," *New York Journal,* August 22, 1897, 1.

64. On the role of women in imperial politics, see Antoinette Burton, "The White Woman's Burden: British Feminists and 'the Indian Woman,' 1865–1915," in *Western Women and Imperialism: Complicity and Resistance,* ed. Nupur Chaudhuri and Margaret Strobel (Bloomington: Indiana University Press, 1992), 119–36; Anna Davin, "Imperialism and Motherhood," *History Workshop* 5 (1978): 9–65; Kaplan, *The Anarchy of Empire,* 40.

65. Quoted in "The Rescue of Miss Cisneros Elicits Enthusiastic Applause," *New York Journal,* October 15, 1897, 6.

66. See discussion in Campbell, *The Year That Defined American Journalism,* 75–87, 161–94.

67. *Washington Times* quoted in "The Cisneros Case Is Still the Centre of Public Interest," *New York Journal*, October 19, 1897, 8; Julian Hawthorne, "Karl Decker ('Charles Duval'), Who Rescued Miss Cisneros, Is Here," *New York Journal*, October 15, 1897, 1.

68. "The Civilized World Approves the Rescue of Miss Cisneros," *San Francisco Examiner*, October 11, 1897, 2; "Reads Like Some Medieval Romance," *San Francisco Examiner*, October 13, 1897, 2.

69. "The Cisneros Reception," *Cleveland Plain Dealer*, section 2, October 24, 1897, 13; "With the Player Folk," *New York Journal*, October 24, 1897, 41.

70. "Theater Gossip," *Atlanta Constitution*, October 24, 1897, 21.

71. "Would Adopt Miss Cisneros," *Chicago Tribune*, November 4, 1897, 1.

72. "Brings Hope to Cuba," *Chicago Times-Herald*, November 14, 1897, 6.

73. Julian Hawthorne, "The Spectacle of Death," *New York Journal*, March 14, 1898, 2; "Human Documents from Cuba," *New York Journal*, March 14, 1898, 6.

74. William A. Smith, "Representative Smith Tells of Dreadful Conditions at Matanzas," *New York Journal*, March 16, 1898, 2; "Tells of Horrors of Cuban Warfare," *San Francisco Chronicle*, January 10, 1898, 2.

75. "Starving Cubans," *Denver Post*, May 13, 1897, 6; "The *Journal* Photographs Fill Congress with Horror," *New York Journal*, April 6, 1898, 5.

76. "Help the Cubans," *Houston Post*, December 3, 1897, 4. See also, for example, "A Group of Starving Natives in Famine-Stricken India," *Philadelphia Inquirer*, January 17, 1897, 1; "Frightful Scenes in the Scourge Stricken Regions of India," *New York Herald*, May 30, 1897, 1; "The Indian Famine. Help!" *Chicago Tribune*, February 7, 1898, 9.

77. "Senator Proctor on Cuba's Desolation," *Literary Digest* 16 (March 26, 1898): 362.

78. *Wall Street Journal*, March 19, 1898, quoted in William J. Donahue, "The United States Newspaper Press Reaction to the *Maine* Incident—1898" (Ph.D. diss, University of Colorado, 1970), 165–66.

79. "Senator Proctor on Cuba," *Boston Herald*, March 19, 1898, 6; "Senator Proctor's Speech," *Chicago Record*, March 19, 1898, 4; "Senator Proctor's Statement," *Chicago Inter Ocean*, March 19, 1898, 6; "Senator Proctor's Statement," *Los Angeles Times*, illustrated magazine section, March 20, 1898, 2; "What He Saw in Cuba," *Washington Post*, March 18, 1898, 1.

80. Thurston's speech quoted from Paul T. McCartney, *Power and Progress: American National Identity, the War of 1898, and the Rise of American Imperialism* (Baton Rouge: Louisiana State University Press, 2006), 103; "Horrors in Cuba Described by *Journal* Envoys," *New York Journal*, March 13, 1898, 41.

81. Sallie Beverley, "Credit to the Camera," *Washington Post*, April 3, 1898, 5.

82. *The Autobiography of William Allen White* (New York: Macmillan, 1946), 305.

83. Ellen Maury Slayden, *Washington Wife: Journal of Ellen Maury Slayden from 1897–1919* (New York: Harper & Row, 1962), 235.

84. Hilderbrand, *Power and the People*, 27.

2. The Spectacle of Disaster

1. Louis Pérez Jr. criticizes the historiography of the Spanish-American War for overemphasizing the impact of the *Maine* on the causes of the war. Louis A. Pérez Jr., "The Meaning of the *Maine:* Causation and the Historiography of the Spanish-American War," *Pacific Historical Review* 58 (1989): 293–322.

2. See George Cotkin, *Reluctant Modernism: American Thought and Culture, 1880–1900* (New York: Twayne Publishers, 1992).

3. Charles D. Sigsbee, *The "Maine": An Account of Her Destruction in Havana Harbor* (New York: Century, 1899), 44.

4. "Minister De Lome's Criticism," *Boston Herald,* February 11, 1898, 6.

5. Gregory Mason, *Remember the Maine* (New York: Henry Holt and Company, 1939), 1–3.

6. *The Chicago Record's War Stories by Staff Correspondents in the Field* (Chicago: reprinted from the *Chicago Record,* 1898), 8.

7. Scovel had obtained a signed blank cable form weeks earlier from a Cuban sympathizer, set with the censor's seal of approval, and had been carrying it with him for just such an opportunity. Joyce Milton, *The Yellow Kids: Foreign Correspondents in the Heyday of Yellow Journalism* (New York: Harper & Row, 1989), 219–20.

8. "A Day and Night in the *Courier-Journal* Office," *Louisville Courier-Journal,* section 4, September 24, 1899, 1.

9. "How a Great Newspaper Gathers Its War News," *Houston Post,* July 24, 1898, 19.

10. "United States Battleship *Maine* in a Gale," *New York World,* February 14, 1897, 11.

11. This point draws from Ulrich Keller's work on Crimean War reporting, which found that the "virtual simultaneity of event and transmission" was a key element in the modernization of mass media in wartime. Ulrich Keller, *The Ultimate Spectacle: A Visual History of the Crimean War* (Australia: Gordon and Breach, 2001), xiii.

12. The Columbia image descends from the graphic icon of the "Indian Princess" of the colonial period, which by the early nineteenth century had come to be viewed as too primitive and natural, and therefore too sexually available; it had to be adapted to a new model of American femininity. By the late nineteenth century, graphic artists had transformed Columbia into a semi-allegorical feminine ideal. Philip J. Deloria, *Playing Indian* (New Haven: Yale University Press, 1998), 29–30, 51–53; John Higham, "America in Person: The Evolution of National Symbols," *Amerikastudien* 36 (1991): 477–82; Rayna Green, "The Pocahontas Perplex: The Image of Indian Women in American Culture," *Massachusetts Review* 16 (1975): 698–714.

13. Robert C. Hilderbrand, *Power and the People: Executive Management of Public Opinion in Foreign Affairs, 1897–1921* (Chapel Hill: University of North Carolina Press, 1981), 18–19.

14. Editorials nationwide spoke of the public's restraint in the immediate aftermath of the *Maine* explosion. The *Scientific American* remarked, "The attitude of the public has been one of anxious and patient expectation, in which hasty conclusions and precipitate actions have met with universal disapproval." "The Official Report of the '*Maine*' Disaster," *Scientific American* 78 (April

9, 1898): 226. The *Louisville Courier-Journal* affirmed: "The American people are a high-spirited and fearless people, but they are also a people of fairdealing and common sense. However suspicious they may think the circumstances of the destruction of the *Maine*, they are not going to act until they know the facts." "Awaiting the Facts," *Courier-Journal*, February 18, 1898, 6.

15. William J. Donahue, "The United States Newspaper Press Reaction to the *Maine* Incident—1898" (Ph.D. diss., University of Colorado, 1970), 152–53.

16. Ellen Maury Slayden, *Washington Wife: Journal of Ellen Maury Slayden from 1897–1919* (New York: Harper & Row, 1962), 14.

17. Louis A. Pérez Jr. elucidates the historiographical dispute over the chronology of public opinion after the *Maine* disaster. On one side, historians such as Foster Rhea Dulles, Hollis W. Barber, Samuel W. McCall, Walter Millis, and Charles Morris claim that public indignation was immediately belligerent, while others, including Harry T. Peck, Thomas A. Bailey, Margaret Leech, James MacGregor Burns, Alfred L. Dennis, William Appleman Williams, Lewis A. Harding, and John Holladay Latane, argue that public opinion was restrained until the naval investigation concluded. See Pérez, "The Meaning of the *Maine*," 302–4.

18. Donahue, "United States Newspaper Press Reaction," 232.

19. See *Chicago Times-Herald* front-page cartoons for March 1, 3, and 4, 1898.

20. W. Joseph Campbell, *The Spanish-American War: American Wars and the Media in Primary Documents* (Westport: Greenwood Press, 2005), 101–6.

21. See Raymond Smith Schuneman, "The Photograph in Print: An Examination of New York Daily Newspapers, 1890–1937" (Ph.D. diss., University of Minnesota, 1966); Kevin G. Barnhurst and John Nerone, "Civic Picturing vs. Realist Photojournalism: The Regime of Illustrated News, 1856–1901," *Design Issues* 16.1 (Spring 2000): 74–77.

22. Milton, *Yellow Kids*, 226.

23. For examples of technical drawings and diagrams of the *Maine*, see *Dallas News*, February 25, 1898, 2; *Scientific American* 78 (February 26, 1898): 133; *New Orleans Picayune*, March 28, 1898, 1; *Charleston News and Courier*, March 29, 1898, 1; *Boston Herald*, February 18, 1898, 3; *Washington Post*, February 17, 1898, 1; *San Francisco Chronicle*, February 23, 1898, 1; *Cleveland Plain Dealer*, February 19, 1898, 1; *Philadelphia Inquirer*, February 18, 1898, 7.

24. Letter to the editor, *Scientific American* 78 (April 23, 1898): 263, in response to drawings published in *Scientific American* 78 (April 9, 1898): 234–35.

25. "The *World*'s Latest Discoveries Indicate *Maine* Was Blown Up by Submarine Mine," *New York World*, February 20, 1898, 1.

26. John C. Hemment, *Cannon and Camera: Sea and Land Battles of the Spanish-American War in Cuba, Camp Life, and the Return of the Soldiers* (New York: D. Appleton and Company, 1898), 1–3, 24–25.

27. *Chicago Tribune*, March 3, 1898, 3.

28. For additional examples of visual representations of the divers, see *Dallas News*, February 26, 1898, 1; *San Francisco Examiner*, February 20, 1898, 13; *Louisville Courier-Journal*, March 1, 1898, 1; *New York Herald*, February 23, 1898, 9; *Chicago Tribune*, March 6, 1898, 3; *Scientific American* 78

(March 12, 1898): 161; *Boston Herald,* March 4, 1898, 1; *Collier's Weekly* 20 (March 19, 1898): 5–6; *Leslie's Weekly* 86 (March 17, 1898): 168–69; *Cleveland Plain Dealer,* February 25, 1898, 1.

29. *San Francisco Examiner,* March 1, 1898, 1; *New York Journal,* February 23, 1898, 1; *Dallas News,* February 27, 1898, 1.

30. John Wall, "How I Rescued the *Maine* Heroes," *Richmond Times,* March 20, 1898, 1, reprinted in the *Philadelphia Inquirer,* March 20, 1898, 26.

31. "Bodies Are Badly Mutilated," *Chicago Record,* February 25, 1898, 2.

32. "Fight for Life," *Minneapolis Journal,* February 22, 1898, 1.

33. "Victims of Spanish Cruelty at the Funeral of the *Maine's* Gallant Crew," *San Francisco Examiner,* February 24, 1898, 3. See also *New York Herald,* February 23, 1898, 5; *Boston Herald,* February 24, 1898, 2.

34. Milton, *The Yellow Kids,* 294. See the appendix for circulation data on other newspapers nationwide.

35. Donahue, "United States Newspaper Press Reaction," 180.

36. Frederick T. Jane, "The '*Maine*' Disaster and After," *Fortnightly Review* 63 (April 1898): 640.

37. "Message from the President of the United States, Transmitting the Report of the Naval Court of Inquiry upon the Destruction of the United States Battle Ship *Maine* in Havana Harbor, February 15, 1898, Together with the Testimony Taken before the Court" (Washington, D.C.: Government Printing Office, 1898), 3–5.

38. Michael Blow, *A Ship to Remember: The Maine and the Spanish-American War* (New York: Morrow, 1992), 174.

39. On theories of the *Maine* explosion, see ibid.; Robert H. Beggs, *The Mystery of the Maine: An Examination of Public Documents Relating to the Destruction of the U.S.S. Maine* (Washington, D.C.: Carnahan Press, 1912); Hyman G. Rickover, *How the Battleship Maine Was Destroyed* (Washington, D.C.: U.S. Government Printing Office, 1976); Thomas B. Allen, ed., "A Special Report: What Really Sank the *Maine?*" *Naval History* 12.2 (April 1998): 30–39.

40. Quoted in James Castonguay, *Film Studies and the Spanish-American War,* http://chnm.gmu.edu/aq/war/fs1.htm.

41. Raymond Fielding, *The American Newsreel, 1911–1967* (Norman: University of Oklahoma Press, 1972), 5.

42. See the following sources by Tom Gunning: "The Cinema of Attractions: Early Film, Its Spectator and the Avant-Garde," in *Early Cinema: Space, Frame, Narrative,* ed. Thomas Elsaesser (London: BFI Publishers, 1990), 56–62; "The Whole Town's Gawking: Early Cinema and the Visual Experience of Modernity," *Yale Journal of Criticism* 7 (1994): 189–201; "An Aesthetic of Astonishment: Early Film and the (In)credulous Spectator," *Art & Text* 34 (Spring 1989): 31–45; and "'Now You See It, Now You Don't': The Temporality of the Cinema of Attractions," *Velvet Light Trap* 32 (Fall 1993): 3–12.

43. On early film as a "visual newspaper," see Robert C. Allen, "Contra the Chaser Theory," *Wide Angle* 3 (1979): 7–8; Charles Musser, *The Emergence of Cinema: The American Screen to 1907* (New York: Charles Scribner's Sons, 1990), 225–26; Charles Musser, *Before the Nickelodeon: Edwin S. Porter and the Edison Manufacturing Company* (Berkeley: University of California Press, 1991), 10, 162–67.

44. Campbell, *The Spanish-American War,* 14.

45. See Jonathan Auerbach, "McKinley at Home: How Early American Cinema Made News," *American Quarterly* 51 (1999): 798–801; Charles Musser and Carol Nelson, *High-Class Moving Pictures: Lyman H. Howe and the Forgotten Era of Traveling Exhibition, 1880–1920* (Princeton: Princeton University Press, 1991), 87.

46. Musser and Nelson, *High-Class Moving Pictures,* 11, 77–78, 86–93; Kathryn H. Fuller, *At the Picture Show: Small-Town Audiences and the Creation of a Movie Fan Culture* (Washington, D.C.: Smithsonian Institution Press, 1996), ix–x; Anne Moray, "Early Film Exhibition in Wilmington, North Carolina, 1897–1915," *Spectator* 17.1 (Fall–Winter 1996): 9–11.

47. Quoted in Musser, *The Emergence of Cinema,* 241.

48. *New York World,* March 27, 1898, 15.

49. Musser, *The Emergence of Cinema,* 240–47; *Chicago Record,* April 9, 1898, 2; "Plays and Players," *Boston Herald,* March 27, 1898, 10.

50. These films can be downloaded and viewed at the Library of Congress American Memory Web site, "The Spanish-American War in Motion Pictures," http://memory.loc.gov/ammem/sawhtml/sawhome.html. See also Musser, *The Emergence of Cinema,* 247–48.

51. Albert E. Smith, *Two Reels and a Crank* (Garden City, N.Y.: Doubleday, 1952), 38, 53–54.

52. Musser and Nelson, *High-Class Moving Pictures,* 326.

53. T. J. Jackson Lears, "From Salvation to Self-realization: Advertising and the Therapeutic Roots of the Consumer Culture, 1880–1930," in *The Culture of Consumption: Critical Essays in American History, 1880–1980,* ed. Richard Wightman Fox and T. J. Jackson Lears (New York: Pantheon Books, 1983), 18; Richard Ohmann, *Selling Culture: Magazines, Markets, and Class at the Turn of the Century* (London: Verso, 1996), 175–85.

54. *Atlanta Constitution,* February 18, 1898, 6; *Houston Post,* April 24, 1898, 23.

55. "Fragment of the *Maine,*" *Atlanta Constitution,* April 10, 1898, 5; "Crowds Looking at a *Maine* Relic in Front of *World* Office," *New York World,* March 19, 1898, 3.

56. *San Francisco Examiner,* May 13, 1898, 4; *Los Angeles Times,* April 24, 1898, 15.

57. *New Orleans Picayune,* July 3, 1898, 1.

58. Louise Imogen Guiney to Herbert E. Clarke, June 4, 1898, in *Letters of Louise Imogen Guiney,* ed. Grace Guiney, vol. 1 (New York: Harper & Row, 1926), 276.

59. "Flashes the *World*'s Cartoon on His Pulpit Screen," *New York World,* February 21, 1898, 8.

60. Reverend A. M. Sherman, *Morristown, New Jersey, in the Spanish-American War* (Morristown: Jerseyman Office, 1900), 25; "Patriotism of the Pulpits," *San Francisco Examiner,* April 25, 1898, 5.

61. Jill DeTemple, "Singing the *Maine*: The Popular Image of Cuba in Sheet Music of the Spanish-American War," *Historian* 63 (Summer 2001): 715–29.

62. "Scene at the *Maine* Monument Matinee at the Tabor This Afternoon," *Denver Post,* March 23, 1898, 1; "The *Maine* Monument Fund," *Denver Post,* March 24, 1898, 1.

63. "No North, No South, No East, No West—All Honor the Martyrs," *San Francisco Examiner,* March 8, 1898, 3; "The Veterans of the G.A.R. Will Help to Build the *Maine* Monument," *San Francisco Examiner,* March 11, 1898, 2; "Help to Build the *Maine* Monument To-Night at Metropolitan Temple," *San Francisco Examiner,* March 16, 1898, 9; "Help to Build the Monument to the *Maine* Martyrs," *San Francisco Examiner,* March 15, 1898, 8.

64. "Drama and Music," *Boston Globe,* August 30, 1898, 2; "All the World's a Stage," *Dallas News,* December 4, 1898, 6; "The New Theatres," *New Orleans Picayune,* September 25, 1898, 7; "Successful Opening," *New Orleans Picayune,* October 18, 1898, 6; "Current Bills," *Chicago Times-Herald,* August 14, 1898, 22.

65. "The Drama," *Harper's Weekly* 42 (September 24, 1898): 939.

66. "Pride of the West," *Nebraska State Journal,* June 2, 1898, 2.

67. James B. Haynes, *History of the Trans-Mississippi and International Exposition of 1898* (Omaha: Committee on History, 1910), 247.

68. James B. Haynes's official history of the fair estimated that 65 million words were written about the fair outside the Omaha press. The fair's Department of Publicity and Promotion provided to publications nationwide over 125,000 bird's-eye views of the exposition, 400,000 large and small pamphlets, and thousands of photographs. Ibid., 251; "Advertising the Exposition," *Omaha Bee,* June 1, 1898, 3. Robert Rydell notes that "local newspaper stories and regional and national magazine articles, often generated by world's fair publicity bureaus, together with the merchandise advertising, carried the gospel of imperial abundance beyond the fairgrounds to a national audience." Robert Rydell, "The Culture of Imperial Abundance: World's Fairs in the Making of American Culture," in *Consuming Visions: Accumulations and Display of Goods in America, 1880–1920,* ed. Simon J. Bronner (New York: W. W. Norton & Co., 1989), 204–5.

69. W. S. Harwood, "The Omaha Exposition," *Harper's Weekly* 42 (August 20, 1898): 823;"Glimpses on the Midway," *Omaha World-Herald,* August 4, 1898.

70. "Spanish-American Fantasie," *Omaha Bee,* September 20, 1898, 4; "Battle Fantasie Very Popular," *Omaha Bee,* September 24, 1898, 5.

71. "Glimpses of the Midway," *Omaha World-Herald,* September 23, 1898, 2.

72. "Glorious Day at Exposition," *Omaha World-Herald,* July 5, 1898, 4.

73. Octave Thanet [Alice French], "Octave Thanet at Omaha," *Los Angeles Times,* illustrated magazine section, August 14, 1898, 10.

74. "The War with Spain, and After," *Atlantic Monthly* 81 (June 1898): 724.

75. "'No More Delay!' Sentiment of the Nation on Cuban Question—The *World's* Poll of Congressional Districts," *New York World,* April 6, 1898, 4.

76. "Asked to Forget the *Maine,*" *Chicago Inter Ocean,* May 24, 1898, 4. Henry Watterson, editor of the *Louisville Courier-Journal,* also noted that many church societies and local organizations protested the adoption of "Remember the *Maine*" as the nation's war cry and argued that the United States must go to war not for vengeance but for loftier goals. Henry Watterson, *History of the Spanish-American War: Embracing a Complete Review of Our Relations with Spain* (New York: Werner Company, 1898), 68. See the cartoon mocking the "Don't-Let's-Remember-the-*Maine*-Society," *Chicago Inter Ocean,* May 26, 1898, 7.

77. Diary of Marian Lawrence Peabody, April 1898, in *To Be Young Was Very Heaven* (Boston: Houghton Mifflin, 1967), 366.
78. Helen Adams Keller to Mrs. Laurence Hutton, January 17, 1899, in Helen Keller, *The Story of My Life: With Her Letters (1887–1901) and a Supplementary Account of Her Education, Including Passages from the Reports and Letters of Her Teacher, Anne Mansfield Sullivan* (New York: Doubleday, 1903), 441.
79. Arnold M. Shankman, "Southern Methodist Newspapers and the Coming of the Spanish-American War: A Research Note," *Journal of Southern History* 39.1 (February 1973): 93.
80. For examples of cartoons on this theme, see *Minneapolis Journal*, April 8, 1898, 1; *Atlanta Constitution*, March 31, 1898, 1; *New York Herald*, March 28, 1898, 3; *Chicago Record*, March 9, 1898, 1; *Denver Post*, March 5, 1898, 1; *Boston Herald*, March 2, 1898, 2; *Washington Post*, February 25, 1898, 1; *Philadelphia Inquirer*, April 10, 1898, 1.
81. David Traxel, *1898: The Birth of the American Century* (New York: Alfred A. Knopf, 1998), 115.
82. Quoted in Lewis L. Gould, *The Spanish-American War and President McKinley* (Lawrence: University Press of Kansas, 1982), 48.
83. Slayden, *Washington Wife*, 15.
84. Quoted in Warren Zimmermann, *First Great Triumph: How Five Americans Made Their Country a World Power* (New York: Farrar, Straus and Giroux, 2002), 262.
85. *Congressional Record: Containing the Proceedings and Debates of the Fifty-fifth Congress*, 2nd sess., vol. 31 (Washington, D.C.: Government Printing Office, 1898), 4062.
86. Ivan Musicant, *Empire by Default: The Spanish-American War and the Dawn of the American Century* (New York: Marion Wood/Henry Holt, 1998), 154.
87. Slayden, *Washington Wife*, 19, quoted in Campbell, *The Spanish-American War*, 165.
88. "Soldier Boys Honored," *Dallas News*, May 4, 1898, 8.

3. *Socializing the Politics of Militarism*

1. *Fulton Weekly Gazette* (Fulton, Mo.), April 29, 1898, quoted in William J. Donahue, "The United States Newspaper Press Reaction to the *Maine* Incident—1898" (Ph.D. diss., University of Colorado, 1970), 241.
2. Edward M. McNulty, "The Cuban Crisis as Reflected in the New Jersey Press, 1895–98" (Ph.D. diss., Rutgers University, 1970), 421.
3. "Dewey Tattooed on Their Left Arm," *Philadelphia Inquirer*, color section, November 27, 1898, 8.
4. This is not an exhaustive study of the battles and events of the war. I focus on Manila Bay, San Juan Hill, and Santiago because these battles figure most prominently in media coverage. I exclude, for example, the battle at Guantanamo and the Puerto Rican campaigns because the press did not grant these events substantial attention.
5. Michael Rogin argues: "Spectacles colonize every day life . . . and thereby

turn domestic citizens into imperial subjects. Spectacle goes private by organizing mass consumption and leisure; it attaches ordinary, intimate existence
to public displays of the private lives of political and other entertainers."
Michael Rogin, "'Make My Day!' Spectacle as Amnesia in Imperial Politics,"
Representations 29 (Winter 1990): 106.

6. See Brenda Murphy, *American Realism and American Drama, 1880–1940*
(Cambridge: Cambridge University Press, 1987); Vanessa Schwartz, *Spectacular Realities: Early Mass Culture in Fin-de-Siècle Paris* (Berkeley: University of California Press, 1998); Miles Orvell, *The Real Thing: Imitation
and Authenticity in American Culture, 1880–1940* (Chapel Hill: University
of North Carolina Press, 1989).

7. In May 1898 the *New York World* reported that the U.S. government had put
into effect censorship rules on information gathered at the front. The Commercial Cable Company released this notice to the press: "The United States authorities declare that all messages containing information of prospective naval
movements and current military operations are inimical to the United States, and
are consequently forbidden. Senders of press or other messages are requested not
to include such matter. If any such is found it will be stricken out by the censor."
"Strict Censorship of Cable News," *New York World,* May 19, 1898, 9.

8. These illustrations fit what W. J. T. Mitchell defines as "metapictures"
because they reflect on the process of viewing images: "The principal use
of the metapicture is, obviously, to explain what pictures are—to stage, as
it were, the 'self-knowledge' of pictures." W. J. T. Mitchell, *Picture Theory:
Essays on Verbal and Visual Representation* (Chicago: University of Chicago
Press, 1994), 35–57, quotation on 57.

9. For other illustrations of the public consumption of military spectacle, see
"Exercises in Independence Square," *Philadelphia Inquirer,* July 5, 1898,
7; "To Review Troops," *Chicago Inter Ocean,* May 23, 1898, 1; "Great
Military Display," *Dallas News,* August 18, 1898, 6; "Our Soldiers at Camp
Dewey," *Boston Herald,* May 8, 1898, 23.

10. Diary of Frederik Holmes Christensen, vol. 6, 7, Collection of the South
Caroliniana Library, Columbia, S.C. On the Christensen family, see Monica
Maria Tetzlaff, *Cultivating a New South: Abbie Holmes Christensen and the
Politics of Race* (Columbia: University of South Carolina Press, 2002).

11. According to Ted Curtis Smythe, the actual number of correspondents in
Cuba varied from 130 to 165 to 198, depending on source and date. Ted
Curtis Smythe, *The Gilded Age Press, 1865–1900* (Westport, Conn.: Praeger,
2003), 190.

12. John T. McCutcheon, *Drawn from Memory* (Indianapolis: Bobbs-Merrill,
1950), 112–15; Charles H. Brown, *The Correspondents' War: Journalists
in the Spanish-American War* (New York: Charles Scribner's Sons, 1967),
188–98.

13. Competitive claims of authenticity were also prevalent in press accounts of
the Civil War. Joshua Brown concludes that "the papers constantly defended
their illustrations as based on eyewitness observation while simultaneously
and ceaselessly accusing their competitors of fabrication." Joshua Brown,
*Beyond the Lines: Pictorial Reporting, Everyday Life, and the Crisis of
Gilded Age America* (Berkeley: University of California Press, 2002), 55.

14. "Photographs from Manila," *Philadelphia Inquirer,* June 18, 1898, 8. Images appeared in the *Inquirer* on June 19, 1898, 33–36.

15. For similar examples of graphic accounts of the battle of Manila Bay, see *San Francisco Sunday Examiner Magazine,* May 8, 1898, 1; *Dallas News,* May 4, 1898, 1; *Leslie's Weekly* 86 (May 12, 1898): 304–5; *Savannah Press,* June 25, 1898, 5; Marshall Everett, ed., *Exciting Experiences in Our Wars with Spain and the Filipinos* (Chicago: Book Publishers Union, 1899), 306, 368; Henry B. Russell, *The Story of Two Wars: An Illustrated History of Our War with Spain and Our War with the Filipinos* (Hartford: Hartford Publishing Company, 1899), 365; W. Nephew King, *The Story of the Spanish-American War and the Revolt in the Philippines* (New York: Peter Fenelon Collier & Son, 1898), page facing 72, 75.

16. "Dewey's Victory Pictured by Pain," *New York Journal,* May 22, 1898, 30.

17. "Battle of Manila Brought to San Francisco: Pyrotechnic Pantomime of the Great Victory, in Aid of the '*Journal*'s' Fund for a Monument of War Heroes," *San Francisco Examiner,* August 14, 1898, 10; "Dewey's Victory Vividly Portrayed," *New York Journal,* May 20, 1898, 6.

18. In addition to Henry Pain's productions, other spectacular reproductions of the battle of Manila Bay appeared nationwide in 1898–99. In Washington Park in Philadelphia, Imre Kiralfy presented "The Bombardment of Manila: The Greatest and Grandest of Water Spectacles," with three hundred cast members and a "monster stage" adorned with a staggering 100,000 square yards of scenery. The *Philadelphia Inquirer* described it as "gorgeous," "thrilling," and "realistic" (July 3, 1898, 16; July 16, 1898, 7). On spectacular reenactments in other cities, see *Richmond Times,* July 11, 1899, 7; *Houston Post,* December 6, 1898, 14; *Chicago Times-Herald,* August 6, 1899, 7; *Dallas News,* November 6, 1898, 6; *St. Louis Post-Dispatch,* August 21, 1898, 15.

19. "A Synopsis and Events of Pain's Great Battle of Manila," *Atlanta Constitution,* October 16, 1898, 7.

20. "Battle of Manila," *Dallas News,* October 9, 1898, 2.

21. "Fighting Top of the *Olympia* during the Battle of Manila Bay," *Chicago Tribune,* December 19, 1898, 7. See also "Battle of Manila," *Chicago Inter Ocean,* December 11, 1898, 13; "Battle of Manila Bay," *Chicago Inter Ocean,* December 18, 1898, 14.

22. Richard Harding Davis, *The Cuban and Porto Rican Campaigns* (New York: Charles Scribner's Sons, 1898), 218.

23. The *Herald* later decided to publish Davis's dispatch on July 7, 1898, but only after Spain's defeat at Santiago made victory seem inevitable. Joyce Milton, *The Yellow Kids: Foreign Correspondents in the Heyday of Yellow Journalism* (New York: Harper & Row, 1989), 334.

24. One notable exception is a drawing published in the *New York Herald* (and in affiliated papers) titled "The 25th (Colored) Infantry Firing on El Caney after the Blockhouse Was Taken," depicting African American soldiers in combat at the Battle of El Caney. *New York Herald,* July 31, 1898, 4. In general, depictions of African American participation in the Santiago land campaigns were rare.

25. See description and painting in H. Avery Chenoweth, *Art of War: Eyewitness U.S. Combat Art from the Revolution through the Twentieth Century* (New York: Friedman/Fairfax, 2002), 81, 85.

26. "The rank and file of the troops are brown and sinewy fellows of the cowboy type, full of the spirit of daring and adventure," reported the *Chicago Inter Ocean*. They were to "be picked from the cowboys of the Wild West, every one of whom will have to give evidence of his ability to cast the terrible coil and rope the enemy before he can enlist," according to the *New York Journal*. See "Uncle Sam's Galloping Regiment of 'Rough Riders,' 'Cow-Punchers' and 'Fifth Ave. Dudes,'" *New York Journal*, May 15, 1898, 20; "Rough Riders Pass Through," *Chicago Inter Ocean*, May 26, 1898, 3; "Another Millionaire Joins 'Teddy Roosevelt's Terrors,'" *New York Journal*, May 14, 1898, 16.

27. John C. Hemment, *Cannon and Camera: Sea and Land Battles of the Spanish-American War in Cuba, Camp Life, and the Return of the Soldiers* (New York: D. Appleton and Company, 1898), 62, 109–10, 160, 171. Photographer James Burton also "found it impossible to make any actual 'battle scenes.'" "Photography under Fire," *Harper's Weekly* 42 (August 6, 1898): 774. On Spanish-American War photojournalism, see Michael L. Carlebach, *American Photojournalism Comes of Age* (Washington, D.C.: Smithsonian Institution Press, 1997), 57–75; T. H. Cummings, "War Photography," *Photo Era* 1.2 (June 1898): 25–26.

28. Albert E. Smith, *Two Reels and a Crank* (Garden City, N.Y.: Doubleday & Company, 1952), 38, 63–64. For another account of a Spanish-American War filmmaker in Cuba (for Edison's Biograph Company), see G. W. Bitzer, *Billy Bitzer: His Story* (New York: Farrar, Straus and Giroux, 1973), 33–38.

29. In a less successful example, a motion picture photographer for Vitascope attempted to reenact the battle of San Juan Hill on film in Orange, New Jersey. He paid eighteen "Negroes" seventy-five cents each and provided them with free beer to impersonate the Spaniards in the charge. But by the time he was ready to shoot, the "Spanish" troops had deserted him, taking two hundred rounds of blank cartridges with them. The police later found a number of the "pseudo Spaniards" playing a game of craps but made no arrests. See "'Spaniards' Would Not Fight: Vitascope Man Badly Treated by Men He Hired to Mimic the Battle of San Juan," *Phonoscope* (April 1899): 15, cited in Amy Kaplan, *The Anarchy of Empire in the Making of U.S. Culture* (Cambridge: Harvard University Press, 2002), 160.

30. "Plays & Players," *Boston Herald*, May 21, 1899, 14.

31. Kaplan, *The Anarchy of Empire*, 148–49; Charles Musser, "The Eden Musee in 1898: The Exhibitor as Creator," *Film & History* 11 (December 1981): 79. See also advertisement for Eden Musee in *New York Journal*, December 4, 1898, 35.

32. "Battle of San Juan," *Chicago Times-Herald*, June 19, 1899, 7; "Mimic Fight a Hit," *Chicago Times-Herald*, July 1, 1899, 7.

33. Jack Rennert, *100 Posters of Buffalo Bill's Wild West* (New York: Darien House, 1976), 14.

34. Robert A. Carter, *Buffalo Bill Cody: The Man behind the Legend* (New York: John Wiley & Sons, 2000), 386.

35. Joy Kasson writes, "Cody projected the capture of Havana as if it were already an act in Buffalo Bill's Wild West; he imagined war imitating the reenactment of war and, in particular, modern war replaying the Indian wars." Joy S. Kasson, *Buffalo Bill's Wild West: Celebrity, Memory, and Popular History* (New York: Hill and Wang, 2000), 249.

36. "Buffalo Bill Writes on 'How I Could Drive Spaniards from Cuba with 30,000 Indian Braves,'" *New York World*, April 3, 1898, 27. See also "Our Best American Fighter," *Richmond Times*, April 24, 1898, 19.

37. Christine Bold, "The Rough Riders at Home and Abroad: Cody, Roosevelt, Remington and the Imperialist Hero," *Canadian Review of American Studies* 18.3 (Fall 1987): 331.

38. David F. Trask, *The War with Spain in 1898* (New York: Macmillan, 1981), 245.

39. On Theodore Roosevelt's celebrity during the Spanish-American War, see Charles L. Ponce de Leon, *Self-Exposure: Human-Interest Journalism and the Emergence of Celebrity in America, 1890–1940* (Chapel Hill: University of North Carolina Press, 2002), 91–92.

40. Richard Schickel, *Intimate Strangers: The Culture of Celebrity* (New York: Fromm International Publishing Corp., 1986), 5; David Brody, "Celebrating Empire on the Home Front: New York City's Welcome-Home Party for Admiral Dewey," *Prospects* 25 (2000): 399. On celebrity in America more generally, see also Joshua Gamson, *Claims to Fame: Celebrity in Contemporary America* (Berkeley: University of California Press, 1993); P. David Marshall, *Celebrity and Power: Fame in Contemporary Culture* (Minneapolis: University of Minnesota Press, 1997); James Monaco, ed., *Celebrity: The Media as Image Makers* (New York: Dell, 1978); Leo Braudy, *The Frenzy of Renown: Fame and Its History* (New York: Vintage Books, 1997).

41. "The Dewey Fad," *New York Journal*, May 22, 1898, 23; "Dewey Honored in Cocktails," *New York Journal*, May 22, 1898, 30; "'Miss Dewey,' the Smartest Bear in the World," *New York Journal*, August 14, 1898, 23; "The Leading War Hero," *Springfield Republican*, August 18, 1898, 6.

42. Another clever satirical comment on the "Dewey craze" is Eugene Zimmerman's cartoon "Deweyville on Dewey Day," *Judge* 36 (June 24, 1899): 392–93.

43. George Dewey, *Autobiography of George Dewey, Admiral of the Navy* (New York: Charles Scribner's Sons, 1913), 289.

44. "Dewey Is Not an Exhibit," *Chicago Times-Herald*, March 24, 1899, 6.

45. See drawing in "The Great Peace Jubilee and Pageant of American History," *Rocky Mountain News*, October 4, 1898, 3.

46. "Philadelphia Honors the Men Who Brought the Nation Peace," *Philadelphia Inquirer*, October 28, 1898, 1.

47. "The Girl Who Kissed Hobson," *Chicago Times-Herald*, August 9, 1898, 3.

48. Remarkable Results of the Great 'Hobson Kiss,'" *New York Journal*, August 14, 1898, 15; "The Arnold Craze in St. Louis," *St. Louis Post-Dispatch*, August 21, 1898, 17.

49. Elizabeth G. Jordan, "4,000 Miles of Railroad Paved with Kisses," *New York World*, December 25, 1898, 23. See also Barton C. Shaw, "The Hobson Craze," *Proceedings of the U.S. Naval Institute* 102 (1976): 54–60.

50. "Efforts to Vindicate Hobson," *Chicago Times-Herald*, May 11, 1899, 6; "The Hobson Kissing Mania," *New York World*, December 25, 1898, 6; "Kissing," *Louisville Courier-Journal*, December 22, 1898, 1.

51. "The Hobson Pace That Kills," *San Francisco Chronicle*, December 22, 1898, 6.

52. "Efforts to Vindicate Hobson," *Chicago Times-Herald*, May 11, 1899, 6; "The Hobson Kissing Mania," *New York World*, December 25, 1898, 6.

53. *Cleveland Plain Dealer,* July 5, 1898, 2.

54. James B. Haynes, *History of the Trans-Mississippi and International Exposition of 1898* (Omaha: Committee on History, 1910), 71.

55. Gurdon Wattles, *Autobiography of Gurdon Wattles* (New York: Scribner Press, 1922), 70.

56. Smith, *Two Reels and a Crank,* 66–67.

57. Hemment, *Cannon and Camera,* 214.

58. See film on Library of Congress Web site, "Spanish-American War in Motion Pictures," http://memory.loc.gov/ammem/sawhtml/sawhome.html.

59. Henry Barrett Chamberlin, "The Destruction of Cervera's Fleet," in *The Chicago Record's War Stories by Staff Correspondents in the Field* (Chicago: reprinted from the *Chicago Record,* 1898), 86.

60. Pamphlet titled "Imre Kiralfy's Grand Naval Spectacle" (New York: Frank V. Strauss, 1898), 8–9.

61. "Our Naval War with Spain Brought to New York," *New York Journal,* August 7, 1898, 23.

62. "Amusements," *Cleveland Plain Dealer,* August 14, 1898, 18; "Our Naval War with Spain Brought to New York," *New York Journal,* August 7, 1898, 23.

63. "Tributes to the Second," *Nebraska State Journal,* September 8, 1898, 5; "Reproduction of the Naval War," *Omaha Bee,* September 7, 1898.

64. Ellen Maury Slayden, *Washington Wife: Journal of Ellen Maury Slayden from 1897–1919* (New York: Harper & Row, 1962), 17–18.

65. "The Theaters," *Louisville Courier-Journal,* section 2, August 21, 1898, 3.

66. "War News Told by 'Fakirs for Fools,'" *New York World,* May 19, 1898, 7. See also "War News at Plays," *New York Journal,* April 24, 1898, 50; "Dramatic Military Bill, Koster & Bial's To-Night," *New York Journal,* May 1, 1898.

67. Cecilia Elizabeth O'Leary, *To Die For: The Paradox of American Patriotism* (Princeton: Princeton University Press, 1999), 186.

68. "Williamson Boys Are Patriotic," *Philadelphia Inquirer,* June 9, 1898, 7.

69. Wilbur Schramm and David M. White, "Age, Education, and Economic Status as Factors in Newspaper Reading," in *Mass Communications,* ed. Wilbur Schramm (Urbana: University of Illinois Press, 1960), 439, 446–47. On the reception of pictorial content, see also George Gallup, "Guesswork Eliminated in New Method for Determining Reader Interest," *Editor & Publisher* 62 (February 8, 1930): 1, 545; George Gallup, "What Do Newspaper Readers Read?" *Advertising & Selling* (March 31, 1932): 22–23; Harvey C. Lehman and Paul Witty, "The Compensatory Function of the Sunday Funny Paper," *Journal of Applied Psychology* 11 (June 1927): 204, 208; Advertising Research Foundation, *The Continuing Study of Newspaper Reading,* no. 138, *Study Summary* (New York: Advertising Research Foundation, 1950), 13, 15.

70. "Our Young Patriots," *Chicago Inter Ocean,* May 15, 1898, 37.

71. Gregory Mason, *Remember the Maine* (New York: Henry Holt and Company, 1939), 47.

72. "The Battleship Craze," *Minneapolis Journal,* August 10, 1898, 4; "The American Boy," *Boston Globe,* November 7, 1898, 2; "School Boys' War Ship Fund," *New York Journal,* August 7, 1898, 38; "President M'Kinley

Indorses the Schoolboys' Plan to Build a War Ship," *New York Journal*, August 8, 1898, 9; "Boys' and Girls' Own Battleship," *Rocky Mountain News*, October 2, 1898, 22; "The American Boy's Contribution to the Navy," *San Francisco Chronicle*, November 20, 1898, 10.

73. *Chicago Times-Herald*, May 1, 1898, 7; *Youth's Companion* 72 (June 9, 1898): 282; *New York World Sunday Magazine*, May 15, 1898, 14; *New York Journal*, July 17, 1898, 24.

74. "Infant Dewey Slain in Battle," *New York Journal*, May 25, 1898, 7; "Boy Shoots Boy in Mimic War," *New York Journal*, May 31, 1898, 12.

75. See ads in *Washington Post*, June 21, 1898, 3; *San Francisco Examiner*, April 17, 1898, 16; *Philadelphia Inquirer*, June 3, 1898, 2; *St. Louis Post-Dispatch*, art portfolio supplement, October 9, 1898, 3.

76. "Red, White and Blue for American Girl," *Rocky Mountain News*, May 15, 1898, 25; "War Fever Has an Influence on Fashions," *Philadelphia Inquirer*, May 1, 1898, 42; *Boston Evening Globe*, October 21, 1898, 12; Rose Hortense, "Patriotic Spirit of the American Woman: Displayed in Her Apparel," *Philadelphia Inquirer*, June 19, 1898, 45.

77. *Chicago Tribune*, April 29, 1898, 12; *Dallas News*, May 22, 1898, 9; "Two Pretty Pictures," *Savannah Press*, May 16, 1898, 4; "The Art of Dressing Windows," *Cleveland Plain Dealer Sunday Magazine*, September 18, 1898, 24.

78. *New York Journal*, color supplement, October 2, 1898, 8; "War's Awful Aftermath—the Souvenir Craze," *New York Journal Illustrated Supplement*, October 2, 1898, 8. See also "The 'Souvenir' Collecting Mania," *New York Herald*, color section, August 14, 1898, 8; "Collections and Recollections of the Quaker City Soldiers," *Philadelphia Inquirer*, October 2, 1898, 34; "Relics of the Spanish War in Demand," *St. Louis Post-Dispatch*, December 4, 1898, 36.

79. *Los Angeles Times*, illustrated magazine section, June 12, 1898, 32; *Los Angeles Times*, June 22, 1898, 10; *Los Angeles Times*, illustrated magazine section, July 10, 1898, 28, and September 18, 1898, 8; *Chicago Times-Herald*, July 15, 1898, 12.

80. Anne Smith, "Women's Wear and Ways in War Time," *Philadelphia Inquirer*, May 29, 1898, 26.

81. Kristin Hoganson delves more deeply into the imperial meanings of American home décor. Not only did homemakers in this period bring patriotic themes into their interior decorations but also they infused international commodities and styles. See Kristin L. Hoganson, *Consumers Imperium: The Global Production of American Domesticity, 1865–1920* (Chapel Hill: University of North Carolina Press, 2007), and "Cosmopolitan Domesticity: Importing the American Dream, 1865–1920," *American Historical Review* 107.1 (February 2002): 55–83.

82. See *War Extra: Catalogue of Edison's Films*, supplement no. 4, May 20, 1898, Thomas Edison Papers, Library of Congress. See also Library of Congress Web site, "Spanish-American War in Motion Pictures," http://memory.loc.gov/ammem/sawhtml/sawhome.html.

83. "Round the Theaters," *Chicago Inter Ocean*, May 8, 1898, 17; "Amusements," *Chicago Inter Ocean*, May 9, 1898, 6.

84. "Stabbed a Play Spaniard," *Chicago Record*, April 13, 1898, 1.

85. "About Plays and Players," *San Francisco Chronicle,* November 29, 1898, 4; "Startling Absurdities of the Spanish-American War in the Popular Drama of the Day," *Sunday Examiner Magazine,* December 4, 1898, 28; "Amusements," *Indianapolis Sentinel,* November 22, 1898, 4; "The Theaters," *Louisville Courier-Journal,* section 2, August 21, 1898, 3; "Current Bills," *Chicago Times-Herald,* August 14, 1898, 22; "Music and the Drama," *Chicago Times-Herald,* August 28, 1898, 22.

86. "Thousands Eager for *Journal* News," *New York Journal,* May 6, 1898, 8. A number of incidents occurred registering public antagonism against Spain. In a saloon in Union Hill, New Jersey, a man named Henry Griningo voiced his sympathies with Spain and deprecated Admiral Dewey, for which he received a hearty beating. In Indianapolis an itinerant Sioux Indian spoke in favor of Spain in a saloon during a card game, causing a brawl, and found himself recovering in the local jail. In Savannah, Georgia, Tinny Smith and Frank Osban, two "colored" men who disagreed about who would win the Spanish-American War decided to "play" war; Smith shot and killed Osban, who had defended Spain, Smith claiming that he did not know the gun was loaded. On a less violent note, in Washington, D.C., a dry-goods merchant filed suit for $10,000 in damages against a rival merchant for calling him a Spaniard in public. See "Called Dewey Cur and Coward," *New York Journal,* May 4, 1898, 9; *Indianapolis Sentinel,* July 16, 1898, 4; "Fatal Play at War," *Savannah Press,* April 25, 1898, 4; "They Called Him a Spaniard," *Chicago Record,* June 2, 1898, 5.

87. John A. Hobson, *Imperialism: A Study* (New York: James Pott & Company, 1902), 227–28, quoted in Kaplan, *The Anarchy of Empire,* 113.

88. Quoted in "Warlike Spectacles Unite All Sections," *New York Journal,* May 28, 1898, 3.

89. See Daniel S. Margolies, *Henry Watterson and the New South: The Politics of Empire, Free Trade, and Globalization* (Lexington: University Press of Kentucky, 2006).

90. Martha Banta, *Barbaric Intercourse: Caricature and the Culture of Conduct, 1841–1936* (Chicago: University of Chicago Press, 2003), 567.

91. Matthew Frye Jacobson's work on the nationalist sensibilities of particular ethnic communities in structuring political discussions of Cuba uncovers yet another dimension to the narrative of nationalism at stake in the project for war and empire; see his *Special Sorrows: The Diasporic Imagination of Irish, Polish, and Jewish Immigrants in the United States* (Cambridge: Harvard University Press, 1995), 141–76.

92. Louis A. Pérez Jr. argues that the very name of the war itself was "palpable evidence of the power of dominant narratives to define the familiar and fix the forms by which the past is recovered, recorded, and received" in *The War of 1898: The United States and Cuba in History and Historiography* (Chapel Hill: University of North Carolina Press, 1998), xii.

4. The Visual Script Changes

1. M. Paul Holsinger, *War and American Popular Culture: A Historical Encyclopedia* (Westport: Greenwood Press, 1999), 190.

2. See, for example, the *New York Journal* editorial "What the National Policy Should Be," May 19, 1898, 10.

3. David Starr Jordan, *"Lest We Forget": An Address Delivered before the Graduating Class of 1898, Leland Stanford Jr. University, on May 25, 1898* (Palo Alto: Published for the University by the Courtesy of John J. Valentine, Esq., August 10, 1898), 9.

4. Virginia Bouvier suggests that war censorship regulations, which the government relaxed in late July, may have contributed to a lack of critical images between April and July 1898. Virginia M. Bouvier, "Imaging a Nation: U.S. Political Cartoons and the War of 1898," in *Whose America? The War of 1898 and the Battles to Define the Nation*, ed. Virginia M. Bouvier (Westport, Conn.: Praeger, 2001), 105.

5. See Thomas J. Osborne, *"Empire Can Wait": American Opposition to Hawaiian Annexation, 1893–1898* (Kent, Ohio: Kent State University Press, 1981), xii and xiii; Merze Tate, *Hawaii: Reciprocity or Annexation* (East Lansing: Michigan State University Press, 1968), 3–14; Elizabeth Buck, *Paradise Remade: The Politics of Culture and History in Hawai'i* (Philadelphia: Temple University Press, 1993), 58, 75; Patricia Johnston, "Advertising Paradise: Hawai'i in Art, Anthropology, and Commercial Photography," in *Colonialist Photography: Imag(in)ing Race and Place*, ed. Eleanor M. Hight and Gary D. Sampson (London: Routledge, 2002), 192.

6. Osborne, *"Empire Can Wait,"* xii.

7. William Adam Russ Jr., *The Hawaiian Republic (1894–1898) and Its Struggle to Win Annexation* (Selinsgrove, Pa.: Susquehanna University Press, 1961), vii–viii.

8. Osborne, *"Empire Can Wait,"* 6, 85.

9. Tate, *Hawaii,* 251–54.

10. Eric T. L. Love, *Race over Empire: Racism and U.S. Imperialism, 1865–1900* (Chapel Hill: University of North Carolina Press, 2004), 78.

11. Ibid., 77–78, 85–88, 95.

12. Jan Nederveen Pieterse, *White on Black: Images of Africa and Blacks in Western Popular Culture* (New Haven: Yale University Press, 1992).

13. Rayford W. Logan, *The Betrayal of the Negro: From Rutherford B. Hayes to Woodrow Wilson* (New York: Collier Books, 1954), 243, 245.

14. "The Hawaiian Question," *New York World,* February 3, 1893, 4.

15. Charles L. Bartholomew, "Symbolical Drawings in Cover Designs and Illustrations," in *Modern Illustrating Including Cartooning: Division 12*, ed. Charles L. Bartholomew and Joseph Almars (Minneapolis: Federal Schools, 1940), 56.

16. See this racial distinction in other popular cartoons, including "Who'll Get the Wishbone?" *New York Journal*, November 25, 1897, 9; "The Unkindest Cut of All," *New York Herald*, December 7, 1897, 7, reprinted in the *Boston Globe*, December 8, 1897, 7.

17. Eric Love, *Race over Empire,* 106, 118, argues that annexationists tried to "safeguard and expand white rule."

18. "Strange Delusions on Hawaii," *New York Journal,* January 5, 1898, 8.

19. "Some of Uncle Sam's New Nieces," *Boston Globe,* July 10, 1898.

20. Jane Desmond, *Staging Tourism: Bodies on Display from Waikiki to Sea World* (Chicago: University of Chicago Press, 2001), 61–63.

21. See Bernard Smith, *European Vision and the South Pacific*, 2nd ed. (New Haven: Yale University Press, 1985), 5; Johnston, "Advertising Paradise," 203–4; Desmond, *Staging Tourism*, 7–8, 11, 79, 95; Christin J. Mamiya, "Greetings from Paradise: The Representation of Hawaiian Culture in Post-cards," *Journal of Communication Inquiry* 16.2 (Summer 1992): 91, 93.

22. Desmond, *Staging Tourism*, 7, 12, 49–51, 54–57.

23. Karina Kahananui Green, "Colonialism's Daughters: Eighteenth- and Nine-teenth-Century Western Perceptions of Hawaiian Women," in *Pacific Diaspora: Island Peoples in the United States and across the Pacific*, ed. Paul Spickard, Joanne L. Rondilla, and Debbie Hippolite Wright (Honolulu: University of Hawai'i Press, 2002), 248–49.

24. "The New Fad of Colonial Expansion," *Denver Post*, June 12, 1898, 4.

25. William Dinwiddie, *Puerto Rico: Its Conditions and Possibilities* (New York: Harper & Brothers, 1899), 14, 111.

26. "Why We Do Not Want Hawaii," *New York World*, June 16, 1897, 6.

27. "It Now Rests with the Senate," *Baltimore Sun*, June 17, 1898, 4; "The Stride of Imperialism," *Boston Transcript*, June 11, 1898, 16.

28. "Views of Many Leading Newspapers on Expansion and Mr. Bryan's Position," *Rocky Mountain News*, December 25, 1898, 4.

29. "A Newspaper Vote on the Philippine Question," *Philadelphia Inquirer*, September 13, 1898, 6. For particular studies, see "A Newspaper Plebiscite on the Philippines," *Literary Digest* 17 (September 10, 1898): 307–8. *Public Opinion* also surveyed newspapers across the nation, but on a smaller scale, with similar results. "The Terms of Peace," *Public Opinion* 25 (August 4, 1898): 132–35.

30. "The Newspapers and the Issue of 'Imperialism,'" *Literary Digest* 17 (July 9, 1898): 32–38.

31. See discussions of this debate in Albert K. Weinberg, *Manifest Destiny: A Study of Nationalist Expansionism in American History* (Baltimore: Johns Hopkins University Press, 1935); Anders Stephanson, *Manifest Destiny: American Expansion and the Empire of Right* (New York: Hill and Wang, 1995); Frank Ninkovich, *The United States and Imperialism* (Malden, Mass.: Blackwell, 2001); Robert L. Beisner, *Twelve against Empire: The Anti-imperialists, 1898–1900* (Chicago: Imprint Publications, 1968); Richard E. Welch, *Response to Imperialism: The United States and the Philippine-American War, 1899–1902* (Chapel Hill: University of North Carolina Press, 1979).

32. "Expansion Not Imperialism: The Outlook Defines the Distinction," *New York Journal*, October 26, 1898, 6. See also "Expansion without Imperialism," *New York Journal*, November 17, 1898, 6.

33. "Expansion vs. Imperialism," *Boston Herald*, August 26, 1899, 6.

34. *San Francisco Examiner*, July 10, 1898, 1. For a few examples of cartoons in the late war period referring to the objective of avenging the *Maine* (and, by extension, leaving out the motivation of ending Cuban suffering), see *Philadelphia Inquirer*, August 1, 1898, 1; *Los Angeles Times*, illustrated magazine section, July 31, 1898, 1; *Judge* 35 (July 30, 1898): 72–73; *Denver Post*, July 5, 1898, 2; *Chicago Tribune*, September 6, 1898, 1; *Minneapolis Journal*, July 13, 1898, 1; *St. Louis Post-Dispatch*, comic weekly, August 21, 1898, 1.

35. This finding supports Louis A. Pérez Jr.'s argument that the mythification of

the *Maine* disaster in the media occurred retroactively, after the declaration of war, rather than as a causal factor. Louis A. Pérez Jr., *The War of 1898: The United States and Cuba in History and Historiography* (Chapel Hill: University of North Carolina Press, 1998). See also Virginia M. Bouvier, "Imperial Humor: U.S. Political Cartoons and the War of 1898," *Colonial Latin American Historical Review* 8 (Winter 1999): 19, 25.

36. Many cartoons and drawings incorporated Cuba Libre symbols and motifs prior to and during the first two months of the war. See examples in *Chicago Tribune,* May 19, 1897, 1; *Denver Post,* April 9, 1898, 1; *Houston Post,* February 15, 1897, 1; *Charleston News and Courier,* May 15, 1898, 14; *Boston Globe,* June 24, 1898, 5; *Judge* 33 (October 23, 1897): 264–65; *Philadelphia Inquirer,* June 5, 1898, 24; *Minneapolis Journal,* April 5, 1898, 2; *Indianapolis Sentinel,* June 3, 1898, 17.

37. *Chicago Record,* April 4, 1898, 1.

38. "We Were Just in Time," *Houston Post,* July 10, 1898, 18.

39. Besides the two images discussed in the text (from the *Syracuse Herald* and *Puck*), only two other cartoons in my sample making reference to Cuba Libre appeared between July and November 1898: *Minneapolis Journal,* July 30, 1898, 1; *Boston Globe,* July 24, 1898, 1.

40. Trumbull White, *Our New Possessions. Four Books in One: A Graphic Account, Descriptive and Historical, of the Tropic Islands of the Sea Which Have Fallen under Our Sway, Their Cities, Peoples and Commerce, Natural Resources and the Opportunities They Offer to Americans* (Boston: Home Library Association, 1898), 583–84.

41. "Gen. Wheeler on the Cuban," *Dallas News,* August 20, 1898, 4.

42. Amy Kaplan maintains that Theodore Roosevelt's writings about the battle of San Juan Hill rendered the Cubans as cowardly and unmanly in addition to erasing their participation in the war. Amy Kaplan, *The Anarchy of Empire in the Making of U.S. Culture* (Cambridge: Harvard University Press, 2002), 128. Kristin Hoganson similarly argues that although Cuban soldiers were depicted earlier in the "chivalric drama" as heroes and knights, later accounts "often wrote Cuban men out of the romance" in deference to the implications of U.S. imperial ambitions. Kristin L. Hoganson, *Fighting for American Manhood: How Gender Politics Provoked the Spanish-American and Philippine-American Wars* (New Haven: Yale University Press, 1998), 45, 62. Louis A. Pérez Jr. makes an important critique of the historiography when he argues that the dominant historical accounts of the Spanish-American War erroneously replicate the erasure of Cuban participation. Pérez. *The War of 1898,* 99–101.

43. Quoted in Ada Ferrer, *Insurgent Cuba: Race, Nation, and Revolution, 1868–1898* (Chapel Hill: University of North Carolina Press, 1999), 188, 189–91. See also David Traxel, *1898: The Birth of the American Century* (New York: Alfred A. Knopf, 1998), 183.

44. "The Cuban Insurgents," *Louisville Courier-Journal,* July 21, 1898, 4.

45. *Chicago Tribune,* August 10, 1898, 1; *New York Times Illustrated Magazine,* August 14, 1898, 16.

46. "The Filipinos and the Cubans," *Washington Post,* January 17, 1899, 6.

47. For examples of drawings of African American army camp life, see *New York Herald,* May 29, 1898, 4; *Boston Globe,* April 27, 1898, 3; *Boston Herald,* May 7, 1898, 9; *Los Angeles Times,* illustrated magazine section, May

1, 1898, 14; *New York Times Illustrated Magazine,* May 15, 1898, 4; W. Nephew King, *The Story of the Spanish-American War and the Revolt in the Philippines* (New York: Peter Fenelon Collier & Son, 1898), 116, 123. On African Americans in Edison films of the Spanish-American War, see Kristen Whissel, "The Gender of Empire: American Modernity, Masculinity, and Edison's War Actualities," in *A Feminist Reader in Early Cinema,* ed. Jennifer M. Bean and Diana Negra (Durham: Duke University Press, 2002), 156–58.

48. Theodore Roosevelt, *The Rough Riders* (New York: Charles Scribner's Sons, 1919), 143. Glenda Gilmore argues that "whites infantilized the soldiers on the one hand and portrayed them as animals on the other." Glenda Gilmore, *Gender and Jim Crow: Women and the Politics of White Supremacy in North Carolina, 1896–1920* (Chapel Hill: University of North Carolina Press, 1996), 81. See discussions in Amy Kaplan, "Black and Blue on San Juan Hill," in *Cultures of United States Imperialism,* ed. Amy Kaplan and Donald. E. Pease (Durham: Duke University Press, 1993), 219–36.

49. Willard B. Gatewood Jr., *Black Americans and the White Man's Burden: 1898–1903* (Chicago: University of Illinois Press, 1975), 16–18. Gatewood acknowledges that upon the return home of the U.S. Army, the black regiments enjoyed a moment of public acclaim in the white press. Still, this recognition was fleeting and not substantial enough to transform the visual and popular culture of the war (102–7).

50. "Proffered Support," *Indianapolis Freeman,* May 7, 1898, 4; "What We Are to Get Out of the War," *Colored American,* April 30, 1898, 4; "An Equal Chance and Fair Play," *Colored American,* May 28, 1898, 4.

51. See advertisements in the *Indianapolis Freeman,* November 20, 1897, 6, and December 11, 1897, 2.

52. *Colored American,* February 4, 1899, 4.

53. "The Color Line in Cuba," *Indianapolis Recorder,* February 18, 1899, 2. The other quotes are from George P. Marks III, ed., *The Black Press Views American Imperialism (1898–1900)* (New York: Arno Press and the *New York Times,* 1971), 115, 131, 154.

54. *Indianapolis Recorder,* February 18, 1899, 2.

5. The War's Final Phase

1. "Richard Harding Davis Writes of the *World*'s Correspondent," *New York World,* February 18, 1897, 1.

2. W. Joseph Campbell, *The Year That Defined American Journalism: 1897 and the Clash of Paradigms* (New York: Routledge, 2006), 143–47, 159.

3. "The War and Its Problems," *Indianapolis Sentinel,* June 29, 1898, 4.

4. Robert I. Fulton and Thomas C. Trueblood, eds. *Patriotic Eloquence Relating to the Spanish-American War and Its Issues* (New York: Charles Scribner's Sons, 1900), 322–23.

5. Daniel T. Pierce, "Does the Press Reflect Public Opinion?" *Gunton's Magazine* 19 (November 1900): 423.

6. Cultural studies of the Spanish-American War have emphasized the importance of masculinity in the gendered politics of war and empire. Kristin Hoganson argues that "policy-makers tried to legitimize their policies by presenting them as conducive to manhood," giving "gender beliefs the power to

affect political decision-making" and essentially "lead the nation into war." Kristin L. Hoganson, *Fighting for American Manhood: How Gender Politics Provoked the Spanish-American and Philippine-American Wars* (New Haven: Yale University Press, 1998), 3–4. Amy Kaplan writes, "Imperial expansion overseas offered a new frontier, where the essential American man could be reconstituted in his escape from modernity and domesticity." Amy Kaplan, *The Anarchy of Empire in the Making of U.S. Culture* (Cambridge: Harvard University Press, 2002), 99. See also Kristen Whissel, "The Gender of Empire: American Modernity, Masculinity, and Edison's War Actualities," in *A Feminist Reader in Early Cinema*, ed. Jennifer M. Bean and Diana Negra (Durham: Duke University Press, 2002), 141–65.

7. Laura Wexler further destabilizes postwar constructions of the male body in a fascinating discussion of the gender play in Frances Benjamin Johnston's photographs of Dewey and his crew aboard the *Olympia* in August 1899. Wexler argues that "domestic visions" of white manhood created a sentimentalized image of U.S. imperial and military power to mask U.S. aggression. Laura Wexler, *Tender Violence: Domestic Visions in an Age of U.S. Imperialism* (Chapel Hill: University of North Carolina Press, 2000), 15–51.

8. Muckraking is a form of journalistic exposé most often associated with the Progressive movement of the early twentieth century. These reformist reporters and writers typically addressed middle-class audiences and aimed to expose corruption in business, society, and politics. See Robert Miraldi, *Muckraking and Objectivity: Journalism's Colliding Traditions* (New York: Greenwood Press, 1990), 6–19; David Mark Chalmers, *The Muckrake Years* (Huntington, N.Y.: Robert E. Krieger Publishing, 1980); Richard Hofstadter, *The Age of Reform: From Bryan to F.D.R.* (1955; repr., New York: Alfred A. Knopf, 1981), 185–212.

9. For additional examples, see *Houston Post*, March 22, 1899, 1; *Philadelphia Inquirer*, August 20, 1898, 1; *Pittsburgh Press*, March 4, 1898 (*Uncle Sam Cartoons: War with Spain*, scrapbooks of mounted cartoons on the theme of the Spanish-American War, assembled by the Manhattan Press Clipping Bureau [New York, 1898], vol. 1, no. 86); *San Francisco Post*, April 14, 1898 (*Uncle Sam Cartoons* scrapbook, vol. 3, no. 147); *Buffalo Enquirer*, May 3, 1898 (*Uncle Sam Cartoons* scrapbook, vol. 5, no. 44).

10. John Dudley, "'The Manly Art of Self-Defense': Spectator Sports, American Imperialism, and the Spanish-American War," in *Convergencias Hispanicas: Selected Proceedings and Other Essays on Spanish and Latin American Literature, Film, and Linguistics,* ed. Elizabeth Scarlett and Howard B. Wescott (Newark: Juan de la Cuesta, 2001), 119–29.

11. Theodore Roosevelt, *The Strenuous Life* (New York: Century, 1900). On the struggles over American manhood in this period, see Michael Kimmel, *Manhood in America: A Cultural History* (New York: Free Press, 1996), 117–88; Gail Bederman, *Manliness and Civilization: A Cultural History of Gender and Race in the United States, 1880–1917* (Chicago: University of Chicago Press, 1995), 77–120; Judy Hilkey, *Character Is Capital: Success Manuals and Manhood in Gilded Age America* (Chapel Hill: University of North Carolina Press, 1997), 75–82, 142–65; David Axeen, "'Heroes of the Engine Room': American 'Civilization' and the War with Spain," *American Quarterly* 36.4 (Autumn 1984): 481–502. On the rise of sport and athletics in the 1890s, see Donald J. Mrozek, *Sport and American Mentality, 1880–1910* (Knoxville:

University of Tennessee Press, 1983); E. Anthony Rotundo, *American Manhood: Transformations in Masculinity from the Revolution to the Modern Era* (New York: Basic Books, 1993), 247–51; Mark Dyreson, "Regulating the Body and the Body Politic: American Sport, Bourgeois Culture, and the Language of Progress, 1880–1920," and Steven A. Reiss, "Sport and the Redefinition of Middle-Class Masculinity in Victorian America" in *The New American Sports History: Recent Approaches and Perspectives,* ed. S. W. Pope (Urbana: University of Illinois Press, 1997), 121–46 and 173–97; Elliott J. Gorn, *The Manly Art: Bare-Knuckle Prize Fighting in America* (Ithaca: Cornell University Press, 1986), 179–94.

12. Camp imagery served the needs of the press, particularly early in the war and between major battles, by providing continuous content to sustain audience interest in military matters. Photographs of camp life were much easier to acquire than battle shots, putting many more of them in circulation for graphic artists to convert into press illustrations. For additional examples of "domestic" camp scenes in the press depicting soldiers praying, eating, washing, resting, and so on, see *New Orleans Picayune,* June 25, 1898, 8; *Collier's Weekly* 21 (May 7, 1898): 12–13; *New York Herald,* June 26, 1898, 3; *Richmond Times,* May 14, 1898, 1; *Houston Post,* July 16, 1898, 8; *Philadelphia Inquirer,* May 8, 1898, 41; *Chicago Inter Ocean,* June 12, 1898, 26; *Cleveland Plain Dealer,* May 5, 1898, 1; *Dallas News,* May 8, 1898, 21.

13. See *War Extra: Catalogue of Edison's Films,* supplement no. 4, May 20, 1898, Thomas Edison Papers, Library of Congress.

14. Alvah H. Doty, "Little Fear of Yellow Fever," *Leslie's Weekly* 86 (May 19, 1898): 323.

15. French Ensor Chadwick, *The Relations of the United States and Spain,* 2 vols. (1911; repr., New York: Russell & Russell, 1968), 1:49.

16. Quoted in Graham A. Cosmas, *An Army for Empire: The United States Army in the Spanish-American War* (Columbia: University of Missouri Press, 1971), 266. See Cosmas's discussion of the problems of army mobilization and camp conditions (ibid., 245–94); Charles H. Brown, *The Correspondents' War: Journalists in the Spanish-American War* (New York: Charles Scribner's Sons, 1967), 428–40.

17. Vincent J. Cirillo, "Fever and Reform: The Typhoid Epidemic in the Spanish-American War," in *United States Military History 1865 to the Present Day,* ed. Jeffrey Charlston (Burlington, Vt.: Ashgate, 2006), 271.

18. Walter W. Ward, *Springfield in the Spanish-American War* (Easthampton, Mass.: Press of Enterprise Printing Company, 1899), 56, 119–20.

19. "Soldier Boys of the 14th Say That Rich Uncle Sam Gives Them Poor Food," *New York Journal,* June 7, 1898, 14. See also "More New York Volunteers Write Home Complaining of Their Experience in Camp," *New York Journal,* June 9, 1898, 14.

20. Poultney Bigelow, "In Camp at Tampa," *Harper's Weekly* 42 (June 4, 1898): 550.

21. "Charges of Incompetence in the Army," *Literary Digest* 16 (June 18, 1898): 721–23.

22. "Teddy Called Down," *Cleveland Plain Dealer,* August 5, 1898, 1–2.

23. "Yesterday's Spectacle in this City," *Springfield Republican,* November 4, 1898, 6.

24. Ward, *Springfield in the Spanish-American War,* 143.
25. David F. Trask, *The War with Spain in 1898* (New York: Macmillan, 1981), 335.
26. Chadwick, *The Relations of the United States and Spain,* 2:259.
27. For additional examples, see W. A. Rogers, "Camp Wikoff," *Harper's Weekly* 42 (September 10, 1898): 890–91; *Philadelphia Public Ledger,* September 16, 1898, 2; *New York Journal,* September 4, 1898, 38; *Boston Herald,* August 21, 1898, 2; *Chicago Inter Ocean,* Sept 11, 1898, 2; *Springfield Republican,* August 23, 1898, 7; *Indianapolis Sentinel,* April 21, 1898, 17.
28. *Richmond Times,* September 11, 1898, 1.
29. "Where to See War Pictures," *New York Journal,* August 13, 1898, 5.
30. "The Horrors of Our War," *Harper's Weekly* 42 (September 10, 1898): 882.
31. *New York World,* September 2, 1898, 3. See also *Leslie's Weekly* 87 (September 15, 1898): 201.
32. This cartoon is based on Homer Davenport's cartoon published in the *New York Journal,* August 26, 1898, 6, and *San Francisco Examiner,* September 1, 1898, 6.
33. "Yellow Journalism and Camp Wikoff," *San Francisco Chronicle,* November 19, 1898, 6.
34. "The Sick Soldiers," *Boston Transcript,* August 25, 1898, 4.
35. "Moving War Pictures," *Wilkes-Barre Record,* September 17, 1898, 5. Cited in Charles Musser and Carol Nelson, *High-Class Moving Pictures: Lyman H. Howe and the Forgotten Era of Traveling Exhibition, 1880–1920* (Princeton: Princeton University Press, 1991), 308–9.
36. "Howe's Realistic Pictures," *Wilkes-Barre Record,* January 25, 1899, 6.
37. "Entertainments," *Philadelphia Public Ledger,* September 13, 1898, 15.
38. "The Eden Musee," *Savannah Press,* October 7, 1898, 2; "American Character: Keep It High," *New York Journal,* August 22, 1898, 6.
39. Burr McIntosh, *The Little I Saw of Cuba* (London: F. Tennyson Neely, 1899), 2–3, 33, 77–82.
40. *Boston Globe,* October 9, 1898, 4; *New York Journal,* October 4, 1898, 6, and October 2, 1898, 31.
41. *New York Journal,* February 28, 1899, 5.
42. Cited in Alexander Nemerov, *Frederic Remington and Turn-of-the-Century America* (New Haven: Yale University Press, 1995), 53.
43. Cited in Peggy and Harold Samuels, *Frederic Remington: A Biography* (Garden City, N.Y.: Doubleday, 1982), 282–83.
44. I credit the football reading of this painting to Peter H. Hassrick, "The Painter," and David McCullough, "The Man," in *Frederic Remington: The Masterworks* (New York: Harry N. Abrams in association with the St. Louis Art Museum, 1988), 122 and 30, respectively; Nemerov, *Frederic Remington and Turn-of-the-Century America,* 54–60.
45. See further discussion in Nemerov, *Frederic Remington and Turn-of-the-Century America,* 62–64. Colonel H. Avery Chenoweth argues that Remington's work, compared to the more typical representations of the battle of San Juan Hill, demonstrates the difference between illustrations produced at home and eyewitness combat art. H. Avery Chenoweth, *Art of War: Eyewitness U.S. Combat Art from the Revolution through the Twentieth Century* (New York: Friedman/Fairfax, 2002), 80–81, 84–85.

46. "Shearing the Locks of Samson," *New York Journal,* August 31, 1898, 6.
47. "The Horrors of Camp Life," *Denver Post,* September 2, 1898, 4.
48. "The Stars and Stripes," *Dallas News,* August 21, 1898, 14.
49. See the discussion of this iconographic trend in Virginia Bouvier's work on *New York Herald* artist Charles Nelan, "Imaging a Nation: U.S. Political Cartoons and the War of 1898," in *Whose America? The War of 1898 and the Battles to Define the Nation,* ed. Virginia M. Bouvier (Westport, Conn.: Praeger, 2001), 106–7, and "Imperial Humor: U.S. Political Cartoons and the War of 1898," *Colonial Latin American Historical Review* 8 (Winter 1999): 28.
50. *Cleveland Plain Dealer,* August 9, 1898, 1. Other cartoons utilizing the "fat" Uncle Sam motif include those in the *Washington Post,* June 26, 1898, 1; *Denver Post,* November 25, 1898, 1; *New York Herald,* color section, November 27, 1898, 1; *Judge* 35 (July 23, 1898): 49; *Life* 32 (November 24, 1898): 1; *Houston Post,* June 9, 1899, 1; *Indianapolis Sentinel,* February 26, 1899.
51. "The Filipinos and the Cubans," *Washington Post,* January 17, 1899, 6.
52. See her visual commentary on this *Life* cartoon in Martha Banta, *Barbaric Intercourse: Caricature and the Culture of Conduct, 1841–1936* (Chicago: University of Chicago Press, 2003), 211.
53. "The War's Aftermath," *Savannah Press,* September 14, 1898, 4.
54. "Civic Parade's Make-Up," *Philadelphia Inquirer,* October 20, 1898, 7.
55. "A Suggestion for the Peace Jubilee," *Chicago Record,* September 21, 1898, 4.
56. See Cheryl Leibold, "Philadelphia's Peace Jubilee Parades of 1898: Celebrating the End of 'That Splendid Little War,'" *Nineteenth Century* 18 (Fall 1998): 4–10. The only known manuscript collection on the Peace Jubilee, the papers of J. Hampton Moore, secretary of the Jubilee, is housed at the Historical Society of Pennsylvania, which also includes a large collection of William Rau's photographs of the event. There are additional photographs at the Library Company of Philadelphia, the Chester County Historical Society, and the Free Library of Philadelphia.
57. "The Peace Jubilee," *Philadelphia Times,* October 26, 1898, 4; "Guns, Flags, Glory Usher in Jubilee," *Philadelphia Inquirer,* October 26, 1898, 1.
58. "Arts of Peace Had Their Day," *Philadelphia Public Ledger,* October 29, 1898, 1–2. On the colonial floats, see "Hawaii in the Jubilee," *Philadelphia Times,* October 18, 1898, 5; "Civic Day's Great Show," *Philadelphia Times,* October 25, 1898, 5; "Civic Day Program," *Philadelphia Inquirer,* October 19, 1898, 7; "A Civic Parade," *Cleveland Plain Dealer,* October 29, 1898, 2.
59. "Philadelphia Honors the Men Who Brought the Nation Peace," *Philadelphia Inquirer,* October 28, 1898, 1; "Parade Incidents," *Philadelphia Inquirer,* October 28, 1898, 3.
60. Susan G. Davis, *Parades and Power: Street Theatre in Nineteenth-Century Philadelphia* (Berkeley: University of California Press, 1986), 159. In his study of working-class sentiment toward British imperial policies in South Africa, Henry Pelling similarly contends that rallies were weak indicators of popular political inclinations. Examining the night of Mafeking in May 1900, Pelling argues that such demonstrations reveal nothing more than the fact that the working class enjoyed displaying emotions in public. Henry Pelling, *Popular Politics and Society in Late Victorian Britain* (London: Macmillan, 1968), 82–100. See also Richard Price, *An Imperial War and the British Working*

    Class: Working-Class Attitudes and Reactions to the Boer War, 1899–1902 (London: Routledge & Kegan Paul, 1972), 46–96.

61. "No Political Significance," *Savannah Press,* December 18, 1898, 4.
62. Trask, *The War with Spain in 1898,* 484.
63. "A Phase of the Fading War Spirit," *Springfield Republican,* September 13, 1898, 6.
64. Ivan Musicant, *Empire by Default: The Spanish-American War and the Dawn of the American Century* (New York: Marion Wood Book, Henry Holt and Company, 1998), 583.
65. Lewis L. Gould, *The Spanish-American War and President McKinley* (Lawrence: University Press of Kansas, 1982), 103.
66. Quoted in James B. Haynes, *History of the Trans-Mississippi and International Exposition of 1898* (Omaha: Committee on History, 1910), 245, 467.
67. David Traxel, *1898: The Birth of the American Century* (New York: Alfred A. Knopf, 1998), 255. John Dobson makes this argument, claiming that McKinley "tried to avoid closing off any options until he was sure his final scheme would have popular support." John Dobson, *Reticent Expansionism: The Foreign Policy of William McKinley* (Pittsburgh: Duquesne University Press, 1988), 101–2.
68. "In This Sign We Conquer," *Chicago Inter Ocean,* October 14, 1898, 6.
69. Robert C. Hilderbrand, *Power and the People: Executive Management of Public Opinion in Foreign Affairs, 1897–1921* (Chapel Hill: University of North Carolina Press, 1981), 34–39; McKinley to Whitelaw Reid, October 31, 1898, Reid papers, Library of Congress, quoted in H. Wayne Morgan, *America's Road to Empire: The War with Spain and Overseas Expansion* (New York: John Wiley and Sons, 1967), 92.
70. For a discussion of how McKinley connected Philippine annexation with ideological notions of duty and destiny in his October speaking tour, see Paul T. McCartney, *Power and Progress: American National Identity, the War of 1898, and the Rise of American Imperialism* (Baton Rouge: Louisiana State University Press, 2006), 213–17.

6. Building an Imperial Iconography

1. "Filipinos at a Mid-Lent Party," *New York Journal,* March 5, 1899, 50.
2. On the diversity of views and constituents of the anti-imperialist movement, see Robert L. Beisner, *Twelve against Empire: The Anti-Imperialists, 1898–1900* (Chicago: Imprint Publications, 1968), 216–22; Richard E. Welch, *Response to Imperialism: The United States and the Philippine-American War, 1899–1902* (Chapel Hill: University of North Carolina Press, 1979); E. Berkeley Tompkins, *Anti-Imperialism in the United States: The Great Debate, 1890–1920* (Philadelphia: University of Pennsylvania Press, 1970); Daniel B. Schirmer, *Republic or Empire: American Opposition to the Philippine-American War* (Cambridge: Schenkman, 1972); Erin L. Murphy, "Women's Anti-Imperialism, 'The White Man's Burden,' and the Philippine-American War: Theorizing Masculinist Ambivalence in Protest," *Gender & Society* 23.2 (April 2009): 244–70; Kristin L. Hoganson, "'As Badly Off as the Filipinos': U.S. Women's Suffragists and the Imperial Issue at the Turn of

the Twentieth Century," *Journal of Women's History* 13.2 (Summer 2001): 9–33; George P. Marks III, ed., *The Black Press Views American Imperialism (1898–1900)* (New York: Arno Press and the New York Times, 1971).

3. Matthew Morrison argues that "due to the nature of the communication process, there is substantive reason to believe that non-verbal symbols can transmit meaning more directly than can verbal symbols." Matthew C. Morrison, "The Role of the Political Cartoonist in Image Making," *Central States Speech Journal* 20 (Winter 1969): 253. See also Alan P. Costall, "Seeing through Pictures," *Word & Image* 6 (July–September 1990): 273–75.

4. W. J. T. Mitchell, *Picture Theory: Essays on Verbal and Visual Representation* (Chicago: University of Chicago Press, 1994), 162.

5. Charles Nelan, *Cartoons of Our War with Spain* (New York: Frederick A. Stokes, 1898), quoted in Virginia M. Bouvier, "Imperial Humor: U.S. Political Cartoons and the War of 1898," *Colonial Latin American Historical Review* 8 (Winter 1999): 7.

6. John J. Appel, "From Shanties to Lace Curtains: The Irish Image in *Puck*, 1876–1910," *Comparative Studies in Society and History* 13 (October 1971): 374, citing Oscar Handlin, *Race and Nationality in American Life* (Garden City, N.Y.: Doubleday, 1957), 72. See also Morrison, "The Role of the Political Cartoonist in Image Making," 253; Martin J. Medhurst and Michael A. Desousa, "Political Cartoons as Rhetorical Form: A Taxonomy of Graphic Discourse," *Communication Monographs* 48 (September 1981): 219–20.

7. Alice Fahs argues that white popular literature in the North during the Civil War used racial caricature to depict former slaves as a means of "containment," to reassure northern whites that African Americans would remain subordinate despite emancipation. Alice Fahs, *The Imagined Civil War: Popular Literature of the North and South, 1861–1865* (Chapel Hill: University of North Carolina Press, 2001), 152–54. On the use of racial and ethnic imagery in late-nineteenth-century cartoon art, see Roger A. Fischer, *Them Damned Pictures: Explorations in American Political Cartoon Art* (North Haven, Conn.: Archon Books, 1996).

8. "Lynchings, Hangings, and Embezzlements of the Year," *Chicago Tribune*, January 1, 1901, 23, cited in W. Joseph Cambell, *The Year That Defined American Journalism: 1897 and the Clash of Paradigms* (New York: Routledge, 2006), 196.

9. "The Flag of the Future," *Baltimore Sun*, June 4, 1898, 2; "The Future of the Philippines," *San Francisco Examiner*, August 6, 1898, 6; "The English-Speaking World," *Atlanta Constitution*, June 6, 1898, 4. See Stuart Anderson, *Race and Rapprochement: Anglo-Saxonism and Anglo-American Relations, 1895–1904* (London: Associated University Presses, 1981), 73–129; Paul A. Kramer, "Empires, Exceptions, and Anglo-Saxons: Race and Rule between the British and United States Empires, 1880–1910," *Journal of American History* 88 (March 2002): 1315–53; Kristin L. Hoganson, *Fighting for American Manhood: How Gender Politics Provoked the Spanish-American and Philippine-American Wars* (New Haven: Yale University Press, 1998), 15–42.

10. See critique of the historiography of "export" and "projection" in Paul A. Kramer, *The Blood of Government: Race, Empire, the United States, and the Philippines* (Chapel Hill: University of North Carolina Press, 2006), 19–21.

11. Stuart Creighton Miller, *"Benevolent Assimilation": The American Con-*

quest of the Philippines, 1899–1903 (New Haven: Yale University Press, 1982), 97, 162.

12. Historian Walter Williams argues that U.S. Indian policy "served as a precedent for imperialist domination over the Philippines and other islands," and urges historians to "accept at face value the argument of the imperialists themselves that they were not making a new departure by holding colonial subjects." Walter L. Williams, "United States Indian Policy and the Debate over Philippine Annexation: Implications for the Origins of American Imperialism," *Journal of American History* 66 (March 1980): 810, 831. On this continuity/discontinuity thesis, see Robert Beisner, *From the Old Diplomacy to the New, 1865–1900* (New York: Thomas Y. Crowell, 1975); Richard Drinnon, *Facing West: The Metaphysics of Indian-Hating and Empire-Building* (Minneapolis: University of Minnesota Press, 1980), 286; Richard Slotkin, *The Fatal Environment: The Myth of the Frontier in the Age of Industrialization* (New York: Atheneum, 1985); Richard Slotkin, *Gunfighter Nation: The Myth of the Frontier in Twentieth-Century America* (New York: Atheneum, 1992).

13. "New Light on the Traits, Character and Customs of the Warlike Filipinos," *New York Herald*, section 5, April 9, 1899, 4.

14. *Houston Post*, April 8, 1899, 1.

15. N. P. Chipman, "Territorial Expansion—II, The Philippines—the Oriental Problem," *Overland Monthly* 35 (January 1900): 29–30, quoted in Williams, "United States Indian Policy," 820.

16. As Michael Hunt notes, "Viewed in the romantic afterglow of his defeat, he [the Indian] emerged near the top, just below whites and far above the lowly blacks." Michael Hunt, *Ideology and U.S. Foreign Policy* (New Haven: Yale University Press, 1987), 55.

17. "A Savage After All," *Louisville Courier-Journal*, February 27, 1899, 4.

18. Slotkin, *Gunfighter Nation*, 12.

19. Paul T. McCartney, *Power and Progress: American National Identity, the War of 1898, and the Rise of American Imperialism* (Baton Rouge: Louisiana State University Press, 2006), 208; Kramer, *The Blood of Government*, 81, 94.

20. The exact same description and similar portraits appeared in *Chicago Times-Herald*, May 4, 1898, 3; *Los Angeles Times*, May 11, 1898, 4; *New Orleans Picayune*, May 6, 1898, 4. For other positive portrayals and descriptions, see *Washington Post*, June 27, 1898, 4; *Los Angeles Times*, May 8, 1898, 10; *Philadelphia Inquirer*, color section, September 4, 1898, 2; *Chicago Times-Herald*, June 9, 1898, 5; *Boston Globe*, June 8, 1898, 7; *Houston Post*, June 11, 1898, 5; *Tennessee Commercial Appeal*, July 23, 1898, 4.

21. *San Francisco Examiner*, June 11, 1898, 5.

22. McKinley's address quoted in Kramer, *The Blood of Government*, 110.

23. See examples of "Asian" depictions of Aguinaldo or Filipinos more generally in *Judge* 36 (June 10, 1899): 360–61; *New York Journal*, August 7, 1898, 21; *Chicago Tribune*, April 10, 1899, 7, February 18, 1899, 11, and February 27, 1899, 9; *Washington Post*, July 19, 1898, 3; *Denver Post*, January 27, 1899, 1; *Chicago Times-Herald*, June 9, 1899, 1.

24. For demographic estimates and discussions of Asian Philippine populations, see Wallace Cumming, "Life in Manila," *Century Magazine* 56 (August 1898): 566; "The Philippine Islands," *Scientific American* 78 (May 7, 1898):

290–91; F. F. Hilder, "The Philippine Islands," *Forum* (July 1898): 541–43; Lucy M. J. Garnett, "The Philippine Islanders," *The Eclectic Magazine of Foreign Literature* 68 (September 1898): 299–309; "Life in Manila," *New York Journal*, June 5, 1898, 28.

25. By the 1890s the United States and Europe developed a fascination with the "Orient" as symbolic of exoticism and decadence, which was integrated into a web of imperial representations that helped Western empires construct an identity in relation to primitive, colonial Others. See Edward Said, *Orientalism* (New York: Vintage Books, 1994); David Brody, *Visualizing American Empire: Orientalism and Imperialism in the Philippines* (Chicago: University of Chicago Press, 2010); Bluford Adams, *E Pluribus Barnum: The Great Showman and the Making of U.S. Popular Culture* (Minneapolis: University of Minnesota Press, 1997), 175–85; John M. MacKenzie, *Orientalism: History, Theory, and the Arts* (Manchester: Manchester University Press, 1995).

26. "Slandering the Colored Soldier," *Los Angeles Times*, June 25, 1899, 4.

27. "Fire from Blackeyes," *Chicago Record*, June 10, 1898, 8. This article and illustration were also published in the *Atlanta Constitution*, May 29, 1898, 19, and the *Philadelphia Inquirer*, May 29, 1898, 26.

28. "Brave to Recklessness," *Boston Globe*, June 10, 1898, 4.

29. Kennett F. Harris, "Landing Troops in Cuba," *The Chicago Record's War Stories by Staff Correspondents in the Field* (Chicago: reprinted from the *Chicago Record*, 1898), 56; "Filipino Women Are All Ugly," *Cleveland Plain Dealer*, March 6, 1899, 7.

30. See Hunt, *Ideology and U.S. Foreign Policy*, 61.

31. For additional examples of cartoons accentuating the potential dangers of a sexual American-colonial union, see *Philadelphia Inquirer*, June 19, 1898, 1; *Chicago Record*, January 11, 1899, 1; *Boston Herald*, January 29, 1899, 1; *New York Bee*, June 22, 1898 (*Uncle Sam Cartoons: War with Spain*, scrapbooks of mounted cartoons on the theme of the Spanish-American War, assembled by the Manhattan Press Clipping Bureau [New York, 1898], vol. 7, no. 124); *Detroit Journal*, September 27, 1898 (*Uncle Sam Cartoons* scrapbook, vol. 11, no. 52).

32. See Gail Bederman, *Manliness and Civilization: A Cultural History of Gender and Race in the United States, 1880–1917* (Chicago: University of Chicago Press, 1995); Ann Laura Stoler, *Carnal Knowledge and Imperial Power: Race and the Intimate in Colonial Rule* (Berkeley: University of California Press, 2002).

33. See Martha Banta's visual commentary on this *Life* cartoon in *Barbaric Intercourse: Caricature and the Culture of Conduct, 1841–1936* (Chicago: University of Chicago Press, 2003), 203–4. For a discussion of ethnic caricature in *Life* magazine, see John J. Appel, "Ethnicity in Cartoon Art," in *Cartoons and Ethnicity*, Festival of Cartoon Art (Columbus: Ohio State University Libraries, 1992), 31–32.

34. On the wider use of the child trope in colonial discourse, see Ricardo Salvatore, "The Enterprise of Knowledge: Representational Machines of Informal Empire," in *Close Encounters of Empire: Writing the Cultural History of U.S.–Latin American Relations*, ed. Gilbert Joseph, Catherine C. LeGrand, and Ricardo D. Salvatore (Durham: Duke University Press, 1998), 83; John J. Johnson, *Latin America in Caricature* (Austin: University of Texas Press, 1980), 116–55; Lester C. Olson, *Emblems of American Community in the Revolu-*

tionary Era: A Study of Rhetorical Iconology (Washington, D.C.: Smithsonian Institution Press, 1991), 125–99; Hunt, *Ideology and U.S. Foreign Policy,* 61–62; Karen Sanchez-Eppler, "Raising Empires Like Children: Race, Nation, and Religious Education," *American Literary History* 8.3 (Autumn 1996): 399–425; William B. Cohen, "The Colonized as Child: British and French Colonial Rule," *African Historical Studies* 3.2 (1970): 427–31.

35. *Autobiography of George Dewey, Admiral of the Navy* (New York: Charles Scribner's Sons, 1913), 285.

36. Olson, *Emblems of American Community in the Revolutionary Era,* 156.

37. See additional examples in *Boston Globe,* June 10, 1898, 6; *Literary Digest* 16 (June 4, 1898): 662; *Boston Herald,* April 10, 1899, 4; *Philadelphia Inquirer,* April 30, 1899, 1; *New York World,* August 2, 1898, 6; *Judge* 34 (June 11, 1898): 379; *New York Herald,* January 12, 1899, 3; *Denver Post,* July 29, 1898, 1.

38. *Boston Globe,* July 29, 1898, 1; August 4, 1898, 1.

39. *Minneapolis Journal,* February 15, 1899, 1.

40. For additional pictorial examples, see *Denver Post,* February 6, 1899, 1; *Dallas News,* May 7, 1899, 18; *Philadelphia Inquirer,* August 18, 1898, 5; *Chicago Tribune,* March 29, 1901, 1; *New York Telegram,* March 22, 1899 (*Uncle Sam Cartoons* scrapbook, vol. 12, no. 132).

41. *Philadelphia Inquirer,* February 10, 1899, 7.

42. Jacob Riis, *How the Other Half Lives: Studies among the Tenements of New York* (New York: Dover Publications, 1971), 153, 160.

43. One of *Judge*'s principal artists, Eugene Zimmerman, commented on this personal relationship in his autobiography. *Zim: The Autobiography of Eugene Zimmerman,* ed. Walter M. Brasch (Selinsgrove, Pa.: Susquehanna University Press, 1988), 88.

44. "Our Course in the Philippines," *Philadelphia Inquirer,* April 9, 1899, 8.

45. Lanny Thompson argues that images of the different colonies varied depending on differing expectations for their integration into the Union. He demonstrates that graphic artists used these tropes purposefully and not uniformly. Lanny Thompson, "The Imperial Republic: A Comparison of the Insular Territories under U.S. Dominion after 1898," *Pacific Historical Review* 71 (November 2002): 539–40.

46. For additional examples of the colonies depicted as white children, see *Chicago Tribune,* November 24, 1898, 1; *Minneapolis Journal,* August 18, 1898, 1; *Atlanta Journal,* April 2, 1898 (*Uncle Sam Cartoons* scrapbook, vol. 3, no. 11). See additional examples of the colonies depicted as black children in *Philadelphia Inquirer,* November 24, 1898, 1; *Denver Post,* January 13, 1899, 1; *Los Angeles Times,* illustrated magazine section, August 7, 1898, 1; *Boston Herald,* October 17, 1898, 2; *Chicago Times-Herald,* November 20, 1898, 3; *Life* 33 (February 23, 1899): 150–51; *Puck* 44 (January 25, 1899): 8–9; *San Francisco Examiner,* July 24, 1898, 1; *Minneapolis Journal,* May 7, 1898, 1; *Chicago Record,* August 18, 1898, 1.

47. Brian McAllister Linn, *The Philippine War, 1899–1902* (Lawrence: University Press of Kansas, 2000), 15, 39.

48. "Can We Govern New Colonies?" *Chicago Times-Herald,* November 30, 1898, 6.

49. "The Philippine Problem," *New York Evening Post,* November 30, 1898, 6.

50. "The Race Question Settled," *St. Louis Post-Dispatch,* November 10, 1898, 6.
51. Christopher Lasch, "The Anti-Imperialists, the Philippines, and the Inequality of Man," *Journal of Southern History* 24 (August 1958): 319–31.
52. "The Cuban in Caricature," *Boston Transcript,* August 19, 1898, 4.
53. For selected graphic examples of the use of minstrel-like representations (with an imperial cast), see *Los Angeles Times,* illustrated magazine section, February 19, 1899, 1; *Life* 33 (April 20, 1899): 337; *San Francisco Examiner,* July 31, 1898, 12; *New York Herald,* January 27, 1899, 7; *Minneapolis Journal,* January 7, 1899, 1; *Chicago Tribune,* January 29, 1899, 14; *Houston Post,* December 23, 1898, 1; *Atlanta Constitution,* December 31, 1899, 5; *Philadelphia Inquirer,* January 10, 1899, 1; *Boston Herald,* January 6, 1899, 8; *Literary Digest* 18 (February 18, 1899): 180.
54. There is an extensive literature on minstrelsy, including Eric Lott, *Love and Theft: Blackface Minstrelsy and the American Working Class* (New York: Oxford University Press, 1993); Alexander Saxton, "Blackface Minstrelsy and Jacksonian Ideology," in *Locating American Studies: The Evolution of a Discipline,* ed. Lucy Maddox (Baltimore: Johns Hopkins University Press, 1999), 114–42; Mel Watkins, *On the Real Side: A History of African American Comedy* (Chicago: Lawrence Hill Books, 1994), 80–133. On the changes in minstrelsy in the late nineteenth century, see Robert Toll, *Blacking Up: The Minstrel Show in Nineteenth-Century America* (New York: Oxford University Press, 1974), 160–263.
55. "Last Night's Plays," *Philadelphia Inquirer,* November 15, 1898, 5; "Amusements," *Indianapolis Sentinel,* December 27, 1898, 6.
56. Kake Walk Program, University of Vermont Libraries' Center for Digital Initiatives, Record Group 53: Fraternities and Sororities, Series: Kake Walk, http://cdi.uvm.edu/collections/item/kwprogram1898.
57. "Much Mirth and Minstrelsy," *Boston Herald,* April 7, 1899, 8.
58. On black characters in comic strips, see Fredrik Strömberg, *Black Images in the Comics: A Visual History* (Seattle: Fantagraphics Books, 2003); Henry T. Sampson, *That's Enough, Folks: Black Images in Animated Cartoons, 1900–1960* (Lanham, Md.: Scarecrow Press, 1998), 1; Appel, "Ethnicity in Cartoon Art," 13–48; Ian Gordon, *Comic Strips and Consumer Culture, 1890–1945* (Washington, D.C.: Smithsonian Institution Press, 1998), 14, 62–63.
59. See extended description of the "Darktown" serial in Joseph Boskin, *Sambo: The Rise and Demise of an American Jester* (New York: Oxford University Press, 1986), 125–26.
60. A few examples of the circulation of the caricatured flag include *Charleston News and Courier,* October 2, 1898, 14; *Savannah Press,* September 23, 1898, 6; *New York Journal,* December 29, 1898, 1; *Boston Morning Globe,* August 9, 1898, 5; *Chicago Tribune,* October 21, 1898, 5.
61. Thomas Riis, *Just before Jazz: Black Musical Theater in New York, 1890–1915* (Washington, D.C.: Smithsonian Institution Press, 1989), 37. The *Chicago Tribune* reprinted this *Herald* cartoon on February 11, 1898, 13. The title, "All Coons Look Alike to Me," also appeared in cartoons in the *San Francisco Examiner,* July 22, 1898, 3, and *Detroit Journal,* August 19, 1898 (*Uncle Sam Cartoons* scrapbook, vol. 10, no. 79).
62. Philip B. Kunhardt Jr., Philip B. Kunhardt III, and Peter W. Kunhardt, *P. T. Barnum: America's Greatest Showman* (New York: Alfred A. Knopf, 1995),

149; James W. Cook, *The Arts of Deception: Playing with Fraud in the Age of Barnum* (Cambridge: Harvard University Press, 2001), 121.

63. Adams, *E Pluribus Barnum*, 158–63. On the "What Is It?" exhibit, see A. H. Saxon, *P. T. Barnum: The Legend and the Man* (New York: Columbia University Press, 1989), 98–99; Neil Harris, *Humbug: The Art of P. T. Barnum* (Boston: Little, Brown, 1973), 167; "The What Is It? Archive," available at *The Lost Museum*, http://chnm.gmu.edu/lostmuseum.

64. See Cook, *The Arts of Deception*, 121–62.

65. "Gen. Otis Is Fighting a Tribe of Missing Links," *Louisville Courier-Journal*, section 3, March 5, 1899, 2; "Some of Our New Citizens in the Philippines May Be Genuine Missing Links," *Philadelphia Inquirer*, section 3, May 14, 1899, 3.

66. "Hideous Practices in the Philippines," *Philadelphia Inquirer*, July 10, 1898, 26; "Evil Dancers and Witch Killers of the Philippines: Hideous Savage Customs of the Native Islanders, Which the Greater United States Will Soon Stamp Out, Described for the *Journal* by the Only American Who Ever Witnessed Them," *New York Journal*, July 17, 1898, 15; "Our Queer New Citizens in the Philippine Islands," *New York Journal*, color supplement, October 2, 1898, 5; "Devil Dance of Filipinos," *New York Journal*, October 2, 1898, 44; "Idols from the Philippines," *Richmond Times*, July 10, 1898, 27.

67. Adams, *E Pluribus Barnum*, 175–85.

68. *Boston Herald*, February 19, 1899, 2.

69. *Boston Globe*, July 21, 1898, 6.

70. McCartney, *Power and Progress*, 255.

71. On the gendering of anticolonialists, see Hoganson, *Fighting for American Manhood*, 174–79; Murphy, "Women's Anti-Imperialism," 253–54.

7. The Spectacular Wrap-Up in Three Postwar Moments

1. "Aguinaldo as a Prisoner at $4 a Day," *New York World Sunday Magazine*, October 5, 1902, 2, cited in David Brody, *Visualizing American Empire: Orientalism and Imperialism in the Philippines* (Chicago: University of Chicago Press, 2010), 64–65.

2. Marshall McLuhan, *Understanding Media: The Extensions of Man* (New York: McGraw-Hill, 1964), 7, 216.

3. Paul A. Kramer, *The Blood of Government: Race, Empire, the United States, and the Philippines* (Chapel Hill: University of North Carolina Press, 2006), 88, 111.

4. Albert G. Robinson, *The Philippines: The War and the People; A Record of Personal Observations and Experiences* (New York: McClure, Phillips & Co., 1901), 73, 93–95; "Washington Views of the Situation," *Louisville Courier-Journal*, March 28, 1899, 1.

5. Quoted in Paul T. McCartney, *Power and Progress: American National Identity, the War of 1898, and the Rise of American Imperialism* (Baton Rouge: Louisiana State University Press, 2006), 210.

6. See film on Library of Congress Web site, "Spanish-American War in Motion Pictures," http://memory.loc.gov/ammem/sawhtml/sawhome.html. Kristen Whissel argues that watching similar films of the Philippine-American War "provided audiences with an imperially inflected panoramic perception" such that "the desired point of view for the camera-spectator is that of the agent-observer of

imperialism as he struggles to bring the disputed territory under control." Kristen Whissel, "Placing the Spectator on the Scene of History: The Battle Re-enactment at the Turn of the Century, from Buffalo Bill's Wild West to the Early Cinema," *Historical Journal of Film, Radio and Television* 22 (2002): 225, 238.

7. See Alan Trachtenberg, *Reading American Photographs: Images as History, Matthew Brady to Walker Evans* (New York: Hill and Wang, 1989), 71–118; William A. Frassanito, *Gettysburg: A Journey in Time* (New York: Charles Scribner's Sons, 1975), 154–229.

8. John Lawrence Tone, *War and Genocide in Cuba, 1895–1898* (Chapel Hill: University of North Carolina Press, 2006), 223.

9. Kramer, *The Blood of Government*, 90; Stuart C. Miller, "Our Mylai of 1900: Americans in the Philippine Insurrection," in *American Expansion: The Critical Issues*, ed. Marilyn Blatt Young (Boston: Little, Brown, 1973), 110.

10. See the discussion of military censorship in Stuart Creighton Miller, *"Benevolent Assimilation": The American Conquest of the Philippines, 1899–1903* (New Haven: Yale University Press, 1982), 82–87.

11. "Press Censor's Work," *Dallas News*, March 19, 1899, 3.

12. Robinson, *The Philippines*, 86.

13. "Otis Censured by War Correspondents," *San Francisco Chronicle*, July 18, 1899, 1.

14. "General Otis Has Bungled the Philippine Campaign," *New York Journal*, July 17, 1899, 3.

15. "A New Policy, but the Old Otis," *Louisville Courier-Journal*, August 18, 1899, 4.

16. John T. McCutcheon, *Drawn from Memory* (Indianapolis: Bobbs-Merrill, 1950), 141; Robinson, *The Philippines*, 92.

17. For advertisements, see *Boston Transcript*, January 3, 1899, 11; *Indianapolis Sentinel*, December 8, 1898, 2; "Come Home from Cuba Shivering," *New York Journal*, April 4, 1899, 5.

18. *Chicago Record*, January 30, 1899, 1.

19. "Uncle Sam, His Show," *Los Angeles Times*, November 5, 1899, 5.

20. "Omaha's New Exposition," *Omaha Bee*, March 30, 1899, 1.

21. *Book of Views, Greater American Exposition, 1899: Omaha U.S.A. July 1 to November 1*, issued by the Bureau of Publicity and Promotion (Omaha, 1899). See also "Greater America to People of Omaha," *Omaha World-Herald*, April 16, 1899, 5; "First Place among Great Expositions," *Omaha World-Herald*, May 31, 1899, 6.

22. *The Time Saver and Catalogue of America's War Museum: Greater America Exposition Omaha, Neb., U.S.A.* (Omaha: A. J. Bishop, 1899).

23. "A Chicago Tribute to the Greater America Exposition," *Omaha World-Herald*, May 26, 1899, 4; "Tour of the Buildings," *Omaha World-Herald*, June 4, 1899, 15; "Glorious Week for Greater America," *Omaha World-Herald*, June 11, 1899, 5.

24. "Sinking of the *Merrimac*," *Omaha World-Herald*, June 25, 1899, 28; "Scenes along the Midway," *Omaha Bee*, June 28, 1899, 7.

25. I have argued elsewhere that Robert Rydell's premise that world's fairs transmitted "ideological messages" that put forward "the essential rightness of imperialism" has been too easily accepted as true in our historical assessments of fairs and their impact. See Bonnie M. Miller, "The Incoherencies of

Empire: The 'Imperial' Image of the Indian at the Omaha World's Fairs of 1898–99," *American Studies* 49 (Fall–Winter 2008): 5–30; Robert Rydell, "The Trans-Mississippi and International Exposition: To Work Out the Problem of Universal Civilization," *American Quarterly* 33 (Winter 1981): 603. For sources making this argument with respect to the Omaha fairs of 1898–99, see Robert Rydell, John E. Findling, and Kimberly D. Pelle, *Fair America: World's Fairs in the United States* (Washington, D.C.: Smithsonian Institution Press, 2000), 46; Sarah J. Moore, "Mapping Empire in Omaha and Buffalo: World's Fairs and the Spanish-American War," in *The Legacy of the Mexican and Spanish-American Wars: Legal, Literary, and Historical Perspectives,* ed. Gary D. Keller and Cordelia Candelaria (Tempe, Ariz.: Bilingual Review Press, 2000), 112, 124; Robert Rydell, "Souvenirs of Imperialism: World's Fair Postcards," in *Delivering Views: Distant Cultures in Early Postcards,* ed. Christraud M. Geary and Virginia-Lee Webb (Washington, D.C.: Smithsonian Institution Press, 1998), 58. For scholarship arguing that U.S. expositions generally rallied support for national imperial objectives, see Robert Rydell, *All the World's a Fair: Visions of Empire at American International Expositions, 1876–1916* (Chicago: University of Chicago Press, 1984); Aram A. Yengoyan, "Culture, Ideology and World's Fairs: Colonizer and Colonized in Comparative Perspectives," in *Fair Representations: World's Fairs and the Modern World,* ed. Robert Rydell and Nancy Gwinn (Amsterdam: VU University Press, 1994), 62–83; Burton Benedict, "Rituals of Representation: Ethnic Stereotypes and Colonized Peoples at World's Fairs," in Rydell and Gwinn, *Fair Representations,* 28–61; Paul Greenhalgh, *Ephemeral Vistas: The Expositions Universelles, Great Exhibitions and World's Fairs, 1851–1939* (Manchester: Manchester University Press, 1988).

26. "Omaha Fair Opened," *Chicago Times-Herald,* July 2, 1899, 5.

27. *Book of Views.* On the purpose of the GAE, see Emma Abbott Gage, *Western Wanderings and Summer Saunterings through Picturesque Colorado* (Baltimore: Lord Baltimore Press, 1900), 224–25.

28. "Big Omaha Show Open," *Chicago Tribune,* July 2, 1899, 13; "Exposition Gates Are Open," *Omaha Bee,* July 2, 1899, 5.

29. "Great Colonial Show Scheme," *Springfield Republican,* December 19, 1898, 10.

30. "Exhibit from Hawaii on Way," *Omaha Bee,* July 5, 1899, 10.

31. "Hawaiians at the Exposition," *Omaha Bee,* July 15, 1899, 5; "Midway Gleanings," *Omaha World-Herald,* August 20, 1899, 5.

32. "Features of the Midway," *Omaha Bee,* June 25, 1899, 5; "Scenes along the Midway," *Omaha Bee,* July 15, 1899, 5.

33. "Midway Gleanings," *Omaha World-Herald,* September 10, 1899, 14; "Cuba's Notorious Choker to Come to Exposition," *Omaha World-Herald,* May 7, 1899, 5.

34. "Fifty Lusty Filipinos," *Omaha World-Herald,* June 25, 1899, 28–29.

35. "Omaha's Filipino Colony," *Omaha World-Herald,* November 11, 1899, 9; "Midway Gleanings," *Omaha World-Herald,* August 31, 1899, 8.

36. *Greater America Exposition: Omaha USA July First to November First* (Omaha: Baker Brothers, 1899).

37. Peter Hoffenberg, *An Empire on Display: English, Indian, and Australian*

Exhibitions from the Crystal Palace to the Great War (Berkeley: University of California Press, 2001), 17, 72; William Schneider, "Race and Empire: The Rise of Popular Ethnography in the Late Nineteenth Century," *Journal of Popular Culture* 2 (1977): 98; Tony Bennett, "The Exhibitionary Complex," *New Formations* 4 (1988): 76.

38. "Scenes along the Midway," *Omaha Bee*, July 20, 1899, 5; "Filipinos Are on the Ground," *Omaha Bee*, August 7, 1899, 5.

39. "That Exposition," *Nebraska State Journal*, November 2, 1899, 4.

40. On the GAE committee and its management of colonial exhibits, see "Greater America to People of Omaha," *Omaha World-Herald*, April 16, 1899, 5; "Exhibits from Philippines," *Omaha World-Herald*, February 16, 1899, 8.

41. "A Day at the Metropolis," *Nebraska State Journal*, September 13, 1899, 7.

42. "Expositions," *Christian Advance* (Council Bluffs, Iowa) 4 (September 1899): 2.

43. "Deep, Deep in the Hole," *Nebraska State Journal*, November 2, 1899, 7.

44. Paul Kramer's analysis of the St. Louis Exposition of 1904 demonstrates that even after the war in the Philippines ended, decisions about the display of Filipinos at American world's fairs remained a contested and complicated process. Paul A. Kramer, "Making Concessions: Race and Empire Revisited at the Philippine Exposition, 1901–5," *Radical History Review* 73 (Winter 1999): 74–114.

45. "Government Takes a Hand in Exposition," *Omaha World-Herald*, May 7, 1899, 1; "Indians for Great Show," *Omaha World-Herald*, May 11, 1899, 5; "Exhibits from Colonies," *Omaha Bee*, April 27, 1899, 5; "Filipinos Cannot Land," *Grand Island Independent*, July 27, 1899, 1.

46. On September 24, 1899, the *Chicago Tribune* published a large portrait of Dewey captioned "The Idol of the American Nation," 50. "Dewey 'Most Popular American Living,'" *New York World*, September 28, 1899, 1; "Dewey Always Brave," *Boston Herald*, September 24, 1899, 45.

47. *Dallas News*, November 25, 1899, 6; "Dewey Is Wrought Up," *Dallas News*, November 23, 1899, 1.

48. Margherita Arlina Hamm, "Dewey's Home-Coming Will Be an Event without Precedent in History of the Nation," *Dallas News*, September 17, 1899, 16; "The School and Children and Dewey," *New York Journal*, May 1, 1899, 6; "Admiral Dewey," *Boston Herald*, October 1, 1899, 16; "Our Dewey Day," *Boston Herald*, October 5, 1899, 6; "The Hand That Smote Spain at Manila," *Chicago Times-Herald*, May 3, 1898, 3; Edgar M. Dilley, "Dewey, Sampson, and Schley's Heads Compared," *Louisville Courier-Journal*, July 17, 1898, 3.

49. David Brody persuasively makes this point in "Celebrating Empire on the Home Front: New York City's Welcome-Home Party for Admiral Dewey," *Prospects* 25 (2000): 396–97.

50. John R. Rathom, "Unrecognized Heroes of the War," *San Francisco Chronicle*, March 26, 1899, 12; Alan Dale, "Dewey and the Stage Hero," *New York Journal*, October 1, 1899, 33.

51. "Dewey's Latest Photograph," *Atlanta Constitution*, March 12, 1899, 6; J.J. Ingalls, "Dewey's House," *New York Journal*, May 21, 1899, 26; "A Photographic Interview with Admiral Dewey on the Olympia at Naples," *New York Journal*, September 3, 1899, 14–15.

52. "Great Naval Pageant," *Houston Post*, September 30, 1899, 4; "New York Greets the Nation's Hero," *Boston Herald*, September 30, 1899, 1.

53. "Patriotic Idiots," *Chicago Tribune,* September 29, 1899, 6.

54. "70,000 Dimes for the Loving Cup," *New York Journal,* September 28, 1899, 8; "$75,000 from the State to Help Welcome Dewey," *New York Journal,* May 25, 1899, 3; "Schoolgirls Spell Dewey's Name in Human Letters," *New York World,* September 9, 1899, 12; *Chicago Times-Herald,* September 12, 1899, 1.

55. "Souvenirs of the Admiral," *Boston Herald,* September 24, 1899, 45.

56. Arthur Hoffman to Assistant Secretary of the Navy Charles H. Allen, September 23, 1899, National Archives, General Correspondence of the Secretary of the Navy, 1897–1915, File 8669-28.

57. "Three New Plays for the Week," *New York Journal,* October 15, 1899, 41; "Vaudeville Week at the Show Houses," *New York Journal,* September 24, 1899, 24; "Dewey in Boston," *Boston Herald,* October 22, 1899, 15.

58. Michele Bogart, *Public Sculpture and the Civic Ideal in New York City, 1890–1930* (Chicago: University of Chicago Press, 1989), 106.

59. "Marble Dewey Arch Sure," *New York World,* October 8, 1899, 9.

60. Bogart, *Public Sculpture and the Civic Ideal in New York City,* 104; "Public Art in New York," *Municipal Affairs* (September–December 1899): 756.

61. "From Dewey," *Boston Herald,* September 28, 1899, 6; "Admiral Dewey," *Boston Herald,* October 1, 1899, 16.

62. "No Dewey Islands, but a House," *Chicago Tribune,* May 25, 1899, 6.

63. See Stanley Karnow, *In Our Image: America's Empire in the Philippines* (New York: Random House, 1989), 163.

64. "The Dewey Home Transfer," *Washington Star,* November 21, 1899, 3.

65. "Want None of Dewey Fund," *New York World,* November 25, 1899, 3; "Angry at Dewey's Act," *Chicago Tribune,* November 21, 1899, 7.

66. For reports of anti-Dewey sentiment in theaters, see "Dewey Home Transfer," *Dallas News,* November 22, 1899, 3; "Dewey Transfers Home to His Bride," *New York World,* November 21, 1899, 1.

67. "Dewey Back in Favor," *Chicago Tribune,* November 23, 1899, 7.

68. George Dewey, *Autobiography of George Dewey, Admiral of the Navy* (New York: Charles Scribner's Sons, 1913), 289.

69. "Naval Arch Fund Is Only $150,000," *New York World,* January 7, 1900, 8. See also "The Navy Memorial Arch," *New York World,* November 22, 1899, 6; "The Navy Arch," *New York World,* November 29, 1899, 6.

70. Michele Bogart and G. Kurt Piehler read these acts of vandalism as symbolic of radical anticolonialist sentiment. I am more persuaded by David Brody's hypothesis that this was a souvenir-seeking effort. See Brody, "Celebrating Empire on the Home Front," 418; Bogart, *Public Sculpture and the Civic Ideal in New York City,* 108; G. Kurt Piehler, *Remembering War the American Way* (Washington, D.C.: Smithsonian Institution Press, 1995), 89.

71. Quoted in John Tebbel, *America's Great Patriotic War with Spain: Mixed Motives, Lies and Racism in Cuba and the Philippines, 1898–1915* (Manchester: Marshall Jones, 1996), 353.

72. "News of Theaters," *Chicago Tribune,* May 29, 1899, 5.

73. Thomas Schoonover, *Uncle Sam's War of 1898 and the Origins of Globalization* (Lexington: University Press of Kentucky, 2003), 85, 95.

74. See Brody, *Visualizing American Empire,* 89–112.

75. "Report by MacArthur," *Chicago Inter Ocean,* March 29, 1901, 5.

76. Duffield Osborne, "The Capture of Aguinaldo," *Harper's Weekly* 43 (December 23, 1899): 1297–99.

77. Arthur Power Dudden, *The American Pacific: From the Old China Trade to the Present* (New York: Oxford University Press, 1992), 88.

78. "Capture of Aguinaldo," *Chicago Inter Ocean,* March 29, 1901, 6; "Funston's Exploit Was Foretold in Fiction," *New York Journal,* April 7, 1901, 52; "Gen. Funston's Alleged Enterprise," *Boston Herald,* March 26, 1901, 6.

79. Miller, *"Benevolent Assimilation,"* 168.

80. "Colonel Funston's Picture: From Original Photograph," *Chicago Times-Herald,* April 27, 1899, 3.

81. "Plan for Funston Day at a Kansas State Fair," *Chicago Tribune,* May 9, 1899, 3; *Los Angeles Times,* April 29, 1899, 8.

82. Quoted in Miller, "Our Mylai of 1900," 107–8.

83. "What to Do with Aguinaldo," *Cleveland Plain Dealer,* March 29, 1901, 4.

84. Philip C. Jessup, *Elihu Root,* vol. 1 (New York: Dodd, Mead & Company, 1938), 335. See also Louis J. Alber, director of the Affiliated Lecture and Concert Association, to Secretary of War Patrick J. Hurley, February 20, 1932, National Archives, Records of the Bureau of Insular Affairs, RG 350, Personal Information File; W. H. Wright to Hon. Elihu Root, Secretary of War, August 11, 1902, National Archives, Records of the Bureau of Insular Affairs, RG 350; "Aguinaldo in Demand," *San Francisco Chronicle,* May 17, 1901, 9. For cartoons on this theme, see *New York Journal,* March 29, 1901, 16; *San Francisco Examiner,* April 3, 1901, 14; *New York World,* March 29, 1901, 6; *Boston Herald,* April 10, 1901, 11.

85. Wallace Irwin, "A Job for Aguinaldo," *San Francisco Examiner,* April 10, 1901, 14.

Index